Saving the Church of England

Saving the Church of England

John Edwards (1637–1716) as Dissenting Conformer

DANIEL C. NORMAN

Foreword by Mark Noll

WIPF & STOCK · Eugene, Oregon

SAVING THE CHURCH OF ENGLAND
John Edwards (1637–1716) as Dissenting Conformer

Copyright © 2022 Daniel C. Norman. All rights reserved. Except for brief quotations in critical publications or reviews, no part of this book may be reproduced in any manner without prior written permission from the publisher. Write: Permissions, Wipf and Stock Publishers, 199 W. 8th Ave., Suite 3, Eugene, OR 97401.

Wipf & Stock
An Imprint of Wipf and Stock Publishers
199 W. 8th Ave., Suite 3
Eugene, OR 97401

www.wipfandstock.com

PAPERBACK ISBN: 978-1-6667-3223-8
HARDCOVER ISBN: 978-1-6667-2567-4
EBOOK ISBN: 978-1-6667-2568-1

APRIL 26, 2022 1:38 PM

Copyright for frontispiece: © National Portrait Gallery, London

Front cover: churches where Edwards served
top: Bury St. Edmunds Church, Suffolk
lower left: Holy Trinity Church, Cambridge
lower right: Church of the Holy Sepulchre, Cambridge

Contents

Foreword by Mark A. Noll | vii
Acknowledgments | ix
Abbreviations | xi

1	Introduction	1
2	Edwards in His Historical Context	11
3	The Life and Legacy of John Edwards	25
4	Edwards and Anti-Trinitarians	44
5	Edwards and Church Parties	94
6	Ecclesiology, Conformity, and Nonconformity	136
7	On Church Unity and Schism	167
8	Conclusion	199

Appendix A: The Works of John Edwards | 207
Appendix B: Scholarship Focused on Edwards | 219
Appendix C: Edwards and His Critics | 221
Appendix D: Was Edwards a Lonely Reformed Voice in the Church of England in 1700? | 229
Bibliography | 240
General Index | 281
Scripture Index | 289

Foreword

JOHN EDWARDS (1637-1716), an English Calvinist who supported state-church Anglicanism, is much less well known than his near namesake, Jonathan Edwards (1703-1758), the colonial British Calvinist who supported the state-church establishment in Massachusetts. Daniel Norman's thoroughly researched and well written study of this "Dissenting Conformist" wants to change that disproportionate awareness by tracking the influence of the English Edwards among his contemporaries (and long afterwards), by documenting the important theological controversies that this Edwards had (especially with John Locke), and by explaining the historical significance of an Anglican who stoutly maintained his Calvinism (though with considerable flexibility) long after the Church of England had mostly turned to other theological positions.

John Edwards, it turns out, was read with appreciation by a number of his British contemporaries who also worried about the theological eurekas of their day. For students of American history, it is notable that Edwards's contemporaries in the English colonies, like Increase and Cotton Mather, also recommended some of Edwards's many works. Even more interesting is that Jonathan Edwards singled out John Edwards as one of the most important authors who fixed his own Calvinist convictions. For George Whitefield, the dynamic itinerant who transformed much of church life in England, Scotland, and the colonies, John Edwards was the author who firmed up the Calvinist convictions that Whitefield would defend in his many tiffs, disagreements, and sometimes slugfests with Arminian Wesleyans.

Daniel Norman's book does a particularly good job at explaining why John Edwards felt compelled to write against John Locke. To Edwards, Locke's plea for a broad religious toleration that took in all but atheists and Catholics represented not a principled defense of liberty but a covert plea to protect himself. As he canvasses the extensive but tangled scholarship on the question, Norman makes a strong case for regarding Locke as heterodox on the Trinity and, therefore, the kind of danger to faithful Christianity and social order that Edwards claimed. In addition to thorough discussion of this important debate, Norman adds a careful discussion of Edwards's writings against several other leading thinkers of the period like Samuel Clarke (for diminishing the divinity of Jesus) and William Whiston (for like Locke casting doubt on the Trinity).

Norman's most surprising revelation, however, concerns the spirit with which John Edwards carried out his polemical writing. In his career as a fellow at Cambridge and as a parish minister, Edwards maintained his loyalty to the English state church. He was a "dissenter" in swimming against the theological novelties of his day, but not a Dissenter in breaking with the Church of England. With a stance that in some aspects carried on with Richard Baxter's definition of "mere Christianity" (and so also anticipated C. S. Lewis in the twentieth century), Edwards believed that belief in the Nicene Creed provided a sufficient basis for ecclesiastical fellowship. Edwards, thus, differentiated between his worries about Locke, Whiston, and Clarke (regarded as outside the pale of orthodoxy) and less serious objections to Arminianism or other forms of Trinitarian Protestantism (regarded as deficient but not fatally so). It was a stance as a "Dissenting Conformist" that others, like George Whitefield in his charitable moments, and then many others, would follow as well.

A decade ago Dewey Wallace enlivened the history of the period before Whitefield, the Wesleys, and the other Edwards in a splendid theological prosopography of six *Shapers of English Calvinism, 1660-1714* (Oxford University Press, 2011). One of the six was John Edwards, whom Daniel Norman has now portrayed as a figure worthy of a book on his own.

MARK A. NOLL
Professor of History Emeritus,
Wheaton College and University of Notre Dame

Acknowledgments

THIS BOOK IS A REVISION of my PhD dissertation. Writing it has been an adventure of discovery, like putting together a large jigsaw puzzle, never before assembled, without having the puzzle pieces supplied, nor the box cover to serve as a guide. Without the puzzle pieces at hand, there was the added dimension of a scavenger hunt. At a sufficient number of points of discovery (i.e., finding a puzzle piece), there have been clues on where to look for related pieces. At the beginning, the picture was not in focus. Details could not seen and entire sections of what would become a finished product were blank. And, of course, it was not clear that the pieces necessary to complete a coherent picture actually existed. Adding to the adventure was the fact that some of the pieces which were discovered meant that the picture turned out differently than originally imagined.

A challenge in ordinary picture puzzles is that at first glance some pieces aren't so easy to distinguish from other pieces. So too here. Two contemporaries named Thomas Burnet became part of this story—also two named Jonathan Edwards, one of whom who has frequently been confused with John Edwards, not the most unusual name, then or today.

Fortunately as evidenced by many footnotes, this was not a solo activity. If Isaac Newton had to stand on the shoulders of giants, how much more the rest of us. I have benefitted from the work of many scholars whose diligent research has provided me with important puzzle pieces and clues about where to find others.

Along my way, my supervisor Richard Snoddy has helped in numerous ways: suggesting places to look for pieces to my puzzle; correcting my fuzzy thinking when I have tried to force together certain pieces which did not actually fit; and recognizing that some pieces that I found do not actually belong in my puzzle at all. He has also helped correct many errors which I did not see. I have also appreciated the assistance and advice of others at London School of Theology, including Tony Lane and Sandra Kahil.

No one could undertake a project like this without libraries. I have been well-served by a number of excellent conventional ones including those located at Cambridge University, St. John's College, Cambridge, Oxford University Bodleian, Queen's College, Oxford, and the University of Washington. In addition to manuscript searches at these, my scavenger hunt has taken me to the Library of Congress, Massachusetts Historical Society, and the American Antiquarian Society. As valuable as those have been, I could not have put this puzzle together without the resources of a number of digital libraries, which have provided a wealth of material from the sixteenth-, seventeenth- and eighteenth-centuries: Early English Books Online, Eighteenth Century Collections Online, The Post-Reformation Digital Library and The Internet Archive.

Finally, I want to thank my wife Judy for her encouragement and patience, which I repeatedly challenged.

Abbreviations

BCP — Book of Common Prayer

CAE — Crisp, Tobias. *Christ Alone Exalted: Being the Compleat Works of Tobias Crisp, D.D.* London, 1690.

DNB — *Dictionary of National Biography.* 63 vols. Edited by Leslie Stephen and Sidney Lee. New York, NY: Macmillan, 1885-1900.

ODNB — *Oxford Dictionary of National Biography.* 60 vols. Edited by H. C. G. Matthew and Brian Harrison. Oxford: Oxford University Press, 2004.

PCR — Whiston, William. *Primitive Christianity Reviv'd in Four Parts.* 5 vols. London, 1711-12.

REM — *Remains of the Late Reverend and Learned John Edwards, D.D. Sometime Fellow of St. John's College in Cambridge.* London, 1731.

WCL — *The Theological Works of the Reverend Charles Leslie.* 7 vols. Oxford: Oxford University Press, 1832.

WGW — *The Works of the Reverend George Whitefield, M.A., Late of Pembroke-College, Oxford and Chaplain to the Rt. Hon., the Countess of Huntington.* 6 vols. London, 1771-72.

WJO — *The Works of John Owen.* 17 vols. Edited by William Goold. Carlisle, PA: Banner of Truth, 1997.

WJT — *The Works of the Dr. John Tillotson, Late Archbishop of Canterbury.* 10 vols. London, 1820.

WWB — *The Theological Works of William Beveridge, D.D., Sometime Lord Bishop of St. Asaph.* 12 vols. Oxford: Parker, 1842-1848.

1

INTRODUCTION
An Unduly Neglected Figure

IT IS WELL KNOWN that the two most prominent voices of the eighteenth-century Great Awakening in the American colonies were Congregational minister Jonathan Edwards (1703–58) and itinerant English preacher George Whitefield (1714–70). What is not so well known is that both men were profoundly influenced by a nearly forgotten English cleric who neither ever met and who died when both men were children. Whitefield credited John Edwards with his conversion to committed Calvinism from a somewhat confused Arminian theology. He was introduced to Edwards in two books by eighteenth-century Church of England dissenter Jonathan Warne (fl. 1740), who quoted at length from John Edwards in several of his works. Whitefield later thanked Warne for giving him the books, stating, "I think the Quotations out of Dr. Edwards are worth their Weight in Gold; I intend to recommend them in my Journal."[1]

Jonathan Edwards scholar Wilson Kimnach identifies four significant influences on young Jonathan during his early years in the pulpit. Two were his father Timothy (1669–1758) and his grandfather Solomon Stoddard (1643–1729), whose pastorate at the Congregational Church in Northampton, Massachusetts Bay Colony he inherited at the young age

---

1. Whitefied's letter to Warne was printed after the preface in the third edition of Warne, *Church of England*.

of twenty-five. The third was Cotton Mather (1663–1728), pastor of Boston's North Church who, though not a blood relative of Jonathan, was, nevertheless, closely associated with the family.² Despite the historic conflict between Stoddard and the Mathers, Jonathan found Cotton Mather's *Manuductio Ad Ministerium* very helpful in his own ministry and recommended it to others. The fourth notable influence was John Edwards, especially *The Preacher*, listed on the first page of Jonathan's "Catalogue," which included his notes on books that were important to him. Kimnach compared sermon attributes such as delivery characteristics (persuasive, intense, and personal), the recognized seriousness and sacredness of being God's convicting messenger, and the critical importance of a clear application to change lives, as advocated in *The Preacher*, to what is known about Jonathan Edwards's preaching. He concludes, "as for *The Preacher*, there are too many echoes of its individualistic expressions throughout Edwards's notebooks to have doubts about its importance to him."³

Not only did John Edwards have a remarkable influence through his published works on later generations of clergymen on both sides of the Atlantic, but he also influenced the course of public debate during his own lifetime. Late seventeenth- and early eighteenth-century England was a time of unprecedented scientific discovery and profound transformations in government, church, and society—unprecedented and profound not only for the small islands of Britain, but for the world. Its two most famous intellectuals of that time, Isaac Newton (1642–1727) and John Locke (1632–1704), were both personally challenged by the religiously unaccommodating culture in which they lived. Troubled by the divisive conflict over theology, both became engrossed in private Bible study, searching for solutions to this conflict which appeared to be caused by irrational hermeneutics.

At a time when nonconformity to the Church of England was most often associated with those who viewed the church as departing in various ways from the Protestant Reformation, neither man fit that mold, but neither did they conform. Newton was fairly successful in his independent divergence, being private about his beliefs. But Locke

---

2. Jonathan's grandfather Solomon Stoddard married Cotton Mather's uncle's widow. Stoddard's support of the Halfway Covenant at his church brought him into sharp dispute with both Cotton Mather and his father Increase.

3. Edwards, *Works of Jonathan Edwards*, 10:16-20. See Chapter 3 for a more complete discussion of the influence of Edwards on Whitfield, Jonathan Edwards, and others.

saw intolerance, especially of a religious nature, as the primary cause of tension and hostility in the world. He launched what he perceived to be a very reasonable campaign to end it, soon discovering that few key members of the church shared his theological convictions or his view of tolerance.

The first person to challenge both his and Newton's biblical exegesis in print was this same John Edwards. Edwards accused Locke of Socinianism, a common slur in late seventeenth-century England, but rarely used by Edwards, Locke being the only one to whom Edwards leveled that charge, at least in print. Locke responded along with a number of other correspondents, some defending and others attacking Locke's orthodoxy. Although the debate over Locke's theology continues today, most observers agree with Edwards's assessment of Locke's heterodoxy.[4] A second round of debate over whether or not trinitarianism was a central and essential element of orthodoxy ensued in the early eighteenth century, with philosopher Samuel Clarke (1675–1729) serving as the primary lightning rod. Again Edwards was at the forefront of the debate, this time linking Clarke's antitrinitarian language found in his defense of his *Scripture-Doctrine of the Trinity* to Newton's "Scholium Generale" essay, appended to his *Principia Mathematica* in its second edition.[5]

In addition to the Great Awakening and the late Stuart trinitarian debate, there is a third pursuit of Edwards which has virtually been ignored. Had he been successful, it would have been his most significant contribution to the church and to posterity. I am speaking of his campaign for church unity and theological toleration within the church. The unity of the church has of course been a continuous concern throughout its history. The problem has been how the conditions or terms for that unity are defined.

The Church of England leadership demanded conformity to their institution, especially to the *Book of Common Prayer* (*BCP*) and its rubric, but were lax on how the XXXIX Articles were to be understood.

---

4. See Chapter 4; also Wootton, "John Locke," 44–58. Some of Locke's defenders have focused on the changing definitions of Socinian historically. For example, did Socinians of late seventeenth-century England strictly follow the teachings of Socinus Faustus (1539–1604)? Edwards charged Locke as a Socinian because it was then generally understood to mean antitrinitarian. Edwards later said that the distinctions between Arian and Socinian were not nearly as important as the fact that men such as Locke and Clarke were clearly intent on corrupting Christian orthodoxy by denying the Trinity. See Edwards, *Some Animadversions*, 4.

5. See Chapter 4.

Many nonconformists followed a narrower interpretation of the XXXIX Articles, but desired reasonable freedom in complying with the *BCP*. Unlike most nonconformists, Edwards accepted the Church of England as legitimate on the basis of its official adherence to central doctrines deemed essential by orthodox Christians historically. Beyond this, he was willing to grant latitude to those with whom he had sharp disagreements over historically divisive understandings of soteriology, ecclesiology, etc.

Edwards was actually quite tolerant in his ecclesiology—to a point. That point was the boundary of traditional Christian orthodoxy as expressed in the Nicene Creed and historically recognized by Protestant, Catholic, and Orthodox bodies. From his own study of the New Testament Locke, by contrast, determined that the essence of the gospel was the belief that Jesus is the Messiah. It seemed to him that, as there was so much confusion and divisive acrimony over doctrines such as the Trinity and deity of Christ, making those doctrines optional would lead to peace and unity. His solution: eliminate theological disagreement and rancor by reducing required beliefs for Christian conversion to an absolute minimum.

Edwards found this completely unacceptable because in his view these doctrines were clearly expressed in Scripture, fundamental to the definition of the Christian faith, and had been used to distinguish orthodoxy from heresy since the early fourth century. Edwards also had a very high view of the unity of the church. But without agreement on historically essential doctrines, on what basis would the identity and therefore unity of the church be based? In Edwards's view, orthodox doctrine as understood and accepted historically expressed immutable truth revealed by God in holy Scripture.

Edwards was certainly not the only one committed to both trinitarian orthodoxy and the unity of the church, at least in principle. Among those who shared Edwards's orthodox convictions (both within the Church of England and nonconformists bodies) however, Edwards was unique. He was unique in that he willingly subordinated many doctrines and practices which he held dear to the unity of the church, while remaining in the church and continuing to defend his Reformed understanding. This was not true for prominent spokesmen among the nonconformists, nor for the Church of England leadership. Conformists and nonconformists all had certain beliefs and/or practices of which they were unwilling to compromise, even though such beliefs had never been widely accepted as defining elements of the Christian faith, nor criteria to distinguish orthodoxy from heterodoxy. These included tenets on church government, sacraments, liturgy, and the relative importance of moral behavior and ceremonies.

For Edwards, many of these contentious issues were also of great concern because he wanted to be faithful to Scripture. Edwards was, after all, a strong Calvinist and Calvinists have often been accused by their opponents of being some of the most exclusive and intolerant Christians, especially on doctrine. Unfortunately Calvinism is not today, nor was it then, a well-defined term.[6] But it is important for this discussion to understand what Edwards meant.

Throughout the seventeenth century, Calvinism became such a tainted label from abuse by Lutherans, Catholics, Laudians, and Latitudinarians that most English Protestants avoided it, but not John Edwards.[7] He identified himself as a Calvinist and wrote about what he viewed to be distortions and errors on the part of some Calvinists as well as critics of Calvinism. Reflecting his ecclesiology, Edwards placed Calvin in the succession of faithful interpreters of Scripture going back to the "Ancient Fathers" and continuing with the sixteenth-century martyrs of the Church of England. He further asserted that in its first eighty years following the break with Rome, none of the prominent men of the Church of England affirmed any Arminian doctrines or rejected any of Calvin's. But, he said, "they must all give way to the Inspired Writers, to the Records of the Old and New Testament: For these alone are the Infallible Standard of Divine Truths."[8] So even though Edwards called himself a Calvinist, Calvin was not his authority, nor was Arminius his nemesis.

> I do not confine my self to *Calvin*, and all his particular Opinions, tho undoubtedly he was a very worthy and excellent Man, and of great Sense and judgment; but we are not to think that he had a Monopoly of Truth, or was Infallible [. . .] As for *Arminius*, it is granted, that he was a Man of great Parts and Learning, and therefore we may observe, that all his great and rational Strokes are on our side.[9]

---

6. Muller, *Calvin*, 51–69.

7. Milton, *Catholic and Reformed*, 407–8.

8. Edwards, *Theologia Reformata*, 1:ii–iv. Note: Quotations from early modern works follow the spelling, punctuation, capitalization, and italicization of the original source.

9. Edwards, *Veritas Redux*, xx.

What did Calvinism mean to Edwards? As he understood it, Calvinism was simply a useful designation for biblical truth, expounded by the Fathers and Reformers and expressed in the XXXIX Articles of the Church of England.

> That which we now call *Calvinism*, is to be found in the Writings of the *Antient Fathers* of the Church, and is the very Doctrine which the *First Reformers* of our own Church profess'd and maintain'd, and which is contain'd in our *Articles, Homilies,* and *Liturgy,* and which our *Archbishops* and *Bishops,* and the whole Body of our *English Clergy* have generally asserted and vindicated.[10]

He emphasized throughout his many discourses that "these Doctrines do not bear date with Mr. *Calvin* [. . . and] neither *Luther* nor *Calvin* were the Authors of our Doctrines, but we received them from the Word of God."[11] Edwards did give particular emphasis to the doctrine of predestination along with divine mercy and justice, not because he saw them as uniquely Calvinistic, but because they "are the brightest Demonstrations of the Truth of the *Divine Attributes*."[12] As he understood it, Calvinism was essentially equivalent in meaning with Reformed theology, having been since the beginning of the English Reformation "the very *Test* of the *Reformed Religion*."[13]

In late seventeenth-century England, however, Edwards's understanding of the term Calvinism was not universally accepted. Some used it only to refer to a Presbyterian understanding of church government or as a synonym for predestination. Even as Edwards had a broader view of Calvinism, he did not subscribe to everything he understood Calvin to say. "*Melanchton* and *Calvin* and some others of the Reformed assert that Christ is Mediator according to his Divine Nature only [. . . but we] assert that Christ is Mediator both as to his Humane and Divine Nature."[14]

By 1700, Calvinism, however it was defined, was not at all popular in England. Yet Edwards wrote numerous lengthy tomes expounding Calvinism as he understood it—works which were highly valued by pastors on both sides of the Atlantic long after he died. He wrote against

10. Edwards, *Veritas Redux*, xix.
11. Edwards, *Veritas Redux*, 496, 498.
12. Edwards, *Theologia*, 1:iii–iv.
13. Edwards, *Preacher, Third Part*, vi.
14. Edwards, *Doctrine of Faith*, 240.

Arminians in the church, but though he believed Arminians to be seriously in error on certain matters, he valued them as fellow believers and refused to separate himself from them. In other words, though Edwards was an unwavering and outspoken Calvinist, he was tolerant of Arminians because of his overriding commitment to the unity of the church. For him, unity was important not only because it was taught in the New Testament, but also because it is evidence of Christian love, which Jesus said was evidence of true faith.

So, unlike virtually all of his contemporaries who were concerned enough to write on the subject, it will be argued that in late seventeenth- and early eighteenth-century Protestant England, Edwards's practice of toleration was unique. Edwards has more often been portrayed as bigoted and unforgiving, especially when compared to his most famous opponent, the pioneer and champion of toleration, John Locke. But what does it mean to be tolerant? John Coffey maintains that toleration is not simply giving each person the freedom to believe as they desire; nor is it merely a matter of "indifference" toward the behavior or beliefs of others. It is "the policy of patient forbearance towards that which is not approved."[15] Edwards practiced genuine toleration toward all who accepted the foundational articles of the Church of England, even though he disapproved of the Arminian interpretation of those articles which was dominant at the time, the High Church ceremonialism of Archbishop Laud (1574–1656), and the Episcopalian form of government. But he was not tolerant of heresy within the church, because he believed that the acceptance of heresy would define the church out of existence. He was not trying to impose his own beliefs on everyone else, but simply limit church membership to orthodox believers as Christian orthodoxy had traditionally been understood. As will become clear, in late seventeenth- and early eighteenth-century England, Edwards was unique within the Church of England as an outspoken Calvinist who subordinated his closely-held Reformed theology to the unity of the church. By contrast, John Locke was himself not so tolerant of those who found his gospel hermeneutics lacking. But more significantly, the issues for which he wanted others to exercise their tolerance were ones toward which he was relatively indifferent.

Being a Calvinist, Edwards was also very committed to the related principle of the doctrinal purity of the church. Purity and unity have never been easily reconciled. Focus on purity leads to pedantic dogma,

---

15. Coffey, *Persecution and Toleration*, 10.

a major contributor to schism. On the other hand, to achieve complete unity would eliminate significant doctrines which necessarily define the Christian faith. Edwards viewed doctrinal purity on two levels. The basic level was defined by acceptance of the three formative creeds of the Church of England (Apostles', Nicene, Athanasian) as both necessary and sufficient. He also saw the creeds as the minimal basis for church unity because, for him, doctrinal truth was central. Ideally however, Edwards believed that moderate Calvinism represented the best understanding of Scripture and it was to that level of doctrinal purity that he worked to persuade others. But he emphasized, "I am not a rigid requirer of a *Perfect Agreement* among us." He referred to Augustine: "There be some things in which the Learnedst and best Defenders of the Catholick Rule may disagree among themselves *Salvà fidei compage*, without breaking the Bond of Faith, as well as of Charity."[16] Given Edwards's prominence in the debate over orthodoxy, his indirect influence on the Great Awakening, and his commitment to church unity which overlooked serious differences with his Arminian brethren and Episcopalian government, why is Edwards virtually unknown today except by a few scholars? This book seeks to help rectify this situation by explaining not only why Edwards was significant in his day, but also presenting him as someone to instruct the present day.

OVERVIEW

The story of Edwards's contribution to preserving the Church of England will unfold in eight chapters. Chapter 2 provides a summary of the cultural, philosophical, and religious climate of seventeenth-century England which gave rise to the revolutionary changes Edwards faced. This turmoil influenced his education at Cambridge, his parish ministry, and especially his public debates with prominent scholars of the day. Among the interrelated movements that he faced, some unique in England, were Cambridge Platonism, Latitudinarianism, Cartesianism, Laudianism, Calvinism, Arminianism, Arianism, Deism, Socinianism, and Unitarianism. In addition to the intermittent military conflicts and political and ecclesiastical convulsions, population centers faced periodic outbreaks of bubonic plague.

---

16. Edwards, *Preacher, Second Part*, 138. Latin: preserving the framework of faith.

Introduction

John Edwards's life and legacy are presented in Chapter 3. As no biography has been written of his life, there is much that we do not know. However from various sources, a clear enough picture emerges, beginning with his father Thomas, who has attracted much more attention for his turbulent life as an intemperate Presbyterian preacher. John followed his father in attending Cambridge and was ordained in 1662 less than a month after the Great Ejection. After serving as a well-regarded preacher in several parishes, he retired due to poor health and began writing, first to help raise biblical literacy among the laity, then to challenge heretics and others whose hermeneutics he faulted, and finally to provide ministers with contextualized Calvinist theology. Before his death he published over forty books, some of which were prized in the libraries of noted churchmen and used to train many pastors for generations after he died.

The fourth chapter is a look at Edwards's response to influential men he saw as undermining the Christian faith by misrepresenting and distorting biblical truth. Edwards became a primary combatant in the pamphlet wars against some of the most determined and gifted intellects of his day who were intent on eliminating what they perceived as rigid dogmatism in the Church of England by dismissing doctrines such as the Trinity as nonessential. These included mathematician and theologian William Whiston (1667–1752) and philosophers Locke and Clarke. Edwards believed that such heresy was a very serious threat to the church, claiming it led to atheism, and was zealous to defend against it. His uncompromising stand led his opponents and their allies to view Edwards as arrogant, angry, and mean-spirited, but a close look at what transpired does not bear that out. More than once, he asked his opponents for clarification and to show him how he may have misunderstood or misrepresented their views.

As described in chapter 5, Edwards also spilled a lot of ink criticizing and debating many within the church, mostly over Arminian theology. In these cases, he was also resolute in stating what he believed, but he exercised unusual tolerance by remaining in the church where his views were clearly the minority. Though Edwards was a vocal and committed Calvinist, he was quick to commend Latitudinarians within the church when they spoke against heresy or when their biblical exegesis made for useful citations. He took the XXXIX Articles to be a sound synopsis of Biblical doctrine and criticized Latitudinarians, high-flyers, and wayward Calvinists for misinterpreting them. Yet, despite serious differences with most of the Church of England leadership, he was determined to remain. Edwards was surprisingly accommodating for the sake of church unity.

Chapter 6 summarizes the primary ecclesiastical issues that led many not to conform. Though Edwards was more concerned with soteriological doctrines and theology proper, he had definite views on ecclesiology. Like most Church of England clergymen, he was strongly opposed to the papacy and Rome's view of the Eucharist. He was understanding of the reasons many dissenters had left the church, generally finding their theology more acceptable than many of his conforming brethren. For example, he was very critical of ceremonialism and Latitudinarian soteriology and opposed the Episcopalian system as unbiblical. In other words, he agreed with many of the dissenters on those very issues which caused them to depart, but he did not.

The seventeenth-century Church of England was rocked by extremist elements on all sides. But as chapter 7 relates, even the seemingly moderate voices who spoke against schism and claimed they were committed to church unity, were committed as it turned out, only on their own terms. Unlike those described in chapter 4 who wanted to make optional those doctrines traditionally considered as essential, such as the Trinity and deity of Christ, people in this category generally agreed on the fundamental essentials. However, they wanted to make certain issues, not traditionally considered as essentials of the Christian faith, essential. Among these were Laudians who demanded Catholic-like ceremonialism and Presbyterians who rejected the Episcopalian system of government. Edwards, by contrast, placed high value on nonessentials found in his Calvinist theology, but not as high as the unity of the church. What he held even higher were essentials as defined by the Nicene Creed because without them, the church would not really be the church. And even though Edwards conformed, he did not condemn those who did not, recognizing that each person must be free to follow their own conscience.

Chapter 8 summarizes Edwards's efforts to save the Church of England.

2

Edwards in His Historical Context

Even before he had to confront the philosophical and theological challenges of the day, as a boy, Edwards found himself in a world of turmoil and intolerance at a personal level. Before John was born, his father Thomas was imprisoned for his rabble-rousing preaching, popular with some, but not the authorities. Later his imprudent preaching again caught the attention of ecclesiastical officials who suspended his license. In 1647, he and some other obstinate ministers occupied Parliament for a few days, leading to his self-imposed exile in the Netherlands where he died before John turned eleven.

During Edwards's youth, England experienced a time of continuing political conflict. From his infancy until he was fourteen, there were domestic military hostilities culminating with the English Civil Wars. They were triggered by the attempt of King Charles I to force the Scots to submit to Church of England liturgy as prescribed by Archbishop Laud's 1637 revision of *BCP* and accompanying rubric. Intermittent conflict with the Dutch and Spanish continued for eight more years over trade and colonial interests and just before Edwards's twelfth birthday, the king was executed.

Not only was there turmoil in the state, but also within the church. When he was six years old, the Westminster Assembly was first convened to make the church more clearly Reformed and quash the Laudian movement. Less than two years later, Archbishop Laud was executed for high treason. When Edwards was nine, the episcopacy was officially abolished followed by the *BCP*. Fifteen years later Charles II had returned with the establishment of the former institutions of church and state.

Like many nearly forgotten men of history, John Edwards had neither a wide following, nor a popular cause. What is surprising is that, were it not for his early retirement, he would be an unknown Church of England cleric to this day. Few people have retired in their fifties due to "ill health" to write over forty scholarly books, many of which were studied and cited for generations after their death. Although little is known of his early life, professional or private, his works leave little doubt about where he stood in relation to many of the intellectual and theological conflicts of the seventeenth century.

THEOLOGY IN THE EARLY STUART CHURCH

Perhaps the best general description of Church of England dynamics since its break with Rome is: conflicted "heterogeneity indeed is arguably of the 'Anglican' essence."[1] It is generally acknowledged that Calvinism was dominant in the Elizabethan church, although the character of said Calvinism was somewhat in flux, partly in response to anti-Calvinist challenges, especially regarding predestination.[2] Two prominent cases involved sermons preached at Cambridge by Chaplain William Barrett (fl. 1595) in 1595 and Peter Baro (1534–99) in 1596. The first questioned predestination and the second advocated semi-Pelagianism. Condemned widely in the university community and by Archbishop John Whitgift (1530–1604), Barrett converted to Roman Catholicism and Baro resigned his Lady Margaret Professorship. The year 1595 was the same year Whitgift drafted the Lambeth Articles to eliminate any doubt that the XXXIX Articles were Calvinistic, but Queen Elizabeth did not approve them, probably to maintain the mystery of predestination and to avoid or at least diminish controversy.[3] It was during this time that William Laud was studying at Oxford. According to his biographer Peter Heylyn

---

1. Tyacke, "Laudians to Latitudinarians," 46.

2. To say that Calvinism was dominant is not to suggest universal agreement or absence of dissent. See, for example, White, "Rise of Arminianism," 33–54.

3. Russell, *Lancelot Andrewes*, 50–51; Doran, "Elizabeth I's Religion," 706–7.

(1599–1662), it was safer in those days "to have been look'd upon as an *Heathen* or *Publican*, than an *Anti-Calvinist*."[4]

But the situation began to change with James I, especially toward the end of his reign. Or did it? Some scholars such as Peter White argue that the "'rise of Arminianism' looks like a puritan alibi for repeated failure to impose rigid predestination doctrines on the Church of England."[5] Others such as Nicholas Tyacke see a seventeenth-century Arminian coup of church leadership initiated by Archbishop Laud: "Without doubt Laud was a passionate anti-Calvinist, who denounced the Lambeth Articles as containing 'fatal opinions.' He also condemned Calvinist teaching on reprobation and perseverance."[6] Edwards often blamed Laud for what to him were England's greatest seventeenth-century problems: the civil wars and the departure in worship and doctrine from the course of reform initiated by Thomas Cranmer (1489–1556).

> In short, our English Divines continued firm and unshaken in the Doctrine of *Calvin* and professed an opposition to the *Arminian* Points till the close of the foresaid King *James's* Reign, and the beginning of King *Charles the First's* at which time and afterwards some Court Doctors and others who saw that the owning and professing of *Arminianism* was the way to Preferment, set up for this Perswasion, and in their Discourses and Writings, were very fierce against *Calvin*: especially this Game was play'd when Archbishop *Laud* mounted the Throne of *Canterbury*. This is the True Date, this was the first Conspicuous Rise of *Arminianism* among our Churchmen.[7]

King James died in March 1625 and within fifteen months, newly-crowned Charles I issued a decree effectively suppressing Calvinism. Charles recognized Laud's potential as a valuable ally and rewarded him accordingly.[8] The only divine in seventeenth-century England to have a

---

4. Heylyn, *Cyprianus Anglicus*, 48.
5. White, "Rise of Arminianism," 54.
6. Tyacke, "Rise of Arminianism," 215.
7. Edwards, *Preacher, Third Part*, 272–73. So it was clear to Edwards that the rise of Arminianism commenced with Laud's appointment as archbishop. He quoted Bishop John Hacket (1592–1670) in his *Life of Archbishop Williams* as saying that Laud "was not only a great Patron of them that maintained Arminius's Doctrine, but a great Discountenancer of the opposite part: and since he shook the Box, they (i.e., the Anti-Arminians) were but Duices and Trais in all Church Preferment." Edwards, *Preacher, Second Part*, 170–71.
8. Tyacke, *Rise of Arminianism*, 202–3, 211–12. Prior to Laud, Tyacke cites as

movement as his namesake, Laud "deserves to rank among the greatest archbishops of Canterbury since the Reformation. Indeed one is hard pressed to think of others in the same league, save the obvious Thomas Cranmer."[9] Both were executed, Cranmer for heresy and Laud for high treason, but despite their premature deaths, both were influential long after they died, significantly altering the theological landscape of England.

Educated at St. John's College, Oxford, BA, 1594; MA, 1598; BD, 1602?; DD, 1608, Laud first came under the influence of Arminian tutor John Buckeridge (1562–1631).[10] Laud's 1611 nomination as president of St. John's College, Oxford was unsuccessfully, but strongly, opposed by Calvinist Archbishop George Abbot (1562–1633), who called him "a papist or, at least, very popishly inclined."[11] With successive promotions (Bishop of London, Chancellor of Oxford, Archbishop of Canterbury), his anti-Calvinism became increasingly bold: endorsing the view of free will held by Semi-Pelagian John Cassian in a 1622 sermon before King James and characterizing Calvinist teachings as *"fatal."* While Laud's motives at the time may be impossible to discern, by 1628 he was censoring sermons at Paul's Cross, "the most public pulpit in the land."[12]

As Laud amassed greater influence, he pushed his agenda forcefully and shrewdly, but in the end, not shrewdly enough. He and Charles cooperated on a common goal: to ally church and king as a unified front against their mutual enemies, like the Puritans. Above all, Charles wanted peace. Laud had three objectives: church unity, recognition of the episcopacy

---

examples, Calvinist works by William Perkins (1558–1602), Gervase Babington (1550–1610), Jacobus Kimedoncius (d.1596), Zacharias Ursinus (1534–1583), Robert Some (1542–1609) being approved, but not those of anti-Calvinist writers such as Peter Baro and Richard Thomson (d.1613).

9. Tyacke, "Archbishop Laud," 51.

10. Adair, "Laud and the Church," 125.

11. Lake, "Calvinism," 50. Despite the fact that Laud continued to be called a papist by his opponents (primarily for his ceremonialist emphasis and his recognition of Rome as the true church), he did oppose Rome strongly at times as in his conference with Jesuit John Percy (a.k.a. Fisher), where he denied the legitimacy of the papacy and on the topic of unwritten tradition, stated "not the Church of England only, but all Protestants, agree most truly, and most strongly in this, *That the Scripture is sufficient to salvation, and containes in it all things necessary to it.*" Quoted in Quantin, *Church of England*, 195. See also, Patterson, *King James VI*, 343–44.

12. Tyacke, "Archbishop Laud," 57–60, 65–66. Indicating the continuing debate over Laud's convictions, Quantin says that "Laud and Charles I did not intend to mount an attack against Augustine but rather to silence controversy on the whole issue." Quantin, *Church of England*, 189.

as divinely instituted, and High Church ceremonialism. He believed that the key to unity was uniformity. So intent was he to achieve unity that he ordered all English churches located in the "*Low-countries*" to "conform in all things to the Church of *England*"; otherwise "there would be a perpetual Seminary for breeding up men in Schism and Faction, to the disturbance of this Kingdom."[13] Not only was preaching censored, but also university lectures and book publishing. A request by Archbishop James Ussher (1581–1656) to publish his edition of the letters of Polycarp and Ignatius was refused by Regius Professor of Divinity John Prideaux (1578–1650) because he feared Laud:

> I am loth to speak, but the truth is, our Oxford presses are not for pieces of that coin. We can print here Smiglecius the Jesuit's metaphysical logic [. . .] but matters that entrench nearer on the true divinity must be strictly overseen.

Prideaux was known as a "moderate Calvinist."[14]

Laud's lieutenants worked to persuade the nation that Laudianism alone best represented the true church by framing the conflict as conformist against nonconformists, sound tradition against error, loyalty versus sedition, and ultimately good opposed to evil. They tailored their message for different audiences. For one they asserted that the Church of England was clearly part of the continental Reformed tradition and therefore to oppose Laudian reforms was to oppose Calvin, Luther, and the Reformation itself. For a second they argued that the Church of England was the most authentic branch of the Reformation, in contrast to Calvin and Luther. By a third message, Laud was correcting faulty interpretations of sixteenth-century canons and church rulings to justify High Church furniture and ceremony revisions. Fourth, they claimed to be following in the footsteps of sixteenth-century heroes who suffered courageously to defend the truth. Anyone who opposed Laud was compared to the despised Queen Mary, while Charles was equated with Elizabeth, who continued popular and revered long after her death.[15]

Laudians advanced their approach to worship under the biblical prescription, "O worship the LORD in the beauty of holiness" (Ps 96:9), reversing many of the sixteenth-century architectural reforms which had been designed to confirm the theological break with Rome. Laud replaced

---

13. Heylyn, *Cyprianus*, 219–20.
14. Prideaux quoted in Trevor-Roper, *Archbishop Laud* 1573–1645, 112–13.
15. Lane, *Laudians*, 72–74.

the wooden communion table of the Lord's Supper with a stone altar, often raised, and set back along the eastern wall. Images of Mary, Jesus, angels, and biblical characters were introduced in stained glass, as well as in wood and stone carvings. Elaborate vestments were brought back. Candles proliferated. What had been relatively plain became ornate. New liturgies and ceremonies, including bowing took on a ritualistic air.[16] Laud argued that the altar was more important than the pulpit because "a greater reverence, no doubt, is due to the body than to the word of our Lord."[17] Laudians referred to clergy as priests.[18] Laud met resistance in the cathedrals where he focused most of his attention, believing that cathedrals should set an example for the churches.[19]

Not everyone was convinced and not all who opposed the Laudian reforms were Puritans. Accused of being a Puritan, conformist Peter Smart simply wanted to follow established church law. He attacked the ceremonialism of Bishop Richard Neile (then) of Durham for departing from the *BCP*. For Smart, the prayer book was about the gospel of Jesus Christ; the new ceremonies and vestments about entertainment and idolatry. His criticisms brought him over eleven years in prison (1629–41).[20]

When Charles reconvened Parliament to pay for the Bishops' Wars of 1639 and 1640, Laud was impeached for high treason.[21] At his trial, Laud pleaded not guilty, taking no responsibility for what he could attribute to others, especially the king.

> They say, *I injoined the wearing of Whites*, &c. Surely I understand myself a great deal better, than to injoin where I have no Power. Perhaps I might express that, which *His Majesty* Commanded me, when I was *Dean* of *His Majesty's Chapel* here.[22]

Given his strong desire for uniformity in the church, it is difficult to believe that Laud was not directly responsible for imposing ceremonial worship on the Scottish and Irish Presbyterians, leading to rebellion in both places. But the cause of the revolt was broader than ecclesiastical tyranny. Protestants and Catholics alike were incensed by English political

---

16. Fincham and Tyacke, *Altars Restored*, 74–125.
17. Laud, *Speech Delivered*, 57.
18. Russell, "Introduction," 21.
19. Atherton, "Cathedrals," 895–918.
20. Lane, *Laudians*, 17–26.
21. Milton, *Laudian and Royalist Polemic*, 107.
22. Laud, *History*, 1:89.

subjection. A riot broke out at St. Giles Cathedral on July 23, 1637 the first time that the new prayer book was used in Scotland, prompting Laud's reaction:

> For though I like the *Book* exceeding well, and hope I shall be able to maintain any thing that is in it, and wish with all my Heart that it had been entertained there; yet I did ever desire, it might come to them with their own liking and approbation. Nay, I did ever, upon all Occasions, call upon the *Scottish Bishops* to do nothing in this Particular, but by Warrant of Law.[23]

The rebellion may have been about English domination in general, but the prayer book was an emotive and clear manifestation of that policy, precipitating violent reactions.[24] Trying to engender sympathy, Laud attempted to cast himself as a martyr, identifying with righteous Job. Parliament was not impressed. They disregarded the king's pardon and allowed him to preach his own funeral sermon.[25]

During Laud's lifetime, judgments about him were quite polarized. Hagiographer and chaplain to the king Peter Heylyn, whom Anthony Milton calls "the most important defender of Laudian policies," concluded his uncritical biography attempting to impart an incomparable legacy, stating that

> it will appear, to an equal and impartial Reader, That he was a man of such eminent Vertues, such an exemplary Piety toward God, such an unwearied Fidelity to his Gracious Sovereign, of such a publick Soul towards Church and State, so fixt a Constancy in Friendship, and one so little byassed by his private Interestes that *Plurarch*, if he were alive, [we] would be much troubled to find a sufficient Parallel wherewith to match him in all the Lineaments of perfect Verture.[26]

Recent assessments are considerably more measured, although generally divided by the following questions: How influential was Laudianism with respect to church and state? Was Laud an ardent Arminian? One assessment doubts Laud's Arminianism, sees him as reasonably tolerant, concluding that his long-term influence was minimal—a perspective which Laud himself would have shared. "Laudianism itself had

23. Laud, *History*, 1:109.
24. Carlton, *Archbishop William Laud*, 192.
25. Laud, *History*, 223-34, 447-51.
26. Milton, *Laudian and Royalist*, 3; Heylyn, *Cyprianus*, 508.

little political momentum" and he became "the obvious scapegoat for Carolinism." As evidence that Laud was not anti-Calvinist, Julian Davies found only three cases where Laud investigated ministers for their predestinarian views in the early 1630s, claiming that Laud's real motivation for any discipline was the peace and unity of the church.[27]

On the other hand, David Como found at least ten such cases against Calvinists, stating that there is "no evidence that he ever disciplined or even questioned any London preacher for Arminian, universalist, or anti-Calvinist statements." If peace and unity was his only concern, why did Laud not go after vocal Arminian anti-Calvinists? No, Laud believed that Calvinism was both a serious theological error and that it led to "political and ecclesiastical discord." Como concludes, "the patterns of evidence presented here suggest very strongly that Laud engaged in a conscious, deliberate, and in many ways devious campaign to silence London's Calvinists."[28] A large majority of those appointed as deans, bishops, royal chaplains, and hundreds of clergy receiving an allowance from the crown were friends and allies of Laud. Fincham concludes, "Laud's commanding influence in patronage reflected his intimate standing with the king, and has no obvious precedent in the post-Reformation Church."[29]

Although Laud favored Arminianism, not all Laudians were Arminians. Robert Sanderson (1587–1663) was a prominent, albeit moderate, Calvinist, who aligned himself with Laud apparently because he placed high value on church unity.[30] In general, Laudians saw Puritans as more disruptive of ecclesiastical concord than Catholics. Laudianism was broader than the theology of the archbishop, sharing some of the characteristics and goals of the Latitudinarians and Cambridge Platonists, such as toleration and church unity. But Laud's toleration was selective. He exhibited wide latitude on doctrine but none on liturgy.[31]

Clearly there is no consensus on the extent of the Carolinian decline of Calvinism, nor Laud's contribution to it. Many, including Edwards, saw Laud's heavy-handed, ambitious campaign as the main contributor to his own demise, the Civil War, and revival of Puritanism. However the interregnum proved to be only a temporary setback for Laud's successors

27. Davies, *Caroline Captivity*, 301–04.
28. Como, "Predestination and Political Conflict," 289, 291, 292.
29. Fincham, "William Laud," 79–81, 92.
30. Lake, "Serving God," 81–116.
31. Abbey and Overton, *English Church*, 1:368.

as the return of Charles II led to the 1662 ejection of some 2000 ministers who would not comply with the new rubric and *BCP*.[32] Mark Goldie points out that ejected Presbyterians had far more in common with conformers remaining in the church than they did with dissenting Baptists. They "adhered to most of the Church's Thirty-Nine Articles and most of the liturgy of the Prayer Book," while many who remained in the church "continued quietly to ignore the rubrics to which they objected," a point reiterated by Edwards.[33]

One thing is clear: whether the debate was between Protestants and Catholics or between Arminians and Calvinists, for the most part, men on both sides appealed to the Fathers to substantiate their own understanding of contentious issues such as the sacraments, soteriology, use of tradition, sufficiency of Scripture, and even the interpretation of the XXXIX Articles. This was especially true in the early seventeenth-century of anti-Arminians such as Robert Abbot (1560–1617), John Davenant (1572–1641), Prideaux, and Samuel Ward (1572–1643), who cited Augustine rather than Calvin, leading their opponents to find fault with their interpretations of Augustine, or of Augustine himself.[34] Few disagreements were resolved because the Fathers were not in agreement and even claims to follow the consensus of the Fathers did not help as disputants on both sides rarely agreed on the interpretation of that consensus. Edwards later observed that none of the Fathers could be depended upon all the time.

THEOLOGY IN THE LATER STUART CHURCH

Citing G. R. Cragg, Daniel Howe states that "most remaining traces of Anglican Calvinism evaporated quickly after 1660." There is little disagreement that Arminianism became dominant in the Church of England following the return of Charles II, but Howe's statement is open to varying interpretations depending on the meaning of evaporate and quickly.[35] Of course, most of the ejected ministers in 1662 were Calvinist, but

---

32. Seed, *Dissenting Histories*, 16–17, 36. Although 2000 ejected is commonly accepted, a more conservative calculation is 1760. See Gatiss, *Tragedy*, 8, 26.

33. Goldie, *Roger Morrice*, 227.

34. Quantin, *Church of England*, 176–87.

35. Howe, "Decline of Calvinism," 310. What Cragg actually wrote was that by the early eighteenth century, "Calvinism in England fell from a position of immense authority to obscurity and insignificance," due largely to some Calvinists' "reckless

there were notable Calvinists who remained, such as Bishop of Lincoln Thomas Barlow (1608/9–91), Vice-Chancellor of Oxford John Conant (1608–1694), Bishop of Derry Ezekiel Hopkins (1634–90), Bishop of Chester John Pearson (1613–86), Bishop of Norwich Edward Reynolds (1599–1676), and Dean of Ripon Thomas Tully (1620–76).[36] However, as the century wore on, retiring Calvinists holding prominent posts tended to be replaced by Latitudinarians. While it has been commonplace to attribute the Calvinian decline to the heavy-handed rule of Laud's successors in the Restoration church, as is often the case, the actual story is more complicated. A recent study argues that the pivotal point in the transition to Arminian dominance occurred when historians least expected it: during the Cromwellian era, fostered by increased religious toleration and the adoption of Arminian soteriology by some influential Puritans, such as John Goodwin, John Horn, Thomas Moore, and Tobias Conyers.[37]

This increased toleration opened the way for another movement to arise within the Church of England following the Restoration, competing not only with Calvinism, but also with Laudianism. Latitudinarianism might be seen as an offshoot of Laudianism because both were insistent on an Episcopalian Church of England and mostly favored Arminian theology. But they differed in important respects, which led to conflict. While the Laudians emphasized High Church ceremonialism and were generally intolerant, Latitudinarians followed Low Church ecclesiology, proclaimed a morality-based soteriology, and were quite tolerant, even toward Puritans (except of their harsh doctrines).[38]

Of Latitudinarians Bishop Edward Fowler (1632–1714) and Archbishop John Tillotson (1630–94), John Spurr wrote,

> The restated doctrine of salvation had no room for [what is implied] about the hopelessness of the human condition. [. . .] The "moderate" divines were proud of the clarity and reasonableness of their own message when compared with the absurd and irrational system of the puritans.[39]

Latitudinarians viewed their mission as saving the church from internal turmoil and external attacks. By presenting the Christian faith as

---

lack of moderation." Cragg, From Puritanism, 30, 31.
36. See Hampton, *Anti-Arminians;* Tyacke, *Aspects of English Protestantism.*
37. Ollerton, "The Crisis of Calvinism," 52–70.
38. Tyacke, "Laudians to Latitudinarians;" Spurr, "Latitudinarianism."
39. Spurr, "Latitudinarianism," 76–77.

reasonable, given that no one can oppose what is reasonable; by persuading people to accept a gospel without controversial doctrines, which lead to dissension and schism; and by employing sermons which emphasize the blessings to society of following Christian ethics, these men were convinced that the church would be strong and well received.[40] A church at peace with itself would make it easier to persuade those who were attracted to Puritanism, Roman Catholicism, Socinianism, etc. to return to the true church.

But lax interpretations of the XXXIX Articles resulted in charges of heresy against Archbishop Tillotson, Bishop Gilbert Burnet (1643–1715), and their associates beginning in the 1690s. Church officials realized that public debate inspired by a pamphlet war was no way to settle important doctrinal issues and finally called a convocation in 1701 to officially and clearly demarcate orthodoxy from heresy, especially with regard to the doctrine of the Trinity. Censured were *Christianity Not Mysterious* by Deist John Toland (1670–1722) and Bishop Burnet's *Exposition of the Thirty-nine Articles*.[41] According to Burnet, people subscribed to the XXXIX Articles with widely different interpretations, which is why the charges of Socinianism against Latitudinarians were both true and false. He wrote that the disputed articles had been

> conceived in such general words that it can admit of different literal and grammatical senses, even when the senses given are plainly contrary to one another, yet both may subscribe the Article with a good conscience, and without any equivocation.[42]

Edwards argued that the XXXIX Articles should be interpreted in a Calvinian sense consistent with the intentions of Archbishop Cranmer. In addition to allowing broad interpretations, Burnet questioned whether the Apostles' Creed was written by the Apostles or the Athanasian Creed by Athanasius, which the church took as questioning their authority.[43] Edwards would have agreed with him when he said, "we receive those Creeds not for their own sakes [. . . but] because we believe that the Doctrine which they declare, is contained in the Scriptures."[44] But the convocation's charges of heresy were too serious for the party of toleration to

40. Kim, "Religion of Reason," 49.
41. Greig, "Bishop Gilbert Burnet," 249–50, 257.
42. Burnet, *Exposition*, 10.
43. Greig, "Heresy Hunt," 586.
44. Burnet, *Exposition*, 128.

tolerate. Soon, prominent Latitudinarians such as Burnet and Benjamin Hoadly (1676-1761) responded by accusing the High Churchmen of treasonous designs with Rome.[45]

Latitudinarians recognized that reason and dogma are not in opposition, but toleration for clearly conflicting doctrinal understandings eventually led to the Latitudinarian inclusion of almost anyone. In the seventeenth century, Latitudinarians generally upheld orthodox doctrines such as the Trinity, Incarnation, and Resurrection, but by the beginning of the eighteenth century, heterodox men such as Locke, Clarke, and Whiston could be considered Latitudinarians.[46] This liberalizing development sheds light on the noteworthy Latitudinarian legacy: "If you ignore the Latitudinarians, you cannot explain the emergence [...] of Deism"; i.e., Latitudinarianism fostered a moralistic interpretation of the Christian faith.[47] From a small minority in the 1660s, Latitudinarians grew to a position of "dominant" influence in the Church of England thirty years later with Tillotson and Thomas Tenison (1636-1715) serving successively as Archbishops of Canterbury.[48] This was the Church of England, in which John Edwards served.

Another strand of this story is the changing nature of Puritan movement following 1662. Although the Puritan reform movement within the Church of England essentially ended in 1662, ejected Puritans refocused their efforts to influence the broader society as Whigs, diffusing their earlier Calvinist emphasis.[49] With their shift toward Arminianism and Socinianism, the Calvinist influence of Presbyterians also declined so that, despite their denials, "by the end of the seventeenth century they construed Calvin's legacy in ways that were distant from the orthodoxies that had prevailed a century earlier."[50]

APPROACH

This book is based primarily on Edwards's published works, along with relevant works of his contemporaries. I have failed to locate a personal

---

45. e.g., Hoadly, *Letter*.
46. Griffin, *Latitudinarianism*, 46-47, 90-91.
47. Cragg, *Puritanism*, 81.
48. Rivers, *Reason, Grace, and Sentiment*, 1:26.
49. Goldie, *Roger Morrice*, 190-93.
50. Goldie, *Roger Morrice*, 254. See also, Bolam, *English Presbyterians*.

diary and there is no evidence that he kept one. Some of the correspondence between Edwards and others is extant and has been incorporated, but it appears that most of it is lost. The situation is similar for letters, diaries, and notes which mention him.[51] Although he freely expressed his views on theological, historical, philosophical, and scientific controversies, he did not think it significant to speak of more personal matters, such as his family or his pastoral ministry, which means that a number of interesting questions cannot be answered. For example, what was his relationship with his mother and father? Both as a child and as an adult, what did he think of his father's work? To what extent was his own outlook and demeanor influenced by his father? How was his worldview challenged and changed during his Cambridge education? Did he have any reservations about being ordained in the Church of England immediately following the Great Ejection? Which men were most influential in his life as a young man with respect to his theology and philosophy of ministry? How did his thinking change during his active pastoral ministry? At which aspect(s) of the pastoral ministry did he feel most successful? Most challenged? How did he divide his time between work and leisure? What sort of husband was he? How did his parishioners view him? Members of the communities in which he lived? What was the nature of the encouragement (or discouragement) that he experienced in writing fifty books? Did he have close friends among the clergy within the Church of England? Among the nonconforming clergy?

Limited biographical information on Edwards comes from both the *DNB* and *ODNB*, along with several biographical dictionaries published in the late eighteenth and nineteenth centuries. The primary source for their material is the second edition of Biographia Britannica edited by Andrew Kippis (1725–95).[52]

Research for this work was directed by the following questions: Given Edwards's strong Calvinist convictions, why was he so loyal to the Church of England when he was so theologically out of step with

---

51. Significant direct references to or of Edwards used in this research include those by Lawrence Fogg (1623–1718), Richard Kidder (1633–1703), Simon Patrick (1626–1707), Jonathan Warne, George Whitefield, John Woodward (1665–1728), and Americans Jonathan Edwards and Cotton Mather. Undoubtedly there were others.

52. Kippis, *Biographia Britannica*. Other dictionaries include Johnson, *New and General Biographical Dictionary*; Aikin and Overton, *General Biography*; Chalmers, *General Biographical Dictionary*; Gorton, *General Biographical Dictionary*; Rose, *New General Biographical Dictionary*. See the conclusion of the Biographical Sketch in Chapter 3 for additional comments.

its leadership? Were there other outspoken Calvinists like Edwards who conformed? What were the primary reasons so many Calvinist did not conform? What was Edwards's position on issues which led other Calvinists not to conform? How did Edwards understand Calvinism? How accurate were Edwards's contemporary critics in their assessment of him? How accurate was Edwards in his assessment of his opponents? To what extent were Edwards's works, particularly those of a polemical nature, influential? How should we best understand his legacy?

To answer these questions, hundreds of primary works by and about Edwards and those with whom he interacted were collected and studied, along with secondary sources which concern Edwards, his contemporaries, and relevant political, scientific, ecclesiastical, philosophical, and theological aspects of Early Modern England. My intention has been to be critically objective and to avoid interpreting Edwards through a theological, philosophical, or historical lens. I did not make a diligent effort to uncover material among unpublished diaries from the seventeenth and eighteenth centuries or in the church and municipal records in places where Edwards lived and worked. It is likely that useful documents may yet be discovered to help answer open questions about Edwards. For example, though he served only briefly in Colchester and though he was not the focus of Timothy Glines's research cited in Appendix A, Edwards makes an appearance in his PhD dissertation.

The overarching question that directed this research was, in the mind of Edwards, what is the church? In answer to that question, Edwards's writing career went in two directions addressing the theological boundaries of the church. On the one hand, the church is defined by certain core beliefs such that to deny them places someone outside the church. On the other hand, schismatic movements were leading some people who held these core beliefs to abandon the Church of England because other beliefs, traditionally deemed nonessential were considered by them to be essential. This schismatic tendency also occurred within the Church of England whereby its leaders were adding nonessentials to these traditionally established core beliefs. In his works, Edwards addressed both positions: those who sought to weaken or diminish the set of core beliefs long-established as orthodox and also those who found those core beliefs to be inadequate. To further explain Edwards's view of the church, I collected and summarized his teaching on ecclesiological conformity, nonconformity, unity, and schism, along with that of some significant contemporaries, who held different views.

3

THE LIFE AND LEGACY OF JOHN EDWARDS

On 25 July 1665 five-year-old John Morley of Holy Trinity parish in Cambridge died. On his chest were found black spots, tokens of the plague. His little brother, who had sat on a stool round-eyed and fearful watching him, also had spots on his face: he was swept from his mother's arms by men dressed in white robes and taken away. He died in the pest house on 5 August 1665, and the distraught parents were shut up in their house with a red cross painted on the door and the words "Lord Have Mercy on Us" written below it. In Cambridge, the nightmare had begun.[1]

THIS TERROR FIRST STRUCK Cambridge in April 1349, nine months after sailors brought it to England. The plague caused panic, death, and disruption at irregular intervals until the seventeenth century, when it appeared in 1625, 1630, 1631, 1637, 1638, 1642, 1646, 1665, and 1666. The cause was commonly thought to be foul air from garbage or manure occurring with the warm weather. Some thought it was simply God's judgment on an immoral culture. Astrologers had forecast the plague's return following comet sightings in late 1664 and early 1665.[2]

As it was believed that the germ agent was airborne, public meetings of all kinds were cancelled, including the traditional late-summer

---

1. Lord, *Great Plague*, 1.
2. Lord, *Great Plague*, 2–6.

fair on Stourbridge Common, located on either side of the Bridge across a slow-moving stream known as Stour. Chartered in 1219, by the seventeenth century, it had become the largest fair in Europe, lasting for nearly a month each September. Writing in 1722, Daniel Defoe (1660-1731) called it "not only the greatest in the whole nation, but in the world."[3]

Besides the fair, morning worship at Cambridge churches was cancelled. City aldermen did not meet to attend to any of their official business.[4] Infected people were kept in isolation. As the incubation period seemed to vary considerably, often entire families were quarantined in their homes if one member was thought to be infected.

It is difficult to know how many died of plague during 1665-66 because neither records nor diagnostics were that accurate, but estimates put the number of deaths at 12% of a population of eight thousand or so. Not only was Cambridge University closed, but when it re-opened, enrollment was lower than at any time during the seventeenth century. Most of the town residents who were able, escaped to the countryside, just like those in London.[5] Isaac Newton left Trinity College (BA, 1665) for his home at Woolsthorpe, where he is reported to have discovered the universal law of gravitation, watching an apple fall from the family tree.[6] Robert Hooke had just proposed a calibration standard for the thermometer when he retired to Surrey.[7]

BIOGRAPHICAL SKETCH

John Edwards had been appointed curate of the prominent Holy Trinity Church the year before this plague began. As a young cleric, he no doubt began this first charge with great enthusiasm and optimism. His preaching was described as "plain, practical and temperate," attracting many from both the town and university, including masters of three Cambridge colleges: Anthony Sparrow (1612-85) of Queen's, Joseph Beaumont (1616-99) of Peterhouse, and John Pearson of Trinity.[8]

---

3. Defoe, *Tour*, 164.
4. Lord, *Great Plague*, 67-69.
5. Lord, *Great Plague*, 101, 128.
6. Mullinger, *History*, 160-61.
7. Purrington, *First Professional Scientist*, 50-51.
8. Robinson, "John Edwards;" Rose, *New General Biographical Dictionary*.

In addition to preaching and administering the sacraments, Edwards had a clear sense of what it meant to care for the flock. When churches were closed by the plague, he realized that he was needed even more to bring God's comfort and encouragement to people isolated and dealing with great anxiety, fear, and grief. So while most who had the means left the cities for the country, he moved from his university residence into the town, where he remained for the duration of the plague in order to better serve the people of Holy Trinity Parish.[9] Subsequent analysis has shown that virtually all deaths from that plague occurred in the area of the town, not the university, no doubt because the university was virtually closed.[10] From his parish residence, Edwards was well situated to help families such as the Morleys, for which he was greatly commended.

His first publication was a sermon preached during this time, *The Plague of the Heart*. Taking his text from Solomon's dedicatory prayer, where he entreated God to hear the future prayers of his people, Edwards focused on First Kings 8:38 where Solomon referred to a man's sin as "the plague of his heart." Dreadful and ominous as this black death was, Edwards admonished his congregants that sin was a far worse curse. Those who escape this present plague face physical death, but the spiritual plague separates one from God for an eternity of unimaginable suffering. By comparison, this present plague is nothing. The plagues with which God struck Egypt are nothing. For these physical plagues, people seek relief from "Quacks and Empiricks [. . .] who can *palliate* the disease," but even St. Sebastian and legitimate doctors provide no cure.[11] Unlike this and other plagues of history, no one can escape this plague of the heart because it is "that originall corruption and pollution which we derived from the loyns of our first Parents."[12] And although we know not the cause nor the cure for the current plague, the cause of the spiritual plague is no mystery and God has mercifully provided a cure for all who believe. Therefore, we face this crisis without fear because our hope is in

---

9. Robinson, "John Edwards."

10. Lord, *Great Plague*, viii.

11. Simpson and Weiner, *Oxford English Dictionary*. Empirick: "A member of the sect among ancient physicians called Empirici (Εμπειρικοι'), who (in contrast to the Dogmatici and Methodici) drew their rules of practice entirely from experience, to the exclusion of philosophical theory." Sebastian (d. c.288) became the patron saint of plagues as the result of a legend describing a plague that subsided when an altar honoring Sebastian was erected at the Church of Saint Peter in Pavia, Lombardy. Edwards, *Plague*, 13.

12. Edwards, *Plague*, 4.

God. Edwards's pastoral words of hope and comfort concluded with, "Be not afraid to take Death by the *cold hand*," because

> if we are *shot* in *Gods service* we can not suffer, if we are *taken off* by the *Arrows of the Almighty*, our end will be unspeakably comfortable; if we are snatched away with the *common calamity*, even then we are safe and secure.[13]

John Edwards was born on February 26, 1637 in Hereford to Thomas (1599–1647) and Mary Edwards. Like his son John, Thomas was ordained as a young man following a Cambridge education. Like John, he began his preaching career at Cambridge, but that was about the extent of the resemblance. Thomas' approach to ministry was that of a recalcitrant, anti-Arminian firebrand, for which he was summoned repeatedly before the ecclesiastical courts, eventually coming to the attention of Archbishop Laud. Finally he received an order to recant, with which he complied on April 6, 1628. But after moving to London, he aligned with others who were "suppressed or suspended" by Laud, but managed to continue preaching in more rural areas, including Christchurch, Hereford, Dunmow, and Godalming.[14]

Although Thomas Edwards refused to abide by prevailing Church of England conventions, neither did he favor the Independents whom he viewed as divisive. He was convinced that only the Presbyterian understanding of church government was biblical, avoiding extremes of the Episcopal Church of England and the fragmented, nonconforming Independents. In 1641, he entered the national debate over church government with a pamphlet, *Reasons Against the Independent Government of Particular Churches*. Provocative though it was, there was little response because ministers meeting at the time with the respected Edmund Calamy the Elder (1600–66) agreed not to quarrel publicly about their theological differences in order to unite against popery. Within two years, however, Independent ministers published a response to which Edwards replied with his *Apologia*, where he attacked Independent ministers by name, including Jeremiah Burroughs (1599–1646), William Bridge (1600?–1670), Thomas Goodwin (1600–80), Philip Nye (1596?–1672), and Sydrach Sympson (1600?–55), increasing his notoriety.[15]

---

13. Edwards, *Plague*, 39, 40.
14. Vian, "Thomas Edwards."
15. Baker, "Thomas Edwards."

His biggest concern, however, was false teaching that seemed to be tolerated everywhere. The year following *Apologia*, *Gangræna* appeared, a hastily written, poorly organized, and extremely contentious defense of orthodoxy as he saw it. Subtitled, "A Catalogue and Discovery of many of the Errours, Heresies, Blasphemies and pernicious Practices of the Sectaries of this time," he condemned over two hundred sects, errors, and heresies. Such a reaction did it set off, that he was compelled to revise and reprint it almost immediately. With the third edition of Part One he added Part Two, in order to respond to his critics.[16] The summer following December 1646 when Part Three was published, he was involved in unsuccessful political agitation against the New Model Army when he and some other ministers occupied Parliament. It generated so much hostility that he thought it best to leave England for Holland. Late in the year, he became ill and died on February 7, 1648 of what was thought to be malaria (*quartan ague*), leaving his widow with five young children.[17] One of those Edwards condemned for his independent polity was John Milton (1608–74) who later ridiculed Edwards, along with Robert Baillie, in his poem, "On the New Forcers of Conscience under the Long Parliament":

> Men, whose life, learning, faith, and pure intent,
> Would have been held in high esteem with Paul,
> Must now be named and printed heretics
> By shallow Edwards and Scotch What d'ye call[18]

What affect the turmoil surrounding his father's activities, not to mention his father's death, had on young John cannot be surmised; neither is it known if his mother remarried. Fortunately he was able to enroll in Merchant Taylor's School in London about that time where he received a good education afforded because his mother had received a sizable inheritance.[19] There John studied seven years before being admitted to St. John's College, Cambridge at the age of seventeen. He arrived at Cambridge shortly after the introduction of Cartesian philosophy

---

16. Hughes, *Gangræna*. *Gangræna* appeared in three parts. Part One was in its third edition when Part Two was added. Part Two appeared in two editions and Part Three in one.

17. Vian, "Thomas Edwards"; Baker, "Thomas Edwards."

18. Cleveland, *Poetical Works*, 510. Scottish clergyman Robert Baillie was known as an impudent member of the Glasgow Assembly.

19. Kippis, "John Edwards."

into the curriculum and came under the influence of Presbyterian Anthony Tuckney (1599–1670). Formerly Tuckney had been a member of the Westminster Assembly where, as a major contributor, he drafted significant portions of the Larger Catechism.[20] When the doctrinal issues were settled, he left for the vice-chancellorship of Cambridge and subsequently professor and master at St. John's, where he was known as a man of integrity, principle, and academic rigor. Although theologically conservative, he treated his opponents with respect and often cooperated with them to further mutual interests. He was appointed a member of the Savoy Conference in 1661 to revise the *BCP*, but did not think it worthwhile to attend. Like many other Presbyterians hoping for some toleration, he welcomed the return of Charles II. But when the *BCP* was re-instituted in chapel at St. John's, he refused to attend. With the return of the royalist faction, Tuckney was dismissed from both positions at St. John's. The reason given was his age and health, even though he was only sixty-two. Tuckney moved to London and preached on occasion to private congregations. To escape the plague, he moved to the Nottingham, but he could not escape official notice of his nonconformity and was briefly imprisoned.[21]

John Edwards excelled as an undergraduate at Cambridge, being named "scholar of the house," twice appointed as moderator, and elected as a fellow while a middle bachelor. He graduated in 1658 and three years later received his MA. Juxtaposed with the Great Ejection of August 24, 1662 was his ordination as deacon on September 11 by Bishop of Lincoln Robert Sanderson (1587–1662), followed ten days later as priest, at which time he was selected to deliver the sermon to his ordination class. There is no record of that sermon nor his thoughts during this momentous time. On May 13, 1664, he was appointed curate, preacher, and vicar of Holy Trinity Church.

After the plague ended in 1666, Edwards was offered a good position in Gloucestershire, which he did not accept, remaining at Trinity for two additional years. Shortly after receiving his BD in 1668, he was selected as lecturer at Bury St. Edmunds at £100 per annum.[22] It seems

---

20. Letham, *Westminster Assembly*, 290.

21. Gordon, "Anthony Tuckney"; Collinson, "Anthony Tuckney."

22. The date for his BD award of April 5, 1671, given in the Clergy of the Church of England Database, but that date is not in accord with Edwards's 1670 departure from St. John's as the result of his conflict with Gunning and Turner. The March-April transition of Gunning to Turner is well-established. http://db.theclergydatabase.org.

that he missed the academic life at Cambridge and so resigned after one year, despite having performed his duties "with great reputation and acceptance."[23] He returned to a fellowship at St. John's, but it was not long lasting due to a strained relationship first with principal Peter Gunning (1614–84) and second with the new master Francis Turner (1637–1700) who succeeded him in April 1670. Apparently neither man was very tolerant of Edwards's Calvinism. Leaving St. John's, he became a fellow commoner in civil law at Trinity Hall and in 1676, married the widow of former alderman and attorney Mr. Lane. On July 6, 1678 he was appointed curate and preacher at the twelfth-century Cambridge church of St. Sepulchers, so-named because of its architectural resemblance to the rotunda of the Church of the Holy Sepulcher in Jerusalem. There "his sermons were as much attended by persons of consequence in the University as they had formerly been at Trinity."[24]

He turned down two other financially attractive positions offered by his friend Sir Robert Carr in Norfolk before taking his final clerical position at St. Peter's Church in Colchester on February 8, 1683. He retired after about twenty-five years of active parish ministry due to deteriorating health. The Edwardses moved into town about 1697 to be closer to markets and also the university, as he did not have much of a personal library. Finally yielding to the prodding of friends he received his DD two years later and two years after that, Mrs. Edwards died. His second marriage was to Catharine Newcombe (1663–1745), niece of his former wife's first husband.[25] During his last years in Cambridge, it is likely that he worshipped at St. Andrew the Great because he is buried in that church. Along with a large engraved tombstone in the floor of the church, there is a large plaque on the wall.

---

uk/jsp/locations/index.jsp?locKey=20846.
  23. Kippis, "John Edwards."
  24. Kippis, "John Edwards."
  25. Kippis, "John Edwards."

Figure 1. Plaque in St. Andrew the Great Church, Cambridge commemorating John Edwards

After his sermon *Plague of the Heart*, printed in 1665, his next published work was *Cometomantia* in 1684. Dedicated to the Bishop Seth Ward (1617–89) of Salisbury, a mathematician and astronomer, Edwards's objective was to affirm astrology's claim that signs in the heavens, particularly of comets, are from God, but deny that the heavenly bodies have any power of their own to direct or influence events, as many non-Christians had taught. Edwards's understanding of astrology was commonly held in his day. In 1665, citing recent disasters of the 1662 ejection, the severe drought of 1665, the 1665 plague and current war with Holland as evidence of God's judgment, Richard Baxter (1615–91) wrote, "Strange Comets (which filled the Thoughts and Writings of Astronomers) did in the Winter and Spring along time appear before these Calamities."[26]

Edwards published only these two works before retiring, but his retirement was not to a life of leisure. He began to write, not as a means of income, but to educate. Initially he wrote to help people like those in his former churches improve their biblical literacy. When Locke's *The*

---

26. Baxter, *Reliquiæ*, Part II, §445; Walsham, *Providence*, 116-66.

Reasonableness of Christianity appeared, Edwards began defending traditional orthodoxy against those wishing to redefine it under the guise of toleration, peace, and unity. Still later, he wrote to explain Reformed theology and counter the Arminian influence in the church. He wanted to correct errors he saw within the church, from those who mandated certain unbiblical or relatively insignificant beliefs or practices, from anti-Calvinists, and from the increasing number of those who simply regarded doctrine as not that important. Responding to his concern for well-educated clergy to serve future generations, Edwards wrote several lengthy volumes which were distributed to many rural parish libraries and used in pastoral training. During the last twenty-five years of his life, he wrote over forty books, the last to be published being a posthumous collection entitled, *Remains of the Late Reverend and Learned John Edwards, D.D.*[27] In all of his books, he drew on his Cambridge education, where he had encountered the various philosophical and theological movements confronting the church.

Many of his works were in dialogue with other men, who had either written something that Edwards found unacceptable or had attacked Edwards on some point of doctrine, but in terms of volume, his corpus was dominated by theological and exegetical works. Those to whom he chose to respond on at least one occasion included Arthur Bury (1624–1714?), Samuel Bold (1649–1737), Clarke, Samuel Crisp (1669/70–1704) and his father Tobias (1600–43), Lawrence Fogg, Anthony Horneck (1641–97), Robert Lightfoote (1666–1726), Stephen Lobb (1647–99), John Locke, Robert Nelson (1656–1715), Newton, Edward Nicholson (?), Stephen Nye (1648–1719), Matthew Scrivener (1622?-88), William Sherlock (1641?–1707), John Spencer (bap. 1630–93), Jeremy Taylor (1613–1667), Whiston, and Daniel Whitby (1638–1726).[28]

Most of the controversy surrounding Edwards erupted from such works. Despite his many critics, Edwards had his allies. Richard Kidder, Bishop of Bath and Wells wrote to Edwards, "I am much pleased that you so Religiously stick to the Text, when some bold Critics *alter pro arbitrio*. I pray God prosper your studies in this kind. Never was there more need

---

27. Kippis, "John Edwards."

28. Edwards recognized Spencer as an accomplished poet and Old Testament scholar, but took issue with some of his theology. For example, he accused Spencer of simply regarding the Sabbath not as a day of worship, but simply one for rest, following the pattern of Genesis 1–2. See Theologia, 2:453.

than now of Laboring this way."[29] In the preface to his second discourse on Ezekiel 21:27, Joseph Jacob wrote of Thomas Burnet and Edwards that none in our age have exceeded them for *"Strength* of Argument, *or Purity of* Style," their "Thought and Language *far exceeding the* usual *Proportion"* and that Edwards *"in an eminent manner, deserves the Thanks of all Christians for his late Excellent Book,"* The Preacher.[30] A good number of others cited Edwards in support of their (mostly polemical) writings.[31]

That assessments of Edwards's legacy varied widely can be easily seen in the biographical entry by nonconformist Andrews Kippis. Referring to an unidentified source he wrote, "he is said to be the Paul, the Augustine, the Bradwardine, the Calvin of his age." Some thought him to be "one of the most valuable writers of his time." By way of editorial comment Kippis added,

> we are now convinced that his works, notwithstanding their [sic] being undoubtedly learned, are too scholastic and calvinistical to be in any considerable degree the objects of present attention. [. . .] One thing which rendered Dr. Edwards unpopular among many of his brethren, was his great zeal for the Calvinistic Doctrines. This matter he undoubtedly carried to a bigoted excess; for he adopted and contended for the absurd notion of the old Puritans, that there is a close connection between Arminianism and Popery.[32]

Kippis disclosed that his source on Edwards was a manuscript provided by an "anonymous benefactor" who responded to a request for information published in the "Gentleman's Magazine." Kippis concluded that the manuscript "appears to have been principally written by [Edwards]," although he did not say why. Although there is no reason to doubt the Kippis entry, much of the biographical material cannot be independently corroborated. Of particular interest is the author of the comments praising Edwards.

---

29. British Library, Add MS 474/49, Richard Kidder, Letter to John Edwards, August 14, 1702.

30. Jacob, *Desolations Decypher'd*, iii.

31. Some examples: Anon, *Censura Temporum*, 41–42, 357–61; Bailey, *Essays*, 70–71; Biddulph, Essays, 66; Bruder, *Evangelical Truth*, 15; Hill, *Apology*, 80–82, 179–86; Owen, *Plain Reasons*, 15–16; Stennett, Answer, 169–70; Walter, *Choice*, 54; Watts, Works, 4.512, 8,209; Wise, *Christian Eucharist*, 50, 149; Witing, *Truth*, 3, 96, 106–07, 111–12, 114, 116, 120, 123, 130.

32. Kippis, "John Edwards."

Eighty years after Kippis, Henry Bradshaw looked into the matter. A series of events are related by which some handwritten papers, including a book fragment and some "scraps of paper" were given to the Cambridge University Library, having passed through several hands over the years. After examining that collection in 1873, Bradshaw concluded that the Kippis biographical entry came from Edwards, but he does not say whether the scraps of paper contained all that is found in that entry, only that it was "drawn up in great measure by himself." Neither does he comment on the section comparing Edwards to St. Paul, etc. Like Kippis, Bradshaw did not have a favorable view of Edwards's theology.[33]

CONTRIBUTIONS TO THEOLOGICAL EDUCATION

Through his writings, Edwards's influence extended far beyond his former parishes in Cambridge, Suffolk, and Essex. In addition to readers in England, some ministers heard about him in the American colonies, aided by a young English clergyman, Thomas Bray (1656–1730). After graduating from Oxford, Bray served in several parishes before he was commissioned in 1696 to establish the Church of England in the colony of Maryland. But as he began to undertake this endeavor, he realized that although theological books were much sought after, young ministers were often too poor to afford a personal library. So he organized an effort to establish parochial libraries as part of the parsonage in rural Britain, colonial America, and other outposts of the Church of England. Before he died, eighty such libraries were started in England and Wales and thirty-nine in the American colonies. His library venture included printing and some translation as well as distribution and was later known as the Society for Promoting Christian Knowledge. In conjunction with this, he also established the first American library classification system.[34] One of his first shipments was to Charles Town, Carolina (now Charleston,

---

33. Bradshaw, *Collected Papers*, 69–73. Edwards was often bold in his writing, a fearless defender of biblical truth as he understood it. He did not respect careless exegesis, defective logic, or ancient language incompetence. However, his works give no hint of self-promotion, over-confidence in his own understanding or abilities, or even concern for his own reputation. Therefore, it seems likely that the comparison of him with St. Paul, etc. was provided by an admirer of his, perhaps his wife Catherine or someone like Jonathan Warne who held Edwards in high esteem and quoted him extensively.

34. Steiner, "Rev. Thomas Bray," 59–75.

South Carolina) in 1698, of which we have fairly complete knowledge. Of two hundred and thirty-three titles sent to Charles Town between 1698 and 1701, four were by Edwards, and this before his more popular theological works appeared.[35]

It seems that many who continued to read Edwards's works during and following his life, whether in England or North America, were involved in theological education. Two of these were Increase Mather (1639–1723) and his son Cotton, who was influential pastor of Boston's Old North Church (Congregational) for over forty years and author of some four hundred and fifty works. Cotton received some of Edwards's books in Massachusetts not only for personal use, but also, as a leading pastor in New England, to prepare young men for the ministry. Although in the early years of Harvard and Yale formal higher education was closely tied to the church, the orientation of the curriculum was more academic than vocational. Consequently, established pastors like the Mathers often provided a couple years of internship as a transition between the BA degree and the pastorate. This not only provided young candidates with valuable experience under an established mentor, but also with additional theological education in the context of a local church.

In his diary of June 17, 1711, Mather wrote of preparing a teaching resource titled *The Old Pathes Restored* by using material from several sources, including John Edwards to whom the short work was dedicated. It was printed in both Boston (1711) and London (1712). His primary audience was the southern colonies "where the Christians cry for Help against the Pelagian Encroachments." The purpose of this publication was to show that

> the Doctrines of Grace, *hitherto preserved in the Churches of the Non-conformists, are not only asserted in the Sacred Scriptures, but also in the* Articles *and* Homilies *of the* Church of England; *And that the General Departure from those Doctrines, especially in those who have subscribed them, is a most unaccountable Apostasy.*[36]

Two years later (October 4, 1713), he wrote,

> I would with mature Advice, prevail on our Booksellers, to become furnished from *England*, with certain Books, that our

---

35. Pennington, "Library in Charles Town," 176–82.

36. Mather, *Diary*, 2:81. See Chapter 7 for an unexpected printing of *Old Pathes Restored*.

Candidates of the Ministry ought in the first place, to be supplied withal. And then see that the said Candidates do therewith supply themselves. This may prove a Service of no little Consequence. Especially *Ravanellus, Turretin*. *Ushers* Body of Divinity. *Alstedii Turris David*, Edward's *preacher And, Theologia Reformata*.³⁷

He also promoted Edwards's works as greatly beneficial in his own books.³⁸ In the preface to one of his son's books, Increase Mather quoted "my worthy friend *Dr. John Edwards*" as saying, "Next unto the Sacred Scriptures, the *Practical Discourses*, which promote REAL and VITAL RELIGION, or *Godliness in the life and Power of it*, are the most Profitable, and the most Valuable." Of Edwards's many books, he wrote, "I earnestly Recommend unto the Reading, especially of our young Students & Preachers."³⁹ Cotton wrote to Edwards on at least two occasions, thanking him for his books, which he often loaned to his friends. In October 1712, "Your works (I must continue to inform you) are of great esteem in this country."⁴⁰ In another letter Mather mentioned how thankful were ministers in the "Southern Colonies" and Pennsylvania at receiving his books.⁴¹ *Manuductio Ad Ministerium*, the book Mather wrote to instruct candidates for ministry recommended Edwards's *Theologia Reformata* as a "treasure [. . .] for all occasions," along with *Veritas Redux*. John Ryland reprinted this work of Mather for London readers sixty-five years after his death and added to the recommendations in the preface *The Preacher* along with a number of other works.⁴² After his death, some of Cotton Mather's library was purchased by Isaiah Thomas and given to the American Antiquarian Society. In this collection are eight of Edwards's works plus the extract of a letter from Edwards to Mather.⁴³

---

37. Mather, *Diary*, 2:243.
38. Mather, *Bonifacius*, 180; Mather, *Minister*, 30; Mather, *Palm-Bearers*, 55.
39. Mather, *Utilia*, Preface.
40. British Library, MS Add 4276, f.49.
41. Undated letter from Mather to Edwards: manuscript identified as II-58, located in the archives of the American Antiquarian Association, Wooster, MA.
42. Mather, *Manuductio Ad Ministerium*, 91, 93, 160.
43. Tuttle, *Libraries*, 59–60. Edwards's works as listed are *Arminian Doctrines*; in Mather's hand, "Extract from a letter of Dr. Edwards to C.M. Jun. 19, 1711," followed by the text of the extract in the same hand; *Some Brief Critical Remarks*; *Brief Remarks on "The Difficulties;" Concio*; *Crispianism Unmasked*; *Divine Perfections Vindicated*; *A Letter*; *Supplement*. *Brief Remarks on "The Difficulties"* does not appear to be extant.

George Whitefield was another prominent preacher who found John Edwards's works especially useful, both personally and for instructing others. He cited Edwards in his letter exchange with John Wesley on the subject of free grace on September 25, 1740 writing from Boston and again on December 24 from Savannah, Georgia, where he had established his "orphan house academy" called Bethesda College. In the latter letter,

> Tis not my design to enter into a long debate on God's decrees. I refer you to Dr. *Edwards* his *Veritas Redux*, which I think is unanswerable—except in a certain point concerning a *middle sort* between elect and reprobate, which he himself in effect afterwards condemns.[44]

Near the end of this rather lengthy letter, Whitefield wrote,

> I referred you, at the beginning of this letter, to Dr. *Edwards's Veritas Redux*, which I recommended to you also in a late letter, with *Elisha Cole* on *God's Sovereignty*. Be pleased to read these [...] and I doubt not that but you will see all your objections answered.[45]

At Bethesda College, Whitefield included Edwards's *The Preacher* and *Veritas Redux* in his list of divinity books to be read by the students.[46] In the preface to the *Works of John Bunyan*, he wrote,

> Among these may be justly reckoned those great luminaries, *Bishop Jewel*, [...] *Edwards*, who, notwithstanding a difference of judgment in respect to outward church–government, all agreed (as their printed works manifestly evince) in asserting and defending the grand essential truths for which the Puritans, though matters of an inferior nature were urged as a pretext, chiefly suffered, and were ejected.[47]

However as a young preacher, Whitefield was not established in his beliefs as he expressed in a letter to some Presbyterians who questioned his theology.

> I think it no dishonour, to retract some expressions that formerly dropped from my pen, before God was pleased to give

---

44. Whitefield, "Letter CCXXI," 1:212; Whitefield, "A Letter to the Reverend Mr. John Wesley," 4:55.
45. Whitefield, "Letter to the Reverend Mr. John Wesley," 4:70.
46. Whitefield, "College Rules," 3:499.
47. Bunyan, "Works," 1:iii–iv.

me a more clear knowledge of the doctrines of grace [. . .] I received the Spirit of adoption before I had conversed with one man, or read a single book, on the doctrine of "Free justification by the imputed righteousness of Jesus Christ." No wonder then, that I was not so clear in some points at my first setting out in the ministry [. . .] and I desire your prayers, that his grace may shine more and more in my heart.[48]

Continuing his confession, "In my sermon on *justification*, I seem to assert *universal redemption*, which I now absolutely deny."[49] The change occurred on Whitefield's second voyage to the colony of Georgia in September 1740. One biographer attributes Whitefield's theological shift to Jonathan Edwards; another to Scottish Presbyterian dissenting ministers Ralph (1685–1752) and Ebenezer (1680–1754) Erskine.[50] No doubt all three were influential to some degree. But the closest indication we have of a Calvinistic influence from the Erskine brothers before 1740 from Whitefield himself is his comment upon receiving a letter from Ralph Erskine that "*some may be offended at my corresponding with him*," but he does not give a reason.[51]

Before leaving on his second voyage to Georgia however, Whitefield acquired two books, *The Church of England Turned Dissenter* and *Arminianism the Back-Door to Popery* by Jonathan Warne. These books contained extensive quotations from Edwards, covering approximately 30 percent and 85 percent of their entire lengths, respectively. Commenting on reading the two books in his journal of September 29, 1740, Whitefield wrote,

> this Afternoon was exceedingly strengthen'd by perusing some Paragraphs out of a Book call'd *The Preacher*, written by Dr. *Edwards* of *Cambridge* [. . .] These are such noble Testimonies given before that University, of Justification by Faith only, the imputed Righteousness of Christ, our having no Free-will, &c. that they deserve to be written in Letters of Gold. [. . .] *Lord, open thou my mouth, that I may henceforward speak more boldly and explicitly, as I ought to speak!*[52]

---

48. Whitefield, "Letter to Some Church-Members," 4:45–46.
49. Whitefield, "Letter to Some Church-Members," 4:47.
50. Tyerman, *Life*, 1:274.
51. Whitefield, "Continuation of the Reverend Mr. Whitefield's Journal, During the Time," 31.
52. Whitefield, "Continuation of the Reverend Mr. Whitefield's Journal, from His

Given Whitefield's later references to Edwards, it is clear that Edwards was the turning point in Whitefield's theological understanding. Clearly his enthusiasm for Edwards influenced many others, including Revs. Jonathan Parsons of Lyme, MA, Joseph Bellamy (1719–90), and Daniel Wadsworth (1704–47), pastor of the First Church of Christ, Hartford, CT, who met Whitefield on his first trip to New England and later reported reading *The Preacher* in his journal.[53]

For his part, Warne was simply passing on what he had discovered. His first encounter with Edwards was a sermon, *One Nation, and One King*, given at Cambridge University on May 1, 1707, celebrating the union of England and Scotland. Following that he read *The Preacher* (all three volumes), which he said "*proves* [. . .] *that the* Arminian *Clergy are apostatized from the Doctrine of the Reformation*." He continued, "*I resolved* [. . .] *to inspect narrowly into the Truth of what the Doctor charges them with*," after which he investigated the views of Bishops Babbington [1615–91], William Beveridge [1637–1708], Downham [d.1634], Hall [1633–1710], Reynolds, Ussher, and "*several others*" which "*caused me to have held many Arguments with the Clergy and Laity; wherein I find them great Enemies to the Doctrines of the Reformation*." Warne concluded his preface appealing to his readers earnestly to buy and read these three volumes of Edwards and "*when you have read them with great Application, then lend them to your Friends and Neighbors; and this will be doing the greatest Piece of Love and Kindness you can possibly do for them* [. . .] *Be like the noble Bereans.*"[54]

Following his 1736 Yale graduation, Joseph Bellamy (1719–90) studied under Jonathan Edwards to prepare for the ministry. According to Bellamy's notebook, John Edwards's *Theologia Reformata* was his primary text. Bellamy's notebook is logically organized by sub-discipline and referenced to *Theologia Reformata*. Though only thirty-two pages long, the first twelve consist primarily of direct quotations from the Edwards text.[55] Bellamy followed Jonathan Edwards's example by mentoring more than sixty college graduates during his fifty years in the pastorate at the Congregational church in Bethlehem, Connecticut.[56]

Embarking," 19.

53. Wadsworth, Diary, 21, 52, 67, 116.
54. Warne, *Church of England*, iv–vi.
55. Schuman, "Training Ministers," 265.
56. Crisp and Sweeney, *After Jonathan Edwards*, 41–42.

Works of John Edwards also found a prominent place in the library of Jonathan Edwards. Six of them are listed in Jonathan Edwards's "Catalogue." Upon discovering these six to be of value, Jonathan Edwards expressed a desire to acquire Edwards's other works.[57] Jonathan's father Timothy, pastor of the Congregational Church in East Windsor for nearly sixty-four years also profited from reading John Edwards, seen in citations from *Veritas Redux* and *Theologia Reformata* in his manuscript notebooks.[58] With the interest of such high-profile ministers in New England, it is not surprising that some of Edwards's works were printed in Boston.[59] Some of his works were taken to Europe as evidenced by translations into German and French.[60]

Back in England, Edwards continued to be widely read. In the introduction to his *A Compleat Body of Speculative and Practical Divinity*, Thomas Stackhouse (1677–1752) wrote that of the "*almost innumerable*" works published as "Bodies of Divinity," two are "*the best known, and most in use*," those written by Edwards and Richard Fiddes (1671–1725). He called Edwards "*very* Learned" and his frequently footnoted works, "*purely* Calvinistical." Stackhouse described his *Theologia Reformata* as a "*Magazine of Knowledge*," but was critical of Edwards's style, being repetitious with too many notes and quotations in Greek and Latin.[61] Writing a half century after Edwards's death, Vicar Thomas Bowman (1728–92) of Norwich commended him, as one of very few Calvinist in the Church of England after 1662, for opposing the rise of Arminianism, Arianism, and Socinianism.[62] Among other Edwards citations, Augustus Toplady (1740–78) quoted him at length to argue that the official doctrines of the Church of England were Calvinistic, and named him first among "Men, the Dust from whose Volumes I am not worthy to wipe."[63]

In the nineteenth century, Edwards's works were still being read. He was the first preacher to be cited at length in Presbyterian S. G. Winchester's essay on Preaching.[64] He was cited favorably in Wesleyan

---

57. Edwards, *Works of Jonathan Edwards*, 26:22, 44.
58. Edwards, *Works of Jonathan Edwards*, 26:286.
59. For example, *Whole Concern of Man* and *Fruits of the Spirit*.
60. Edwards, *Der Socinianische Glaube* (*The Socinian Creed*). Also see Chapter 4.
61. Stackhouse, *Compleat Body*, i.
62. Bowman, *Review*, 118–27.
63. Toplady, *Church of England*, 21–23, 52, 60–62, 67–69, 74, 80–81; Toplady, *More Work*, 67.
64. Winchester, *Importance*, 8–11.

Thomas Powell's work on apostolic succession.[65] Edwards's *The Doctrines Controverted between Papists and Protestants* was published in 1850 as the sixth of seven supplemental volumes to the nineteenth century edition of Edmund Gibson's *Preservative against Popery*—a response to the Tractarian movement. William Farrer (1820–1908) published *First Lines of Christian Theology* in two editions (1854, 1860) using manuscripts of nonconformist theologian Dr. John Pye-Smith (1774–1851). Pye-Smith left a historical overview, commenting on those men who made significant contributions in systematic theology. In the seventeenth, eighteenth, and nineteenth centuries, he listed Edwards with four others from the Church of England, calling him "a divine of eminent piety, learning, and literary activity, and a strenuous defender of the Calvinistic system." Pye-Smith recommended Edwards's *Theologia Reformata* and his *Discourse of Episcopacy*.[66] Charles Spurgeon (1834–92) referenced *Theologia Reformata* several times in his commentary on the Psalms.[67] Charles Ryrie cites Edwards as one of the pre-Darby contributors to dispensationalism, even though Edwards viewed the millennium reign as spiritual rather than physical.[68] Edwards's hermeneutical insights have even contributed to very recent scholarly works.[69] In addition to the aforementioned works, Edwards was cited by dozens of other writers in works published throughout the eighteenth and into the nineteenth and twentieth centuries. Reflecting the wide consensus of so many who have appreciated probably the most popular work of Edwards, Richard Muller wrote, "Edwards's *Theologia reformata* stands as the summation of an orthodox approach, born of controversy in the declining years of the Commonwealth and the troubled times of the Restoration."[70] Thus, it is fairly clear that Edwards's influence in theological education and therefore the church both in England and her American colonies was fairly significant and continued long after he died.

Aside from pastors and theologians, Edwards influenced other notable individuals, such as philosopher George Berkeley (1685–1753) and

---

65. Powell, *Apostolical Succession*, 56, 124, 199.
66. Pye-Smith, *First Lines*, 42, 627.
67. Spurgeon, *Treasury of David*, 2:374–75; IV:169, 192, 218; 5:362–63.
68. Ryrie, *Dispensationalism*, 66.
69. Thiselton, *First Epistle*, 1243; McKim, *Dictionary*, 1051.
70. Muller, *Reformed Dogmatics*, 3:149.

jurist William Blackstone (1723–80).[71] Emanuel Swedenborg's disciples cited Edwards as an authority, among other issues, in defining truth and also holding with other authorities from Augustine to Isaac Watts that infants who die could face eternal damnation, which Swedenborg thought to be a serious error.[72]

---

71. Pearce, "Berkeley's Lockean Religious Epistemology," 417–38; Prest, "The Religion," 162.

72. Clissold, *Spiritual Exposition*, 299–302; Barrett, *Beauty for Ashes*, 27–28, 33.

4

Edwards and Anti-Trinitarians[1]

BELIEVING THAT HIS HEALTH was in decline, Edwards retired from the pulpit and began what was to become his writing career, seeking to help people like his former parishioners become more biblically literate. In the first of these works published at age fifty-five, he expounded on four perplexing New Testament passages.[2] That was followed by a longer, similar work, dedicated to Latitudinarian Bishop Simon Patrick of Ely.[3] A three-volume, rather apologetic overview of the Bible was next, where he explained why Christians accept it as true and authoritative, how to interpret its many genres and figures of speech, how the Bible has influenced the world, and concluding with translation errors found in the Septuagint, Vulgate, and some English translations.[4] But aside from sermons, most of the rest of his extant forty-odd published works were divided between theological exposition and responses to other publications. Edwards saw the church threatened from within and without. Although he often railed

---

1. Most of the men covered in this chapter were ordained by the Church of England and thought of themselves as Christians. But in Edwards's judgment (and by the standards of traditional orthodoxy) they denied doctrinal essentials such as the Trinity and therefore were outside the church.

2. Edwards, *Four Remarkable Texts*.

3. Edwards, *Farther Enquiry*. Patrick is credited with coining the term "latitudinarian." P[atrick], *Brief Account*. Patrick replied in a letter, "You could not have made a more acceptable project than your former treatise wherein you enquire into several difficulties in the Holy Scripture." See Simon Patrick to John Edwards, 1692.

4. Edwards, *Discourse Concerning*, 3:477–569.

against Atheists and Arminians, he clearly distinguished between heresy and what he viewed as flawed doctrine.

Among his prominent contemporaries were those whose understanding of the Christian faith Edwards saw as fundamentally wrong. He became increasingly alarmed that writers with Arian, Socinian, and Deist views were boldly masquerading as mainstream Christians, intent on redefining orthodoxy to incorporate their antitrinitarian doctrines and therefore posing a great danger to the church by leading many astray.[5]

These public debates which Edwards hoped would persuade people to follow orthodox Christianity, though, were actually part of a larger Edwards project to articulate and promote a Christian worldview and show its superiority to competing worldviews. Influenced by philosophical materialism, his opponents distorted Christianity and even atheism itself. His first response to Locke's *The Reasonableness of Christianity* was an appendix to a new book where he intended to show how the created order points us to God. Drawing on his insights in teleology, astronomy, meteorology, agriculture, geology, zoology, and human physiology, he intended to *"carefully trace and discover the Footsteps of the* Divinity *every where"* in contrast to naturalistic explanations of Descartes, Hobbes, and Copernicus.[6] Like many of his contemporaries, Edwards did not accept Copernicus' heliocentric model, seeing it as contrary to God's revelation.

As has been noted, various heterodox labels were often misused to attack and discredit one's opponents. The most common charge of heresy in the late seventeenth century was Socinianism. Often used carelessly, it became such a label of ill repute that the Socinians adopted the Unitarian label. Conservative High Churchman Charles Leslie (1650–1722), unhappy with the direction of the church since the time of Archbishop Laud, called Archbishop Tillotson a Socinian. He accused him, along with Bishop Gilbert Burnet, of following the rationalism of Spinoza and Hobbes to the extent that, as for example, one could not distinguish the preaching of Dr. Tillotson from Hobbes. In his *Charge of Socinianism Against Dr. Tillotson*, Leslie associated Tillotson closely with Deist Charles Blount (1654–93), calling Tillotson his "tutor."[7]

---

5. Edwards was widely read and often criticized men such as Thomas Hobbes and Baruch Spinoza, but they will not be included here, being officially outside the church.

6. Edwards, *Some Thoughts Concerning Atheism*, Preface.

7. Leslie, *Charge of Socinianism*, 547, 595, 603; Leslie, *Some Reflections*; Leslie, "Supplement," 640.

Edwards never called Tillotson a Socinian, but some with heretical views happily agreed at least in part with Leslie's assessment. When he published his *magnum opus*, radical freethinker John Toland left his own name off the title page, but featured a quotation from the archbishop: "*We need not desire a better Evidence that any Man is in the wrong, than to hear him declare against Reason and thereby acknowledg that Reason is against him.*"[8]

JOHN LOCKE

Similarly in 1695 John Locke published *The Reasonableness of Christianity* anonymously, no doubt because he knew that it would cause an uproar and above all else, Locke hated controversy. The underlying message of this work reflected the outlook of many of his contemporaries who wanted an end to the religious strife that had plagued Europe, especially since the Protestant Reformation. Upon studying the New Testament, Locke decided that the essence of the gospel of salvation could be found in the four Gospel accounts and the book of Acts, thereby separating the question of how one becomes a Christian from what one should believe and how one should live as a Christian, which he determined was answered in the epistles. He reasoned that as the Christian faith was open to everyone including the illiterate, anyone ought to be able to understand what is required for Christian conversion without having to fathom theological mysteries. The thrust of his book is substantiating from the Gospels his belief that the essence of the gospel is that Jesus is the Messiah, although he did not clearly state what Messiahship means theologically.

> This was the great Proposition that was then controverted, concerning Jesus of *Nazareth*, whether he was the *Messiah* or no; And the assent to that was that, which distinguished Believers from Unbelievers. [. . .] Whereby it is plain, that the Gospel was writ to induce men into a belief of this Proposition, *that Jesus of Nazareth was the Messiah*; Which if they believed, they should have life.[9]

And how do we know he is the Messiah? Locke: "There is a three-fold declaration of the *Messiah:*" by miracles, by "Phrases and Circumlocutions"

---

8. Toland, *Christianity Not Mysterious*.

9. Locke, *Reasonableness*, first ed., 26–29; Locke, *Reasonableness*, critical ed., 23–24.

[by which he meant Jesus' references to the Kingdom of God and Old Testament messianic prophecies], and by direct declarations, which were few. Locke's emphasis is clearly on the "the multitude of Miracles he did before all sorts of People [. . .] that what he delivered cannot but be received as the Oracles of God, and unquestionable Verity."[10]

In addition Locke said that once converted, people should subscribe to reasonable beliefs, including that God exists as the eternal and omnipotent creator and merciful ruler and that we should repent of our sins and live obedient lives. Doctrines such as the Trinity, original sin, and purgatory he argued were difficult to understand and divisive. Therefore we should be tolerant of all who disagree with us on such matters. This book was the logical development of his thinking, first expressed in his *Essay on Toleration* in 1667 or 1668, which evolved into four *Letters Concerning Toleration* published between 1689 and 1704.[11]

The Reasonableness launched a major pamphlet war on the Trinity—major not only because it involved John Locke, but also because it eventually involved, among others, a second prominent English philosopher (Clarke), a former archbishop (Tillotson), three bishops (Edward Stillingfleet [1635-99], Fowler, Burnet), the Dean of St. Paul's Cathedral (Sherlock), four prominent mathematicians (Newton, Gottfried Leibniz [1646-1716], John Wallis [1616-1703], Whiston), and an outspoken Unitarian (Nye). And John Edwards, the first to respond to Locke in print, was in the middle of it.[12] Locke's book appeared as Edwards was about to publish, *Some Thoughts Concerning the Several Causes and Occasions of Atheism*, dedicated to Thomas Tenison, Archbishop of Canterbury, who four years earlier had preached *A Sermon Concerning the Folly of Atheism*. Edwards was not theologically aligned with Latitudinarian Tenison on many issues, but as he demonstrated repeatedly, he was happy to make alliances with anyone in the church to combat heresy.

For Edwards, atheism was a very serious threat which was promoted through heretical teaching, especially concerning the nature of God.[13]

---

10. Locke, *Reasonableness*, first ed., 55–61, 256; Locke, *Reasonableness*, critical ed., 37–40, 143.

11. Marshall, *John Locke*, 230, 287, 310, 336–44, 454.

12. Philip Dixon writes that Stillingfleet "dragged Locke into the trinitarian controversy of the decade," seemingly unaware of the timing, namely that Stillingfleet's first response to Locke did not appear until after Edwards had attacked Locke in three or four separate publications. See *Nice and Hot Disputes*, 139.

13. Edwards's concern about public apathy and the influence of atheistic writers

He believed that atheism was spread through a variety of agents, which he explained by characterizing the attitudes and practices of the people who were most susceptible: the ignorant, including those of low and high rank who do not take time "to think of a God" (he noted that practicing scientists and philosophers were less likely to be atheists); the disingenuous, who make feeble excuses about mysteries of the spiritual world even though there are many things in physical world that they cannot see or explain; those who make light of spiritual matters, essentially by mocking God; the proud; those who, like the pagans, define God according to their own thinking; those who live as though they are immortal, which goes hand-in-hand with atheism, as he cited Psalm 53:1; those who observe the wicked prospering or the righteous suffering and conclude by their weak minds that God must not exist; those who think they must understand everything, yet cannot explain the Trinity and other mysteries; and those whose intellectual and prosperous context prevent them from being "content with what the *Bible*" tells us. In addition to these nine, he mentioned three other contributors to the spread of atheism, directly attributable to members of the church: division and disputes in the church, including those caused by heresy; even worse than disputes, hypocrisy and bad behavior of *"Professors of Christianity,"* which many use as an excuse not to believe; and the less-than-exemplary lives of leaders and teachers in the church, which Edwards noted was the category that Jesus condemned most harshly.[14]

Continuing his analysis of atheism's causes, Edwards said that Socinianism is also one, since *"in the very Socinian Doctrine it self there seems to be an Atheistic Tang,"* which follows from denying or seriously compromising some of God's essential attributes such as self-existence, omnipresence, omniscience, spirituality, and especially his triunity. Socinians deny certain aspects of biblical truth because they are unable to resolve apparent theological contradictions, which arise from holding reason higher than revelation. To believe in a false God is to be an atheist with respect to the true God.[15]

---

like Thomas Hobbes was shared by many, including prominent (and fairly tolerant) Latitudinarians; e.g., Gilbert Burnet, Joseph Glanville (1636-80), Patrick, Stillingfleet, Tillotson, and Bishop John Wilkins (1614-1672), all of whom opposed unbelief in their books and sermons. See Griffin, *Latitudinarianism*, 52.

14. Edwards, *Some Thoughts*, 3-64.

15. Edwards, *Some Thoughts*, 64-71.

Before Locke's book was printed Edwards had already in his new work attacked Nye, a prominent exponent of Unitarianism who rejected trinitarian theology as irrational: "'Tis not true, that we prefer our Reason before Revelation." God would never deceive us. "Therefore, we conclude that [. . .] what is false in Reason, can never be true in Revelation [. . .] So that whatsoever in Revelation doth seem to contradict Reason, can be nothing but our Blunder."[16] Again Nye:

> We do not reject the Doctrines of the Trinity and Incarnation, because they are Mysteries; but because they are plain Contradictions to Reason and common Sense, and consequently Untruths: for (without doubt) Reason and Truth are but two Names, for the same thing; and clear Reason is no other thing, but clear Truth.[17]

In establishing the link between Socinianism and atheism, Edwards wrote that if you deny God's essential attributes you are denying God.[18] He further claimed that Descartes and "Modern Philosophers" in general contributed to atheism by their efforts to reduce everything to natural and material causes. "Some take occasion thence to believe, that Men as well as Brutes are no other than Engines and Machines, mere Neurospasts and Senseless Puppets." From Descartes's own words, Edwards wrote that we can see that even he was not confident in some of his metaphysical speculation.[19]

With his book nearly finished, it was easy for Edwards to write an addendum in response to this new book which some suggested had been written by Locke. Edwards found this difficult to believe because previously Edwards had a very positive opinion of him from reading *Some Thoughts Concerning Education*. Among other positive comments, Edwards referred to Locke as "that very Thoughtful and Ingenious

---

16. Nye, *Letter of Resolution*, 1. Edwards contended that it is futile for Socinians to depend on their reason to resolve their difficulties because the Bible makes it clear that because God is an infinite God, "it is impossible that the Apprehensions of finite Creatures could reach these things." It is not that the doctrine of the Trinity is so contrary to sound reason, but that it is "above their Reason" (and anyones'). Edwards, *Some Thoughts*, 71–74.

17. Nye, *Considerations*, 30.

18. Edwards, *Some Thoughts*, 67.

19. Edwards, *Some Thoughts*, 87–89. A "neurospast" was a little puppet controlled by a string.

Gentleman," following "all the Great and Renowned Philosophers of our Age."[20] In his transition to attack this new work, Edwards remarked that others had been paving the way: Bishop Jeremy Taylor, author of *A Discourse on the Liberty of Prophesying*, whom he called a *"Learned, but Wavering Prelate"* along with Arthur Bury who was fired from his rectorship at Exeter College, Oxford about the time he published *The Naked Gospel*.[21] In that work, Bury, who later called himself "The Rational Deist," sought to strip the gospel of what he identified as theological and philosophical trappings added by the church. Officials were not impressed and had it publicly burnt at Oxford just after it was published. Locke, on the other hand, was pleased to be associated with Taylor and Bury whom he characterized as "Eminently Pious and Learned."[22]

In attacking *The Reasonableness*, Edwards emphasized two points clearly taught in the Gospel accounts and central to the faith, which Locke chose to ignore: the doctrines of the Trinity and the Incarnation. Edwards argued that these must be taught and believed, if only with very limited understanding. Equally serious and lacking a coherent rationale was Locke's decision to ignore the epistles which are integral to the message of the New Testament.[23]

The first of many books, tracts, and sermons to similarly criticize *The Reasonableness*, Edwards's book provoked two anonymous responses: *A Vindication of the Reasonableness of Christianity* (Locke) and *The Exceptions of Mr. Edwards, in His Causes of Atheism* (Nye) almost immediately. Locke did not fancy being accused of Socinianism, much less atheism. He challenged Edwards's ability to determine which articles of faith are necessary to believe because in the epistles the necessary ones are "promiscuously delivered with other Truths, and therefore cannot be distinguished."[24] Locke's goal was to determine "all that is required, and no more than what is absolutely required to be believed by all Christians, without which Faith they cannot be of Christ's Church."[25] He accused Edwards of reading into this book what the author did not write, but he

---

20. Edwards, *Some Thoughts*, 96–97, 115.
21. Edwards, *Some Thoughts*, 104.
22. Locke, *Vindication*, first ed. 3; Locke, *Vindications*, critical ed., 8.
23. Edwards, *Some Thoughts*, 104–15.
24. Locke, *Vindication*, first ed. 16; Locke, *Vindications*, ed. by Nuovo, 15.
25. Locke, *Vindication*, first ed. 21–22; Locke, *Vindications*, ed. by Nuovo, 17.

did not appear to have much respect for Edwards's critique as the general tenor of his response was one of satirical derision:

> I must acknowledge his excess of Civility to me; He shews me more kindness than I could expect or wish, since he prefers what I say to him my self to what is offered to him from the Word of God [. . .] I should in return [. . . entreat] him, that when he takes next in hand such a Subject as this is, wherein the Salvation of Souls is concerned, he would treat it a little more seriously, and with a little more Candor; lest Men should find in his Writings another cause of Atheism, which in this Treatise, he has not thought fit to mention.[26]

Locke concluded that Edwards failed to convince him of any errors, although he regretted that he was not able to read Ely Bishop Patrick's *Witness to Christianity* prior to writing *The Reasonableness*. For Locke to endorse Patrick's work so enthusiastically seems a bit incongruous, leading one to wonder how much of the thirteen hundred pages he actually read. Though Latitudinarian, a major theme of Patrick was that Jesus is the incarnate Son of God.

> For we are assured by those who heard him, and were with him from the beginning, and were witnesses of his Resurrection, and received the Holy Ghost from him that He was the WORD MADE FLESH; and that the Word was God, and all things were made by him, and is the Son of God not by office only, but in his nature and essence.[27]

Patrick introduced his second volume by assuring the reader,

> that *these three are one* in their Essence; then it is certain there are *Three Persons*, whose Essence is one and the same. For else there would not be *three* Witnesses in heaven, but onely *one*: which would cross the design of the Apostle; whose scope is, to shew that our Faith doth not rely upon a single Testimony.[28]

Shortly after Locke's *A Vindication* appeared, Edwards replied, pointing out that by reducing Christianity to one article of faith, the author had ignored essential doctrines such as the fall and original sin, the Trinity, and the atonement and that he failed to clearly explain what it

---

26. Locke, *Vindication*, 25–26; Locke, *Vindications*, ed. by Nuovo, 20.
27. Patrick, *Witnesses*, 1:595–96.
28. Patrick, *Witnesses*, 2:To the Reader.

actually means for Jesus to be the Messiah. This writer might think that traditional Christian doctrines are confusing, yet his explanation of Messiah is no less obscure. Did he really think that his religion was very different from that of "Mahometans" who believe Jesus was a prophet sent by God? He accused Locke of ignoring catechisms which have described Christian beliefs historically while instead espousing universal salvation free from accountability to the church. Edwards did not accuse the author of *The Reasonableness* of atheism, but only that "he hath mightily gratified the *Atheistical* Rabble."[29] Locke claimed, "I took not my sense of those texts [Luke 3:38; 4:3] from those writers [antitrinitarians], but from the scripture it self."[30] Conceding to Locke that he may not have read any Socinian works, Edwards called him an "*Ignoramus Socinian*."[31]

From passages like John 20:31, it seemed obvious to Locke that somehow "Jesus is the Messiah" was equivalent with "Son of God."[32] Evidence for either one, such as miracles, Jesus' birth in Bethlehem, and the resurrection, Locke took to be evidence for the other.[33] Edwards stressed that though these supernatural events are evidence that he was divine, Jesus is not the Son of God because of them. He is the Son of God by virtue of "*his Eternal Filiation:* he was begotten from Eternity of the substance of the Father by an ineffable Generation." It is therefore critical to understand the distinction between Messiah and Son of God. He is the Christ as part of his "Office" because of his "Divine Mission," resulting from being the Son of God.[34]

> He was not *God* (a *Metaphorical God*, as the *Socinians* sometimes make him) because he was *Christ* or the *Messias*: but he was the *Messias* because he was *God*, even the *True God*. He was the *Christ of God* because he was *the Son of God*.[35]

---

29. Edwards, *Socinianism Unmask'd*, 69. In this work, Edwards had yet to identify Locke as the author.

30. Locke, *Vindication*, 22; Locke, *Vindications*, critical ed., 18.

31. Edwards, *Socinianism Unmask'd*, 93.

32. Locke, *Reasonableness*, first ed., 28–36; Locke, *Reasonableness*, critical ed., 24–26.

33. Locke, *Reasonableness*, first ed., 26–29, 54–56, 95; Locke, *Reasonableness*, critical ed., 23–24, 36–37, 60.

34. Edwards, *Socinianism Unmask'd*, 89.

35. Edwards, *Socinianism Unmask'd*, 90.

In his reply to Edwards, Locke did not respond on this point; he never addressed the question of why Jesus is the Messiah or Son of God ontologically. He simply continued to reiterate his point that "by his Miracles declar'd himself to be the King of that Kingdom."[36]

On Edwards's charge of Socinianism, Locke was not so ignorant regarding that teaching as he claimed: a significant part of his library and a major part of his reading consisted of Unitarian works, including eight by Nye.[37] Writing in his personal notebook, 1694-95, almost all of the entries of a trinitarian nature he credited to two books by John Biddle, often called "the father of English unitarianism."[38] Also, Locke was "very intimate" with the family of Thomas Firmin 1632-97) who helped print many of the Socinian works.[39] Locke's associations and correspondence, especially on matters of biblical hermeneutics with other heterodox apologists such as Collins, Newton, Matthew Tindal (1656-1733), and Toland are also a bit incriminating.[40]

In *Socinianism Unmask'd*, Edwards also addressed "*another (professed) Socinian writer*," who had come to Locke's defense attacking Edwards with his own book. Nye basically saw only two alternatives to understand the Trinity: modalism or tritheism, both of which were deemed heretical in orthodox thinking. In response to Edwards's accusation that Locke failed to actually define messiah, Nye did not define it either. He simply said that "the most illiterate Fishermen and Shepherds, and Women knew what was meant by *JESUS* and what was meant by *Messiah*."[41] Nye often betrayed his own theological ignorance: "The Fa-

36. Locke, *Second Vindication*, 252; Locke, *Vindications*, critical ed. by Nuovo, 141.

37. When Locke died in 1704, his library contained over one hundred Socinian and Unitarian works. Marshall, "Locke, Socinianism," 118.

38. Marshall, "Locke, Socinianism," 119; Biddle, *Confession of Faith*; Biddle, *Twelve Arguments*.

39. Bourne, *John Locke*, 1:310, 2:405.

40. Snobelen, "To us," 128; Champion, "Directions," 225.

41. Locke did equate Messiah with Son of God, but never affirmed the full divinity of either the Messiah or Son of God. Son of God does not have a single meaning in the Bible as Adam is also called *"the son of God"* in Luke 1:38. Later in his reply to Edwards, Locke said that the term Messiah "needs no more explication of it, than what our English bible gives of it, where it is plain to any *vulgar capacity*, that it was used to denote that King and deliverer, whom God had promised." Locke, *Second Vindication*, 108; Locke, *Vindications*, critical ed., 83. Edwards responded that first century Jews had no thought of equating Messiah with Son of God. That percipience is associated with conversion as evidenced by the testimony of the Ethiopian eunuch when he replies to Philip, Acts 8:37: "And Philip said, If thou believest with all thine heart,

ther was God too, and if God was *Incarnate*, how will it be avoided that the Father was *Incarnate?*"[42] Reacting against the "Atheistic Tang" accusation, Nye completely missed Edwards's logic and attempted to make Edwards appear inconsistent.

> Mr. *Edw.* is no less Injurious in his Censures upon other Writers: *In the very Socinian Doctrine it self* (saith he) *there seems to be an Atheistical Tang.* For proof, he cites the *Considerations on the Explications of Doct. of Trin.* pag.5. Where (saith he) *the Self-existence of God, which is the Primary, Fundamental, and Essential Property—of the Deity, is peremptorily pronounc'd by them to be a* CONTRADICTION. It's strange a Man of Mr. *Edwards's* Undertaking, should give forth such a Calumny. His Ldp. of *Worcester* [Stillingfleet] says, *If God was from Eternity, he must be from himself.* That Author answers, that *that is an Espousing the Cause of the Atheists,* and he gives this Reason; *If God is from Eternity, he must be of none; neither of (or from) himself, nor from any other; not from himself, for then he must be before he was; and neither from himself, nor from any other, because all Origination of what kind soever is inconsistent with an Eternal Being.* Is this now peremptorily to pronounce, that the *Self-existence* of God is a Contradiction? or is it not to vindicate the Self-existence of God from a false Notion of it, occasion'd by the Bishop's words? But what will Mr. *Edw.* say to the Author of the XXVIII Propositions, &c. (who, they say, is the Bishop of *Glouc.*) who peremptorily denies, nay says, *It is a flat Contradiction, to say that the second and third persons* (of the Trinity) *are Self-existent?* (Prop. 8.) Consequently neither of them is God: because (as Mr. *Edw.* says) *Self-existence is the Primary, Fundamental, and Essential Property of God,* which yet neither the Son nor the H. Ghost have. I wish Mr. *Edw.* would either reconcile himself to the Bishop, or the Bishop to him, before he charges an *Atheistical Tang* upon the Socinian Doctrine, upon account of the denial of God's Self-existence, which he may see strongly affirm'd in the Reflections on the said Propositions, &c.[43]

---

thou mayest. And he answered and said, I believe that Jesus Christ is the Son of God." Edwards, *Brief Vindication*, 83–85. Edwards said that Locke "makes *Christ and Adam* to be *the Sons of God* in the same senses, viz. by their Birth as the *Racovians* generally do." Edwards, *Some Thoughts*, 112. Locke: "He being by Birth the Son of God." Locke, *Reasonableness*, first ed., 199–203; Locke, *Reasonableness*, critical ed., 113–15; Nye, *Exceptions*, 15.

42. Nye, *Exceptions*, 10.

43. Nye, *Exceptions*, 17–18. The author of the *XXVIII Propositions* was Edward

The source of Edwards's quote, "God's *Self-existence* is a Contradiction," was a Socinian Tract, whose author had misinterpreted a sermon of Bishop Stillingfleet.⁴⁴ In his sermons, Stillingfleet repeatedly tried to explain the mystery of the Trinity and Incarnation, but in no way intended to "*espouse the cause of the atheists.*" He responded directly to their charge of holding a contradiction:

> God was from all Eternity, although we cannot conceive in our minds how he could be from himself. Now what saith the *Unitarian* to this, who pretended to answer me? He saith, "*If God must be from himself then an Eternal God is a Contradiction; for that implies that he was before he was, and so charges me with espousing the cause of Atheists.* [. . .] This is malicious cavilling [. . .] My design was only to shew [. . .] that it is a thing that we are bound to believe stedfastly, although it is above our comprehension."⁴⁵

Nye then enlisted Gloucester Bishop Fowler to the debate, no doubt assuming that, because Fowler was trinitarian, Edwards would agree with him. But Fowler was a subordinationist as evidenced by proposition four (and others) of his twenty-eight: "God the Father alone, is in reference to His *Manner of Existence* an Absolutely Perfect Being; because He alone is Self-Existent."⁴⁶ On the mystery and unity of the Trinity, Edwards was consistent with Stillingfleet and himself, but not with Fowler. Edwards wrote to Locke: "As to the *Examinator's* question, How the *Second* and *Third Persons* can be *Self-existent?* I answer, They are Self-existent as they are eternally from the Self-same Deity" because according to the Nicene Creed, self-existence has to do with "the *Essence* of Christ which is common to him with his Father."⁴⁷

Before responding to Nye, Edwards had begun his conclusion to *Socinianism Unmask'd* by noting that although the author of *The Reasonableness* may not consider himself to be a Socinian, Nye actually "applauds him for his being so serviceable to the *Socinian* and *Antitrinitarian* Interests."⁴⁸ Edwards had accused the Socinians of denying God's

---

Fowler.

44. Edwards, *Socinianism Unmask'd*, 122; Hunt, *Religious Thought*, 2:216.

45. Stillingfleet, *Discourse in Vindication*, 60.

46. Fowler, *Certain Propositions*, 3. By traditional orthodoxy, God is self-existent, but the three persons of the Trinity are not individually self-existent.

47. Edwards, *Socinianism Unmask'd*, 123.

48. Edwards, *Socinianism Unmask'd*, 115. Similarly, he called Deism "the Atheist's

foreknowledge, immensity, omnipresence, self-existence, and spirituality, and in his response, Nye either dismissed those doctrines as unimportant or admitted that neither Socinus or Crellius held them. Edwards concluded, "I hope the Reader is convinc'd that I was not *Unjust* [. . .] when I charg'd them with *Atheism* or a *Strong Tendency* to it in some Points."[49]

Locke did not reply to *Socinianism Unmask'd* immediately, allowing Edwards time to publish another work *The Socinian Creed*, this time dedicated to another Latitudinarian leader in the church, Bishop Stillingfleet of Worcester. Nearly three decades earlier Stillingfleet had refuted Socinian teaching in *A Discourse Concerning the Doctrine of Christ's Satisfaction* and, perhaps because no one had replied, he seemed to think that Socinianism had been fading away.[50] Stillingfleet was initially prompted to address the Socinian issue directly by an error-filled letter he received from an unnamed Socinian writer, accusing him and others of failing to read Socinian works.[51] In his preface to the reprint twenty-seven years later, Stillingfleet noted that having him read their literature was not such a good idea, since *"if I had not read their books I might peradventure have entertained a more favourable Opinion of them, than I now have,"* concluding *"that if the New Testament* [books] *are to be our Rule of Faith, they were extreamly mistaken."* More measured and diplomatic in his critique than Edwards, his verdict was not much different, namely that their books undermine the New Testament, leading to Deism.[52]

But Stillingfleet's earlier concern was not only about the abuse of reason by atheists and Socinians, but the lack of reason by Catholics. Against Catholic polemicists such as John Sergeant (1622–1707) who argued that the answers to all theological questions arising from doctrinal mysteries such as transubstantiation or from textual variations in biblical manuscripts rest with the infallibility of the Pope and the Catholic Church, Stillingfleet charged Rome's apologists with fideism, calling Rome's doctrine of infallibility "an egregious piece of sophistry."[53] Stillingfleet maintained that the source of infallibility for the Christian faith

---

Tool" in *Preacher*, 33.

49. Nye, *Exceptions*, 18–19; Edwards, *Socinianism Unmask'd*, 124–27.
50. Stillingfleet, *Works*, 1:8.
51. Stillingfleet, *Six Sermons*, 259–61.
52. Stillingfleet, *Two Discourses*, iii–iv.
53. Stillingfleet, *Rational Account*, 1:8.

is the Bible which is an eminently reasonable foundation.[54] By defending Christianity's reasonableness in this way, Sergeant said it was impossible to arrive at the truth. For evidence, Sergeant said that Protestants, Socinians, and other heretics all use the same hermeneutical "Rule": "You [all] fight with that ambidextrous Weapon, *Scripture's Letter interpretable by Private Judgments*."[55] He challenged Stillingfleet to show that Protestants could establish the "Ground of Absolute Certainty for their Faith."[56]

After reading more Socinian books, Stillingfleet described their words against the Trinity as "*so spiteful, so unjust, so unreasonable* [. . .] *especially since they are addressed to me* [. . .] *towards clearing the fundamental* Mystery of the Athanasian Religion, *as they call it.*"[57] His aim was to show that trinitarian theology is based on Scripture, was held by the early church, and in no way results in a contradiction. Stillingfleet was similar to Edwards in both his sense of mission to defend the Trinity and his conclusions regarding the Socinian doctrine:

> I do not charge their Writers with a professed design to advance Deism *among us; but their way of managing their Disputes, is as if they had a mind to serve them.* [. . .] *In such a Nation as ours* [. . .] *there is no opening professed schools of* Atheism; *but the design must be carried on under some shew of Religion. And nothing serves their turn so well, as setting up natural Religion in opposition to Revealed.* [. . .] *I call it* Deism, *because that Name obtains now, as more plausible and modish; for* Atheism *is a rude unmannerly Word and exposes Men to the Rabble.* [. . .] *But to be a* Deist, *seems to be only a setting up for having more Wit.*[58]

In addition to this unnamed Socinian writer, Stillingfleet criticized Locke's *Essay Concerning Human Understanding* which subsequently generated a series of letters between them. This new offensive against Locke was occasioned by the publication of Toland's *Christianity Not Mysterious*, which Stillingfleet found to be inspired by Locke's *Essay*, particularly with respect to how reason is used to determine the validity of revelation and dismiss theological mysteries. Behind the emphasis on Christianity being reasonable, was the view that doctrines like the Trinity and Incarnation were unreasonable. Such thinking alarmed Stillingfleet. While not

54. Stillingfleet, *Rational Account*, 1:1–461.
55. Sergeant, *Five Catholick*, 71.
56. Sergeant, *Five Catholick*, Preface.
57. Stillingfleet, *Discourse in Vindication*, ii.
58. Stillingfleet, *Discourse in Vindication*, xlviii–l.

explicitly denying the Trinity, Toland contended that *"there is nothing in the Gospel contrary to Reason, nor above it; and that no Christian Doctrine can be properly call'd a Mystery,"* which sounded to Stillingfleet very much like the Socinians.[59] Speaking of the Trinity, Toland wrote,

> This famous and admirable Doctrine is the undoubted Source of all the *Absurdities* that ever were seriously vented among *Christians*. Without the Pretence of it, we should never hear of the *Transubstantiation*, and other ridiculous Fables of the Church of *Rome*.[60]

Locke responded with a letter to Stillingfleet, complaining that his book was neither about the Trinity nor theological mysteries and that he could not be liable for Toland's work. Stillingfleet answered Locke's letter, which was followed by a second letter and reply, but nothing was resolved between them, though their language was more respectful than it was between Edwards and Locke. Stillingfleet told Locke that he could clear his name if only he would make it known that "you owned the *doctrine of the Trinity* as it hath been Received in the Christian Church."[61] Locke spent 300 prevaricating pages in his last letter to Stillingfleet avoiding a direct answer, beginning by pleading ignorance concerning how the doctrine of the Trinity has been received historically. Stillingfleet's conclusion was that Locke's "Notion of *Ideas* is inconsistent with [. . .] the *Trinity* and the *Incarnation of our Saviour*."[62] The bishop obligingly declined to accuse him of denying those central doctrines, but he did "charge" him "with laying such Foundations as do tend to the Overthrow of them; of which we have had too much Experience already."[63]

Edwards wrote his *Socinian Creed* to state as clearly possible how Socinianism fails the standard of orthodoxy, reiterating his claim that it leads to atheism by proving that it denies central doctrines, especially regarding the character of God. First, he cited examples where Socinians not only said that the Bible is full of errors, but refuse to accept what it does say when it conflicts with their beliefs. He quoted Socinus' view of the atonement from his book *De Jesu Christo Servatore*: "though it were

---

59. Toland, *Christianity Not Mysterious*, 6; Stillingfleet, *Discourse in Vindication*, 230–71; Wallace, "Socinianism," 63.

60. Toland, *Christianity Not Mysterious*, 26–27.

61. Stillingfleet, *Bishop of Worcester's Answer*, 4.

62. Stillingfleet, *Bishop of Worcester's Answer*, 44–45.

63. Stillingfleet, *Bishop of Worcester's Answer*, 177.

extant in the Sacred Monuments of the Scripture, and there were written not only once, but many times, I would not for all that believe it."[64] Edwards acknowledged that, although there is considerable confusion by some of their writers, most Socinians hold to God's self-existence. But the major defect in Socinian theology was their denial of the Trinity and related doctrines of the propitiation and atonement of Christ, held historically by all orthodox Christians. Edwards quoted numerous passages of Scripture which clearly teach the Trinity, including 1 John 2, which says that the deity of the Father and the deity Son cannot be separated. Reject one and you reject both. The Christian God is necessarily triune. "He that denies the existence of the True God is an Atheist, the *Socinian* doth the former, therefore he is the latter." And if the deity of the Son is denied, there is no salvation because salvation depends on the satisfaction of Christ, the result of his propitiatory sacrifice on the cross, which is of no avail if he is only a man.[65]

He continued his exposition by further discussing various false beliefs of Socinians along with biblical counterpoints regarding: human nature before and after the fall, including original sin and final judgment; the unbiblical reduction of Christian theology to one tenet and their faulty notion of what messiah means; their subjection of every doctrine to the judgment of human reason in order to eliminate mystery; what amounts to a sacrilegious inconsistency to deny the divinity of Christ yet enjoin worship of him; their declaration that "there is no collation of any Grace, no Confirmation of our Faith, no bestowing of any Spiritual Blessing in the use of the Sacraments";[66] and their lack of church government or discipline. He noted how they have borrowed ideas from Arians, Ebionites, Macedonians, and other heretics and also find areas of agreement with very questionable Catholic teachings, such as Transubstantiation and distinguishing between venial and mortal sins.[67]

In this work, Edwards wrote that all doubts regarding Locke's authorship have vanished, but he had heard rumors that some believe he has "mistaken Mr. Lock," in linking him to the Socinians. Edwards therefore invited a response that "would oblige the world by shewing the

---

64. Edwards, *Socinian Creed*, 21–22.
65. Edwards, *Socinian Creed*, 54–59.
66. Edwards, *Socinian Creed*, 166.
67. Edwards, *Socinian Creed*, 205, 221.

Mistake, and letting men see wherein and in what instances I have misapprehended his sense and meaning."[68]

Shortly thereafter Locke began his second response to Edwards, a rambling 400-page essay, which began, "A Cause that stands in need of Falshoods to support it, and an Adversary that will make use of them, deserve nothing but Contempt."[69] He was clearly agitated by Edwards, especially for saying that Locke had reduced Christianity to a single article of belief. Previously Locke protested, "But where did you find *I contended for one single Article*, so as to *exclude all the rest?* [. . .] I did not so *contend for one* Article of Faith [. . .] However you insist on the word *one* with great vigour."[70] It appears that Locke was correct in claiming that he never uttered those exact words regarding the single article of belief, but it is not too difficult to make that inference. After attempting for forty pages in his *Second Vindication* to rebut and discredit Edwards, Locke demonstrated that his notion of what it means to be a Christian had not changed.

> For I will be bold to say, that every one, who considers the matter, will see, that either only the Article of his being the *Messiah* their King, which alone our Saviour and his Apostles preach'd to the Unconverted World, and received those that believed it into the Church, is the only necessary Article to be believed by a *Theist* to make him a Christian; Or else that all the Truths contain'd in the New Testament, are necessary Articles to be believed to make a Man a Christian; And that between these two it is impossible any where to stand.[71]

Neither would Locke accept Edwards's contention that the New Testament epistles have always been acknowledged as essential to understanding the gospel.[72] Little progress was made between Edward's approach to restate Locke in his own words and draw logical conclusions from what Locke did not say vis-a-vis Locke's approach of parsing Edwards's language to infer conclusions he believed Edwards was drawing, conclusions which Locke did not intend to be drawn, or of Locke searching in Scripture and failing to find the precise theological terminology that Edwards used, such as "satisfaction." Locke continued to be offended

68. Edwards, *Socinian Creed*, 128.
69. Locke, *Second Vindication*, 1; Locke, *Vindications*, critical ed., 39.
70. Edwards, *Socinianism Unmask'd*, 58; Locke, *Vindication*, 27–28; Locke, *Vindications*, critical ed., 20–21.
71. Locke, *Second Vindication*, 82; Locke, *Vindications*, critical ed., 73.
72. Locke, *Second Vindication*, 126–43; Locke, *Vindications*, critical ed., 91–97.

by Edwards's criticisms of his theology and Edwards was equally disturbed by his belief that Locke falsely represented the gospel.[73]

Locke closed his *Second Vindication* requesting Edwards to provide "an Answer to these Questions" and Edwards obliged with *A Brief Vindication of the Fundamental Articles of the Christian Faith*, which he dedicated to Oxford and Cambridge universities, whom he felt Locke had insulted for saying that for most people the great effort made learning Greek and Latin serves "no purpose" and that logic and metaphysics are "fitter to amuse, than inform the understanding."[74] Edwards took this opportunity to suggest that Locke's unsound theology resulted from his deficiency in Greek, Latin, and especially logic, where "he makes the Blessed Apostle contradict himself, meerly to contradict me."[75] He also saw Locke using his "New Education" to introduce his "New Religion," essentially perversions disguised as reforms.[76] Transitioning to his debate with Locke over the essence of the Christian faith, Edwards said that in his *Second Vindication*, Locke had not answered any of his charges or questions posed in *Socinianism Unmask'd*. Edwards believed one of Locke's basic problems was, like the Deists and Socinians, that he refused to accept that there are mysteries in Christian theology which we do not understand and therefore "there are some Doctrines in the Gospel which are not plain and clear, and yet are of a necessity to be believ'd."[77] Furthermore, if Locke managed to prove that only one article of faith is necessary to become Christ's disciple, he had proved what no one has ever proved.[78]

In Edwards's view, the impasse in their debate was due in part to Locke's method of exegesis. Locke claimed he had not reduced the gospel to one article and challenged Edwards to list the necessary articles

---

73. Locke, *Second Vindication*, 155–58; Locke, *Vindications*, critical ed., 102–03. In his *Second Vindication*, Locke defended his decision not to speak of the satisfaction of Christ because the term "satisfaction" was not used by "the Holy Ghost in the Scripture" and even though it is "hard for a Christian to deny" it, it is disputed. However Locke stated that satisfaction is implied by the doctrine of redemption and in an undated manuscript, he affirmed it. Locke, *Second Vindication*, 157–58, 465–66, 103, 227; Nuovo, *Christianity, Antiquity and Enlightenment*, 85.

74. Locke, *Second Vindication*, 478; Locke, *Vindications*, critical ed., 232; Locke, *Some Thoughts Concerning Education*, 225, 244.

75. Locke, *Brief Vindication*, 6, 11, 41–42, 50–51.

76. Locke, *Brief Vindication*, 18–19.

77. Locke, *Brief Vindication*, 39–41.

78. Locke, *Brief Vindication*, 75–76.

of belief.[79] Edwards answered with the resurrection of Christ, citing Romans 10:9: "If thou shalt confess with thy mouth the Lord Jesus, and shalt believe in thine heart that God hath raised him from the dead, thou shalt be saved." Locke insisted that to believe in the resurrection is the same as believing that Jesus is the Messiah, as miracles confirm his messiahship. Edwards replied that these are two separate articles, not to be equated. He accused Locke of "inventing" this linkage after reading Edwards's response where he quoted Romans 10:9.[80]

To illustrate their conflicting hermeneutics, consider Locke's exegesis of Peter's sermon in the second chapter of Acts. Of the twenty-six verses recorded of that sermon, Locke honed in on verse 36: "Therefore let all the house of Israel know assuredly, that God hath made that same Jesus, whom ye have crucified, both Lord and Christ."

> We may observe, that the Preaching of the Apostles every where in the *Acts*, tended to this one point, to prove that Jesus was the *Messiah*. Indeed, now, after his death, his Resurrection was also commonly required to be believed, as a necessary Article, and sometimes solely insisted on: it being a mark and undoubted Evidence of his being the *Messiah*, and necessary now to be believed by those who would receive him as the *Messiah*. [. . .] And therefore those who believed him to be the *Messiah*, must believe that he was risen from the Dead: and those who believed him to be risen from the Dead, could not doubt of his being the *Messiah*.[81]

Edwards argued that Locke was simply wrong in thinking that Peter's answer to their question of what they should do to be saved is to believe that Jesus is the Messiah. For it "is not expressly mention'd throughout the whole Sermon, only the substance of it is in ver. 36, after the other Grand Articles of Christs Passion and Dying and Rising had been amply discourse'd of and urg'd." Locke's single-minded focus on this point shows how he had, in fact, reduced the gospel to that.[82]

Edwards concluded his debate with Locke and wrote two addenda to *A Brief Vindication*, one to Samuel Bold (see below) and the second to a "Nameless Socinian" who had replied to his *Socinian Creed* in a tract,

---

79. Locke, *Vindication*, 20–21; Locke, *Vindications*, critical ed., 17–18.

80. Edwards, *Brief Vindication*, 78–79; Locke, *Second Vindication*, 305; Locke, *Vindications*, critical ed.,

81. Locke, *Reasonableness*, 30–31; Locke, *Reasonableness*, critical ed., 25–26.

82. Edwards, *Brief Vindication*, 73–74.

The Agreement of the Unitarians with the Catholic Church. That nameless Socinian is believed to have been Stephen Nye.[83] In his *Socinian Creed*, Edwards had given thirteen propositions describing Socinian doctrine, which Nye claimed were not worded with sufficient care or clarity. Typically Nye's responses fell into one of four categories: he said that a particular statement of Edwards was wrong because it was not precisely nuanced, or he refuted a position incorrectly attributed to Edwards, or he defended his own view against an accusation that Edwards did not make, or he simply skipped over some statements that he did not want to discuss.

As examples of the disjointed debate, Edwards said of the Socinians that "they maintain that the First Man was not created in a State of Uprightness."[84] Nye responded: "In the next Article, he makes us believe a great many things; as that 'the first Man was not created in a State of Uprightness,'" which was not what Edwards believed, but what he accused the Socinians of believing. Nye did not dispute Edwards's description of the Socinian view of Adam's fall, wherein he said that they denied the doctrine of original sin. Instead he accused Edwards of believing that neither Adam's bad example nor the curse of the earth has been detrimental to all people.[85] Edwards wrote that they believe that "there is no distinction of *Persons* or *Subsistencies* in him, and that the *Son,* and *Holy Ghost,* are not God."[86] Nye responded by claiming to be in agreement with the Catholic Church by denying tritheism, of which Edwards did not accuse him:

> The Question is not at all concerning three *Persons*, or three *Subsistencies*, in God, but whether there are three Infinite *Substances*; three eternal *Minds*, and *Spirits*? [. . .] We say the Lord Christ is *God*, and *Man*. He is *Man*, in his respect of his reasonable Soul, and human Body; *God*, in respect of *God in him*. Or more scholastically, in respect of the Hypostatical (or Personal) Union, [. . .] the Divinity was not only *occasionally* assisting unto, but was (and *is*) *always* in Christ.[87]

83. So attributed in Wing's Short-Title Catalogue.
84. Edwards, *Socinian Creed*, 73.
85. Nye, *Agreement*, 7–8.
86. Edwards, *Socinian Creed*, 207.

87. Nye, *Agreement*, 6–7. There are many trinitarian heresies. Nye cleverly attempted to defend his orthodoxy by claiming to deny some of them, which Catholics and Protestants also deny. However, his description of Christ as human and divine fails

The following year, Nye wrote a short work attempting to explain the views of himself and Firmin as Unitarian, but not Socinian nor Arian. But on the fifth page, his attention switched to Edwards who, throughout the entire work, is named more often than Firmin. Edwards and others are accused of misinterpreting Scripture and misunderstanding and misrepresenting the views of both Unitarians and Socinians. To his credit, Nye refrains from innuendo and insult, complimenting Edwards for "having published divers good books," but now unable to "resist of contriving a New Religion [. . .] and of imputing it to the *Socinians*. By whom he means (it appears) the *Unitarians*."[88]

Besides Nye, another writer which came to Locke's defense against Edwards was Samuel Bold. Generally thought to be orthodox, Bold was so zealous a preacher for toleration and against persecution that in 1682 he was sentenced to seven weeks in prison for libel and sedition.[89] Bold's first defense of Locke essentially consisted of three short essays responding to Edwards's works against Locke.[90] He included lengthy quotes from Edwards, to which he responded, but focused mainly on the question of what belief is required to make someone a Christian. Near the end, he refuted two ideas which he incorrectly inferred that Edwards held:

> I think it appears evidently enough [. . .] that there is no just ground to accuse any Man to be an *Anti-Trinitarian*, or a *Socinian*, because he asserts that believing Jesus to be the *Messias* is all that is necessarily required to make a Man a Christian [. . . and] that the belief of the *Trinity*, and that Jesus *the Son of God, is God* doth not constitute a Man a Christian.[91]

Though Bold proclaimed his great respect for Edwards, he was not convinced by his arguments, suggesting that it might be because "I am too dull to perceive what his Reasons are, and wherein the strength of them doth lie."[92] After restating Locke's reasons why Edwards was in error, he again admitted that he was not confident in his understanding of Edwards, writing, "I confess I am not sagacious enough to perceive

---

in his description of "Hypostatical Union" as "*God in him.*"

88. Nye, *Account*, 8

89. Ball, "Samuel Bold."

90. Bold, *Some Passages*. This was published in two editions, the second of which also contained a sermon, to which Edwards also responded.

91. Bold, *Some Passages*, 45–46.

92. Bold, *Some Passages*, 9.

it."[93] He agreed with Locke that his intentions were to "enquire, not what points are proposed to be believed by Christians, but what is necessary to be believed, to make a Man a Christian," which accomplished very little in Locke's defense.[94]

Edwards answered Bold in two different publications, each of which began with separate replies to Locke. The *Socinian Creed* contained a postscript of two short essays addressed to Bold. In the first, a critique of Bold's Philippians 3:8 sermon, Edwards said that it is essentially self-contradictory to claim on the one hand that only one article must be believed to make someone a Christian and on the other that one who becomes a "Sincere" or "True" Christian must believe several additional articles.[95] The second was a response to Bold's essay, "Some Animadversions on Mr. Edwards's Book Entituled, Socinianism Unmask'd." Here Bold continued to belabor Locke's belief that asking *"what Articles a Convert to Christianity may be obliged necessarily to believe?"* is entirely different than asking *"what is necessary to be believed to make a Man a Convert to Christianity?"*[96]

Edwards began his response to the last essay, "Reflections on the Animadversions," by doubting its authenticity: "I can scarcely believe that Mr. *Bold* would offer such a Crude and Shallow thing to the publick."[97] Edwards gave several reasons for doubting Bold's authorship: (1) he recalled hearing the arguments of that essay from other sources; (2) the writing style, including vocabulary and phrasing, was markedly different from the rest of the book; and (3) the font type of the last piece set it apart as a separate printing. Edwards suspected that it came from "J.L. or A.&J.C."[98] Edwards repeated some of his previous arguments against Locke's single article of belief formula. He pointed out that he had spent twelve pages describing the essence of the gospel in *Socianism Unmask'd*, namely that all have sinned, that Jesus is truly God and truly man, that saying Jesus is the Messiah does not mean that he is truly God, that the atonement was made possible only by the death and resurrection of Christ, that salvation

---

93. Bold, *Some Passages*, 19.
94. Bold, *Some Passages*, 45.
95. Bold, *Short Discourse*, 29–33; Edwards, *Socinian Creed*, 240.
96. Bold, *Some Passages*, 21.
97. Edwards, *Socinian Creed*, 250.
98. Edwards, *Socinian Creed*, 250–51. Initials refer to John Locke and Awhsham and John Churchill, Bold's publishers, whom Edwards perceived to share Socinian views; see Wallace, *Antitrinitarian Biography*, 1:321.

is available only by the unmerited grace of God through faith, and that the evidence of true faith is obedience. Edwards mocked Bold's response as no response at all:

> This *Sham-Animadverter* attends not to any one of the Particulars which I had mention'd, nor offers any thing against them, but only in a Lumping way dooms them all in these Magisterial Words, *I do not see any Proof he produceth*, p.21. This is his wonderful way of Confuting me, by pretending that he can't see any Argument of Proof in what I alledg; and all the world must be led by his Eyes.[99]

Edwards's use of the epithet above points to another dimension of their debate. Was Edwards an angry and abusive disputant? It is true that Edwards himself was the source for some of his reputation, but aside from his interchange with John Locke and his refusal to countenance Arianism, Socinianism, and Deism, he was not that strident in his writing. Locke, however, must bear some responsibility for a less than amiable interchange by writing anonymously. When Locke published *A Vindication* he again failed to identified himself. Neither did he, in Edwards's view, answer Edwards's critique of *The Reasonableness*. So, with *Socinianism Unmask'd*, Edwards began to taunt him with amusing nicknames including, "this Guilty Man," "our Nameless Author," "this Upstart Racovian," "this Flourishing Scribbler," "our good Ottoman Writer," "this Inferior Inquisitor," "this Censorious Gentleman," "a Pupil of Socinus," "this Vindicator," "an Egregious Whissler," "a Notorious Dissembler," "the Criminal," "this Judicious Casuist," and "a Stubborn Dissembler."[100] Locke was not entertained, continuing nameless in his *Second Vindication*. He accused Edwards of laying "Stress on Matters of Fact foreign to the Question, as well as to Truth; and [stuffing] it with Scurrility and Fiction" and calling him "*Skimmington*," the "*Unmasker*," and "*Creed-maker*."[101]

Neither did Stephen Nye identify himself in his first or second defense of Locke. In response, Edwards named him "the Reverend Examinator," "a Dabbler in Grammar and Criticism," and "triply a Blunderer."[102] Edwards referred to men like Whitby and Whiston as "Enthusiastic

---

99. Edwards, *Socinian Creed*, 256.

100. Edwards, *Socinianism Unmask'd*, 5, 24, 41, 53, 61, 97, 98, 102, 105, 112.

101. Skimmington: a mock parade made through a village intended to bring ridicule on and make an example of a nagging wife or an unfaithful husband; Locke, *Second Vindication*, Preface, 2, 415; Locke, *Vindications*, critical ed., 33, 40, 207.

102. Edwards, *Socinianism Unmask'd*, 118, 128, 130.

Imposters, and Pretenders to a Prophetick Spirit."[103] In his attacks on Edwards, Nye skipped colorful titles to focus on Edwards's presumed inability to reason clearly: "Mr. Edw. in asserting there are three such Persons in one Divine Nature, renders in effect the whole Bible void and useless for the proof of any Proposition whatever it may be."[104] Certainly Edwards was not very winsome and a more diplomatic approach like that of Bishop Stillingfleet was clearly more civil, even if it was not in the end more compelling with adversaries such as Locke.

A contemporary assessment of approaches taken by Edwards, Locke, and Stillingfleet in their debate was given by an anonymous writer self-identified as "F.B., M.A. of Cambridge." Portraying himself as evenhanded in his analysis, he wrote, "I was inclined to Mr. *Lock's* side, before I read and well perused the Bishops remarks upon him." Some had thought Edwards "too severe" with Locke, but upon reading Stillingfleet "all men of consideration and due thoughts conclude, that Mr. *Edwards* had just occasion (tho we knew it not so well as he did) to alarm the World with the apprehensions of the danger of Mr. *Lock's* Writings." He did fault both Edwards and Locke for failing to recognize anything of value in their opponents, but he excused Edwards as not being among those "hum-drumming Authors" who feel compelled to "compliment and flatter their opponents." He concluded by judging each man's performance against a standard "borrowed from an eminent Pen" who said that "Writers of Controversies should *use soft Words and hard Arguments.*" By this writer's estimate, he concluded that Stillingfleet did so, while Locke used hard words for soft arguments and Edwards used hard words for hard arguments.[105]

One can only imagine the conversation and correspondence that accompanied publication of these works. Lady Masham (Ralph Cudworth's (1617–88) daughter), a good friend and frequent correspondent of Locke, received an anonymous letter informing her of the printing of *Socinianism Unmask'd.* The identity and intentions of the writer remain

103. Edwards, *Some Brief Observations*, 1.

104. Nye, *Exceptions*, 23.

105. F.B., *Free but Modest Censure*, 7, 8, 14, 15–16. Both Samuel Bold and Victor Nuovo believe that Edwards wrote this anonymous work to restore his damaged reputation: Locke, *Vindications*, critical ed., lxvii. While such a conjecture is possible, weighing against it are two considerations: there is no other evidence of Edwards ever failed to identify himself in print and no evidence that he wrote to advance his reputation, for which he professed to have little concern. See for example, Edwards, *Preacher, Third Part*, 224.

a mystery.[106] Thomas Burnett (1656–1729) kept Leibniz informed on Locke's difficulties resulting from *The Reasonableness* in a series of letters from London. He asked that Leibniz "not name him in this connection" because "the novelty of his manner there might scandalize the clergy, etc., etc." Burnett referred to Edwards and others as the source of "some excellent sermons."[107]

Although Edwards's last work on Locke's dilution of the gospel was published in 1697, he continued to point out other errors of Locke in later works. For example, he attacked Locke for contradicting the clear teaching of Scripture as traditionally understood by denying the doctrine of innate ideas; for thinking that some people in Africa have no religion; for objecting to certain doctrines simply because their common theological terms are not found in Scripture, such as "*Satisfaction of Christ*" and "*Hypostatical Union*"; for his confused teaching on the bodily resurrection; for implying that "*a mere Material Being may think*"; for denying the soul's immortality; for opposing children reading the Bible, "*either for the perfecting their Reading or principling their Religion, that perhaps a worse could not be found*"; for stating that God's death sentence to Adam was nothing more than a change from the state of immortality to mortality; for dismissing the New Testament epistles as "*Occasional*" rather than essential; for reducing God's infinite nature to a numerical concept; for writing that people are not punished "*for unbelief, but only for their misdeeds*"; and for elevating reason above revelation because everyone can clearly understand "*Natural Religion*," but what we learn from revelation is obscure and difficult to understand, as he quoted Locke:

> Whatsoever Truth we come to the Discovery of, from the Knowledge and Contemplation of our own clear *Ideas*, will always be certainer to us than those that are conveyed to us by *Traditional Revelation*. For the Knowledge, we have, that this *Revelation* came from GOD, can never be so sure, as the Knowledge that we have from the clear and distinct Perception of the Agreement, or Disagreement of our own *Ideas*.[108]

106. Hutton, "Debating the Faith," 171.

107. Quoted in Duncan, "Toland and Locke," 129, 132. Burnet was a diplomat trusted by Locke and also a cousin of Gilbert Burnet.

108. Edwards, *Free Discourse*, 42; Edwards, *Theologia*, 1:26, 553; 2:5, 24–25, 48, 489; Edwards, *Veritas*, 311; Edwards, *Some Brief Observations*, 20; Edwards, *Some New Discoveries*, 9; Edwards, *Doctrine of Faith*, 63; Edwards, *Free Discourse*, 83–84.; Locke, *Concerning Human Understanding*, fifth ed., 582; Locke, *Concerning Human Understanding*, critical ed., 169.

Besides reiterating many of Locke's theological errors, in a sermon at Cambridge he attacked him for declaring that words such as virtues and sins have an "uncertain signification" and accused him of being a Hobbist, "in whose steps he affects to tread."[109]

Some argue that Locke was more a Latitudinarian than a Socinian and that critics like Edwards were way off the mark in calling Locke a Socinian, but there was a significant divide between Locke and the Latitudinarians.[110] Although Latitudinarian Tillotson's orthodoxy was open to question on a number of issues, he did defend the doctrine of the Trinity, divinity of Christ, Incarnation, and atonement in several sermons, which Locke continued to refuse to do.[111]

> A man must not deny what God says to be true; though we cannot comprehend many things which God says: as particularly concerning this mystery of the Trinity. [. . .] The words thus explained, contain that great mystery of godliness, as the Apostle calls it, or of the Christian religion, viz. the incarnation of the Son of God, which St. Paul expresseth by the appearance of manifestation of God in the flesh [. . .] and this will not only infer his existence before his incarnation, but from all eternity.[112]

Similarly, William Chillingworth (1602–44), sometimes seen as a founding father of Latitudinarianism, clearly and repeatedly affirmed the doctrines of the Trinity, Incarnation, resurrection, etc.[113]

Was Locke a Socinian? Obviously not a self-identified one as he adamantly rejected that label. Nevertheless, from what he wrote and refused to say, others besides Edwards and Stillingfleet saw clear similarities, such as conservative nonconformists like John Owen (1616–83) and Stephen Lobb. Others calling Locke a Socinian include Church of England clergymen Thomas Beconsall (1663/4–1709) and William Payne (1650–96); Henry Felton (1679–1740), principal of St Edmund Hall, Oxford; Winch Holdsworth (1679–1761), DD, fellow of St. John College, Oxford; Scottish Presbyterian Robert Ferguson (1637–1714), and nonjuring minister

---

109. Edwards, *Eternal and Intrinsick Reasons*, 26–28; Locke, *Concerning Human Understanding*, 32; Locke *Concerning Human Understanding*, critical ed., 77–80.

110. Tetlow, "Theological Context," 7.

111. Tillotson, "Concerning the Divinity," 3:281–442. (Sermons XLIII–XLVIII).

112. Tillotson, "Concerning the Incarnation," 3:430; "Concerning the Divinity," 3:283, 324.

113. Chillingworth, *Religion of the Protestants*, 159, 169.

John Milner (1628–1702).[114] Even German mathematician and philosopher Godfried Leibniz wrote that Locke "inclined to the Socinians because of a diminished view of who God is.[115] Recent concurrence comes from Nicholas Wolterstorff, along with others such as David Wootton and Allison Coudert: "It is indeed fairly clear that in his theological views Locke was a Socinian (unitarian) for the last decade and a half of his life."[116] Others suggest he may have been closer to Arianism.[117] Among Locke's other contemporary critics was Richard Willis, later Bishop of Winchester. He accused Locke of borrowing his one article of faith from Hobbes, but Locke maintained that his only source was the New Testament.[118] Likewise Bishop Stillingfleet suggested the influence of Hobbes upon him since they both had similar ideas regarding the immortality of the soul.[119]

Those who came to Locke's defense were, except for Samuel Bold, non-trinitarians or those who, like Locke, refused to commit themselves, including poet Catherine Cockburn (1674?–1749) and Cambridge mathematics professor William Whiston (1667–1752).[120] But in the late seventeenth century, neither prevailing public opinion nor civil courts were willing to tolerate Locke's theology. The XXXIX Articles were established by law, not to be disputed, much less "*absolutely denied.*" On May 17, 1697, the Grand Jury of Middlesex handed down a decision to punish "to the utmost severity of the law" the "Authors, Printers and Publishers" of publications that are

---

114. Dacome, "Resurrecting Numbers," 82–83; Marshall, *John Locke*, 286, 417.

115. Quoted in Jolley, "Leibniz on Locke," 233, 237, 239, 243. In commenting on this observation by Leibniz, Jolly says that "*this remark* [. . .] *has received far less attention that it deserves.*" Indeed. Three decades later, Maria Rosa Antognozza demonstrates this to be the case: "Leibniz does not endorse the suspicion of Anti-trinitarianism brought against Locke in several quarters." One of these, she identifies as Edwards, who she says, "unduly deduces that he [Locke] wishes to deny the other revealed truths on the basis of rationalistic premises of a Socinian kind." See her *Leibniz on the Trinity*, 132, 133.

116. Wolterstorff, "Locke's Philosophy," 185; Wootton, "John Locke," 39; Coudert, "John Locke," 101.

117. Marshall, *John Locke*, 426; Hudson, *English Deists*, 160.

118. Savonius-Wroth et al., *Continuum Companion*, 117; Locke, *Second Vindication*, 470–72; Locke, *Vindications*, critical ed., 228–229.

119. Stillingfleet, *Bishop of Worcester's Answer*, 54–57.

120. Sell, *John Locke*, 211–26.

either directly contrary to the said Doctrine, or by consequence in opposition to them, denying all the Mysteries of the Christian Religion, and resolving all into such Notions as are to be made good by Humane Reason, and thereby making void the whole revealed Religion, and destroying the Necessity of Faith in order to Eternal Salvation.

As Arian, Socinian, atheistic, and Deist proselytes were causing a "great Scandal of the Church of England" the decision called for the suppression of books already printed and the prevention of future such books, including *The Reasonableness* and *Christianity Not Mysterious*.[121]

For many of his accusers, Locke's problem was his general practice of agnosticism on issues deemed critically important to his opponents, which means that many of them may have feared the worst and may have misjudged him. But he did not seem to interested in understanding perspectives other than his own. And despite the efforts of some, no prodding would entice him to commit on controversial issues like the Trinity.[122]

Reverberations from the Locke-Edwards debate crossed the channel where abridged versions of *The Reasonableness, A Vindication,* and *Socinianism Unmask'd* were translated into French and published in the scientific journal *Acta Eruditorum* in Leipzig.[123] Locke maintained his anonymity even in private correspondence with friends, perhaps because he wanted their unbiased opinion. He wrote to Remonstrant theologian Philipp van Limborch, asking his opinion of the French translation. In his generally positive, but less than glowing reply from Amsterdam, Limborch reported that the *Acta* editors were critical of *The Reasonableness*, which they attributed to someone named Pockius, but no one had doubts about his opponent:

> Extollunt magnifice Joannem Eduardum, quod præclare hactenus in Anglia contra Socinianam hæresin variis scriptis militaverit, librumque ediderit Meditationum quarundam de causis & occasione atheismi, hodierni præsertim fæculi; in quo passim autoris hujus anonymi sententias, ut periculosas & á socinianismo ac atheismo non alienas perstrihxit.[124]

121. Gailhard, *Epistle and Preface*, 82–83.
122. Locke, *Mr. Locke's Reply*, 100–7.
123. *Acts of the Erudite*, published 1682–1782.
124. They praise John Edwards very highly because he has hitherto fought gloriously in England against the Socinian heresy in various writings and has published a

The editors were disappointed that they were unable to include Edwards's initial attack on Locke, which appeared in *Some Thoughts Concerning the Causes of Atheism.*

Locke had also requested that his friend, philosopher William Molyneux (1656–98), review *The Reasonableness.*[125] As late as May 1697, following an active letter exchange in which Edwards is repeatedly derided and following publication of Locke's *Second Vindication,* of which Molyneux had received a copy, he still did not know that Locke was the author of his trilogy.

> If you know the Author thereof, (as I am apt to surmise, you may) be pleased to let him know, that I think he has done Edwards too much Honour in thinking him worth his Notice, for so vile a Poor Wretch certainly never appear'd in Print.[126]

Philip Dixon's view of Locke's opponents in the controversy reflects Locke's view: disappointed but respectful of Stillingfleet; angry and dismissive of Edwards. Failing to acknowledge any similarity between the charges of Edwards and Stillingfleet, Dixon characterizes Edwards's arguments as "of little intellectual worth, proceeding largely by calumny, insinuation and innuendo." After briefly trying to discredit Edwards with little in the way of substantive evidence, candid admissions follow: that "modern historian" Justin Champion "concluded that Edwards was correct"; that Locke did believe that only one article was necessary for salvation; that Locke scholar John Higgins-Biddle is "at pains to exonerate Locke from charges of heterodoxy;" that Stillingfleet "may not have been wide of the mark," and that it is "highly implausible" that Locke never read Socinian books.[127] Furthermore, Dixon reports that in planning for a future book, Locke left notes containing references to Biddle and two arguments against the Trinity in outline form. "More conclusive proof about Locke's clandestine unitarianism" is seen in his letters with

---

book of *Some thoughts concerning the causes and occasion of atheism, especially in the present age,* in which he has everywhere found fault with the opinions of this anonymous author, as dangerous and as no different from Socinianism and atheism. From, Locke, *Correspondence,* 6:43; Letter from Limborch to Locke, March 16, 1697.

125. Locke, *Correspondence,* 5:667–68; Locke to Molyneux, July 14/24, 1696.

126. Locke, *Correspondence,* 6:123; Molyneux to Locke, May 15, 1697; 5:652–55; Molyneux to Locke, June 6, 1696; 6:82–83; Molyneux to Locke, April 6, 97; 6:191–93; Molyneux to Locke, Sept. 11, 1697.

127. Dixon, *Nice and Hot,* 162–65.

Limborch, who edited Socinian Samuel Przypkowski's (1592–1670) works.[128] Dixon fails to acknowledge that both Locke and Edwards based their position on Scripture with Edwards's understanding in line with orthodox Christian tradition and Locke's interpretation following his own way akin to a literalistic Socinianism. Concluding the chapter, as if to restore Locke's slandered reputation, Dixon writes, "Accusations of Socinianism by his contemporaries should definitely not be taken at face value."[129]

SAMUEL CLARKE

Another major philosopher whose orthodoxy Edwards found wanting was Samuel Clarke. Like many in the previous generation, Clarke wrestled to resolve the tension between reason and revelation. Like Locke, he did so by undertaking a serious and independent study of Scripture. Like a number of other intellectuals of his day, he identified his primary opponent as rising Deism, which had virtually eliminated any sense of divine revelation. He set off another round of debate beginning with his Boyle Lectures in 1704 on the *Being and Attributes of God* and in 1705 with *Evidences of Natural and Revealed Religion*.

Clarke has been called a high Arian by nineteenth- and twentieth-century scholars to distinguish his view from classical Arianism. Recently it has been shown that his trinitarian theology was closely related to Eusebius of Caesarea and Origen, whereby the essence of the Son is subordinate to the Father, not created, but derived from the Father in eternity past and is of similar (ὁμοιούσιος), but not identical (ὁμοούσιος) essence to that of the Father.[130] For Edwards however, such distinctions were essentially irrelevant to the fact that Arians and Socinians all denied the traditional understanding of the doctrine of the Trinity.

In 1712 Clarke published *The Scripture Doctrine of the Trinity*, where in fifty-five propositions he laid out his understanding of the Trinity, enumerating twelve hundred and fifty-one New Testament passages in support of his view.[131] He also drew upon many of the Fathers. Public reaction

---

128. Dixon, *Nice and Hot*, 165–67.
129. Dixon, *Nice and Hot*, 168.
130. Pfizenmaier, *Trinitarian Theology*.
131. A summary of Clarke's view:
   a. "Father" implies supreme cause of everything else, including the Son, who was

was swift and dramatic, comparable to Locke's *The Reasonableness* nearly twenty years earlier. The first response, published anonymously, was from Edward Wells (1667–1727), questioning Clarke's orthodoxy. Wells was no mere pamphleteer. He recognized that the unavoidable mystery of the Trinity makes easy comprehension impossible and that familiarity with the original languages is essential for serious analysis. The objective of his response to Clarke was to defend the established orthodox doctrine of the Trinity and deity of Christ from the Old Testament: that the Son was eternally begotten; that the Spirit proceeds from the Father and the Son; that each member of the Trinity is equally divine both in essence and attributes. He called attention to Clark's weak hermeneutics, for example in ignoring numerous Old Testament passages where divine titles are used for the Son or where Elohim is plural.[132]

Shortly after Wells, Edwards published his first of three critiques. He began with a summary of the debate since Locke, very thankful for certain men that had opposed the Unitarians, including Bishops Gilbert Burnet, Fowler, and Stillingfleet, along with Wallis and John Williams (1636?–1709). Edwards said that though Arianism and Socinianism are not equivalent, their theological differences are insignificant relative to their common desire to "destroy the true and proper Divinity of the Son of God, and of the Holy Ghost."[133] Verse-by-verse he showed how Clarke had misinterpreted Scripture and ignored the clear teaching of many prominent trinitarians among the church fathers, while citing words of "*the Arian Hereticks* of Old."[134] He closed by explaining how all of church liturgy was clear and unambiguously opposed to Arianism, concluding

---

not created *ex nihilo* (like man), but derived by a deliberate act of the Father (i.e., not filiation) in eternity past.

b. The Son was given the power and attributes of the Father, except for aseity, independence, and absolute supremacy.

c. The Son is known as God in the New Testament not because his substance is derived from the Father, but because of his divine attributes and authority.

d. We worship the Son not because of his divine essence, but because of his works and communicable attributes. To the Father alone is due supreme worship.

132. Wells, *Essay*, 3, 5, 27–33 (*Elohim* being plural). Wells, BD, DD, Oxford, was a High Churchman, mathematician and linguistic scholar. He produced one of the first critical editions of the Greek New Testament, the basis for future critical editions, along with a revised English translation (not based on Textus Receptus). His careful scholarship and expertise were clearly sufficient to challenge Clarke's hermeneutics; see Katz, *God's Last Words*, 185.

133. Edwards, *Some Animadversions*, 4.

134. Edwards, *Some Animadversions*, 10.

that Clarke wanted "*a New Liturgy, New Creeds,* and *New Articles,* as well as *New Scriptures.*" And for those who understand the Creed of Athanasius, to reject it as Clarke had is "*Damnable.*"[135]

Exactly what was the nature of Clarke's near muted reply to *Some Animadversions* is not clear, but in his next salvo against Clarke, Edwards noted that while some writers "think their Security lies in being silent," he interpreted it as weakness: a "Tacit Confession from Dr. Clarke [who] owns himself unable to make any reasonable Opposition to my *Animadversions.*"[136] Before discussing Clarke's views, Edwards described what he saw as the three main contributors to Arianism: Platonists who see "Three distinct Principles in the Deity" in a subordinationist relationship, following the teaching of Justin Martyr and Origen; some of the Fathers who used terms like "*Cause*," "*Principle*," "*Fountain*," "*Root*," and "*Author*" when expressing the relationship between the Father and the Son and Spirit; and some of the Fathers who saw divine paternity too much like human paternity.[137]

In his *Scripture-Doctrine,* Clarke critiqued the Creed of Athanasius line-by-line, concluding, "tis not consistent with Scripture, nor with Expressions of the Liturgy cited in the foregoing chapter." For example, he stated that neither the Son nor the Holy Ghost was "uncreated"; both were derived. Though the Son and Holy Ghost are immortal, only the Father "hath immortality" (1 Tim 1:17) because only he is "independent and underived." Though the Son and Holy Ghost are both Good, we read, "*there is None Good but One* [. . .] because He Only is the original absolute underived Good."[138]

Therefore,

> the Meaning of these Words, [*Three Persons and* yet but *One God,*] understood consistently, must be; that the *Power and Divine Authority* of each of the *three Persons* in their several Operations, being distinctly acknowledged; there is yet nevertheless but *One God* or One Supreme unoriginated independent absolute Governour of all things, viz. *God the Father Almighty.*

---

135. Edwards, *Some Animadversions,* 46–47.
136. Edwards, *Supplement,* Preface.
137. Edwards, *Supplement,* 4, 6, 14.
138. Clarke, *Scripture-Doctrine,* 428–34.

The only other alternatives he could see were modalism or tri-theism, neither of which make sense.[139] Edwards was not impressed.

> For a Sophister this is commendable and brave enough; but for a grave Professor of Divinity, it is ridiculous and to be hiss'd at. For how could it come into any Man's Thoughts, that when our Church expressly professes her Belief of *Three Persons and One God*, the only Thing that Is to be understood by it, is, That She acknowledges the Power and Divine Authority of each of the Three Persons, without owning them to be One God? [...] Any one that hath read the other Parts of our Liturgy [...] cannot but know [...] that the Church plainly affirms the Father, Son and Holy Ghost to be One God, according to what we profess in the *Athanasian* Creed.[140]

Referencing Scripture and the Fathers, Edwards explained the difference between functional and ontological subordination, between temporal and eternal generation and between logical and hierarchical order of the Godhead.[141] Regarding subordination, he acknowledged that there is a sense of it in Scripture and the liturgy, but that sense refers not to his divine nature, but only to the mission of Christ to redeem sinful man.

> He was sent, not by Nature of His Deity, but by the Oeconomy and Disposition of His Humanity. [...] All those places mention'd in our Liturgy which imply the Subordination of Christ to His Father, are generally to be understood of His Humane Nature, and of His Office of Mediator. In these Capacities, He is Subordinate and Inferior to the Father, but in no other Respect.[142]

He corrected Arian thinking on generation and begetting, observing that for human beings, a father is superior to his son because of his prior existence. But with God, there is no similar priority because all persons of the Trinity exist eternally and the same substance is "common to them all."[143] The problem of understanding this arises when we use a human relationship to explain a divine relationship, whereas the reverse provides the proper understanding.

---

139. Clarke, *Scripture-Doctrine*, 455.
140. Edwards, *Supplement*, 71–72.
141. Edwards, *Supplement*, 76–78.
142. Edwards, *Supplement*, 78.
143. Edwards, *Some Animadversions*, 21–23.

The Son was produc'd or generated out of the Substance of the Father, but that Substance did not exist before the production of the Son, for the production was from all Eternity. The Existence could not precede that generation, because they were both together.[144]

He stressed that though the three persons are equal in essence, power, glory, etc. there is a logical order to be observed, given to us by Christ himself. This logical order reflects our understanding of the history of redemption: the Father in electing and creating, the Son in redeeming and mediating, and the Holy Ghost "as executing the decrees concerning our Salvation." Thus, "there is a Priority of Order or Rank, but no Prelation or Preeminence as to Excellency," clearly "an absolute Co-equality."[145]

Concerning the Arian interpretation of Colossians 1:15, Edwards explained that "first-born" in Scripture carries the idea of "Chiefest and Principal kind." Israel, for example, is called God's firstborn not because they were the first people in human history, but because they were chosen by God for special purposes and honor, ultimately to bless the rest of the world through the birth of Jesus. So Christ is "Head of all the Elect" and "Heir of all things," according to Hebrews 1:2.[146] He reiterated that the Son is God with respect to both his essence and his person and that as self-existence is a *"natural Property"* of God, it is certainly a *"natural Property"* of the Son because he is God.[147] He concluded by criticizing the way Clarke attempted to show that the church liturgy is Arian: by misinterpreting certain passages to show subordination, while ignoring other passages which are clearly contrary. Again, he cited men with whom he did not agree on a number of theological issues against Clarke, whom Clarke had misused to support his understanding of subordination, in this case Bishops Pearson of Chester and George Bull (1634–1710) of St. David's.[148]

Sometime after Edwards's second response to Clarke, another work critical of Clarke appeared, in which Robert Nelson penned a surprisingly accommodating introductory letter, introducing its anonymous author as his friend. That friend was James Knight (1672–1735). Citing

144. Edwards, *Some Animadversions*, 36.
145. Edwards, *Supplement*, 29–30.
146. Edwards, *Some Animadversions*, 29.
147. Edwards, *Supplement*, 47.
148. Edwards, *Supplement*, 65; Clarke, *Scripture-Doctrine*, 51 (marked 49), 62, 161–62, 177–78, 256–57, 266, 268–71.

various Fathers, in a manner similar to Edwards, Knight refuted Clarke's interpretation of about forty texts that Clarke had used to support his Arianism.[149] That work elicited responses from both Edwards and Clarke.

In Edwards's essay, which appeared as an appendix in *Some New Discoveries of the Uncertainty, Deficiency and Corruptions of Human Knowledge and Learning*, he called Nelson "that worthy Gentleman" and a man of "wonderful Self-denial and Moderation" and "great Faithfulness and Probity."[150] But he wondered why Nelson was complaining to Clarke about him as the "very Zealous and Learned Divine in our Church" as though Nelson and Clarke were united against Edwards.[151] Nelson, he reminded his readers, was known as "a zealous Defender of the receiv'd Doctrines of the Church of England," but now "he applauds and extols Dr. Clarke," leading Edwards to conclude that he was appeasing a heretic. Is it possible that he "would bear the Censure of Arianism without saying one Word for himself"? Is he trying to avoid the "rough" treatment that Dr. Wells received for discrediting Clarke? Would it not be better to have been "friendly and charitable to advise Dr. *Clarke* to absent himself from the Lord's Supper, till he hath better Thoughts of the Sacred Trinity"—and not only the Lord's Supper, but from exercising any office in the church until he decided to repent? Edwards reminded Nelson the words of the fifth canon of the church:

> Whosoever shall affirm that any of the Nine and Thirty Articles are in any part erroneous, let him be excommunicated ipso facto, and not restored, but only by the Archbishop after his Repentance and public Revocation of such his wicked Errors.[152]

Clarke replied to Nelson, commenting not only on the Knight book, but also on earlier remarks about Clarke made in Nelson's biography of Bishop Bull and a book by the new Bishop of Chester Francis Gastrell (1662–1725).[153] Clarke had asked Gastrell to review his book and Gastrell expected to give a positive review, especially after learning in the introduction to the book that Clarke's purpose was to help people avoid

---

149. Knight, *Scripture Doctrine*.

150. Edwards, *Some New Discoveries*, 233, 236, 241.

151. Knight, *Scripture Doctrine*, x–xi.

152. Edwards, *Some New Discoveries*, 234–37.

153. Clarke, *Reply*; Nelson, *George Bull* (Nelson's first response to Clarke); Gastrell, *Remarks*.

the heresies of "*Tritheism, Sabellianism, Arianism and Socinianism.*"[154] Instead Gastrell was greatly dismayed, especially after reading Clarke's twenty-seventh proposition, which says that "*All Divine Powers* [are ascribed to the Son] *excepting absolute Supremacy and Independency*." Of this Gastrell remarked, "*All Divine Powers excepting absolute Supremacy* is, in the utmost Latitude of Terms, more than an *Arian* will allow. [. . .] Whoever reads the *Second Part* of Dr. *Clark's* Book [. . .] will [. . .] rank him in some *Arian* Class."[155] For Gastrell to call Clarke an Arian is noteworthy because, although he defended the doctrine of the Trinity against freethinking Deist Anthony Collins, he had a favorable view of Locke.[156]

Nelson was prompted to write about Clarke in his biography of Bishop Bull because of Clarke's attempt to support his Arianism by misrepresenting the views of prominent church leaders, especially Bull and Pearson.[157] In Clarke's response, he commended Nelson for his "Candour," "Civility," and "Fairness and Temper," but he was upset with Nelson for writing that

> *almost all* my Citations out of that Learned Author *are represented in a very different View from That which the Author had certainly* [intended] *in writing those Passages; as are also the Citations out of the Fathers themselves, which Dr. Clarke here met with, and hath accommodated to his own purpose, and That frequently without so much as the least Notice taken of the Explications and Answers given to them by* Bishop Bull.[158]

Clarke also objected to Knight's selection of only forty of the more than three hundred texts from Scripture included in his book "wherein either the word [GOD] absolutely, or the title [*One God*] is, in the express words of the Text itself, put in *contradistinction*" [. . .] to either the Son or the Spirit or both.[159]

Edwards's final response to Clarke, which came after he read Clarke's reply to Nelson, began by rephrasing Nelson's assessment of Clarke that "*he hath an Artful way of citing Authors and Books*" in more direct terms: "He is Artful indeed, in perverting their true Sense and Meaning, and

---

154. Clarke, *Scripture-Doctrine*, xxviii; Gastrell, *Remarks*, preface.
155. Gastrell, *Remarks*, 3–4.
156. Gastrell, *Defence*; Collins, An Essay; Pyle, *Dictionary*, 329–31.
157. Nelson, *George Bull*, 322–23.
158. Clarke, *Reply*, 3, 4.
159. Clarke, *Reply*, 7.

where the Matter will not bear any Reply, he betakes himself to mere Evasions and Shufflings."[160] Edwards proceeded to call out Clarke's mistranslations, such as of First John 5:20, which reads, "οἴδαμεν δὲ ὅτι ὁ υἱὸς τοῦ Θεοῦ ἥκει, καὶ δέδωκεν ἡμῖν διάνοιαν ἵνα γινώσκωμεν τὸν ἀληθινόν καὶ ἐσμεν ἐν τῷ ἀληθινῷ, ἐν τῷ υἱῷ αὐτοῦ Ἰησοῦ Χριστῷ. Οὗτός ἐστιν ὁ ἀληθινὸς Θεός, καὶ ἡ ζωὴ αἰώνιος."[161]

Clarke:

> I read and understand the Text thus: *The Son of God is come, and hath given us an Understanding*, [has enlightened the Eyes of our Understanding, as 'tis *Eph*.1,18,] *that we may know the True God*, [viz that we may know and acknowledge the Father revealed by the Son;] *And we are in him that is True*, [viz. in That True God,] *by* (or, *through*) *his Son Jesus Christ. This is the True God, and Eternal Life*, [viz. This God, whom the Son has given us an Understanding to know, is the True God; and to know and acknowledge him, and to be In him in (*or by*) his Son, this is eternal Life:] Οὗτός ἐστιν ὁ ἀληθινὸς Θεός, καὶ ἡ ζωὴ αἰώνιος." [slightly illegible in original]: This is the True God, and This the Way that leads to him.[162]

Edwards was quick to point out that to understand Christ as merely the way to God and not God himself is neither the natural reading, nor is it how Hilary, Jerome, and Augustine read it. Edwards accused Clarke of searching only for texts to "favour his pre-conceived Opinion."[163]

Another point of contention was over the meaning of θειότης in passages such as Romans 1:20 and Colossians 2:9 where it is translated "Godhead." According to Clarke, "θειότης signifies nothing else but *Divine Power* or *Dominion*; not the *Substance* of *God*, which this learned Author seems erroneously to think the Word *Godhead* signifies."[164] Further he said that both θειότης and Θεός have "in Scripture [. . .] *a relative Signification*; and not [. . .] an *Absolute* One." He summarized, "the word

---

160. Nelson, *George Bull*, xii; Edwards, *Some Brief Critical Remarks*, 3. Clarke was also offended by Nelson's characterization, inferring that he was accusing him of not being trustworthy when making citations. See Clarke, *Reply*, 5.

161. And we know that the Son of God is come, and hath given us an understanding, that we may know him that is true, and we are in him that is true, even in his Son Jesus Christ. This is the true God, and eternal life.

162. Clarke, *Reply*, 97.

163. Edwards, *Some Brief Critical Remarks*, 22–23.

164. Clarke, *Reply*, 283.

God in Scripture, is indeed always a relative word of Office, signifying personal *Dominion, Dignity* or *Government*."¹⁶⁵

Edwards objected that this understanding turns the Romans passage into a tautology: "*his Eternal Power and Power*." He cited Athanasius, the Cappadocian Fathers, and others to say that θειότης refers to God himself subsisting in three persons. God is an absolute term of essence, implying his power, attributes, etc.¹⁶⁶ Then in a postscript, Edwards reported that he had recently concluded that Clarke borrowed this idea that God is a relative term from the Polish Socinain Johannes Crellius (1590–1633), increasing his disrepute.

Not only that, Edwards discovered that in his second edition of *Philosophiae Naturale*, Clarke's friend Isaac Newton appended a short essay "Scholium Generale" which contained the same idea, expressed as, "*Nam deus est vox relativa & ad servos resertur; & deitas est dominatio dei, non in corpus proprium, uti sentiunt quibus deus est anima mundi, sed in servos*."¹⁶⁷ Edwards translated the passage of interest as,

> God is a *Relative* Word, and hath Reference to *Servants*: And the *Deity* is the *Dominion* of God, not on his own Body, but on Servants. The *Supreme God* is an Eternal, Infinite, and absolutely Perfect Being; but a Being tho' never so Perfect, without Dominion, is not *Lord God*—It is the *Dominion* of a Spiritual Being that makes *a God*. If this Dominion be true, it makes a True God; if Supreme, it makes a Supreme God, if False and Counterfeit, it makes a False God.¹⁶⁸

Edwards was shocked to read such words from the revered Newton. He was baffled by what they might mean and consulted some scholarly associates who were unable to help. Following additional study, he concluded that Newton was saying that God has a body, that "*Organs of Sense and Motion* belong to God," but he does not have dominion over them. By his reference to a "Supreme God," Newton meant the Father, implying there were lesser gods (Son and Holy Ghost). He concluded that Newton held to the "very same [Arian heresy] which Dr. *Clarke* and Mr. *Whiston* have publicly asserted," though he hoped that his understanding was in

---

165. Clarke, *Reply*, 284, 290.

166. Edwards, *Some Brief Critical Remarks*, 26–28.

167. Edwards, *Some Brief Critical Remarks*, 36–37; Newton, *Principia Mathematica*, 528.

168. Edwards, *Some Brief Critical Remarks*, 37.

error. Although he first thought that Newton's phrase "God is a Relative Word" came from Clarke, he discovered that it was "borrow'd from Crellius."[169] This is believed to be the first time in print where Newton was named a heretic.[170] With access to Newton's library, to his private manuscripts and following careful study of Newton's close association with Clarke and Whiston, recent scholarship has concluded, "Edwards was right: there is Socinianism in the General Scholium" and "Newton almost certainly used the 'General Scholium'" [. . .] to influence Clarke and "support his interpretation of the Trinity, further detailing their shared theology in this matter." By stating, "*Deus est vox Relativa*," Newton understood that the Son could be God in some lesser divine sense, but not absolutely and not ontologically. He did not follow Socinian or Arian doctrine entirely, but he was clearly antitrinitarian.[171]

As in the early church, disagreement over the extent of subordination within the Trinity was not limited to heresies like Arianism. In his biography of Bishop Bull, Nelson thought that Edwards's understanding of subordination from John 14:28 as applying to Christ's human nature was too limited. He defended Bull and Pearson's teaching on subordination, claiming that only a minority of the Fathers agree with Edwards.[172] Edwards believed that Nelson had erred in thinking that an inferiority in order was the same as inferiority in dispensation. But as "every one that hath read [the Fathers] can tell" only dispensation refers to the Incarnation. It is clear that the Son is inferior to the Father in his humanity, but the orthodox Fathers did not hold that he was inferior with respect to his divine filiation.[173]

Edwards complained that Bishops Pearson and Bull had helped lead Clarke and Whiston astray "by urging the Inferiority of the Son to the Father, in respect to his Divinity."[174] Nelson's conclusion: Edwards failed

169. Edwards, *Some Brief Critical Remarks*, 36, 38, 40. Whether or not Clarke or Newton were separately inspired by Crellius, Newton had formulated his idea prior to Clarke. See Pfizenmaier, *Trinitarian Theology*, 184.

170. Kassler, *Seeking Truth*, 319.

171. Snobelen, "God of Gods," 191–96; Wigglesworth, "Samuel Clarke's Newtonian Soul," 47; Pfizenmaier, "Was Isaac Newton?," 57–80.

172. Nelson, *George Bull*, 333–35.

173. Edwards, *Supplement*, 63–64. As with Scripture, the Greek and Latin Fathers were used to support virtually any theological view. Some such as Scrivener believed that they were especially necessary because Scripture could not serve as its own interpreter. See, for example, Quantin, *Church of England*, 331–41.

174. Edwards, *Some Animadversions*, 21.

in his attack on Clarke regarding subordination.[175] In Edwards's response to Nelson, he put the matter of subordination in perspective, making it clear that he did not hold a personal grudge:

> I am glad to find that this learned Gentleman hath no more to say against me for my opposing the Doctrine of Subordination. It appears from his Way of managing this Cause, that he is a generous and yielding Adversary, and scorns to be a Slave to his Hypothesis.

And despite his significant differences with Bishop Bull's theology, Edwards took the opportunity to commend him: "I would not say one Syllable to derogate from the real Worth of this learned Prelate, for he was certainly a very great Man, and Mr. *Nelson* hath taken great Pains to let the World know it."[176]

Meanwhile Wells, who was pleased to learn that he was not the only one thinking that Clarke's book could be the source of "great Mischief," wrote a second book. He criticized Clarke's attempt to support his views from Tillotson, Chillingworth, and Bishop William Wake (1657–1737), in whose diocese he worshipped. Accusing Clarke of misrepresenting their views, he suggested that his bishop (as the only one of the three still living) "could Free himself from Dr. Cl.'s Imputation, by yet declaring what is his True meaning in those Words of his cited by Dr. Cl."[177] Wells followed with a third work, again charging Clarke with ignoring the Old Testament teaching on the Trinity and exhibiting poor scholarship. Comparing words from Nelson's biography of Bull side-by-side with how Clarke quoted them in his letter to Wells, he told Clarke that "Mr. *Nelson* had but too just Reason to complain of your *Quotation* being *FOUL*, even to such a degree as *NOTHING can be FOULER*." Similarly he accused Clarke of dealing "with me in *so* Foul a manner as *NOTHING can be FOULER*."[178] Other published critics of Clarke's *Scripture-Doctrine* during Edwards's lifetime included rectors Thomas Bennet (1673–1728), Richard Mayo (1690–1727), and Edward Welchman and Edward Potter

---

175. Nelson, *George Bull*, 333–39.
176. Edwards, *Supplement*, 66.
177. Wells, *Remarks on Dr. Clark's Introduction*, Preface, 38.
178. Wells, *Second Letter*, 14.

(d.1715), fellow of Emmanuel College, Cambridge.[179] Wells was the only one besides Nelson to whom Clarke published a reply.[180]

Like Locke, Clarke was concerned that his book would cause an uproar. Before making it public, he sent a review copy to the highly respected lawyer and biographer Roger North (1653–1734). North probably became acquainted with Clarke through the Boyle lectures and as translator of some of Newton's works. North consulted his friend, theologian George Hickes (1642–1715). Neither of them approved of Clarke's trinitarian theology, nor his close association with Newton and the implications of Newton's radical, anti-Cartesian theory of celestial mechanics. Newton's mathematics was praised, but not his physics or theology. In a letter to his nephew, North wrote that words like "attraction" and "inertia" seemed occult-like, harkening back to Aristotle: "He hath broached a sort of philosophy more occult than that of the Peripatetic scool."[181] Descartes' plenist universe seemed much more intuitive than Newton's with his concept of vacuum and space. Newton contrasted the absolute (space, time, motion) in which he associated the absolute with God who is eternal, infinite, sovereign, etc. with the relative, whether relative time where man lives or the relative deity of Jesus Christ. So it seemed obvious to many of his orthodox contemporaries like Hickes and North that Newtonianism led to Arianism and Deism.[182]

Within two years of publishing the *Scripture-Doctrine*, Clarke's trinitarianism attracted the attention of Parliament, which resulted in a series of letters between themselves and Archbishop Tenison and his bishops to deal with this attempt "to subvert our Common Faith."[183] Clarke realized he was in trouble and sent to the bishops a paper which appeared to be a surrender to his critics, at least publicly:

> I am willing to promise [. . .] not to Preach any more upon this Subject. I do not intend to Write any more Concerning the Doctrine of the Trinity, but if I fail [. . .] I do hereby willingly submit my self to any such Censures as my Superiors shall think fit to pass upon me. [. . .] I am sorry that what I sincerely intended for the Honour and Glory of God, and so to Explain this

---

179. Bennet, *Discourse*; Mayo, *Plain Scripture-Argument*; Potter, *Vindication*; Welchman, *Dr. Clarke's Scripture Doctrine*.

180. Clarke, *Letter to the Reverend Dr. Wells*.

181. North, *Autobiography*, 255; Stewart, "Newtonianism," 53–61.

182. North, *Notes of Me*, 18–19.

183. Laurence, *Apology*, 9–12.

great Mistery, as to avoid the Heresies in both Extremes, should have given any Offence to this Synod, and particularly to my Lords the Bishops; I hope my Behaviour for the Time to come, with Relation hereunto, will be such, as to prevent any further Complaints against me.[184]

He further denied reports that he had omitted trinitarian liturgy in his church or engaged in antitrinitarian private conversation. But whether or not he had significantly changed his views seems in doubt because the outrage over his views continued long after 1714, even after Clarke died in 1729. Beginning in 1719, his primary combatant was Daniel Waterland who served as Master of Magdalene College, Cambridge and Archdeacon of Middlesex. Between Clarke, Waterland and John Jackson (1686–1763), who wrote that Clarke's book gave him "the true Faith of the ever-blessed Trinity" and subsequently did most of the writing to defend Clarke, over twenty pieces were published between them, aside from sermons—with no concessions from Clarke.[185] Jackson also defended Clarke against Edwards's earlier critiques, particularly regarding the meaning of persona.[186] Waterland expressed frustration after three and a half years of intransigence on the part of Clarke and Jackson for dismissing his arguments from Scripture and church authorities. Near the end of his *Second Defense*, he told Jackson, "you have not been able to acquit the Doctor of the Charge of *equivocating* or *contradicting* Himself; nor to take off the Force of our Arguments built upon Gal. iv.8 for the *essential* Divinity of God the Son." From that key verse (Galatians 4:8), he said that Clarke's position on the dominion and personhood of God had been previously answered sufficiently by a "learned Gentleman" (Edwards).[187]

DANIEL WHITBY

The same year of Clarke's crisis with Parliament, he gained a new ally in the person of clergyman Daniel Whitby, a recent convert from Arminianism. Four years earlier, Whitby recalled spending seven years in

---

184. Clarke, *Dr. Clark's Sentiments*, 2–4.

185. Jackson, *Three Letters*, 1; See, for example, Clarke, *Observations*; Waterland, *Critical History*.

186. Jackson, *Examination*, 18–26.

187. Waterland, *Second Vindication*, 467, 472; Edwards, *Some Brief Critical Remarks*, 18.

the university under Calvinist men, but had finally rejected their understanding of original sin, reprobation and election.[188] From two works attributed to Whitby, both published in 1714, it appears that he underwent a significant transformation upon reading Clarke.[189] In the first, prior to Clarke, he encouraged a friend "to hold fast the *Orthodox* Faith" for,

> Dr. *Clarke* being censured by the *August Assembly* of our Lower-House of *Convocation*, we doubtless shall receive from some of the *Reverend* Persons who compose that learned *Assembly*, a full and clear Confutation of all that He hath offered in Defense of his *Heretical* Doctrines.

He advised his friend,

> Consider seriously the great and constant Trouble you may bring upon your self, should your narrow Search pervert you, as it hath done Mr. *Whiston* and Dr. *Clarke*, Men of unquestionable Sincerity in their Endeavours to find out the Truth; and yet how miserably have they miscarried? And how happy was it for the *old Orthodoxy* that the Heads of our *Church* rose up against them, and condemned them.[190]

But after reading the *Scripture-Doctrine*, Whitby was persuaded by Clarke's understanding and began defending Clarke in an anonymous work now attributed to Whitby. The general thrust of this second work was an assessment of a "Learned Layman" who had been critical of Clarke's use of ante-Nicene sources to support his theology. This work argued that Clarke's, rather than the Learned Layman's theology more closely agreed with the ante-Nicene Fathers.[191]

Given that these two works are Whitby's, it seems a reasonable speculation that a third anonymous work favorable to Clarke might also be his. In favor of this conjecture are the following facts. All three books were published in 1714. The author of both works favorable to Clarke identified himself as a "clergyman." Both begin with somewhat

---

188. Whitby, *Discourse Concerning the True Import*, iii.

189. *Eighteenth Century Collections Online*.

190. Whitby, *Dissuasive*, 9–10, 22.

191. Whitby, *Discourse Shewing*. That "Learned Layman" was Robert Nelson. Secretan, *Memoirs*, 269; Edwards judged Nelson to be "*a person of wonderful Self-denial and Moderation*," known as "*a zealous Defender of the receiv'd Doctrines of the Church of England*" and was very surprised and disappointed at how accommodating he was to Clarke. Edwards, *Some New Discoveries*, 235–36.

obsequious, self-deprecating introductions addressed to Clarke. And this third book fits the narrative of Whitby's Arian conversion, in which he credited Clarke for turning him away from his former, generally accepted, belief in the "Vulgar Explication of the Doctrine of the Trinity." Finally, after 1714 Whitby is no longer defending Arminianism, but Arianism.

> When I apply'd my self to the reading of the present Controversy, I cou'd not but observe how the Prejudice of my former Notions byass'd my Understanding in favour of the *Explanation* of the Doctrine *generally receiv'd*; and I could hardly forbear censuring it as a presumptuous Undertaking, to bring that Doctrine into a Subject of Debate, which has for many Centuries past obtain'd an undoubted and quiet Possession in most Christian Churches.[192]

In 1720 and 1721, Whitby published two other works, defending Clarke when the debate was renewed by Daniel Waterland.[193]

WILLIAM WHISTON

In his first work against Clarke, Edwards also condemned William Whiston as a co-heretic. In 1702 Whiston had, with Newton's help, succeeded him as Lucasian Professor of Mathematics at Cambridge. Unlike Locke and Newton, Whiston had no apprehension about making his theological views clear, resulting in his 1710 expulsion from Cambridge for Arianism.[194] Whiston's first work *A New Theory of the Earth,* published in 1696, was an attempt to harmonize the biblical accounts of creation and the flood with Newtonian science.[195] This book was written in response to an

---

192. Philalethes, *Reflections,* 4–5. Another possibility for Philalethes is John Jackson who wrote three letters to Clarke beginning in July 1714, but in the first, he addressed him as "brother." His language is respectful, but not fawning. Other less likely candidates: Arthur Ashley Sykes (1683/4–1756) who wrote fifteen identified works before defending Clarke in 1718; John Lewis (1675–1747) and William Wake—neither wrote about Clarke and appeared to be too orthodox; and Francis Atterbury (1662–1732) who was involved in political, rather than theological controversy.

193. Whitby, *Reply*; Whitby, *Second Part of a Reply.*

194. The 1662 Act of Uniformity required ordination of all church and government officials confirmed by an oath of adherence to the *BCP*. Newton had done so in 1669, but by 1675 had decided that agreeing to the XXXIX Articles was tantamount to worshipping the Beast of Revelation 20:4. He would have been dismissed were it not for a royal dispensation making ordination optional only for the Lucasian post by Secretary of State Joseph Williamson. See Westfall, *Never at Rest,* 330–34.

195. Whiston, *New Theory.*

earlier attempt by Thomas Burnet (c.1635–1715) to reconcile the Genesis accounts of the creation and flood with the mechanistic naturalism of Cartesianism.[196] Burnet had taught Cartesian philosophy at Cambridge, having studied at Clare College and Christ College, Cambridge under Tillotson and Cudworth. In addition to the Bible and Descartes, his cosmogony drew from ancient sources including Plato and Augustine. He corresponded privately with Newton who thought his interpretation of Genesis too free. His novel explanations of the creation, fall, and coming millennium brought criticism from many in print, including Edwards, but it appears that he replied in any detail only to Erasmus Warren (d.1718) and John Keill (1671–1721).[197]

Burnet believed he properly accounted for God's providential role, but Whiston thought he was far too accommodating to Deists. Whiston claimed to offer a literal, historical interpretation of Genesis, but it was not literal enough for Edwards, who called it "wholly inconsistent with the History of *Moses*."[198] Edwards was particularly troubled by Whiston's claim that Moses could not give the ancient Jews the truth of the creation because they were incapable of understanding it. For example, Whiston claimed that we read of the heavenly bodies being created on the fourth day of creation because Moses wanted to prevent people from worshipping them. Actually they were created before the account in Genesis 1. He also argued that six days of creation were actually six years.[199] Whiston did not reply to Edwards at that time.

Edwards's second work against Whiston came in 1712, the year following Whiston's *Primitive Christianity Reviv'd*.[200] For Whiston and many others in church history, considerable effort has been made to discover true first-century Christianity, before it was "corrupted" by theologians and philosophers. It seems that his interest in primitive Christianity began with his interest in Arianism following discussions with Clarke in 1705. Three years later he discovered the *Apostolic Constitutions*, a fourth-century work on ecclesiastical polity, purported to have come directly from the twelve Apostles. Even then it was generally considered

196. Burnet, *Sacred Theory*; Burnet, *Archaeologiæ Philosophicæ*. Note, this Burnet is not the Thomas Burnet associated with Locke.

197. Mandelbrote, "Thomas Burnet;" Edwards, *Discourse Concerning*, 2.34–39; Edwards, *Polpoikilos Sophia*, 661, 767–69.

198. Edwards, *Brief Remarks*, 8.

199. Edwards, *Brief Remarks*, 15.

200. Edwards, *Some Brief Observations*.

a forgery, but Whiston concluded it was authentic as it validated his Arian faith and from 1715 to 1717 held weekly meetings in his home for the "Serious and Impartial Discovery of True Religion and Genuine Christianity."[201] Edwards himself referred to primitive Christianity in at least half of his works, but exercised great discernment in distinguishing between sources that were authentic and orthodox and those that were spurious or heretical. In addition to Edwards and Whiston, at least dozen other writers wrote on this subject between 1695 and 1719 and five of them like Edwards in opposition to Whiston.[202]

By 1711, Whiston had published his four-volume work which attempted to authenticate the larger *Epistles of Ignatius*, along with the *Apostolic Constitutions* and prove that the traditional understanding of the Trinity and Incarnation was incorrect, in part by arguing that the current views developed after the early church.[203] Prior to publication, Whiston sent letters to the Archbishops of Canterbury and York and some other notables—letters which he later printed in his preface along with their responses. The enthusiasm with which he launched his mission to secure endorsements from learned divines to return the church to its original doctrine is expressed in a letter to the Vice-Chancellor of Cambridge:

> If you, Sir, with the rest of the Heads and Members of this University please [be pleased] to encourage that fair Examination which I desire and insist upon, I will immediately apply my self to the Governors of the Church, the Archbishops and Bishops, for their Permission and Directions therein, which I have good Hope they will not deny in so important a Matter. And indeed, I look upon it as the peculiar Duty and Business *of the Clergy*, to reform and amend the Corruptions which at any Time appear to be crept into the Faith or Practice of the Church.[204]

---

201. Force, *William Whiston*, 15–16, 19; Whiston, *Proposal*.

202. Michael Mattaire, 1711; James Knight, 1712; Conyers Place, 1713; William Berriman, 1719; John Hancocke, 1719.

203. Whiston began his dissertation on primitive Christianity with an account of his efforts to enlist Church of England and university support for his project. He included copies of correspondence and the events leading to his banishment from the university.

204. Whiston, "Historical Preface," 1:civ. Note: Page numbering begins with Roman numerals, but beginning with the second appendix through the postscript (of the preface), Western Arabic numerals are used. Commencing with the main section of the text, there is a page numbering reset.

His correspondents either did not reply or expressed their opposition or great caution regarding his project. The Vice-Chancellor denied use of the university's imprimatur for Whiston's book and on October 23, 1710, Whiston was summoned to appear before him and other university officials. Whiston requested six weeks to prepare his defense after receiving the charges against him, but that request was denied and on October 30, he was "Banished from this University" for "having asserted and spread abroad divers Tenets contrary to Religion receive'd and establish'd by Publick Authority in this Realm."[205] He was spared excommunication, but in 1747 finally left to become a Baptist.

Following Whiston's lengthy preface, a report of his tribulations surrounding publication of his *Primitive Christianity Reviv'd*, is the four-volume body of his work, followed a year later with a fifth volume. Volume 1 contains his commentary on the *Epistles of Ignatius*. Whiston argued that all ten were genuine and reliable, but Edwards cited authorities like Archbishop Ussher who said that only six were genuine and others who questioned the integrity of all ten.[206] The second volume consists of a parallel Greek and English text of the *Apostolic Constitutions,* followed by Whiston's commentary in volume 3, introduced with his personal view:

> I cannot read them [the Constitutions] without the same regard that I pay to any Book of the Bible: Since I have fully satisfy'd my self that they are Genuine, Sacred, and Apostolical; and the Original Repository of these sacred laws of Christ, by which he will govern his Church in that her glorious and happy State, which I look upon as now approaching.[207]

The fourth volume consists of twenty-three articles articulating the doctrines of the Trinity and Incarnation as Whiston believed they were understood in the early church. He supported each article with commentary and Scripture. Following his translation of *The Recognitions of Clement, or the Travels of Peter* in the final volume are two appendices, which contain Whiston's favorable response to Clarke's *Scripture-Doctrine*, Whiston's appeal to Bishop Thomas Manningham (1651?–1722) to be reinstated in the church (rejected), and his reactions to those who commented on the first four volumes (which were mostly negative).

---

205. Whiston, "Historical Preface," 1:clxvi.

206. Whiston, "Dissertation," 1:2, (second p. sig. B); Edwards, *Some Brief Observations*, 13.

207. Whiston, "Essay," 3:11.

According to Whiston, the *Constitutions*, also known as "Christian Laws" were given to the disciples by Christ himself in the period between his Resurrection and Ascension, but not written down until AD 64 to 67. One reason for the latter date is that the *Constitutions* do not refer to any book in the New Testament written after that date (according to Whiston's estimate on when they were written).[208] In his attempt to convince doubters that the *Constitutions* were genuine, Whiston cited internal and external evidence and attempted to link them to biblical prophecy. The fourth volume contains references to the first and second century writers and provides evidence and arguments for Arian theology, concluding with an English translation of the apocryphal second book of Esdras. Whiston was convinced that Second Esdras was wrongly categorized as apocryphal and believed that it was superior to the canonical Ezra.[209]

Edwards was a serious student of church history, particularly of the patristic era. The majority of his printed works contain numerous references to the Fathers. He was especially critical of men like Scrivener "who calls those that pay not extravagant Reverence to the Writings of the Fathers *the blind Worshippers of the Scriptures*" (*caeci Scripturarum Veneratores*) while elevating the authority of the Fathers so as to "justify many of the Abuses and Corruptions of the Papal Communion."[210] He quoted Latitudinarian Chillingworth as saying "There are Popes against Popes, Councils against Councils, some Fathers against others, the same Fathers against themselves [. . .] In a word, there is no Sufficient Certainty but of *Scripture* only, for any considering Man to build upon."[211]

Edwards's response to the *Primitive Church Reviv'd* began with a question which Whiston might seem to ask, namely, how *"the Ancient Fathers of the Christian Church understood the Nature and Essence of God."*[212] Edwards's approach was to take the fathers as a whole, i.e., the church, not simply individual Fathers in their writings, as not all Fathers are held in equal regard, particularly not on a given subject, and they certainly were not all in agreement any more than church leaders of any era. Edwards identified some as "Learned and Tried Pillars" which Whiston rejected in favor of those "he concludes to be Authentic, and in a manner

---

208. Whiston, "Essay," 3:20, 23, 30, 194.
209. Whiston, *Collection*, 62.
210. Edwards, *Patrologia*, 124–25; Scrivener, *Apologia*, 87.
211. Edwards, *Patrologia*, 126–27.
212. Edwards, *Some Brief Observations*, ii.

Infallible."[213] But more fundamental than that for Edwards was the fact that in the New Testament, "we have a Model and Platform of the Primitive Church of Christ [. . .] There is nothing appertaining to Natural or Moral Religion, and more especially supernatural and reveal'd, that is not fully deliver'd in these Writings"—in essence, the original primitive church.[214] But Whiston dismissed the New Testament record as unreliable because it was not presented in a "Systematic Way," and, according to Edwards, considered the *Apostolic Constitutions* to be his "New Bible."[215]

Edwards recognized that an important role of the church is to serve as an authenticator of truth "for the Writings of the Fathers both before and after the *Nicene* Council are no authentic Standard of Truth" because "we can't name one of the Fathers that is not tainted with some false Notion of Religion."[216] Bishop Bull confessed bewilderment at trying to ascertain true doctrine from the ante-Nicene Fathers. Edwards paraphrased him as saying that it is "not possible to determine [. . .] what is Orthodox, from the writings of the Fathers." We are left to conclude individually, "the Testimony of the Fathers is not to be relied upon."[217] And though the Councils are generally more dependable than individuals, Edwards referenced Article XXI of the Church of England which states that "Councils may Err, and sometimes have erred, even in things pertaining to God." Therefore, "the testimony of the Scriptures is of that nature, that commands our Assent and Veneration and all the authority of the (church) depends wholly on this."[218] Edwards accused Whiston of ignoring the collective, historical wisdom of the church, along with the clear teaching of Scripture and instead using "*Unwarrantable and Suspected Authors*" (those men that church leaders have named as spurious or apocryphal) who wrote such works as the *Epistle of Barnabas*, the *Shepherd of Hermas*, *Recognitions of Clement*, *Epistles of Ignatius* and the *Apostolical Constitutions*, and other books that even Rome had rejected.[219]

---

213. Edwards, *Some Brief Observations*, 29.

214. Edwards, *Some Brief Observations*, 19–20.

215. Edwards, *Some Brief Observations*, 21–22.

216. Edwards, *Some Brief Observations*, 46–47.

217. Edwards, *Some Brief Observations*, 50. In another context, Edwards referred to the "unwary and unsafe Language of some of the Fathers," by which he meant that in some cases their words may be open to misinterpretation on controversies which erupted after they wrote them. Edwards, *Supplement*, 3–4.

218. Edwards, *Some Brief Observations*, 59.

219. Edwards, *Some Brief Observations*, 2.

Like Clarke, Whiston did not enter the pamphlet war against Edwards, perhaps because his focus was promoting his version of Arianism, or perhaps because his income depended primarily on book sales, or perhaps because he saw nothing to be gained. He did refer to Edwards in at least three books. In 1712, he published a fifth volume of *Primitive Christianity Reviv'd*, where he dismissively spoke of Edwards as not simply writing against himself, but "against all the Antients."[220] He mentioned Edwards in another as one of a dozen "otherwise very considerable Persons" engaged along with "pious Frauds in Translating and publishing of the Scriptures" and the "Heretick Athanasius" in perpetuating the "long Antichristian State of the Church."[221] His most extensive comments appeared in the preface to a book of Cotton Mather's which Whiston had reprinted in London (see Chapter 7). Edwards commented that Whiston thinks he has easily dismissed him, but the sobering reality is that he not only has "no Respect or Regard for the Fathers," including the Council of Nicaea, but along with Dr. Clarke, has condemned the central doctrines of the Trinity and divinity of Jesus Christ and "is of the true Race of the *Arians*, who were Infamous for their *Slandering* of the Orthodox."[222]

Common to all of the above opponents of Edwards was a professed reverence for Scripture and strong desire to study it for their own understanding and for the good of the church. That they were intellectually gifted can be seen in their scholarship, insights, and discoveries. Some of their contributions to human knowledge were clearly pioneering and innovative. But when those innovations altered the foundations of Christian theology, the very identity of the church, Edwards could not remain silent.

He was skilled in Hebrew, Greek, and Latin. When his opponents stumbled in their logic or inaccurately translated a passage in Greek because of weak grammatical skills or a limited vocabulary, Edwards pointed out their errors and refuted their arguments. He understood that the link between Scripture and church doctrine must be based on careful exegesis, on expertise in the ancient biblical languages, on systematic, meticulous, and comprehensive methodology, consistent with what has been received through the centuries as orthodox tradition.

---

220. Whiston, *PCR*, 5:40 (appendices).
221. Whiston, *Reflexions*, 44–45.
222. Edwards, *Supplement*, Preface.

5

Edwards and Church Parties

A NUMBER OF WRITERS among Edwards's contemporaries and continuing to the present have accused him of being insolent and mean against those with whom he disagreed. He has been vilified as unjust, bigoted, and angry in attacks on his theological opponents. He did, after all, use language that at times appeared to be imprecise, harsh, disrespectful, and downright rude. But is it possible that some critics are not able to distinguish John Edwards from his father Thomas, whose behavior and writings did match his disagreeable and unpopular reputation? Thomas exhibited no interest in church unity or cooperating in any way with those who did not completely conform to his own views. Both John and his father saw themselves as Calvinists. They agreed that the form of church government most true to Scripture was Presbyterian, but John conformed during a period when Arminianism was dominant in the church while his father did not when Calvinism was dominant. Both were concerned about heresy, but were quite different in how they drew the bounds. John's standard was expressed in the Apostles', Nicene, and Athanasian Creeds. A standard for Thomas would be difficult to describe, given his preoccupation with "Errors, Heresies, Blasphemies and pernicious Practices of the Sectaries" which he catalogued in a single list and included items such as "That Christ shall come and live again upon the earth, and for a thousand years reign visibly as an earthly Monarch over all the world, in outward glory and pomp, putting down all Monarchy and Empires."[1] A careful reading of John demonstrates that his Calvinism was quite

---

1. Edwards, *Gangræna, First Part*, 19, subtitle.

moderate, accommodating many who did not share his understanding, whereas his father demonstrated no latitude or toleration.

As noted briefly in Chapter 3, there were quite a number who blessed Edwards's memory for the firm stand he took defending Reformed theology and condemning heresy. A survey of Edwards's commentators' views probably reflects more on their own theology than it does on Edwards's personality. He was not the only one to be accused of using slanderous language against his opponents and he was far from the worst. But was he slanderous? Slander includes what is false and damaging. Edwards did not falsely accuse, nor misrepresent his foes by exaggeration. He did intend to damage the reputation of heretics because their teachings were false and because he placed a high value on truth, not by exaggeration, but by accurately representing their views. Those who saw him in a positive light agreed with his judgments and viewed his sarcasm as tolerable or insignificant in light of his bold defense of orthodoxy. In Edwards's defense, several points can be made.

1. One litmus test that Roman Catholic, Orthodox and Protestant bodies have agreed upon historically to judge heresy has been the Nicene Creed. Edwards was not using Calvinism, nor some personal standard to judge heretics. He simply compared the statements of his opponents to the standard of Nicaea, particularly with respect to their view of divinity of Jesus Christ and accordingly, those men Edwards named as heretics failed this standard of orthodoxy.

2. Edwards's view that influential heretics are a serious threat to the church was also consistent with the church as a whole throughout history, particularly in eras when divine revelation and objective truth were highly valued.

3. Those he named as heretical relied principally on their own biblical hermeneutics. They did so by either ignoring the traditional understanding and importance of the Nicene Creed and other accepted standards, or by attempting to elevate works traditionally viewed as spurious to an authoritative role. Or they simply claimed that the established understanding of contentious, but traditionally considered essential, doctrines such as the deity of Christ should be optional, viewing tolerance and peace as of the greater value. William Whiston, for example, took great lengths to elevate extra-biblical sources and dismiss traditional interpretations of Scripture.

4. Despite holding to a traditional view of the Nicene Creed and appearing to be overly confident with superior scholarship toward his opponents, Edwards did not claim to be infallible in his theology. More than once when addressing those within the church, he expressed sentiment such as the following:

> Far be it from me to arrogate to my self any worth and excellency above my Brethren of the Clergy: I own my self the Meanest of all the Ministers of Jesus, and I doubt not but there are many mistakes, defects, and oversights to be discerned in my Writings, which I shall most readily own when they are discovered to me.[2]

5. It must be recognized that in the debating culture of the day, the use of slander and hyperbole to gain some advantage over opponents was not uncommon on all sides of many debates. Though no one could accuse Edwards of euphemising his assessments, compared to most others, he was moderate and accurate. His charges of heresy were leveled only at those who refused to affirm essential doctrines such as the Trinity and Incarnation.

6. Furthermore, Edwards did not use such strong language against those with whom he had serious theological differences, but did not consider unorthodox. Rather he commended many such men for their stand against heresy. At the beginning of his first public criticism of Clarke, he recalled with gratitude those who had "manfully engag'd in this just Cause," among them Bishops Stillingfleet, Fowler, and Burnet, then Dean of St. Paul's, Archbishop Tillotson, Wallis, and John Williams.[3] He did not name prominent Latitudinarian prelates like Tillotson Socinians, as some did, even though Tillotson and others were at times ambiguous and vague on critically essential doctrines.

7. Edwards recognized that he was not so diplomatic with his opponents (especially heretics), but claimed it was necessary because he saw himself as a lonely voice in a world where the Christian faith was under attack, within the church and English society in general. "Posture-masters *rather than Divines*," he said, were following the

---

2. Edwards, *Preacher, Third Part*, preface.
3. Edwards, *Some Animadversions*, 3.

modernizing trends of other disciplines by abandoning their Reformed heritage and adopting *"some unheard-of Doctrines in Divinity"* and giving us *"a New Christianity."* There are essentials such as the *"Real and Proper Divinity of Christ"* which, if we lose, *"the Gospel will be mere Cypher, and the* Church *an Insignificant Term."*[4]

8. At times, Edwards reflected on his role in the controversy. *"If the Reader reminds me of my Promise not long since made,* to cease from all Hostilities and Disputes," Edwards continued, he must not forget that it was conditional—the condition being that the situation not continue to deteriorate. He described his work as unpleasant and hazardous *"Drudgery,"* which *"I long to be releas'd from,"* but it is necessary because few are willing to speak boldly against *"those profess'd Enemies and Corrupters of the Christian Doctrines."* He compared his work of refuting the errors of Arianism and Arminianism to those who *"discover and apprehend Robbers and Highway-Men."* He closed this particular preface by emphasizing that in his campaign against the opponents of truth, he held no personal grudge against anyone. To the contrary, *"I bear a great Respect to their Persons, and value their Learning and Abilities."* He admitted to at times being *"displeas'd with my self"* for strong language that may have caused offense. Far worse and regretful would be failing to speak the *"Plain Truth,"* which some do *"by a sort of Sneaking Mildness, or downright flattery."*[5]

LATITUDINARIANS IN THE CHURCH

It might be thought that some of Edwards's dedicatory prefaces were disingenuous when those so honored were not his Calvinistic kin. He did, after all, dedicate books to Bishop Simon Patrick and Archbishop Thomas Tenison, commending the latter for exposing the *"Vanity and Inconsistency of the* Hobbian Creed" as it relates to the Christian faith.[6] He also praised Tillotson for at length exposing John Sergeant a controversial Roman Catholic and close friend of Hobbes in *The Rule of Faith* as "a Man of very weak intellects, void of ordinary Logic" and for standing

---

4. Edwards, *Some New Discoveries*, i–iv.
5. Edwards, *Some New Discoveries*, v–vi.
6. Edwards, *Demonstration*, iv.

against heretical doubters by preaching that "*necessary Existence is Essential to the Notion of God.*"[7] On the other hand, he took great exception to Tillotson's view that faith is the easiest word "*in common use*" to understand[8] and to Patrick, for thinking that God instituted the use of altars and sacrifices in Christian worship since it was the "*Custom of Heathen People to feast with their Gods in their Temples, or near their Altars.*"[9]

Whether Edwards was complimenting or taking exception to what was said depended on the context. When commending Tillotson or Tenison, it was because they refuted heretical notions, as noted in Chapter 4. Edwards viewed heresy as a much greater concern than any differences within orthodox theology. But it was especially difficult for Edwards to accept Tillotson. While he did preach against heresy at times, there were other times when his message was far from clear. When questioned why he had not included Tillotson's works in his recommended reading list for young theology students, Edwards responded that in some sermons he treated the

> Subject of Christ's Divinity and the Doctrine of the Trinity so cautiously and gingerly, and with such Apologies that it may make him Suspected: and his extravagantly High Encomium which he fixes on the Socinian Writers is but a bad sign.

During his life, many within the church viewed the archbishop as "*a Lurking Socinian.*" In Edwards's estimation, "*he was reckoned by the Unitarians themselves as one of theirs,*" but Edwards did not so accuse him.[10]

Within the context of the Arminian and Calvinistic debate, Edwards had little positive to say about the Latitudinarian clerics. He was often critical of Tillotson for errors of logic[11] or simply being wrong in his interpretations, such as when he contended that God may grant us faith to believe, but it is not necessary because

> our understandings are naturally endowed with a sufficient power to assent to any truth that is sufficiently propounded to

---

7. Edwards, *Some New Discoveries*, 199; Tillotson, "Rule," 10:225–446. Tillotson issued an anti-Catholic proclamation, prompting Sergeant to escape to France. See also, Southgate, "John Sergeant"; Edwards, *Supplement*, 34; Tillotson, "Concerning the Unity," 3:418

8. Tillotson, "Nature of Faith," 9:180; Edwards, *Doctrine of Faith*, 2.

9. Edwards, *Theologia*, 2:410; Patrick, *Christian Sacrifice*.

10. Edwards, Preacher, *Third Part*, 280–81.

11. Edwards, *Doctrine of Faith*, 364.

them; then there can be no necessity to assert, that the Spirit of God doth, in the work of faith, raise and elevate our understandings above their natural pitch.[12]

To Edwards "nothing" was "more repugnant" to biblical teaching than being told something contrary to the fact that in our "lapsed State," we are "weakened and enfeebled, depraved and corrupted, and we are able to do nothing in Religious and Divine Matters, without the help of the Spirit."[13]

But Edwards did appreciate Tillotson's message at times. Though Tillotson was known to moralize the gospel, Edwards recognized that Christianity was the answer to the rampant immorality present in the culture. He pointed to Tillotson as an example of "perswasive and penetrating [. . .] Exhortations and Reasonings about Practical Duties" delivered "with so popular an Air, that he marvelously insinuates into the Minds of all his Hearers and Readers."[14] In both contexts, Edwards was speaking clearly and honestly, given what was at stake. When speaking to those within the church with whom he disagreed, his rhetoric was much more restrained and even respectful.

William King

On May 15, 1709, Dublin Archbishop William King preached a sermon on predestination and free will, which Edwards thought was off the mark.[15] He wrote a courteous letter to King which began by stating the great respect "Judicious" people have for "your Lordship's Judgment." But after his polite introduction, Edwards quickly challenged King's initial premise of how we understand divine attributes, such as "*Fore-knowledge, Predestination, Understanding, Will* and *Wisdom*," which are "*not to be taken strictly and properly*" but "only by way of *Analogy*." Edwards did not gloss over his objection:

> My Lord, All these seem to be very bold and irregular Strokes, and not expected from such an Accurate and Masterly Hand

---

12. Tillotson, "Testimony of the Spirit," 9:250.
13. Edwards, *Doctrine of Faith*, 18.
14. Edwards, *Preacher*, 65.
15. King, *Divine Predestination*. The printed version of the sermon dates it as given May 15, unlike Edwards's critique, which has May 5.

as yours. First, this is a plain Perverting of your Text [Rom. 8:29–30] and the Apostle's meaning in it.[16]

Edwards told him that his use of the analogy was backwards. God's attributes are absolute and ours are but a poor shadow of his, but by referring to God's attributes as a shadow, King's interpretation "seems to have risk'd the Chief Articles of our Christian Faith." Edwards also challenged King's contention that literal descriptions of God, such as he at the same time "hath all things in his view which can happen," are meant for simple minds, but others know that "this Literal Description is false." Generating additional confusion regarding God's sovereign grace was how Edwards took yet another point. Quoting from King's sermon,

> We are as much oblig'd to magnify his free Mercy and Favour to us, to humble our Minds before him, and return our tribute of Gratitude to him, as if our Salvation intirely proceeded from his mere good Will and Pleasure, without any thing being requir'd on our part, in order to do it.[17]

Edwards asked how this could possibly make sense. We are to act *as if* salvation depends entirely on God's grace, even though it does not and "we are not to be concern'd whether the Scripture represents the Case as in *Truth* it is." For Edwards the truth of Scripture was absolutely essential and foundational and it is only by God's grace that we are saved.[18]

Edwards was further alarmed by how the prelate understood what it means for us to do all things for the glory of God in a figurative sense. King said that,

> it is not meant that the Desire of his Glory is the real End of his Actions, but that he hath order'd all things in such an excellent Method, that if he had design'd them for no other end, they could not have set it forth more effectively. Now to make this figurative Expression the foundation of so many harsh Conclusions [. . . is] the same kind of mistake, that the Church of Rome commits in taking the words of Scripture, *This is my Body*, literally.[19]

Edwards asked whether we have been mistaken all along to think that the chief end of man is to glorify God, yet when the angels sang, "*Glory to*

---

16. Edwards, *Divine Perfections*, 3–5, 8.
17. Edwards, *Divine Perfections*, 7, 9, 13, 14, 16; King, *Divine Predestination*, 20.
18. Edwards, *Divine Perfections*, 18.
19. King, *Divine Predestination*, 32; Edwards, *Divine Perfections*, 20.

God in the Highest" at the birth of our savior, these words had no literal meaning. Are these words are but a *"Metaphorical* Complement"? To Edwards, such loose interpretation of Scripture meant that we could no longer complain about how Roman Catholics, Deists, Skeptics, and Socinians abuse it. Attempting to close on a positive note, he commended the archbishop for seeking to be a *"Peacemaker* and *Reconciler,"* given the conflict between Arminians and Calvinists. But "tis not advisable to disguise the *Truth* for *Peace* sake."[20]

It is not known whether King ever acknowledged Edwards's review, but more than a hundred years later, Oriel College, Oxford provost Edward Copleston (1776–1849) wanted the world to know of the great injustice done to the archbishop. Referring to Edwards as "bitter" and "insolent," his "entirely unprovoked" attack "raises the clamour about the [divine] moral attributes, as if *their* nature also must be held to be different in kind from human virtues."[21] Although American Jonathan Edwards never commented on King's sermon, Copleston thought he would bolster his defense of King by criticizing *The Freedom of the Will* and point out "how vigour of intellect, when once entangled in a snare of words, only tends by its struggles to increase its own embarrassment."[22]

Gilbert Burnet

Latitudinarian and Arminian Bishop Gilbert Burnet wrote a commentary on the XXXIX Articles, which he submitted to the public with considerable modesty, stating that he hoped to unify Lutherans and Calvinists. Two statements in his preface, however, would have alarmed anyone with Calvinist inclinations: first, that "two of the best Books that we yet have" on the Protestant faith were by Laud and Chillingworth and second, that the subject to which he devoted the most *"Care"* and wrote in a most "uncommon Method" was predestination. By "uncommon Method" he meant that he employed Greek Orthodox rather than Augustinian thinking, which he believed would be acceptable to everyone. Edwards took exception to his departure from Augustine because it was from

---

20. Edwards, *Divine Perfections*, 21–25, 31.

21. Copleston, *Enquiry*, 119–20, 136. Of course, Edwards did not contend that human and divine virtues are essentially different, but that human virtues are a shadow of the divine.

22. Copleston, *Enquiry*, 39–46.

that perspective that the XXXIX Articles were written, as Burnet himself clearly admitted.[23]

Edwards began by referring to Burnet in respectful terms, calling him "Learned and Reverend" and "This Worthy Author," but wishing "there were not occasion to complain that the late *Exposition of the Thirty Nine articles* is Sceptical and hovering," by which he meant that Burnet was at best imprecise and obscure. With the latitude of this expression, "we don't know the meaning of a great part of our Articles," not only is our understanding of doctrine bewildering, but also the "Devotionals and the Discipline" of the church. In addition, this exposition dishonors our godly reformers who first drafted these Articles. Here Edwards was not speaking arrogantly as one with absolute knowledge. He used the phrase, "seems to me" and said he was submitting his conclusions "to the Judgment of others." But he warned that such loose hermeneutics would lead us down a slippery slope whereby Catholics and eventually Socinians, Unitarians, and atheists would use the Articles to "maintain their cause."[24]

Following Edwards's critique, an anonymous response appeared in Burnet's defense, arguing that Burnet's commentary was not vague in its entirety; moreover some of the Articles were not clear because the doctrines themselves were enigmatic. For example, does anyone exactly know what is meant by Christ's descent into hell? Certainly there is mystery in the doctrines of election, the Trinity and Incarnation, the writer claimed. Can the bishop be held at fault because neither Scripture nor the Articles answer every question we might have? Appealing to Edwards's sense of unity, he asked,

> In good troth, would the Doctor desire that so moderate a Church as ours is esteem'd to be, should absolutely decide that Christ went locally into the Lake of Fire and Brimstone; that whatsoever Calvin has asserted concerning Predestination, is true, and the like; and should make a Schism with and actually divide from all other Christians who are of a different Sentiment as to these particulars?[25]

The writer continued to say that as far as papists and Unitarians are concerned, let them join with us, if they can in good conscience

---

23. Burnet, *Exposition*, iv–vii, 151.
24. Edwards, *Free Discourse*, 424–28.
25. Anon., *General Exceptions*, 3–6.

subscribe to the Articles and agree that they are consistent with Scripture. Our schism with Rome was caused by the pope. Yes, the first Reformers were self-sacrificing, wise, and good, but does that make them infallible? "Must all those, of our Clergy, be Equivocators, Dissemblers, and Hypocrites, who are not *Calvinists?*"[26] Edwards responded briefly as part of a larger work, again stating that no one who "is sober, and in good ernest, and is not byass'd by Prejudices, can deny that [the Articles] speak the Mind of the *Calvinists*." He was not suggesting that Burnet was indefinite on every Article, but wondered why he, who "freely confesses" that the XXXIX Articles clearly reflect Reformed doctrines, especially "*Justification by Faith alone*," would equivocate as he has. Edwards equated the failure to clearly assert justification by faith alone with rejecting the Pauline epistles of Romans and Galatians.[27]

Benjamin Hoadly

The Bangorian controversy erupted just after Edwards died, initiated by a posthumous work of non-juror George Hickes and a countering sermon by Benjamin Hoadly, then early in his career as Bishop of Bangor.[28] Latitudinarian Hoadly would later serve as Bishop of Hereford, Salsbury, and Winchester, continuing to provoke controversy with his prolific pen, sympathetic of dissent, and critical of High Church authority. In an early collection of sermons, Hoadly answered the lawyer's question of Luke 10:25, "What shall I do to inherit eternal life?" Saying he was sorry to "mention another Learned and Noted writer" who has introduced such confusion about justification, Edwards recalled rectifying this before. He summarized Hoadly's view as defining faith as "sometimes a believing of the Truths of the Gospel, and sometimes the whole Gospel-Dispensation, but never a relying on Christ's Merits."[29]

In "The Mistake of Relying upon Faith, Considered, &c.," (Eph 2:8), Hoadly asked his congregants, "In what Sense it is that Christians may be said to be saved by faith?" He called faith "a Privilege which peculiarly belonged to the first Christians converted, at years of Discretion, from a Life of Sin and Impurity [. . .] But this doth not concern those who have been

---

26. Anon., *General Exceptions*, 8–12.
27. Edwards, *Some New Discoveries*, 130, 242.
28. Hickes, *Constitution*; Hoadly, *Nature of the Kingdom*.
29. Edwards, *Some New Discoveries*, 130; Hoadly, *Several Discourses*, 5–6.

educated, and instructed, in the Knowledge of the Christian Religion."[30] Edwards's briefly responded that this means there are two gospels. Jews and heathens are saved by faith, but we who are enlightened are saved by "Obedience and Good Works," concluding, "I conceive that the bare mentioning of this, is a sufficient Confutation."[31]

Robert Lightfoote and William Tillotson

Edwards's book *The Preacher* was actually three books, published separately, with the second and third volumes subtitled "Second Part" and "Third Part." Following publication of the first two parts, Edwards reported that he "was sincerely insulted by some of my Brethren of the Clergy," initially in their preaching and later by some in print. Edwards said he was not surprised and viewed their abuse more like a commendation because "Applause from some Persons is a Scandal and Disgrace."[32] The first of these critical authors named was Robert Lightfoote, rector of Odel in Bedford, who challenged Edwards's judgment on about thirty-five issues, some at a rather superficial level. In an addendum to *The Preacher, the Third Part*, Edwards replied to Lightfoote and others who he felt had misrepresented his views, after which Lightfoote responded.

In the first part of *The Preacher*, Edwards thought it obvious that "some Reformation" in preaching was needed.[33] Lightfoote disagreed: "there never was better Preaching since the Reformation."[34] Edwards agreed that many of his contemporaries were gifted preachers, but the problem was the sermon topics. Instead of making relevant the doctrines of faith, forgiveness, grace, law, etc., too many sermons were "about the *Truth* of the *Christian Religion*, as if we were Preaching to mere *Pagans* and *Infidels*." Edwards believed that such "shallow," "Inconsistent," and relatively irrelevant preaching was "one great Cause of that *Deism* which reigns among us at this time."[35] Lightfoote replied that Edwards was the inconsistent one, pointing out that only five pages after his charge that contemporary sermons were too often directed toward unbelievers, he

30. Hoadly, *Several Discourses*, 197.
31. Edwards, *Some New Discoveries*, 131–32.
32. Edwards, *Preacher, Third Part*, 223–24.
33. Edwards, *Preacher*, ii.
34. Lightfoote, *Remarks*, 2.
35. Edwards, *Preacher, Third Part*, 228.

wrote that "we have many at this day who bear the name of *Christians*, but are really *Infidels*, and in their Lives shew themselves to be *worse than Pagans*."[36] Neither man stated how many of these pagans actually attended church.

Edwards also accused Archbishop Tillotson (and others) of essentially equating morality with the essence of Christianity by preaching that *"the Fruits of the Spirit are the same with Moral Vertues and that Grace and Verture are but two Names that signify the same thing."*[37] Edwards complained that "some of my brethren," take their sermons more from Pufendorf than Scripture.[38] He reminded his readers that morality can come from "Natural Principles," but uniquely Christian virtues only come from the supernatural grace of God.[39] Edwards also charged Tillotson with elevating human reason and experience over revelation as the basis for religious knowledge. Once Tillotson said that a mother nursing her child is "a natural duty; and because it is so, of a more necessary and indispensable obligation than any positive precept of revealed religion." Edwards wondered how nursing a baby could be "more necessary and indispensable" than "*Trusting in Christ for Life and Salvation.*"[40]

In his *Remarks* to defend Tillotson, Lightfoote proceeded with a lengthy quotation where Tillotson explained "*that* [Christian] *Moral Virtues are the Graces and Fruits of the Spirit,*" but he failed to distinguish between natural morality and supernatural fruits of the Spirit. Lightfoote concluded that Edwards was unjust in comparing Tillotson to "*mere Ethick Lecturers,*" as Edwards described them.[41] Lightfoote asked, "Can any Conclusion be more false than this, That because Two things are given by the same Person, therefore there is no difference between them?"[42] Edwards retorted that Lightfoote blindly defended the archbishop, quoting Article XIII to show that such thinking is completely contrary to the

---

36. Lightfoote, *Dr. Edwards's Vindication*, 6; Edwards, *Preacher, Third Part*, 233.

37. Edwards, *Preacher*, 78; Tillotson, "Fruits of the Spirit," 8:476.

38. Edwards, *Preacher*, 79. Samuel Pufendorf (1632–94) was a political theorist who based social order on natural law. He associated natural law with natural religion, which informs us of God's law by reason. He rejected Calvinism, believing it to be deterministic. See, Pufendorf, *Divine Feudal Law*.

39. Edwards, *Preacher*, 78–82; Tillotson, "Fruits of the Spirit," 8:481.

40. Tillotson, "Education of Children," 3:488; Edwards, *Free Discourse*, 81.

41. Lightfoote, *Remarks*, 44–56.

42. Lightfoote, *Remarks*, 48.

gospel, which emphasizes the difference between good works done before and after conversion:

> Works done before the Grace of Christ, and the Inspiration of his Spirit are not pleasant to God, for as much as they spring not of Faith in Jesus Christ: yea rather, for that they are not done as God hath willed and commanded them to be done, we doubt not but they have the nature of sin.[43]

Edwards referred to a sermon of Bishop Sanderson who made a great distinction between natural and supernatural morality, citing Augustine: "*Altho' a Man may seem to do things that are Good, yet because they are void of Faith, they are not to be called Good.*" Of Tillotson, Lightfoote wrote that Edwards seemed to be concluding mistakenly that Tillotson was equating moral virtue as it is seen in "Heathens" with the "Fruits of the Spirit." The archbishop he claimed was only speaking of "the Moral Vertues of good Christians produced in them by God's Spirit" and not "of the Works of the Heathens."[44] Lightfoote never clarified whether the archbishop's "heathen" included British citizens whose lives had not been changed by the divine grace of which Article XIII spoke.

In another example of Edwards's tangle with Lightfoote over Tillotson, Edwards claimed that Tillotson did not teach the biblical doctrine of justification by faith alone. For some reason Lightfoote responded by quoting part of a sermon by Baxter, wherein he clearly stated that justifying faith consists of two articles: assent to the gospel as revealed in Scripture and trust in God. Lightfoote then proceeded to claim that this was exactly what Tillotson preached in his sermon "Of Justifying Faith" from John 20:31. But in fact, as Edwards pointed out, Tillotson did not. Tillotson preached concerning "the influence which faith hath upon the pardon of sin" and "that repentance and obedience are conditions of our pardon, and consequently of our justification." Although at one point he implied that human merit counts for nothing, he interpreted James to say that justifying faith "must not only be a bare assent" of Gospel truths, "but must include in it obedience to all the commands of the gospel."[45] For Edwards a holy life was the result of justifying faith, not part of it. Along with Baxter, "Faith is, not only to believe all Things of God which

---

43. Edwards, *Preacher, Third Part*, 250.

44. Edwards, Preacher, *Third Part*, 253–54; Lightfoote, *Dr. Edwards's Vindication*, 38.

45. Tillotson, "Justifying Faith," 9:312–13, 319.

are contained in Holy Scripture, but also an earnest Trust and Confidence in God" that he will grant us mercy because of the work of Christ. He concluded that Lightfoote was simply not up to the task of defending Tillotson, naming him Tillotson's vindicator with the comment, "tho it is certain that no Man ever deserv'd it [the title of vindicator] less."[46]

Daniel Whitby

Although Edwards challenged a number of Arminians, his work *Arminian Doctrines Condemn'd* was primarily a response to Whitby before he converted to Arianism.[47] Their debate was launched in 1707 when Edwards criticized Whitby's views on divine decrees, grace, free will, and eternal security found in annotations to his *Paraphrase and Commentary on the New Testament.*[48] Whitby's response appeared in two different publications and Edwards answered both in a two-part book. The first response of Whitby's was a hastily written postscript to a work where he gave his own views on the so-called five points of Calvinism. The thrust of the postscript was to attack Edwards for his "weak Attempts" to defend the doctrines of Calvinism and "to demonstrate, that not one of them was, in his sense, maintained before St. *Austin's* time, and that some of them were not owned by any *Ecclesiastical* writer for a long time after." To argue against Edwards's view that divine grace is completely unmerited, Whitby quoted Gerardus Vossius (1577–1649) as saying that,

> all the Greek Fathers always, and all the Latin fathers, who lived before St. Austin, held that they were predestinated to Life, whom God foresaw that they would live piously and righteously, or, as others say, whom he foresaw, would believe and persevere to the end.[49]

Edwards replied quickly, informing his readers that it was Augustine who stated that some earlier fathers such as Cyprian, Gregory Nazianzen, and Ambrose believed in absolute predestination and for some reason,

---

46. Edwards, *Arminian Doctrines*, 218, 219.

47. See Chapter 4. For a detailed analysis of the debate between Edwards and (Arminian) Whitby, see Yoo, *John Edwards*.

48. Edwards, *Veritas*, 107–09, 336–38, 460. Yoo incorrectly states that the dispute began three years later in 1710 when Whitby attacked Edwards in his *Four Discourses*. See Yoo, *John Edwards*, 61.

49. Whitby, *Discourse Concerning*, 556.

Whitby ignored that fact in *"profound silence."* And to clarify the matter about foreknowledge, Edwards noted,

> I do not deny that the Fathers frequently say that God *foresaw* who should be holy; but I do not remember that it is maintain'd by them, that God was moved to predestinate Man to Life *because of* their foreseen Holiness, or *on account of* their foreknown Faith and Repentance. [. . .] And therefore Holiness is the Fruit of Election, and not consequently the Cause of it.[50]

Edwards also challenged Whitby's use of Vossius. According to Edwards, Vossius did not say *all*, either of the Greek or the Latin fathers, nor did he say that those fathers *"held that they were predestinated to life* [. . .] but only, *they are wont to say,"* which Whitby missed because he apparently "can't construe a plain Piece of Latin." But more significant was Whitby's failure to include what Vossius said immediately after the part Whitby quoted, namely that the Fathers

> *did not think that on Man's Part there is any Cause of Predestination unto Preventing Grace.* [. . .] *It is very probable that all, or most of the Catholic Fathers, when they make Faith prior to Election, do not consider Faith as a Cause properly so called of Election.*[51]

Whitby read works of Augustine's disciple Prosper of Aquitaine (c.390–c.455), but according to Edwards, in citing Prosper, he not only misrepresented his assertion that "Predestination is from Free Grace," but also confused Augustine's views with those of some French Divines who disagreed with Augustine.[52] Edwards proceeded to answer Whitby's objections to divine decrees, original sin, free will, grace, and perseverance, providing additional examples of how he misrepresented and ignored evidence of other Fathers, including Origen, Gregory of Nyssa, and Jerome. Edwards accused him of at best being very careless, but more likely prejudicial in his approach, basically scholarship unbecoming a scholar for using quotations second hand, not checking to see if they agree with the original, and simply ignoring evidence which did not support his own views such that "when he is silent [regarding certain Fathers which

---

50. Edwards, *Arminian Doctrines*, 3–4.
51. Edwards, *Arminian Doctrines*, 5.
52. Edwards, *Arminian Doctrines*, 8–9.

Edwards had quoted], we may conclude that the Quotation is perfectly against him, yea that it is such that he thinks it unanswerable."[53]

Whitby began his second rebuttal of Edwards ridiculing Edwards with a quotation from a recent magazine which referred to Edwards "*as one being very well known to be a warm, tho' a weak Defender of the Calvinistical Doctrines.*"[54] Edwards saw Whitby's *Four Discourses* after he had written his response to Whitby's postscript and so wrote another long essay which he titled *An Answer to Dr. Whitby's Second Pretended Defence of his Arminian Doctrines*. Calling him a *"feeble Adversary,"* Edwards wrote, "*I never met with a Man that made a greater Noise of Learning and Reading, and yet hath a lesser Share of them, and abused and perverts them more, than the Doctor.*" As for the substance of the first discourse, Edwards called it nothing more than a repetition of his earlier paraphrase of that chapter, which he described as an attempt "to disparage and vilify" what is "contain'd in our Church's Article of *Predestination.*"[55] According to Edwards, Whitby's second discourse, which argued that election in the Old and New Testaments pertains to the calling of groups of people (e.g., the Jewish nation, the church) not individuals, even contradicted Whitby himself. Whitby wrote that for God to "have fav'd Jacob without doing any Good, and damn'd Esau without doing any Evil [. . .] is contrary to the whole Tenour of the Scripture," which tells us that God is a righteous judge who will reward each person according to their works.[56] In his discourse on election, Whitby recognized Jacob and Esau as individuals and cited several church fathers including Origin and Chrysostom who also did so.[57]

In his third discourse he called "*blasphemous*" Edwards's teaching that God's foreknowledge depends on his decrees and that God decreed the commission of all sins in the world. Whitby argued that God foreknows the future, but he does not decree it because that would "plainly destroy the Liberty of those Actions" and make "God the Author of Sin."[58] Edwards responded that if God did not decree his saving grace upon someone, he would not know whether that person would repent,

---

53. Edwards, *Arminian Doctrines*, 69–70.
54. Whitby, *Four Discourses*, i–ii.
55. Edwards, *Answer*, 119, 128–29.
56. Whitby, *Four Discourses*, 1, 12.
57. Whitby, *Four Discourses*, 136; Whitby, *Discourse Concerning*, 44, 97–98.
58. Whitby, *Four Discourses*, 37, 39, 50.

referring to Origen who pointed to Jesus's betrayal by Judas as a clear example.[59] From that Whitby mockingly concluded that since God wills us to sin, we should pray that we would sin.

Whitby also rejected that idea that God could be glorified even in the committing of sin and that sin could be used to punish sin "because all Punishments, being from God, must be just and whatsoever is just is good."[60] Edwards countered that Whitby twists his ideas to make God the author of sin. God wills sin only in a secondary sense and "only so far as he is able to order and dispose it to great and good Purposes; yea even to his own Glory." Following a detailed exegesis of several passages, he charged Whitby with conceit and perverting Scripture to think that "evil Agents and their sinful Actions" are not under God's "over-ruling Providence," by which God is diminished to be neither sovereign nor all-wise.[61] In his final discourse, Whitby defended various places in his annotations on the New Testament against Edwards's "Ignorance," "want of Logick," and "Denial of the Truth," which was on display in Edwards's initial attack. Edwards offered little in response, claiming that Whitby was again repeating his earlier arguments and accused him of continuing to mistranslate various passages from the Greek text in order to support his theology.[62]

Whitby had a second Edwards opponent, Welshman Jonathan Edwards (1629–1712), principal of Jesus College, Oxford. Whitby took him to task for his defense of original sin, which he had directed against Whitby in *The Doctrine of Original Sin As It Was Always Held in the Catholick Church*: "*I have had of late two keen Adversaries, differing but little in the Names, and less in the Civility of their Deportment toward me; both full of bitter* Calvinistick Zeal." Portraying himself as unjustly persecuted like Jesus, Whitby wrote, "*I therefore rather chuse to be falsely represented as* a Pelagian Heretick, a Banterer of St. *Paul's* Epistles, an impious, malicious Person, guilty of fraudulent, dishonest Practices," etc.[63] Defending Jonathan Edwards as having "great Judgment and Strength of

---

59. Edwards, *Arminian Doctrines*, 139–46.
60. Whitby, *Four Discourses*, 51, 62, 65.
61. Edwards, *Arminian Doctrines*, 154, 165.
62. Whitby, *Four Discourses*, 97; Edwards, *Arminian Doctrines*, 199–203.
63. Whitby, *Full Answer*, iii.

Reason," John Edwards called Whitby pitiful for being unable to respond with substantive ideas, only "abusive and scurrilous Language."[64]

Edward Nicholson

Little biographical material is available on the Rev. Edward Nicholson, MA, although it is likely that he served in Ireland, given his Dublin printers. His rather scathing review of Edwards's *Veritas Redux*, which he said should have been titled *Scabies Ecclesiæ Redux*, indicates that he had no use for Edwards, nor Calvinism. In his preface, he left off pleasantries, calling Edwards an enemy of the church and accusing him of thinking he was "*learneder than all the Ancients of the first Three hundred years put together.*" Ad hominem attacks appear to be the main theme from beginning to end. Near the beginning, Edwards is likened to the Giant Polyphemus, Ahithophel, and "*an Angel of Light*" and called "*a common Barretor in Divinity* [. . .] *incoherent to himself.*"[65]

Nicholson saw Edwards as arrogant, stating, "*he would fain make his Readers believe, he's the only Man of this Age to Instruct them,*" quoting Edwards as saying, "*I tell the Reader that I reckon there are few Persons in a greater Capacity to enquire impartially into Truth, and Consequently to attain to it, then* [sic] *I am.*"[66] What Nicholson left out was Edwards's context for that statement. What Edwards attempted to explain in the preface was not that he was the greatest authority, but what pains he had taken in his research, consulting commentaries on the creeds and other theological treatises, not only of those with whom he agreed, but also of

> our Adversaries. For I know 'tis usual with some Persons to take up one side of a Question, and to read, to furnish themselves with Arguments to confirm them in the belief of it. But I never perused Authors on that account, I look'd for the Truth on which side soever I thought I could find it; and when I lighted on it in the Adversary's Quarters, I gave it fair reception.[67]

Edwards claimed to be constantly seeking God's help in prayer and to have carefully subjected everything he wrote to the standard of Scripture. Nicholson also ignored Edwards's stated purposes in all of his works.

64. Edwards, *Some New Discoveries*, 132–33.
65. Nicholson, *Short Notes*, Preface, 9.
66. Nicholson, *Short Notes*, 16.
67. Edwards, *Veritas*, iii–iv.

> Every where my design is to *Reconcile* the quarreling People of the World [...] Some have writ Books to uphold Controversies; my aim in writing is, to compose and allay them. Others are for giving Battle, I am for Cessation of Arms. [...] My business is always to stop the fury of these Combatants, and to enquire where we may most peaceably find the Truth. [...] Tho' it be an invidious and perilous Task, yet it is a Christian and necessary one, to unite and reconcile Dissenting Brethren. And tho' 'tis likely I shall displease different Parties, yet I shall be satisfied with discharging my Duty. I would be at quiet with all Men, but rather at peace with my own Conscience.[68]

Nicholson was full of reckless charges, calling Edwards "this snarling Man" who treats Dr. Hammond with "mortal hatred."[69] He said that Edwards was opposed to the entire church and was imposing a foreign doctrine "so as we cannot thereby make our Religion as the Scripture would have it." Certainly Nicholson being Arminian could take issue with Calvinist Edwards. But he seemed so intent on defaming Edwards that what Edwards actually wrote was irrelevant.

> This Author will not own himself the Member or Subject of our living Church, but only of the dead part, for it's that only he calls the Church of *England*, [...] scorning the Church Militant, that is the church now alive, he'll be only of the Church Triumphant, or none.[70]

Upon reading what Edwards said, such fabrication is difficult to imagine. As noted elsewhere, Edwards did not view the church as perfect, but he defended it and never left it. He wrote that "every true Member of the Church Militant [...] must fight upon his Knees" and speaking the truth was an important characteristic of anyone "fit to be a Member of the Church militant."[71]

Nicholson frequently appealed to reason to the point of claiming that "the Trinity Doctrine [...] squares with common Reason in the highest Degree," quite the opposite of Unitarian thinking. He wrote,

---

68. Edwards, *Veritas*, iv.

69. Nicholson, *Short Notes*, 12. See below to check the veracity of charge regarding Henry Hammond (1605–60).

70. Nicholson, *Short Notes*, 21, 31.

71. Edwards, *Theologia*, 2:140, 593.

We have often found it true, that when Reason is against a Man, the Man will be against Reason. Thus the excellent and pious Arch-Bishop Tillotson stands very odious in his [Edwards'] sight, because he had a peculiar faculty of discovering and choaking Absurdities by his Reason.[72]

Edwards was quite critical of those who elevated reason, "abusing and scandalizing Reveal'd Religion," characterizing them as "shrouding themselves under Mr. *Chillingworth's* Wing."[73] Edwards certainly did not view Tillotson's theology favorably, but there is no evidence that he viewed anyone "odiously." Chillingworth's rational theology, spelled out in *The Religion of the Protestants: A Safe Way to Salvation* is clearly far removed from Edwards's understanding. But it is interesting to hear Edwards's comments on Chillingworth, especially on his personal attributes, in light of Nicholson's words.

And who was this Mr. Chillingworth? Not to disparage his Personal Worth, Parts, and Learning (which none ought to question) he was one that refused to subscribe to the Nine and Thirty Articles, and was dissatisfied with the Church of England, and embraced that of Rome.[74]

Nicholson finally brought his ranting tirade to an end, admitting that

I could not read this Book without indignation. [. . .] I will not yet believe that he is a Jesuit in Masqurade; but do believe that if he were one, he could not contrive more mischief to our Church, than by casting the itchy Disputes of these Doctrines among us, in such a manner, with such virulent Reflections upon all our living Bishops and Clergy.[75]

Edwards, if he did see Nicholson's book, did not bother to respond directly. However Edwards's comments on various church officials throughout his writings is further evidence that not only did he not hold "all our living Bishops and Clergy" in disrepute, but that his efforts to

---

72. Nicholson, *Short Notes*, 25, 21.

73. Edwards, *Veritas Redux*, 491; Carter, *The English Church*, 111-13; Griffin, *Latitudinarianism*, 89-104; Rupp, *Religion in England*, 36.

74. Edwards, *Veritas*, 491–92. Chillingworth became a Roman Catholic briefly in his late 20s. Four years before his death he signed the XXXIX Articles, not because he fully believed them, but "as a basis of peace and union," after which Laud appointed him chancellor of Salisbury. See Creighton, *ODNB*.

75. Nicholson, *Short Notes*, 80.

build unity were consistent. In Edwards's commentary on the Apostles' Creed, Bishop Stillingfleet was cited as "a Worthy Prelate of our Church" for demonstrating that the extra-biblical accounts of the creation, which challenge Genesis 1 are fables. For the fourth article (of the Creed), Edwards referenced Bishop Wake of Lincoln as "most Learned" in his "Excellent Comment on the Church Catechism." The scholarship of Dr. Henry Hammond (1605–1660) was commended in the ninth. Also in his discussion of the ninth article, John Hales (1584–1656) was called by Edwards "a Great Man of our Church."[76] Bishop Wilkins of Chester was commended for his understanding and teaching on prayer. These are just some of the men whom Edwards mentioned favorably in specific contexts in only one of his works—none of them Calvinists. At times Edwards pointed out his disagreement with some of them, but it was generally done with respect. For example, in answering the question of how penalty for sin could be infinite when committed by finite beings, Edwards argued that it was against an infinite God, noting that Hammond and others disagreed.[77]

Edwards did not publicly criticize all the prominent Latitudinarians simply because he had significant disagreements with them. On the contrary, for the sake of church unity, he often spoke of them in positive ways. To Ely Bishop Patrick, Edwards dedicated two more volumes, first and second of his *A Discourse on the Authority, Stile and Perfection of the Books of the Old and New Testament*, calling him "Vertuous and Learned":

> The Design of the Dedication is to let the World know, that such a Person is really Praiseworthy, and that even to a Wonder; that he is one that ought to be extremely honoured and venerated for his Transcendent Excellencies, and that he is to be a Pattern to the rest of Mankind.[78]

He dedicated the third volume of that work to Archbishop Tenison, praising him greatly for his stand against Rome.[79]

---

76. Edwards, *Theologia*, 1:9, 393, 557, 619.
77. Edwards, *Theologia*, 2:94, 118, 121.
78. Edwards, *Discourse Concerning*, 2:vi–vii.
79. Edwards, *Discourse Concerning*, 3:v–viii.

FELLOW CALVINISTS IN THE CHURCH

Being a Calvinist, Edwards had his differences with Armenians. But he also disagreed with some Calvinists. But as mentioned in the introduction, he did not feel bound to a particular theologian or a theological label; his objective was to carefully and faithfully understand Scripture, using insights from whichever side he could discover them.[80] Conversely, he took the time to not only critique specific views of some Arminians, but certain positions of others identified as Calvinists. Although accused by some of being extreme, nonconformist Ralph Thoresby (1658-1725), member of the Royal Society, did not find Edwards's works to be at all extreme. On the contrary, "though much depreciated by some because of his moderation, for which reason I visited him."[81]

Tobias Crisp

Not only was Edwards's moderation evident relative to other Calvinists, but also in his charity toward those with whom he had sharp disagreement such as Tobias Crisp. The sermons of the controversial Calvinist were republished by his son Samuel in 1690, precipitating a series of lectures and books attacking and defending Crisp. Richard Baxter was one of the first in a lecture at Pinner's Hall to condemn Crisp as antinomian.[82] The following year after Baxter's death, Presbyterian Daniel Williams (1643-1716) joined the debate, generally following Baxter's thinking. Hostilities became increasingly contentious over most of the decade, engaging more than a dozen ministers, along with Bishop Stillingfleet who also wrote a book refuting Crisp.[83] The unity among nonconformists which Pinner's Hall was supposed to foster was shattered, beginning with Williams being expelled from the lectureship.

According to Edwards, Crisp so emphasized the sovereignty of God and the preeminence of Jesus Christ that there was nothing, including exercising faith to believe, that man could do for salvation or good works. Crisp said,

---

80. Edwards, *Veritas*, iii-iv.
81. Thoresby, *Diary*, 2:75, 231-32.
82. Toon, *Hyper-Calvinism*, 50.
83. Stillingfleet, *Two Discourses*.

> You will ask, is *not* unbelief *a bar to have a part in Christ*? Answ. It is a bar to hinder the Manifestation of Christ in the Spirit; but it is not a bar to hinder one from having a part in Christ. [...] Unbelief is not simply a bar to the bestowing of Christ [...] He [God] bestows him without any regard to belief, or unbelief.[84]

Edwards interpretation:

> He asserts that *Christ may be received*, and that *a Man may have a Part in him*, though he be destitute of *Faith*. And what is this but to be *justified without Faith*? For, *to have a Part in Christ*, is to be justified in him.[85]

Edwards also charged him with antinomianism for separating justification and sanctification to the extent that a Christian can do nothing to offend God or to please God.[86] Crisp argued that God is pleased only with the righteousness of Christ, which covers all the offenses of the believer to the extent that a believer's sin is not a problem: "God doth no longer stand offended nor displeased; though a believer after he be a Believer doth sin often, yet I say, God no longer stands offended and displeased with him, when he hath once received Christ."[87] Crisp reasoned that if Christ died on the cross for my sins, the penalty was paid; additional punishment of the person committing the sin renders the cross ineffectual. Edwards did not disagree at all with the sufficiency of Christ's sacrifice. God does not punish us to atone for our sins, but for "fatherly Corrections and Chastisements, so that they prove the greatest Kindnesses and Favours that can be bestowed upon us." Punishment is actually evidence of God's grace.[88]

Not only did Crisp dismiss a believer's sin as inconsequential, but he identified man's righteous acts as sin, preaching, "There is not one righteous action a man doth perform, but he doth therein anew throw dirt in the Face of God."[89] To Edwards such a belief was the result of focusing on one aspect of theology, while ignoring other clear teaching of Scripture.

---

84. Crisp, *CAE*, 100.

85. Edwards, *Crispianism Unmask'd*, 4. Pederson, *Unity in Diversity*, 237: "What infuriated Crisp's critics most was his seeming careless words about the forgiveness of God."

86. Edwards, *Crispianism Unmask'd*, 47.

87. Crisp, *CAE*, 15.

88. Edwards, *Crispianism Unmask'd*, 41.

89. Crisp, *CAE*, 322.

He did not deny that all our righteous deeds are imperfect and gave three reasons why Crisp was wrong: 1) Citing Second Corinthians 8:12, he said that "God is pleased with the sincere (but imperfect Endeavours of his Servants;" 2) God is pleased with our good works when they are inspired by the Holy Spirit; 3) God is pleased because "Christ makes our Righteousness to be accepted."[90]

Though Edwards believed Crisp's book of sermons was "as *dangerous* and *pernicious* a Piece as hath appear'd in Print in this Age; and it is the more so, because it is in other parts so good and excellent," he did not question his motives or standing before God.

> *Far be it from me, to censure or arraign the State and Spirit of the Reverend Dr. Crisp, whose Soul I take to be in heaven, and whose Intentions and Designs might be sincere and good.* [. . .] *I believe his Heart was warm and honest, as to the Name and Cause of Christ.*[91]

Edwards again opened himself to those critics who found his understanding to be wrong. If I "*have mistaken the Doctor's Mind, mis-quoted his Book, or wrested and perverted what he quotes, or forc'd his Inferences unduly* [. . .] *let such things be discover'd and expos'd.*"[92] Edwards's estimate of Crisp was similar to that of Jonathan Edwards of Oxford who, in a letter to Williams, wrote of Crisp's distortion that it was "false, absurd, impossible, but likewise an Impious and Blasphemous Opinion; as being highly Dishonourable to our Saviour, repugnant to the Wisdom and Justice of God, and tends plainly to subvert the whole design of Christianity."[93]

Lawrence Fogg

Lawrence Fogg was a fellow Calvinist and author of books which Edwards had praised, in part. In a brief essay included in *Some New Discoveries*, he reviewed Fogg's latest work *Theologiæ Speculativæ Schema*, intended for beginning theology students. He began by commending Fogg for his clarity, for addressing the important issues, and for a succinct question and answer format which he characterized as "Scholastical and Metaphysical." Edwards was very pleased that he mostly stayed with

---

90. Edwards, *Crispianism Unmask'd*, 48.
91. Edwards, *Crispianism Unmask'd*, To the Reader.
92. Edwards, *Crispianism Unmask'd*, To the Reader.
93. Williams, *Answer*, 72.

the "old Divinity," but was quite critical of the few times when he did not, remarking that "where our Moderns have innovated [. . .] he is so complaisant as to tread in their steps." Among his infractions, "He falls in exactly [. . .] with the *Remonstrants* and *Arminians*, [. . .] *Papists* and *Socinians"* in his exegesis of Romans 9, not seeming to understand that the will of a regenerate person is free from its bondage to sin.[94] And after reading "*Nihil absurdi est, si potentiam non parendi Deo, Christum, in diebus carnis suae, habuisse dicatur* (*modo* actu & integritate dispositionis semper Deo obedisse statuatur) alioqui non fuisset per omnia fratribus suis fimilis*,"[95] Edwards concluded that Fogg believed that Christ, "tho' he be *God*, and *most Holy*, can sin if he will; and he can *will* the Commission of Sin, because his Will is indifferent to Good and Evil."[96] Edwards concluded his brief review, expressing surprise and dismay at where this sort of thinking was leading the church.

The following year Edwards wrote a more detailed critique of Fogg in a letter, which appears to be in reply to a letter of Fogg responding to the essay in *Some New Discoveries*. In this letter, Edwards called him to account for "gross Inconsistencies and Absurdities" found in some of his writings. Although viewing these inconsistencies as serious infractions of sound doctrine, Edwards almost seemed more personally annoyed than theologically offended, referring to his "just Resentment of the ill Treatment which I have met with from you," and writing that he did not intend to "mispend my Time and Leisure in tracing you, Paragraph by Paragraph, but I will only offer some brief Remarks on those Passage in your *Letter*, which are most obnoxious to the Censure even of the most moderate Judges."[97] Edwards expressed little sympathy for the elderly Fogg who seemed to be preoccupied with his ailments, teasing him as

> one that is always talking of his *decay of Sight*, the *defect of his Eyes*, his *being almost Stone-blind*, &c. (as if he thought it material that every one should take Notice of this Misfortune) and

---

94. Edwards, *Some New Discoveries*, 134, 137.

95. Fogg, *Theologiæ Speculativæ*, 409. It is not strange that Christ, in the days of his flesh, is said to not have had the obligation to obey the power of God (with a disposition of integrity, he was always obedient to God) otherwise he could not have been in all things like his brethren.

96. Edwards, *Some New Discoveries*, 138.

97. Edwards, *Letter*, 6–7. The nature of Fogg's "ill treatment" is not known as Edwards's letter references two previous pieces of correspondence between them, neither of which seem to be extant.

yet is wholly insensible of a greater and more notorious Decay, that of his Mind and Judgment.[98]

Edwards was especially bothered by how Fogg explained the doctrines of grace and election. Fogg wrote against those who "assert a *Sufficient*, but not an *Irresistible* Operation of Grace, [and therefore] they assert Grace that may be Opposed, and the Holy Spirit thereby Grieved, Quenched, or Provoked to Strive no longer."[99] He also wrote, *"But God will Aid effectually, if Man resist not."*[100] Such inconsistency, Edwards found intolerable. How could Fogg both favor and oppose the theology of God's irresistible grace? But despite his frustration and his harsh, condemning language, Edwards closed his letter on a conciliatory note:

> Let us part as Christian Friends and Brethren in our Lord Jesus Christ, and who were once *Collegues* in the same *Learned* and *Renowned Society* [. . .] and I can assure you, passionately condoles, with me, the Infirmity you at present labour under, and we heartily wish you some degree, at least, of Recovery from it, if it be the Divine Pleasure.[101]

HIGH-FLYERS

According to an eighteenth-century French scholar, high-flyer was a term used to describe a minority party of Tories: ambitious and passionate men who favored absolute power of the monarchy, "taken from Birds that by soaring above the common flight, lose themselves in the clouds," like men "who cannot contain themselves within the limits of established Government." They were especially influential during the sixteenth and early seventeenth centuries, having curried favor with the king. They built their base by attacking Presbyterians thereby stoking fears of church Tories, while concealing their real intentions, such as repealing the Succession to the Crown Act of 1707.[102] It seems that the term was first used in print ecclesiastically in 1680 as a precursor to the term "High

---

98. Edwards, *Letter*, 5.
99. Fogg, *God's Infinite Grace*, Preface.
100. Fogg, *Two Treatises*, 23, 65.
101. Edwards, *Letter*, 32.
102. de Thoyras, *History of England*, 2:801–05.

Churchman," referring to those with strict allegiance to the church and generally aligned with their Tory counterparts.[103]

Henry Dodwell

In 1706 Henry Dodwell (1641–1711) created a stir with his book, which argued from Scripture and the church fathers that the human soul was mortal before Adam's fall.[104] Samuel Clarke quickly responded to refute that idea because it was associated with Socinianism and materialism.[105] Clarke's opposition was mainly metaphysical based on the divisibility of matter. Edwards noted Clarke's response and commented of Dodwell, "He hath other Conceits which are very odd and indigested."[106] The following year in his commentary on the Apostles' Creed, Edwards discussed human immortality at length and described several "Perverse and Dangerous Notions," including Dodwell's, which he called "that wild Attempt to prove out of the Antient Fathers that the *Soul of Man* is naturally Mortal."[107]

Dodwell was not ordained in the church and only employed briefly as a prælector at Oxford before being dismissed as a non-juror in 1691. Edwards recognized him as well-read and knowledgeable in "Ancient History, Geography, Chronology, Ecclesiastical Antiquary" and "well versed in the *Fathers* Writings; but then it is as true, that he hath wretchedly perverted them," particularly in his view of Adam's fall, human nature, hell, and the resurrection. Furthermore, similar to Whiston, he had written in such a way as to make it seem that his "extravagant Notions" were those of the Fathers, such as claiming that very few died as a result of early church persecutions, which Edwards said "is perfectly against the Sense of the *Fathers*."[108]

Edwards nicknamed him chief of the "*High-Church Fanaticks*" and "Oracle of the high-flyers" for his theological eccentricity and adherence to Laudian essentials such as "*Hypercanonical Ceremonies*," signing the cross "at all Times," "the indispensable Necessity of *Sacerdotal Absolution*,"

103. Ollard, *Dictionary*, 115.
104. Dodwell, *Epistolary Discourse*.
105. Clarke, *A Letter to Mr. Dodwell*.
106. Edwards, *Some Brief Observations*, 4.
107. Edwards, *Theologia*, 2:48.
108. Edwards, *Patrologia*, 113.

and "*the Real and Corporal Presence* of Christ in the Eucharist."[109] Edwards also charged Dodwell with hypocrisy for writing in his 600 page book "*that those who separate from our Church are guilty of sinning against the Holy Ghost, and unto death,*" while at the same time he did not attend services because of his nonjuring principles. He returned to the church the year before he died.[110]

George Hickes and J. Scandret

Nonjuring George Hickes lost his deanery at Worcester and later attacked both Tillotson and Burnet while commenting on Burnet's funeral sermon for the archbishop.[111] He called Burnet an "Apostate by his own Confession" and inexcusably duplicitous for preaching against "all sorts of Treasonable Doctrines and Practices" while at the same time working to bring William and Mary to the throne, "one of the Deepest and most Heinous Treasons that Subject was ever engaged in against his Sovereign."[112] Hickes quoted from two of Tillotson's sermons, one of which he designated "down right *Hobbism*," citing influential support for his assessment: gloating by "Atheists, Deists and Socinians"; Bishop Gunning of Ely: "a Doctrine that would serve the Turn of Popery"; Bishop Patrick of Chichester: "treacherous Doctrine"; and Arch-deacon Samuel Parker (1640–88) of Canterbury: "I cannot but have a love to Dr. *Tillotson's* Person, though I have none for his Opinion."[113] As an indication of his contentious approach, he found alliance with Presbyterian rebel Thomas Edwards calling him as "a mighty Bigot for the Cause" (of exposing heretics).[114] Hickes and other high-flyers provide evidence that John

---

109. Edwards, *Preacher, Third Part*, v; Edwards, *Discourse of Episcopacy*, 220; Edwards, *Some New Discoveries*, 142–44.

110. Edwards, *Arminian Doctrines*, 215; Dodwell, *Separation of Churches*; Harmsen, "Henry Dodwell."

111. High-flyer was not a complement, but Hickes redefined it in responding to his opponent Matthew Tindal: "I also profess to be a high-flyer, whose Endeavour is to fly upon the wings of the old Principles, which you ridicule as upon the Wings of angels, to my Saviour, to the General Assembly, to the Church (the High Church) of the Firstborn who are enrolled in Heaven, and to the Spirits of Just Men made perfect." Hickes, *Two Treatises*, 1:56.

112. Hickes, *Some Discourses*, 11, 12.

113. Hickes, *Some Discourses*, 45–49.

114. Hickes, *Apologetical Vindication*, 119.

Edwards was clearly not the most strident critic of the Latitudinarian church, but surprisingly tolerant and mild in his criticism.

Like Dodwell, Hickes "inveigh'd with uncommon Zeal and Fierceness against the *Dissenters*" who had left the church. Yet he "openly and publicly" refused to participate. And like Dodwell, Edwards accused him of misrepresenting the Fathers; i.e., fabricating a "*Trojan* Horse" to justify the use of "Popish Tenets and Practices" in the church.[115] From his works, it is clear that establishing the altar, the eucharist as a sacrifice, and the clerical priesthood ranked very high in Hickes's agenda.[116]

Edwards did not simply oppose such practices because they were associated with Rome, but because he believed them to be clearly unbiblical. With regard to priests, he maintained that from the time of the New Testament, all believers were called a "holy" or "Royal Priesthood, 1 Pet. 2:9." Formerly there were no clerical priests. The confusion stemmed from the English word priest, which he said "is derived from and is an Abbreviature of the French *Prestre* or *Prêtre*, and the German *Priester*, which are from the Latin *Presbyter*, an *Elder*."[117] Quoting Bacon, he said that the ambiguity was caused by having one word in a translation serve for two in the original. In this case, priest is used for both πρεσβύτερος (minister) and ἱερεὺς (sacrificer). Furthermore said Edwards, the word for priest in the New Testament was closely associated with both pagan sacrificing and Jewish sacrificing. Both deny that Christ had come.[118] Edwards enlisted Bishop Stillingfleet in support of his understanding:

> When in the Primitive Church, the Name of *Priest* came to be attributed to Gospel Ministers, in the process of Time, Corruptions increasing in the Church, those names that were used by the Christians by way of Analogy and Accommodation, brought in the Things themselves primarily intended by those Names: So by the Metaphorical Names of *Priests* and *Altars*, at last came up the Sacrifice of the Mass, without which they thought the Names of *Priest* and *Altar* were insignificant.[119]

Then to be clear, he added that although Christians are to offer their bodies as a living sacrifice (Rom. 12:1), the Cross means that there is no

---

115. Edwards, *Arminian Doctrines*, 215–16; Edwards, *Patrologia*, 15.
116. Hickes, *Two Treatises*; Edwards, *Preacher, Third Part*, 11–13.
117. Edwards, *Brief Confutation*, 332, 343.
118. Edwards, *Brief Confutation*, 332–44.
119. Edwards, *Brief Confutation*, 345; Edward Stillingfleet, *Irenicum*, 265.

longer any repeated sacrifices for sin as practiced before Christ. Although there were certainly errors among some of the early Fathers, most, including Cyprian, Ambrose, Chrysostom, and Augustine, understood that the words sacrifice or oblation in a Christian sense must be metaphorical. And historically in the Church of England Articles, liturgy, catechism, or homilies, "she doth not any where call the Sacrament a Sacrifice," but a "*continual Remembrance.*"[120] In fact recalled Edwards, even in the Old Testament, the physical sacrifice was given as a symbol of the spiritual reality of obedience and a broken spirit (1 Sam 15:22; Ps 51:16–17).[121]

Even more extreme than Hickes, was J. Scandret (fl. ca. 1700) whom Edwards cited for arguing that Christians must have physical sacrifices because Jews and Pagans did. Scandret concluded that "the offering of the Material Oblations by earthly Priests, in the great Christian Service, is not only [. . .] the chief Office [of the Priesthood]; but it is the whole." Edwards's reaction: "It is vain to talk with a Man who professes himself to be of the Church of *England*, and yet knows not that it is a *Christian* Church, not a *Pagan* or *Jewish* one," hoping that Hickes and his colleagues would do the necessary rebuking.[122] Commenting on the coherence of the sacrificial system, Edwards reasoned that without a physical sacrifice or traditional priest, there is clearly no need for a physical altar in the gospel and those early Fathers who spoke of it were in error. The early church only used a wooden table for Holy Communion, which is why the Church of England liturgy speaks of "*the Lord's Table*," never an altar. Men like Hickes and Scandret argued for the altar "by alledging the very *same Texts*, and using the very *same Arguments* that the Popish Writers" use. About the only difference these men had with Rome was the doctrine of Transubstantiation, but Edwards noted that at times, "they speak favorably of it."[123] It does not appear that Hickes or Dodwell replied to Edwards in print. Unlike Dodwell, Hickes did not return to the church. He was consecrated a suffragan bishop by three deprived bishops and remained in what he believed to be "the surviving remnant of the true apostolic church" until he died.[124]

---

120. Edwards, *Brief Confutation*, 360–61.
121. Edwards, *Brief Confutation*, 347–61.
122. Edwards, *Brief Confutation*, 365; Scandret, *Sacrifice*, 104–06, 114.
123. Edwards, *Brief Confutation*, 370, 373.
124. Harmsen, "George Hickes," *ODNB*.

William Oldisworth

Edwards was compelled to respond to another high-flyer, William Oldisworth (1680–1734), who wrote against heresy, which he believed was caused by men who view their private interpretation of Scripture as "*the Sole Absolute, Arbitrary and Uncontrollable Umpire, the only Rule, and last Resort in Matters of Religion: and under that Shelter Bully the Church and its Councils*." Among those he had in mind were Locke, Hobbes, Spinoza, Milton, and Toland.[125] Oldisworth was the son of a rector and had studied at Lincoln College, Oxford under George Hickes, but did not graduate. He wrote his three-volume *A Dialogue between Timothy and Philatheus* against Matthew Tindal's *A Defence of the Rights of the Christian Church*, which had provoked a literary outburst for its attack on ecclesiastical authority and on Christianity in general, leading the House of Commons to order it burned. Late in life, Tindal published *Christianity as Old as the Creation*, the definitive work on Deism.

While Edwards certainly did not agree with the elevation of reason in theology by Locke, Tindal, and others, he was just as offended by Oldisworth's opposite position, a distortion of 2 Peter 1:20, which Edwards illustrated with a number of quotations, such as "No man is to judge for himself what he is to believe and practice" and "*Private Judgment* cannot in Verture of its own Authority, Determine a Man in his Religion." In place of private judgment, Oldisworth substituted "Implicit Faith" in the "Authority of the Church," which has been entrusted with "a Sacred *Depositum*."[126] To Edwards this was senseless in that "we may *enquire* whether there be a God, and a Future State, and a Judgment to come, but we are not allow'd to *say* and *affirm* that there are such Things."[127] Such faith, he argued, is blind faith and contrary to biblical commands to understand and defend what we believe.

In quoting Oldisworth's attempt to substantiate his position with his own interpretation of how Jesus operated on earth, Edwards confessed that he wasn't sure "whether [these words] betray more Ignorance or Presumption."[128]

---

125. Oldisworth, *Essay*, xiii–xiv.
126. Oldisworth, *Essay*, 32, 41, 89–90.
127. Edwards, *Some New Discoveries*, 147–49, 151.
128. Edwards, *Some New Discoveries*, 153.

> Our *Saviour* and his *Apostles* [...] where-ever they came, they always began their Mission by applying to the Church: thus Christ *resorted* to the *Synagogues*, taught in the Temple, and reasoned with the *Doctors*, even at his first setting out in the Exercise of his Priestly Office [...] Such regard had our Saviour and his Inspired followers to the Publick, that the first thing they attempted to obtain, was the Judgment and Authority of the Church, etc.[129]

Edwards found it ironic that Oldisworth as a layman advocated vesting complete authority in the corporate church so that no individual Christians, whether clergy or laity, have even the right to think or speak for themselves—including members of the Church of England. But what Oldisworth wrote concerning the Presbyterians, Edwards found slanderous and offensive: "They breed their Pupils [...] to an Aversion for Philosophy and Sound Reasoning, [...] more Dangerous [...] than that of the *Papists* and *Schoolmen*." Oldisworth also accused them of completely rejecting the church fathers, treating other churches with contempt, while calling themselves alone the elect and claiming to be omniscient.[130] Edwards reassured himself that anyone who knows the author will see this caricature of Presbyterians as "malicious Fiction." Unfortunately, by essentially "locking up the Bible," Oldisworth is destroying the foundation of the Reformation and "paving the way to Rome."[131]

Charles Leslie

A fourth individual who appears throughout Edwards's complaints against the high-flyers is Charles Leslie, whom Edwards identified as a friend of Oldisworth.[132] Leslie was so alarmed in studying Tillotson's sermons that he wrote *The Charge of Socinianism against Dr. Tillotson Considered* to expose him as a closet Socinian. Commenting on Tillotson's sermon on Philippians 2:6, Leslie accused him of inverting the meaning of the text to essentially deny the Incarnation:

> Instead of *he thought it not robbery*, οὐχ αρπαγμὸν ἡγήσατο, the doctor would have the sense to be, *he did not arrogate to*

---

129. Oldisworth, *Essay*, 142.
130. Oldisworth, *Essay*, 161–62.
131. Edwards, *Some New Discoveries*, 156, 159.
132. Edwards, *Some New Discoveries*, 159.

himself to be equal with God, though it is quite contrary to the words which are literally translated, *he thought it not robbery to be equal* [. . .] i.e., he did make himself equal: he did not arrogate himself to be equal [. . .] *He did*, says the text: *he did not*, says Dr. T.[133]

Tillotson had paraphrased the text as "he made no ostentation of his divinity" and commented that this was the "true meaning [. . .] because it makes the sense much more easy and current."[134] Leslie viewed Tillotson's understanding of this passage as the same as that given in *The Brief History of the Unitarians* and concluded his analysis by calling Tillotson a Hobbist, hoping to arouse the faithful to action: "These are not tares sown in the night, and by stealth; but it is rooting up all revealed religion in the noonday, and exposing of Christianity to the contempt and buffoonery of atheistical wits."[135] In addition to railing against the deceased archbishop, Leslie also named Bishop Burnet as a Socinian for explaining the meaning of John 1:14 just like the Unitarians.[136] As noted earlier, Edwards had difficulty with the exegesis of Latitudinarians, but he refused to call them Socinians.

Leslie came to the defense of Bishop Ofspring Blackall (1655–1716) of Exeter in a pamphlet war with Bishop Hoadly over the Glorious Revolution. Blackall and Leslie argued against the legitimacy of the revolution, which eventually resulted in a warrant for Leslie's arrest, which he evaded by traveling incognito and writing under aliases. An outspoken opponent of Roman Catholics, not to mention Deists, Jews, Quakers, and Socinians, Leslie followed the high-flyer line of thought regarding the central importance of High Church ceremonialism with as much provocation and invective as any of his associates.[137]

During 1704–09, Leslie published a semi-weekly, successively named "The Observator," "The Rehearsal of the Observator," and "The Rehearsal" under the pseudonym Philalethes. Structured as a dialog between the publication and a "country-man," it served Leslie's objective of promoting his views on selected theological and ecclesiastical issues. Featured in the issues from August 2, 1707 to September 3, 1707 were

133. Leslie, *Charge of Socinianism*, 2:559.
134. Tillotson, "Concerning the Divinity," 3:319.
135. Leslie, *Some Reflections*, 2:604–05.
136. Leslie, *Some Reflections*, 2:607.
137. Cornwall, "Charles Leslie," *ODNB*.

attacks on Edwards regarding predestination, his positive comments on dissenters who conform in doctrine compared to the conforming clergy who do not, his representation of Archbishop Laud's theology and Arminianism in general, and his view of the unity of the church. Of the latter, "The Doctor is very Angry at any who mention the Unity of the Church," citing a sermon where Edwards said, "But it is high time to learn Sobriety, and to be sensible of the infinite Mischief that hath lurk'd under the pretense of advancing the Unity of the Church." The context of Edwards's words were,

> That to maintain the *Unity* of the *Church*, every thing must give way [to] the Scriptures themselves. *The Unity of the Church*, saith Mr. Thorndike [1598–1672], *is the Sovereign Law, to which all other Laws, tho' never so much Enacted by the Apostles, never so evidently couched in the Scriptures, are necessarily subordinate.* A very strange Passage! But it expresses the Sence of too many among us. And so does that of another of our Divines, *It is better*, saith he, *to indulge Mens Vices and Debaucheries than their Consciences.* A wretched saying! But too much in vogue among them that prefer Ceremony to Substantial Religion and Godliness.[138]

Along with his nonjuring brethren, Edwards mocked him for his commitment to church unity:

> Mr. Leslie, mauls the Dissenters and Nonconformists, and roars against them as Schismatics, and yet lives in a profess'd Separation from the Church of *England*. Is it not entertaining, to hear a Man cry *the Church, the Church*, and yet to see him abandon the Church of which he was a Member?[139]

Edwards also found fault with Leslie's scholarship when he attempted to prove not only that Annas and Caiaphas held the office of high priest simultaneously, but that there had been two high priests from the time of Aaron's sons Eleazar and Ithamar.[140]

---

138. Edwards, *One Nation*, 18; Leslie, *View*, 4:49; Thorndike, *Epilogue*, Book 3:378.
139. Edwards, *Arminian Doctrines*, 216.
140. Edwards, *Exercitations*, 247–48.

HENRY HAMMOND

Of all the seventeenth-century authors Edwards referenced favorably, perhaps the most common and surprising (to those who view Edwards as a rigid Calvinist) was Henry Hammond. From Thomas Edwards's generation, Hammond was polished, respected, and about as widely influential as any churchman in his day, not only as a biblical scholar but in church and state political circles. He was appointed to the Westminster Assembly, "his invincible Loyalty to his Prince and Obedience to his Mother the Church not being so valid arguments against his nomination, as the repute of his Learning and Verture were," but he did not attend, perhaps because he anticipated the impending peril to conformers.[141] King Charles I said of him, that he was "the most natural Orator he ever heard."[142] Although influenced like most of his generation by Puritan and Reformed teachers, "by the end of the 1630s, Hammond, like Chillingworth, had begun to move away from Reformed Christianity," influenced to some degree by Dudley Diggs (1610–43), who had "probably the largest collection of Socinian works in England at the time."[143] In part because of his theological reorientation, Hammond is not easy to categorize.[144]

Read superficially, it might seem that Hammond was Reformed. Surprisingly prominent in his theological discourse was the Covenant of Grace. He was unwavering that salvation comes by grace alone.[145] He wrote that anyone who thinks that justification or salvation can be attained by personal righteousness or good works done by the grace of God "deceives himself." It is only "the free mercy of God in Christ, 'not imputing of sin;' and so I am to deny my own righteousness, renounce all trust in that for salvation."[146] He spoke of "the second Person" as "this fountain of all inherent and imputed righteousness, of sanctifying and justifying grace, [who] takes its flight, and rests upon the Christian soul."[147] He affirmed belief in the Trinity, Incarnation and original sin, but upon closer examination, it can be seen that his underlying definitions of familiar Reformed terms differed from common understanding. In addition, the

141. Fell, *Life*, 26.
142. Fell, *Life*, 97.
143. Mortimer, *Reason and Religion*, 89.
144. McGiffert, "Henry Hammond," 255–57.
145. Allison, *Rise of Moralism*, 99.
146. Hammond, *Practical Catechism*, 73.
147. Hammond, *Thirty-One Sermons*, 1:302.

sophistication of some of his theological ideas challenge easy classification. For example, in Hammond's covenant of grace,

> there is pardon reached out to all truly penitent sinners, and assistance promised and engaged, and bestowed upon very easy conditions, humility and prayer and affiance in Him; and this in a degree proportionable to what now is required of us, as far as is truly sufficient, and can reasonably be desired by a rational agent, and as is reconcileable with that liberty which is necessary to be reserved to the will of man, to make him capable of virtue and vice, and consequently of reward and punishment.[148]

So saving grace for Hammond was not actually the unconditional imputation of the righteousness of Christ by God's sovereign election, but rather contingent on the individual's penitence and obedience. In effect, it was the imputation of the individual's own imperfect righteousness supplemented by that of Christ as a "gloss or tincture" by which sins are forgiven.[149]

The central objective of Hammond's theology was to help sustain the Church of England, which became very challenging during Parliamentary rule. Not unlike Roman Catholicism, for Hammond Episcopalian government was not simply one option among many, but the only acceptable form, an essential means for establishing the authenticity and authority of the church since the time of Christ. Accordingly, his soteriology supported his ecclesiology from the position that the church was necessary for salvation because original sin could be forgiven only through baptism and if people did not join the church, there was no salvation.[150] Furthermore,

> Hammond realised that the ideas of Socinus could be used to defend an episcopal church far more effectively than the theology of Arminius, not least because Socinus divided the natural from the supernatural in a way that Arminius did not.[151]

Supernatural grace involved too much mystery for Socinus, which is why he emphasized natural ethics. But Hammond only appropriated from Socinianism what he found useful. Unlike Socinians, he believed

---

148. Hammond, *Miscellaneous Theological Works*, 2:175. In seventeenth- and eighteenth-century usage, affiance meant to trust in God. See Johnson, *Dictionary*.
149. Hammond, *Practical Catechism*, 26.
150. Mortimer, *Reason and Religion*, 138–39.
151. Mortimer, *Reason and Religion*, 119.

that salvation through Christ applied to all, even those who lived before the Cross. Actually, "Grotius (not Arminius) was his favourite modern theologian and it was Grotius's blend of Arminian and Socinian ideas that Hammond most admired."[152]

The practical implication of Hammond's Covenant of Grace is what Neil Lettinga has called the Caroline Anglican Moralism, promulgated by his *Practical Catechism*, which effectively merged the Puritan doctrines of the Covenant of Grace into the Covenant of Works, thus requiring obedience for salvation. In Hammond's view, this made sense since he did not believe that Adam's fall meant that his posterity was unable to take any positive steps toward salvation as taught in traditional Reformed theology. However he rejected the view that anyone could earn their salvation, stating that it was by grace alone and charged Puritans with antinomianism for separating justification from sanctification.[153]

Traditional Protestant understanding differed from that of the Catholics in two important respects: by grace alone, the righteousness of Christ was *imputed* to the sinner resulting in the *event* of justification after which God's grace followed to enable the *process* of sanctification. In Catholic thinking justification and sanctification were integrated into a single process and by the grace of God, the righteousness of Christ is *infused* into the sinner enabling him to live an increasingly righteous life. Hammond rejected the doctrine of imputation since

> if Christ's active obedience were thus imputed to me, then by that I should be reckoned of, and accepted by God as if I had fulfilled the whole law, and never sinned; and then I should have no need that Christ should suffer for my sins.[154]

Thus Hammond reasoned that the doctrine of imputation makes the atonement unnecessary. Instead we should understand that Christ's own active obedience simply demonstrated that he was able to "suffer or satisfy for us" but "not supply the place of ours, or make ours [. . .] less necessary [. . .] Our renewed obedience and sanctification [. . .] is still most indispensably required."[155] In essence, our weak faith and imperfect obedience (provided it is "sincere, honest, faithful"), worthless though they be, are imputed to us by "free grace purchased and sealed to

---

152. Mortimer, *Reason and Religion*, 120, 137.
153. Lettinga, "Covenant Theology," 659, 662, 664.
154. Hammond, *Practical Catechism*, 25–26.
155. Hammond, *Practical Catechism*, 26–27.

us by the death of Christ" so that our obedience is accepted and we are pardoned.[156]

As holy living is necessarily part of sanctification, Hammond realized that the Covenant of Grace (Works) would have been irrelevant to justification since Protestants (in Hammond's view) understood justification occurring prior to sanctification. Citing Ezekiel 18:24 and Matthew 18:34-45, he solved this problem by making sanctification a two-step process, teaching that

> the first part of sanctification, the beginning of a new life, must be first had before God pardons or justifies any: then when God is thus reconciled to the new convert upon his vow of a new life, He gives him more grace, enables and assists him for that state of sanctification, wherein if he makes good use of that grace, he then continues to enjoy this favour and justification; but if he perform not his vow, proceed not in Christian holy life, but relapse into wasting acts or habits of sin, then God chargeth again all his former sins upon him.[157]

Clearly, Hammond's soteriology did not comport with Edwards, but by the time Edwards discovered it, Hammond's ideas had been spread by a number of his disciples. *A Practical Catechism* inspired Richard Allestree (1619–81), Adam Littleton (1627–94), Jeremy Taylor, Herbert Thorndyke (1598–1672), and others to popularize and liberalize the Caroline Anglican Moralism. Most sought-after among their works was Allestree's *The Whole Duty of Man*. With approximately forty-five editions printed during Edwards's adult life, it was estimated that there were enough copies for 10 percent of English households.[158] *The Preacher* contained Edwards's critical comments of this work, which he said was well received because it did not mention the "Principles" or "Doctrines" of Christianity. Edwards was emphatic that Christian ethics is necessarily based on Christian truth. "Fearing and loving of God and keeping his Commandments, are Duties that can't be practised aright without a due Knowledge." False doctrine will not provide the foundation for good ethical behavior or happiness.[159] What people need to know is: who God

---

156. Hammond, *Practical Catechism*, 27, 79.

157. Hammond, *Practical Catechism*, 79. For a more complete discussion of Hammond's soteriology, see Lettinga, "Covenant Theology" and McGiffert, "Henry Hammond," 255–85.

158. Sommerville, *Popular Religion*, 32.

159. Edwards, *Preacher*, 49–52.

is, who Christ is, what does it mean to be saved, and what happens after we die. He said that *The Whole Duty* talks about trusting in God, but Hammond makes no mention of saving faith. It talks about the duty of people to their magistrates and ministers, but not of the officials' duty to the common people. It defines fasting as punishment and allows cheating in business because that practice has been so engrained in the culture of commerce.[160]

Without referencing Allestree, Edwards responded with his own version of the whole duty of man in a third volume of *Theologia Reformata*, organized into four parts, each part containing between six and twenty-four discourses. The first part covered sanctification, regeneration, good works, the conscience, diligence in work, and imitating Christ, and for each he clearly linked theological principles to behavior. For example, in the discourse on regeneration, after beginning with Jesus telling Nicodemus that he must be born again, Edwards explained how that leads to right living, citing Paul's words "if any Man be in Christ, he actually is a new Creature" (2 Cor 5:17), explaining from 1 Corinthians 4 and Ephesians 3 that the "three Principal Faculties which are to be Chang'd are the Understanding, the Will, and the Affections."[161] The second part began with the beatitudes from the Sermon on the Mount followed by various biblical admonitions to "walk circumspectly" (Eph 5:15–16), for fathers to lead their families (Josh 24:15), to deny one's self as a true disciple (Matt 16:24), and to persevere (Rev 3:11). Discourses of the third part, subtitled "*the Helps and Assistances which are serviceable towards the promoting of all other* Graces *and* Duties," included topics such as religious vows (Ps 66:13–14), not associating with the wrong sort of people (Ps 119:115), and avoiding gluttony and drunkenness (Luke 21:34). The final part contained essays for motivating Christians to be diligent because of the rewards of joy and wisdom resulting from obedience in addition to the judgment that comes from continual sin.[162]

Despite Hammond's anti-Calvinistic views and his influence on men like Allestree, there is something especially interesting in how Edwards used Hammond's works. Clearly Hammond was neither Calvinist nor even a solid Arminian, yet Edwards referred to him in a positive manner more often than he did negatively. More than half of his works contain

---

160. Edwards, *Preacher, Third Part*, 301–28.
161. Edwards, *Theologia*, 3:25, 28.
162. Edwards, *Theologia*, 3:The Table.

dozens of references to Hammond, most of an exegetical nature. In responding to Whitby's *Four Discourses*, Edwards used Hammond several times to support his case against Whitby.[163] Refuting Whitby's claim that if God had decreed the commission of sin (as implied by the Westminster Confession of Faith), he would then be the author of sin, Edwards analyzed one Hebrew word and three Greek words often translated as "suffer" or "permit." Reviewing the sense of numerous passages along with Hammond's paraphrase of four different texts, Edwards concluded that the confession is biblical because the examples consistently show that "God *wills* that which he doth *not approve of*."[164]

Perhaps Hammond himself did not always realize how his own exegesis might be used. Interpreting Acts 4:27–28, Edwards said that Hammond was

> forc'd to yield to the Conviction which these words carry'd with them [that certain people would arrest, torture and crucify Jesus] yet after this he staggers and falters, and tells us that tho' God decreed these things, he *decreed not that the Jews should do them, but only permitted them to do them*.[165]

In the appendix to that essay in *The Arminian Doctrines Condemn'd*, Hammond continued to be cited against Lightfoote's defense of Whitby. It was not as though there were no solidly Reformed writers for Edwards to use—and he did use them. Rather it appears that he was attempting to promote church unity in his works by demonstrating consensus on various questions from theologically diverse scholars. At times Edwards spoke favorably of Hammond's theology, though it was not always what he expected. In his catechism, Hammond asked why God would have allowed everyone to suffer for the sins of one man. Edwards found Hammond's answer "very remarkable" in that he "freely own's God's *wisdom* in the matter of Original Sin, and the Punishment that attends it."[166]

Despite the numerous instances where Hammond's insights proved useful to Edwards, such was not always the case and Edwards did not hesitate to point them out. He thought Hammond too narrow in his understanding of the coming of the Kingdom of God as referring to

---

163. Edwards, *Arminian Doctrines*, 158–61, 218, 234–43.
164. Edwards, *Arminian Doctrines*, 160.
165. Edwards, *Veritas*, 109–10.
166. Edwards, *Veritas*, 302; Hammond, *Practical Catechism*, 4.

God's judgment on Jews beginning in the first century.[167] He accused Hammond of "corrupting the Text" by seeing the destruction of Jerusalem in scriptural passages where it is clearly unwarranted.[168] He found Hammond in error for failing to understand imprecatory passages (e.g., David's psalms) in a literal sense; instead, he saw them as "really no more than so many Testimonies of his [David's] assured Confidence that God that hath made him such sure Promises, will make them good to him in his preservation, and that Disappointment and Discomfiture of his Enemies."[169]

Edwards was well aware of Hammond's Reformed shortcomings as noted in his comments on the correspondence between Bishop Robert Sanderson and Hammond over the former's Reformed credentials. Edwards accused him along with others of trying to pressure Sanderson "by foul Play" "to quit *Calvinism*, and to declare on the *Arminian* side." According to Edwards, Hammond had "persuaded himself" from some documentation that Sanderson "was an Arminian as well as himself," but Edwards said Sanderson was diplomatic in representing all sides fairly and another letter proves that the bishop "retain'd his *Calvinistical* Sentiments to the Day of his Death."[170] Edwards quoted Sanderson:

> The manifold cunning of the Arminians to advance their own party [. . .] in bragging out some of their private tenets, as if they were the received, established Doctrine of the Church of England, by forcing the words of the Articles or Common Prayer Book to a sense which appeareth not to have been intended therein.[171]

Certainly Sanderson was not a strict Calvinist, but in Edwards's judgment, he was a "*Calvinist* as to the main, which is enough for my purpose."[172] In his final letter to Hammond, Edwards quoted Sanderson as saying that "it is Impossible to maintain the Doctrine of Universal

167. Edwards, *Theologia*, 2:163.

168. Edwards, *Veritas*, 57.

169. Hammond, *Paraphrase*, 2:136; Edwards, *Theologia*, 2:202.

170. Edwards, *Arminian Doctrines*, 240–43.

171. Sanderson, *Pax Ecclesiæ*, 5:263–64; Edwards, *Arminian Doctrines*, 112.

172. Sanderson is difficult to categorize. He clearly did not like Puritanism, but he preached Puritan themes. He did not like Arminianism, but "he seemed to assimilate certain linguistic or rhetorical habits typical of the Arminians" and made common cause with Laud. In short he was a moderate with very definite views. See Lake, "Serving God," 104; Edwards, *Arminian Doctrines*, 244.

Grace in that manner as the Remonstrants are said to assert it." According to Edwards, Sanderson's Calvinism "forced Dr. *Hammond* to forsake some part of *Arminianism,* at least in appearance."[173]

---

173. Edwards, *Preacher, Third Part,* 291–94.

6

Ecclesiology, Conformity and Nonconformity

Despite Jesus' emphasis on the unity of the church in John 17, differences over ecclesiology have been a major cause of church division throughout Christian history. Although the immediate cause in 1054 is often given as the addition of the filioque clause to the Nicene Creed, Rome's long-standing claim of papal supremacy was no doubt fundamental to all of the East-West tension. Following the Protestant Reformation itself, much of the unresolved discord was over ecclesiastical doctrines, particularly church government and the sacraments. Thomas Cranmer made a heroic attempt to forge a theological reformation within the Church of England, while Henry VIII only wanted an administrative break. But almost as soon as the Catholic threat was no longer so imminent, English Protestants began to quarrel, dividing over liturgy, sacraments, church government, and other doctrines. With the return of Charles II, there was hope by many who would eventually be part of the Great Ejection that a peaceful settlement was possible. But Charles was not strong enough to withstand pressure from the Anglican Royalists who wanted revenge after their suppression during the Commonwealth era and Parliament of 1660 had little sympathy for dissent.

During the latter part of the seventeenth century, there were a number of prominent voices calling for peace and unity in the church, generally from three perspectives. As explained in the previous chapter, high-flyers strongly condemned dissent and nonconformity, especially on matters of liturgy, to the point of equating separation from the church with "*sinning against the Holy Ghost.*" Edwards found their hypocrisy telling since later as non-jurors, they refused to attend services, protesting the exile of James II.[1] Like some Puritans, they were firm in their convictions regarding worship and unwilling to compromise.

A second perspective at the other extreme may be seen in John Locke, who thought of himself as a Christian, despite challenges from Edwards, Stillingfleet, and others. Locke emphasized toleration to the point that he regarded most all doctrines traditionally considered as essential as nonessential. In addition to believing Jesus to be the Messiah, a Christian should believe that God is our omnipotent and merciful creator and be sorry for personal sins. But for the sake of peace, we must simply agree to disagree on controversial issues such as the deity of Christ.

Those holding a third perspective, not as accommodating as Locke, were the Latitudinarians. With Locke, they emphasized peace and unity and called on everyone to use their God-given reason to understand apparent mysteries of the faith. They valued ethical behavior as the essence of Christianity over doctrine and liturgy and had favored accommodation for those ejected. Although they claimed allegiance to the XXXIX Articles, their understanding of it was at odds with most traditional interpretations.

This chapter primarily concerns Edwards's position on those aspects of ecclesiology which figured prominently in seventeenth-century schisms, namely the sacraments, liturgy, and church government. Not included here are other topics of ecclesiology, which Edwards did address, including the church understood as visible and invisible, the church militant and triumphant, the keys of the kingdom, authority and power of the church, church discipline, qualifications for ministers, and the use of Sunday.[2]

THE SACRAMENTS

In his *Theologia Reformata,* Edwards systematically covered the attributes of God, the nature and work of Christ, soteriology, the church, sacraments, and church liturgy. This work was not the only place where these doctrines were addressed, but for most, it was his most thorough development. He began his discussion of the sacraments in the third discourse

---

1. Edwards, *Arminian Doctrines,* 215–16; Dodwell, *Separation of Churches,* 17.
2. Edwards, *Preacher, Third Part,* 38–40.

of "Article IX - I believe in the holy Catholick Church" by placing them in the context of public worship. Though not explained in detail until Moses, Edwards believed that we can see the sacraments being established by *"Divine Command"* when God blessed the seventh day of creation.[3] Regular worship was reinforced by Jesus' regular attendance at the synagogue and by the practice of the early church. Both the Old and New Testaments teach that the sacraments are to be observed publicly.[4]

Before discussing his own understanding, Edwards refuted two views at variance with the standard Protestant position. In the first group were those who opposed using any term not found in Scripture, including sacrament. Edwards referred to Jerome who said that when a concept in Scripture is clear, the name given it is irrelevant. Sacraments, Edwards said, are important spiritual matters symbolized by a physical sign or event, some he called *"Occasional"* and others, *"Extraordinary."* In addition to circumcision and the Passover, manna, for example, was a sacrament of God's supernatural provision in the wilderness.[5]

Rome by contrast, abused the notion of sacrament, fixing the number at seven, though no writer before Hugh of St. Victor spoke of seven. Edwards noted that in the patristic church, there were a variety of opinions. Cyprian said there were two sacraments and according to Jerome, *"there are as many Sacraments as Words"* in the book of Revelation. In Edwards's thinking a sacrament required both a *"Word of Institution"* and a *"visible sign"* and by those two criteria, only baptism and the Lord's Supper qualify for the New Testament church.[6]

Edwards saw these two sacraments as *"so sacred and venerable, so solemn and remarkable, and of so great use in the Church"* that they were foreshadowed in various forms in the Old Testament: the Eucharist, not only in the Passover, but in the bread and wine of Melchizedek, manna and shewbread of the tabernacle and temple; and baptism in the Red Sea crossing (1 Cor 10) and in the laver of regeneration (Tit 3:5). In his sermon on Song of Solomon 7:2, he even saw them symbolically represented by the heap of wheat and naval. He used the example of a unborn child receiving nutrients through the umbilical cord to illustrate to anabaptists

---

3. Edwards, *Theologia*, 1:541.
4. Edwards, *Theologia*, 1:541–53, 581–82.
5. Edwards, *Theologia*, 1:553.
6. Edwards, *Theologia*, 1:554–55.

that baptizing infants of Christian parents is also valid.[7] Citing Maimonides and Dr. Hammond, Edwards saw baptismal ceremony as derived from the Jewish practice of baptizing proselytes from paganism. More obvious, the Lord's Supper was a fulfillment of the Jewish Passover.[8]

With the ancient church, Edwards defined sacrament as "a visible *Sign* of an invisible Grace."[9] Not only are the sacraments mystical and spiritual signs, but Edwards believed that they speak so as to make the inward grace effectual, with respect to the Eucharist, as "Spiritual Nourishment and Refreshment."[10] Furthermore, they remind us of our covenant "with God, with his Church, and of the Church with God," clearly illustrated in the life of Abraham and some of his descendants, proclaiming the intrinsic unity of God's people. Finally, the sacraments serve as seals of God's covenants. Sacraments confirm to us all the promises of God's Word. Those who disregard or belittle the sacraments, like the Quakers and Socinians, "rob us of our Assurance of Happiness."[11]

Baptism

Edwards said that baptism was given to us by Christ so that we might better understand the gospel. The water reminds us that because of sin, we need to be spiritually cleansed—a work of divine grace.[12] The importance of baptism can be seen in that it (along with belief) was explicitly commanded by Christ as a "Condition of Salvation" (Mark 16:16; John 4:1), the baptism being "made effectual by the Spirit of Regeneration."[13] A recurring emphasis throughout his discussion is the relationship between the physical sign and the spiritual reality.

Against Catholic teaching, Edwards reasoned that the baptism of John was "of the same Nature" as that of Jesus, as both concerned repentance and forgiveness (Mark 1:4). Some objected that John's subjects had never heard of the Holy Spirit. Edwards replied that John's baptism implied the promised Spirit just as Abraham's faith the promised Savior.

---

7. Edwards, *Exercitations*, 130–40.
8. Edwards, *Theologia*, 1:556–57.
9. Edwards, *Theologia*, 1:560.
10. Edwards, *Exercitations*, 134, 378–94.
11. Edwards, *Theologia*, 1:560–61.
12. Edwards, *Theologia*, 2:175.
13. Edwards, *Theologia*, 1:562.

And despite the debate over the nature of John's baptism, nowhere does Scripture mention someone being rebaptized.[14]

Edwards began his list of duties for Christian parents by instructing them to have their children "admitted into the Church by Christian Baptism," the church being regarded as a covenant community. He compared infant baptism to Jewish circumcision and cautioned parents and godparents to view baptism as a most "sacred and solemn" sacrament, so as to avoid "mocking God."[15] Just as circumcision brought infants into the covenant community beginning with Abraham, so baptism functions under the New Covenant. Not only does baptism bring us into the church, but it sets us apart so that "we ought to be consecrated to God [...] from our very Infancy," like Samuel and Josiah.[16] From 1 Corinthians 7:14 he concluded that there is "a Federal and External Holiness under the Gospel, whereby the Children of the Faithful are Holy, and born so, and therefore are fit to be Partakers of the Privileges of the Church."[17]

Edwards acknowledged that those baptized as infants are not conscious of what is happening, the vow before God having been made on behalf of the child. But when we grow older, "we must take it upon Ourselves" and make it "our own." It is a vow to conscientiously obey God's law so as to walk "in the Ways of Holiness and Righteousness." We must not forget that as these vows are public vows, the Christian faith is not only about belief, but application and behavior in the public arena. Therefore he emphasized that each Christian must "let the World see that you are performing the Vows you made."[18]

Like circumcision, water baptism is a sign, signifying our membership in the covenant community of the church. But though baptism is seen as a physical act, "it is not a Ceremonial and Outward Purgation, but an Inward and Spiritual one that is able to make a Change in the Minds and Faculties of Men. And that is the Baptism of the Holy Ghost."[19] Edwards noted that Clarke thought that infants were qualified for baptism because of their innocence. Edwards reminded his readers that the

---

14. Edwards, *Theologia*, 1:562-63. Edwards apparently overlooked Acts 2:41; 18:25; 18:3-5 and other debatable passages.

15. Edwards, *Theologia*, 3:270-71.

16. Edwards, *Theologia*, 3:289.

17. Edwards, *Theologia*, 1:569-70.

18. Edwards, *Theologia*, 3:389. Note: irregular pagination, second occurrence; page signatures also reoccur.

19. Edwards, *Theologia*, 1:576-77.

fundamental reality of baptism is sin—original sin, which is the reason for the washing metaphor. "There can be no reason for [baptism] unless we believe [there is sin]."[20] "If infants were clean and pure," there would be no reason to baptize them.[21] Catholics teach that "Original Sin is wholly abolish'd by Baptism," but according to Edwards that is not what Augustine taught. For the truly regenerate, guilt is forgiven, but our corrupt nature and tendency to sin remains.

Although he did not agree with anabaptist practice of limiting baptism to adults, he did not think of them as such heretics as they had been called, noting that adult baptism was the practice of many in the ancient church.[22] In addition to distinguishing himself from anabaptists, Edwards also differentiated his view from Lutherans and Catholics in how faith is understood vis-à-vis infant baptism. "Our church holds that the faith of Parents [. . .] is to be interpreted to be the Faith of the Infants." By contrast, Lutherans believe that infants have the "Act of Faith" and Catholics the "Habit of Faith." The problem with these two views, said Edwards, is that both require some understanding and it is clear that infants have none. Therefore it is best to understand their faith as having been imputed from their parents, which is sufficient until they are able to exercise their own. In response to the anabaptist question of how conversion is possible for those with no understanding, Edwards answered from Luke 1:15: "God can communicate his Spirit to Infants and conferr Divine Blessings upon those that are not come to Years of Understanding."[23]

When we read that "baptism now saveth us" (1 Pet 3:21), it is not that there is some supernatural power in the waters of baptism. Water simply represents the "Cleansing and Purifying of the Soul by the grace which is exhibited by the Holy Ghost"[24] Regeneration is only by the power of the Holy Spirit; there is no "Physical Efficacy" in this sacrament.[25] Like most Protestants, he was very critical of Catholic sacramentalism, charging them with unbiblical idolatry.[26] As to the mode of baptism, Edwards

---

20. Edwards, *Preacher, Third Part*, 243.
21. Edwards, Veritas, 1:286.
22. Edwards, *Theologia*, 3:270–71.
23. Edwards, *Theologia*, 1:571.
24. Edwards, *Theologia*, 2:175.
25. Edwards, *Theologia*, 1:580–81.
26. Edwards, *Doctrines Controverted*, 391–92.

found sprinkling, pouring, immersion, and even substituting sand for water all equally acceptable.[27]

He was quite critical of the all too common problem of people coming to the ceremony too casually, a practice Edwards described as "abuse" and "profane."[28] He called upon his readers who had forgotten or failed to perform their vows to repent of their negligence, reminding them of Ecclesiastes 4: God takes no pleasure in fools who do not pay their vows.[29] To emphasize the seriousness of the matter, Edwards spoke of those who were properly baptized, but failed to pay their vows. "It is not baptism that will save them, if they neglect the Answer of a good Conscience." Citing Matthew 7:23, he said, "That sacramental water will be insignificant, if we defile and pollute ourselves with a sinful Life," naming Simon the Sorcerer and Julian the Apostate as baptized but unregenerate.[30]

Though Edwards addressed various issues regarding infant baptism, he did not directly address the controversy over baptismal regeneration and perseverance that erupted in England following Dort.[31] Responding to sermons by Bishop Ofspring Blackhall (1655–1716) and Dean of Canterbury George Stanhope (1660–1728), which had taught justification and regeneration being conferred in baptism, Edwards wrote,

> For any man sees, that if St. Paul, who so often speaks of *Justification*, had meant it of being entred into into [sic] Church of Christ by *Baptism*, he would at one time or other, or in one place or other have intimated as much. [. . .] But there is not one Syllable concerning this.[32]

He did say that baptized infants share in the New Covenant and that "baptism makes children visible Christians," but he did not believe

---

27. Edwards, *Theologia*, 1:575, 579. Edwards cited a Greek Orthodox account from the seventh century of a Jew being baptized with sand.

28. Edwards, *Theologia*, 2:416.

29. Edwards, *Theologia*, 3:390.

30. Edwards, *Theologia*, 3:503.

31. Collier, *Debating Perseverance*, 59–92. Probably a greater concern for Edwards than baptismal regeneration was not only that baptism was not taken seriously, but that it had become a social inconvenience and embarrassment, as William Sherlock noted: "Publick Baptism is now very much grown out of fashion [. . .] To baptize our Children privately, looks as if we were ashamed of the Christian profession." Sherlock, *Practical Discourse*, 305, 309.

32. Edwards, *Doctrine of Faith*, 433–34; See, Blackall, *Fourteen Sermons*, 347 and Stanhope, "Sermon VIII," 247.

that "Infants are *made Disciples* by being baptiz'd."[33] He qualified the efficaciousness of baptism with, "Infants are by the Holy Spirit cleans'd and purified in the right Use of Baptism."[34] Although we do not know in any given case whether a spiritual change accompanies baptism, "we must distinguish between Infants that are design'd for Happiness, and consequently partake of the real Vertue and efficacy of the Ordinance of Baptism, and others that partake only of the outward Rite, but are not Regenerate." In other words, for some infants, physical baptism truly signifies baptism of the Spirit, but for others, there is no regeneration.[35] On the other hand, he was not willing to "pronounce all Children damn'd that are not baptiz'd."[36] Fundamental to him was the profound mystery of many doctrines of the faith including the sacraments.

The Lord's Supper

Like baptism, there has been confusion historically regarding the Lord's Supper, the term Edwards preferred, although Eucharist was also acceptable because it is important to bring attention to the fact that it is a feast of thanksgiving. He rejected the notion of Jerome and others that "daily bread" in the Lord's Prayer refers to the bread of the sacrament. Like baptism, the Lord's Supper also calls our attention to our grievous sin, which caused the incomprehensible suffering and death of our Savior. Christ commanded us to observe it often, bringing us to hate our sin, "excite us to Holiness of Life" and instill in us a continual love for and thankfulness to God.[37] In an indirect criticism of the Catholic Church, Edwards made it clear how the elements should be understood. It is not necessary to use wine and the type of bread is not important. What is important is that the bread be broken, following Jesus' example, symbolizing that his body was broken for us.[38]

It was Laud who wanted to revert back to the stone altar, which Cranmer had replaced with a wooden communion table.[39] Edwards re-

---

33. Edwards, *Theologia*, 1:567, 569, 576.
34. Edwards, *Theologia*, 1:571.
35. Edwards, *Theologia*, 1:578.
36. Edwards, *Theologia*, 3:270.
37. Edwards, *Theologia*, 2:176.
38. Edwards, *Theologia*, 1:586–87.
39. Lane, "Before Hooker," 320.

sponded to the Laudian altar controversy by saying that the best way to determine how the Lord's Supper should be administered is to look at the teaching and example of Jesus. Jesus did not use an altar nor did he speak of one. Neither is there any mention of a sacrifice (associated with such an altar) in the New Testament except for Christ fulfilling the promises of the Old Covenant. Therefore we should not have a physical altar. Although some claim that an altar was used by the apostolic or patristic church and even the reformers, this, he argued, was unsubstantiated speculation.[40] Some attempted to introduce the idea of an altar by placing the communion table along the east wall of the church, but Edwards said, "the *Rubrick* Orders that *the Table at the Communion time shall stand where Morning and Evening Prayer is appointed to be said*" and pointed out that the *BCP* did not permit the communion table to be called an altar, nor did it permit the placing of candles on it.[41]

Edwards rejected both the Catholic teaching of transubstantiation and Lutheran consubstantiation as "unreasonable and absurd," stating that Calvin "subscrib'd" to the Augsburg Confession's position that "Christ's Body is truly, really, and substantially present in the Sacrament."[42] Although Lutherans often understand this statement to refer to the corporal presence of Christ, Edwards emphasized that Theodore Beza (1519–1605) understood Calvin to believe only in Christ's mystical and spiritual presence. Edwards named several Church of England leaders such as Bishop Andrewes and Archbishop Laud who leaned toward the Lutheran position, but Edwards said,

> when we come to examine the real Sense of *our Church* about this matter which some have done; yea, we find that we are not to interpret her Words in that manner which some have done; yea, we find that she utterly rejects the *Real Presence* of Christ's Body in the Sacrament.[43]

Edwards explained that the Lutheran view is a misunderstanding because a sacrament by definition has an outward part signifying an inward part. It is the bread and wine representing the body and blood, of which we partake by faith, that are the physical sign of the invisible

---

40. Edwards, *Preacher, Third Part*, 18–19.

41. Edwards, *Preacher, Third Part*, 22.

42. Like other Protestants, Edwards was also strongly opposed to the Mass and the Catholic practice of withholding the cup from the laity. See Edwards, *Theologia* 1.590.

43. Edwards, *Theologia*, 1:590–91.

and spiritual reality of the atonement. To avoid confusion, Edwards recommended saying that Christ's body is "*Sacramentally and Spiritually* present."[44]

He reminded his readers that this is consistent with what we read in the Old Testament, where the Passover was given as the physical sign of redemption. The Old Testament symbols prefigured the New Testament spiritual reality, as the Rock in the wilderness representing Christ (1 Cor 10:4) and the mothers of Ishmael and Isaac representing the Old and New Covenants. In the Exodus, a lamb died to deliver each family from bondage from Egypt; Christ died to deliver his people from bondage to sin. The themes of both the Passover and the Lord's Supper are sin, substitutionary death, and life renewed.[45] Edwards dwelt at length on the biblical admonition for self-examination so as not to partake unworthily and incur divine judgment.[46]

After addressing those who partake, but should not, Edwards spoke of four groups of people in his day who "*excuse themselves*," from Communion, but not for good reasons. Some think this sacrament was for an earlier time when the church was not mature or that physical signs are out of order in the new, spiritual dispensation. Another group refused to participate because they are unwilling to repent of their wayward living. A third group is simply negligent and apathetic. Finally, Edwards said there are those who are "*Scrupulous* and *Doubting*."[47] These people fall into one of four categories: those who are overly apprehensive because the sacrament signifies that which is too awesome, those who continually judge themselves to be unworthy and insufficiently prepared, those who object to taking communion with others whom they deem unworthy, and those who object to some ceremonial aspects, such as kneeling.[48]

To this last objection, Edwards said that kneeling should not be an issue simply because those with Catholic sympathies require it. Scripture does not require standing or sitting or prohibit kneeling. Edwards noted that all Protestants in the various continental churches do not follow the same practices regarding posture and it seems likely that Jesus might have conducted the Last Supper "*Leaning or Lying along*." Just because

---

44. Edwards, *Theologia*, 1:592.
45. Edwards, *Theologia*, 1:593–96.
46. Edwards, *Theologia*, 1:597–604.
47. Edwards, *Theologia*, 1:604–07.
48. Edwards, *Theologia*, 1:604–10.

"Papists kneel and worship the Hostie" does not mean that Protestants must worship it if they kneel. Should we refrain from sitting because that position is "abused by the *Socinians*"? Even the Pope "sometimes received the Communion *sitting*." Edwards continued to his logical conclusion, "And then we must not kneel at our *Prayers,* because the Papists do so." On the contrary, he argued, "The Lord's Supper is always receiv'd with Prayer and Thanksgiving [. . .] This Posture of Kneeling is enjoined only as a Thing Decent and Reverent, and not with the least Respect to the fond Opinion of the Church of *Rome*."[49] Edwards concluded by saying that he favored freedom because it is best not to cause offense to each person's conscience. The real issue is not posture, but whether people come to the Lord's table with a spiritual hunger to be satisfied. We must come in faith with a repentant heart.

On this point Edwards was not at all flexible. He recalled how Protestants like to compare Catholics to Pharisees for their outward display of religious pomp although there is no spiritual reality.

> Let me tell you, we have a great deal of this Popery among Protestants, and among ourselves in particular. We content ourselves with the naked Performance of Praying, Hearing, receiving the Sacrament, but we do not sufficiently concern ourselves for the mental and spiritual Part of these holy Exercises; and therein we discover our *Insincerity* and *Hypocrisy*.

He reminded his readers what Jesus thought of hypocrites, that such persons are not fit for the Kingdom of Heaven.[50]

The Lord's Supper is one of the means "appointed by God and Christ" to help us to grow in grace. It does so by reminding us of who we are and who God is. To grow in grace means that "we shall have every Day a *greater Sight and Sense of our sins*."[51] And therefore when the Supper is administered, "*The Body of our Lord Jesus Christ which was given for thee*" should not be heard as doctrine but as words of "Hope and Charity."[52]

Despite Edwards's emphasis on the importance of the sacraments and the urgency with which clergy insure that people understood their importance, it was not simply the ceremonialism of the Catholics and Laudians that he opposed. He was opposing the elevation of the

---

49. Edwards, *Theologia*, 1:610–12.
50. Edwards, *Theologia*, 3:226 (2nd occurrence, p. sig. Ff2).
51. Edwards, *Theologia*, 3:350–51.
52. Edwards, *Letter*, 19.

sacraments to a position of supremacy in worship. Citing various authorities including the apostle Paul, Aquinas, and Bishop Stillingfleet, Edwards stressed that administering the sacraments be subordinate to preaching the Word. Preaching is the most important work of a minister.[53] It is through preaching that people are convicted of their sins, that they hear the gospel, and that they hear the truth in order to reject false teaching. Sermons, therefore, should always precede administration of the Lord's Supper.[54]

Edwards believed his teaching on the sacraments was faithful both to Scripture and to tradition within the Church of England. He was clear to set it apart not only from Catholics, Lutherans, Anabaptists, Quakers, Laudians, and heretics, but also those with a casual and nominal faith. He stressed the importance of self-examination according to 1 Corinthians 11:28 in order to partake "by Faith and True Repentance." His concluding admonition: "Come prepared, or come not at all."[55]

LITURGY

Prescribed liturgy was a third major contributor to dissent. It is noteworthy that the English Civil War was provoked in part by the imposition of the prayer book on the Scots and Irish.[56] Edwards was convinced that the root cause of the political conflict was religious. He dated the beginning of the Civil Wars to 1631 when Bishop Laud "came to be great with the Prince."[57] Showing that he was not alone in this view, he quoted from the *"Eminent"* Dr. Nicholls: "The Miseries of the Civil War were not now owing to the Separatist and Sectaries (for these were afterwards brooded in *Cromwell's* Army) but to the Quarrels and Distinctions made between the Church of *England* Men themselves." Edwards believed that the resulting rise of sectarianism and heresies could have been prevented had the church adopted a Presbyterian form of church government.[58]

53. Edwards, *Preacher*, 16–18.
54. Edwards, *Preacher*, 20, 25, 31–32, 283.
55. Edwards, *Theologia*, 1:613.
56. Carlton, *Archbishop William Laud*, 192.
57. Edwards, *Doctrines Controverted*, 126. Laud did not become archbishop until 1633. Edwards may have selected the year 1631 because of the frequent manifestations of Laud's increasing powers, such as censorship and influence over the Star Chamber. See, for example, Carlton, *Archbishop Laud*, 118; Trevor-Roper, *Archbishop Laud*, 168.
58. Edwards, *Doctrines Controverted*, 126; Nicholls, *Comment*, xiii.

The focal point for much of the controversy over liturgy was the *BCP* which was composed with the three-fold purpose of establishing uniformity among all churches in worship and belief, defining the Church of England as distinctly Protestant, and providing a transition to Protestantism for the people, who were generally comfortable with the Roman Catholic liturgy. The *BCP* was first called, *The godly and pious institution of a christian man*, the work of a committee appointed by the 1537 Church of England Convocation.[59] Under the influence of continental reformers, especially Martin Bucer (1491–1551) and Peter Martyr Vermigli (1499–1562), Archbishop Cranmer transitioned in his own understanding from Erasmian humanist to Reformed Protestant. As Cranmer's convictions were coming into focus, he faced a nearly insurmountable challenge of persuading the church to move with him. Working with his committee, the liturgy was gradually revised, purging it of Catholic practices such as prayers for the dead and using oil in baptism.

Cranmer accomplished the revisions in a series of convocations held in the 1530s and 1540s.[60] While making the liturgy more biblical, he also moved from Latin to English. It seemed that retaining a format similar to the Roman Catholic service, but altering its content in steps to be increasingly Reformed, would make for a smooth transition by gradually introducing the parishioners to Protestant theology. When Edward VI became king, more significant reforms were instituted, including offering full communion to the laity. Edward's early death resulted in the accession of Queen Mary I, bent on returning England to the Catholic fold. But when she died five years later in 1558, Elizabeth rescinded Mary's work. Following the *BCP* first edition of 1549, there were major revisions in 1552, 1559, and 1604.

With the Presbyterian takeover in 1645, the *BCP* was officially outlawed by Parliament. Some opposed prescribed liturgy or simply wanted a clean break with all that Laud represented. Some opposed the use of prescribed prayers, but it was argued, there is no evidence that Jews or members of the early church used anything but precomposed prayers, examples being the Lord's Prayer and the Psalms. Frequent reference to the latter is made in the epistles and we have numerous liturgies from the Patristic era as well.[61] Edwards found some editions of the *BCP* re-

---

59. Wheatly, *Rational Illustration*, 20.
60. MacCulloch, *Thomas Cranmer*, 173–513.
61. Wheatly, *Rational Illustration*, 1–15.

pugnant because they were printed with "*Crucifixes* and *Images*." He also objected to the use of pictures of Mary and Jesus, "drawn with a *Roman Aire*." He recalled an incident when Bishop of Ely Richard Cox (1500–81) refused to conduct a service in Queen Elizabeth's chapel because of the crucifix there.[62]

On the positive side, Edwards saw the liturgy as a great blessing because through it, along with the XXXIX Articles, published homilies and writings of some church leaders, central doctrines are "plainly delivered."[63] These received documents not only taught and reviewed truths of the faith for both laity and ministers, they also served as a guard against some ministers who "live in an open Detestation of some of the Doctrines of the Church [. . .] and work to abuse the best Church in the world, and to shape it into what Form they fancy most." These same men, Edwards said, claim that the church is in great danger unless it follows their way. He responded that the articles and liturgy are biblically sound and a guard against error. He challenged his allies to hold firm, or "you are no Sons of the Church."[64] For Edwards, the stakes were clear: setting aside these doctrines was not only abandoning the Church of England, but going "over in part to that of Rome," which he believed had been Laud's intent.[65]

On balance, Edwards was pleased to use the liturgy. He defended it against dissenters, but also pointed out the failings of the conforming ministers to follow it. For example, the *BCP* instructs the minister to read Scripture in a loud voice, but Edwards said that commonly, ministers do not raise their voice when reading it. Similarly, the people are to repeat after him their confession in a "*humble Voice*," but typically they do so in a loud voice.[66] In many other ways, there were deviations from the *BCP*: some kept Lent, others did not; some spoke the prayers, while others "artificially" sing; some fast on certain days, others neglect to do so. Practices of ministers differed so much that "some of them can scarcely walk in the House of God as friends."[67]

---

62. Edwards, *Preacher, Third Part*, 33.
63. Edwards, *Preacher, Second Part*, 154.
64. Edwards, *Preacher, Second Part*, 154–55.
65. Edwards, *Preacher, Second Part*, 158–60; Heylyn, *Cyprianus Angelucus*, 50.
66. Edwards, *Preacher, Third Part*, 144.
67. Edwards, *Preacher, Third Part*, 145–48.

Edwards reported that conforming minister Thomas Bennet admitted that he did not follow the liturgy and complained that it was too long. On the other hand there were those ministers who placed "such an extraordinary Value for the Publick Liturgy, that they are willing it should exclude Preaching." This was certainly not a problem with "our Dissenting Brethren" and Edwards called upon his fellow ministers to learn from them and "correct that Fault which is so common among you."[68] Edwards noted that no liturgy exists that provides a suitable prayer for every situation and encouraged ministers to "more frequently exercise the Gift of Prayer," especially when visiting people in their homes.[69]

Although he valued the *BCP* and followed the prescribed liturgy, he would have altered this practice if given the freedom to do so. In defining "*Perfect Agreement in the Publick Worship*" as desirable and contributing to real reformation of the church, he meant that the church should not require anything beyond "what Christ and his Apostles have thought fit to appoint and ordain." What he did not propose was freedom for each church to do whatever they desire, but rather to "conform to the Pattern of Devotion prescribed us in the Gospel." Exactly what this means, he did not say, but he was convinced that both Tertullian and Justin Martyr experienced it.[70]

CHURCH GOVERNMENT

When Archbishop Cranmer found himself in the position to lead the reformation in England, he was faced with the difficult and delicate task of prioritizing desirable and necessary changes and then determining how to institute them in a manner that was prudent and shrewd enough to avoid a major schism like Europe had experienced. But of all the changes which occurred in the continental reformation, altering the form of church government to a congregational or Presbyterian structure was not a realistic option if Cranmer was to have the authority and power to effect reform while keeping English Christians united. Like many on the continent, there were those in England who adamantly believed that the reformation was incomplete in a number of ways, including church government. Given the intensity of convictions and the wide range of

---

68. Edwards, "Hearer," 18.
69. Edwards, "Hearer," 65.
70. Edwards, *Time of Reformation*, 424–25.

opinions on what should or should not happen, what Cranmer was able to accomplish was quite remarkable.

Like other doctrinal controversies of his day, Edwards addressed ecclesiological issues to the extent that he believed that they were important and sources of conflict. Church government was one of the most divisive. Published posthumously was *A Discourse of Episcopacy*, a careful look at the Episcopalian system, both biblically and historically, because its proponents defended it from both perspectives. He began his discussion by considering the use of various biblical terms translated into English, such as bishop, presbyter, and overseer, of which the following is a summary.

In the Septuagint, the word ἐπίσκοπος (translated as overseer or officer) is applied to both ecclesiastical and non-ecclesiastical leaders—basically those having some responsibility for the work of others such as in military (Num 31:14), construction (2 Chr 34:12), or priestly (Neh 11:22) contexts. Edwards called it a title of "Honour and Respect."[71] Outside of the Old Testament, ἐπίσκοπος and its Latin derivative *episcopus* were widely used by both Greeks and Romans, referring to various positions of prominence, including kings, civil magistrates and plenipotentiaries (Hesychius, Tully), pagan gods and high priests (Homer, Plutarch), military leaders and spies (Andromache, Eustathius), and officials of the Olympic Games (Pollux). Constantine called himself Ἐπίσκοπος. So when the New Testament was written, ἐπίσκοπος was in common use and an obvious candidate to designate a leader in the church.[72]

Πρεσβύτερος or *presbyter* (translated as elder) was also commonly used prior to the New Testament. In the Septuagint, it is used as a title of honor for respected elders in many communities, beginning with Abraham and Sarah. Similarly we find it used in ancient Greek and Roman literature for notables such as Aristotle and later for members of the Roman Senate. In the New Testament, much of the usage is similarly general, referring to an old person (e.g., Acts 2:17) or a religious leader (e.g., Matt 15:2). Edwards concluded his Old Testament-era survey by saying that bishop and presbyter have been used "among all People" as "Titles of Honour and Worth; and therefore they are most fitly applied to the Ministers of the Gospel, and the Rulers of Christ's Church."[73] But

71. Edwards, *Discourse of Episcopacy*, 150.

72. Edwards, *Discourse of Episcopacy*, 150–52. In the context of the temple or church, the KJV translates the Hebrew word that the Septuagint translates as ἐπίσκοπος as overseer in the Old Testament and bishop in the New Testament.

73. Edwards, *Discourse of Episcopacy*, 155–56.

for Edwards the significant point was that the title of presbyter is actually more honorable than bishop. Bishop implies duty and oversight, whereas presbyter adds to that responsibility, "Gravity and Prudence, together with Power and Authority," which is why the Apostles used presbyter. Edwards cited Bishop Stillingfleet who said that in the New Testament, bishop is used "by way of Diminution, and Qualification of the Power implied in the Name of *Presbyter*."[74]

The prevailing view articulated by Hammond and others was that in the apostolic era, there were only bishops and deacons, presbyters being the same as bishops. But around the turn of the century, arose a third order, designated as presbyters or priests, so that the distinct offices of bishop, priest, and deacon corresponded to the Jewish offices of high priest, priest and Levite. Edwards found this to be "a weak and precarious Notion" because it meant that there was no biblical basis for presbyters as defined by seventeenth-century English Episcopalians. In his New Testament exegesis, Edwards concluded that there was essentially no distinction made between bishop and presbyter as both terms were often used interchangeably for the same persons. For example, Paul called church leaders in Ephesus both presbyters and bishops. Edwards argued that in the opening of Philippians, only bishops and deacons are mentioned because to add presbyters would be redundant. In Titus 1:5 and 1:7, presbyter and *episcopus* are used successively in the same context to mean the same thing: "ordain elders [. . .] For a bishop." First Peter 5:1–2 instructs elders (πρεσβυτέρους) to oversee (ἐπισκοποῦντες), again suggesting no difference in office. In Acts 20:17–28, Paul sent similar instructions to the elders at Ephesus.[75]

If the two offices were distinct, asked Edwards, why does Paul provide qualifications for bishop and deacon only (1 Tim 3)? Supporting his view, Edwards referred to *A Vindication of the Rights and Privileges of the Christian Church* which stated that there were only three offices in the New Testament: apostles, bishops, and deacons.[76] Edwards also noted that in no passage of Scripture where elders or overseers are mentioned is there any indication of rank. Edwards concluded that the apostolic era provides no basis for more than the offices of deacon and elder. If there

---

74. Edwards, *Discourse of Episcopacy*, 157; Stillingfleet, *Irenicum*, 286.

75. Edwards, *Discourse of Episcopacy*, 160–72.

76. Edwards, *Discourse of Episcopacy*, 161. Edwards incorrectly identifies Edward Potter as the author. Actually it was Vicar John Turner (1660–1720) of Greenwich. See Turner, *Vindication*, 42–55.

is no biblical basis, these offices are merely human inventions and therefore, serve human purposes.[77]

Edwards supported his analysis of Scripture from the writings of ancient church authorities, including Clement, Polycarp, Irenaeus, Eusebius, Chrysostom, Jerome, Theodoret, Oecumenius (–990), Tertullian, Origen, Theophylact (1050–1107), Cyprian, and Justin Martyr. The men Edwards cited were active during the second to fifth centuries and perhaps even later. All of them also understood that in the biblical text, bishops and presbyters cannot be distinguished. Beginning with Clement we find similar teachings and reports of church activity: bishop, elder, and presbyter are used interchangeably and only two offices are appointed: deacon and bishop or presbyter.[78]

Yes, not everyone agreed with Edwards. Bishop Pearson of Chester claimed there is no evidence from the early church to support Edwards's view. He said that although a bishop is sometimes called a presbyter in the New Testament, the reverse is never the case. Edwards found his explanations "False and Frivolous," again because his view ignored the undifferentiated use of the terms throughout the biblical text.[79] Edwards pointed out that although some of these Fathers, who understood that bishop and presbyter referred to the same office, nevertheless thought that the "*Episcopacy* is a different Order or degree from *Presbytery* or *Priesthood*." His response was that when this was done, it was not a universal practice and those who did so were following their own contemporary ecclesiology, not careful biblical interpretation.[80]

Aside from the fact that Scripture does not clearly distinguish between bishop and presbyter, Edwards suggested the teaching of Jesus was relevant. When he issued the great commission, it was issued to all of his followers on the same basis. No one was given a special assignment; there was no mention of any hierarchy related to authority, power or gifts. Neither did any of the New Testament writers indicate any such thing. To those who referenced the Old Testament with its high priest, Edwards said that the entire Levitical system had been superseded.[81]

77. Edwards, *Discourse of Episcopacy*, 160.
78. Edwards, *Discourse of Episcopacy*, 163–71.
79. Edwards, *Discourse of Episcopacy*, 173.
80. Edwards, *Discourse of Episcopacy*, 174–75.
81. Edwards, *Discourse of Episcopacy*, 176–80.

Jesus was also very explicit in Matthew 20:25–26 where he instructed his disciples that their chief should be their servant, so as not to mimic the Gentile world. Edwards said that it is the natural human tendency for some ambitious people to seek authority over others and that was the immediate cause of establishing the episcopacy, which in turn led to instituting the papal office, but this is not what Jesus intended. The episcopacy prevailed because of human ambition: "Some Presbyters affected to be above the Rest, labored to make themselves Great, and consequently other Presbyters were to be under them, and to truckle to them." Supporters of the existing Episcopalian system argued that the twelve Apostles were greater in rank than the seventy disciples. Edwards agreed that there were certainly differences between the two, but not in the sense of "Power and Jurisdiction."[82]

Neither did Edwards believe that Jesus intended to distinguish clergy from laity as it had developed—again from Matthew 20:26, "But it shall not be so among you." He understood this to mean that in the secular world, such hierarchical structures may be acceptable, but they are not acceptable in the church.[83] Also, Scripture indicates that in some cities such as Jerusalem, Antioch, Ephesus, and Philippi, the number of bishops (or elders) was greater than one, which does not conform to later practice that there be only one diocesan bishop per city. In James, the elders of the church are called upon to anoint the sick. Paul instructed Timothy to ordain elders in every city of Crete. Edwards concluded that the only reasonable interpretation is that elders were like ordinary pastors.

Edwards acknowledged that a few of the Fathers taught that there could be only one bishop in a given city, among them, Ignatius, Cyprian, and Chrysostom, which is clearly at odds with Scripture, where we read of a plurality of bishops (ἐπισκόποις) in Philippi (Phil 1:1) and a plurality of elders (πρεσβθτέροθς) in Ephesus (Acts 20:17), given that bishop and elder are equivalent. Thus Edwards concluded that men such as Hammond and Pearson who argue that the office of bishop is distinct from presbyter are unable to be consistent in their textual exegesis. The weight of evidence clearly leads to the conclusion that bishop in the New Testament is not the same as the contemporary diocesan bishop; in other

---

82. Edwards, *Discourse of Episcopacy*, 180–82.
83. Edwards, *Discourse of Episcopacy*, 180–83.

words, there were no bishops in the ancient church as they are established today.[84]

Those defending the prevailing bishop/presbyter understanding in the Church of England agreed with Edwards that the duty of both bishops and presbyters included prayer, preaching, and administering the sacraments. But they insisted that it was not permitted for presbyters to ordain others to the ministry. Edwards pointed out that the ordination at Antioch of Paul and Barnabas was performed by certain men, not called bishops, but presbyters and prophets. Similarly was Timothy ordained (1 Tim 4:14). Besides these examples, Edwards reasoned that if presbyters were authorized to offer the Lord's Supper, pray, preach and baptize, they certainly should be able to ordain, a function clearly inferior to these other duties. Edwards remarked that Chrysostom and Jerome distinguished the duties of bishop and presbyter only with respect to ordination, but only because it was the custom in their day. Neither claimed that there was any difference during the first century. Edwards quoted from Jerome's commentary on Zephaniah "that Priests who baptize, and who consecrate the Lord's Supper, which is greater Employment, lay on Hands, and ordain, and make Levites and other Priests, which in Truth is but the less."[85]

Again quoting Jerome, Edwards mentioned that presbyters in Alexandria ordained their own bishops and presbyters for nearly 200 years and it seems that such was the case throughout Egypt. From various sources, he gave examples showing that differences between bishops and presbyters, especially regarding the authority to ordain, were recognized gradually, but not uniformly throughout the Christian world. The *Constitution of the Chorepiscopi*, for example, authorized presbyters to ordain lecturers and subdeacons in villages and country towns, but not presbyters and deacons.[86] In the mid-sixth century, Bishop Pelagius I of Rome was ordained by two bishops and a presbyter. And in England, the practice had been for both presbyters and bishops to ordain. Edwards named some of the "Greatest Men of the Church of *England*," who believed that presbyters should be authorized to ordain: Archbishop Cranmer, Bishops

---

84. Edwards, *Discourse of Episcopacy*, 183–88.

85. Edwards, *Discourse of Episcopacy*, 190–96.

86. Cross and Livingston, *Oxford Dictionary*. Chorepiscopi were men appointed to assist bishops in rural areas of large dioceses beginning in the third century, but controversy over their rank and authority led to their disappearance by the thirteenth.

John Jewel (1522–71), George Carleton (1559–1628) of Chichester, and John Davenant (1572–1641) of Salisbury, along with some other clerics. As recently as 1609, Archbishop Richard Bancroft (1544–1610) of Canterbury stated that ordination by presbyters was "esteemed lawful" if a bishop was not available.[87]

Guidance from tradition is similar for other clerical duties, such as ruling, teaching, and exercising discipline. Edwards quoted Bishop Stillingfleet as saying that "the Power of Ordaining, of Excommunicating, and whatever else is said to be proper to a Bishop, belongs habitually and *in actu primo* to every Presbyter."[88] Even when bishops were elevated above presbyters, there was not a second ordination for a presbyter to become a bishop. Edwards argued this is how it should be, since there are not separate ordinations for bishops and presbyters in Scripture, as Jerome stated. In fact, the ancient church reflected this practice. There are many examples of men being ordained as bishops without having first been a presbyter, including Athanasius. None who were made bishop from presbyter received a second ordination.[89]

Edwards observed that according to the Church of England, the offices of deacon, priest, and bishop are distinct and hierarchical. No one is permitted to hold more than one at the same time. Thus the Church of England is inconsistent in attacking Rome for instituting papal power and authority over the other bishops, while it maintains a similar system of Protestant bishops exercising authority over the rest of the clergy. Rome even maintains that priests, bishops and the pope are of the same order, but not the Church of England.[90]

Casting even more doubt on current policy, Edwards showed that leadership in the patristic church was divided over whether or not deacons could baptize, administer the Lord's Supper, hear confessions, or offer absolution to the dying. Even high-flyers did not always agree with their church. Edwards cited Hickes who "expressly tells us, that Deacons are not a Distinct Order from Presbyters or Priests, for *their ministry is truly and properly Sacerdotal.*" Dodwell wrote, "during the first Times of the Apostle, they did, for a while, forbear the Setting any Bishop up in

---

87. Edwards, *Discourse of Episcopacy*, 198–203. Edwards was referring to a 1610 consecration of three Scottish bishops in London, who were not previously ordained as presbyters by a bishop. His source: Spottiswoode, *History of the Church*, 3:209

88. Edwards, *Discourse of Episcopacy*, 207.

89. Edwards, *Discourse of Episcopacy*, 208–9.

90. Edwards, *Discourse of Episcopacy*, 210–14.

any way considerable Superiority over his Brethren."[91] In fact, tradition did not provide a consistent guide on how we ought to interpret Scripture regarding these questions.[92]

Edwards then presented arguments given by those who defended the Church of England's Episcopalian system. They claimed that Timothy and Titus were Bishops of Ephesus and Crete, respectively, and certainly not presbyters. For example, in addition to his general responsibility of oversight, Timothy is called to teach the clergy (1 Tim 1:3), insure that bishops and deacons were well qualified (1 Tim 1:2–13), reprove those clergy that sin (1 Tim. 5:10), ordain (1 Tim 5:22), and even conduct court (1 Tim 5:19). Certainly, they say, Timothy must have been a bishop to have such great responsibility. After all, a judge is superior to the one being tried.[93]

Edwards replied that he had already stated that all presbyters are ordained to perform all such duties. Just because Timothy was "Censuring, Commanding, Ordaining, Ruling," etc. does not mean that he was in a different order than presbyter. He was simply an example in Scripture for all presbyters and he was not acting unilaterally, but in conjunction with the other presbyters. This is evident from the laying on of hands by Paul (2 Tim 1:6) and also by the presbytery (1 Tim 4:14). Edwards concluded that Timothy was a pastor and that Paul's instructions are meant for the entire presbytery, but were merely sent by way of Timothy. Timothy may have been serving as "president" of the presbytery at that time or it may be that he was simply the elder closest to Paul and therefore entrusted to convey these instructions. Edwards's opponents argued that Timothy was instructed to institute an ecclesiastical court and serve as its judge (1 Tim 5:19). Edwards countered that such judicial action should be understood as pertaining to the entire presbytery. We cannot infer that Timothy was superior to the others; it may have been that the person serving as judge rotated among the presbyters.[94]

Edwards also argued that a bishop, following the diocesan view, would normally be assigned to a given jurisdiction and spend most of his time in the main city. Edwards observed that although Timothy was sometimes in Ephesus, he seems more like Paul's emissary to various

91. Edwards, *Discourse of Episcopacy*, 218, 220.

92. Edwards, *Discourse of Episcopacy*, 216–21. Edwards cited Tertullian, Jerome, Cyprian, and others.

93. Edwards, *Discourse of Episcopacy*, 221, 229.

94. Edwards, *Discourse of Episcopacy*, 222–23.

churches. After Paul sent him to Ephesus, Scripture records him being in Rome (Col 1:1), Thessalonica (1 Thess 3:2), Berea (Acts 17:14), Corinth (1 Cor 4:17; 16:10), Macedonia (Acts 18:5; 19:22), Troas (Acts 20:5, 6), and Miletus (Acts 20:17). At none of these locations does it appear that Timothy is serving as a bishop in the Episcopal sense.[95]

The argument that Titus was a bishop comes from the authority given to him by Paul to *"set in order the things that were wanting"* (Tit 1:5) and to ordain. But as in the case of Timothy, Edwards suggested that Titus was the one selected by Paul to communicate to the entire presbytery of Crete. Edwards's opponents asserted that Titus was charged to control those "Whose mouths must be stopped, who subvert whole houses, teaching things which they ought not, for filthy lucre's sake" (Tit 1:11). He replied that such was the task of every pastor and the presbytery and likewise for other duties such as to *"rebuke with authority"* (Tit 2:15) and to discipline heretics (Tit 3:10).[96] Episcopacy proponents thought that Titus must have set up an ecclesiastical court, which they understood to be a function only of a bishop. Edwards:

> No Such Thing [. . .] You may call this an Ecclesiastical Court, if you will; but you can't thence infer, that he that caused it to be held, was a *Bishop*, or that the holding of such a Court is a Proof of Episcopacy [. . .] *Titus*, as he was a bare Pastor, might exercise this and all the other Acts of Discipline and Government.[97]

Like Timothy who was in Ephesus, Titus did not remain in Crete. After about a year in Crete, Edwards reports Titus being sent to Nicopolis (Tit 3:12), Troas (2 Cor 2:12-13), Macedonia (2 Cor 7:6), Corinth (2 Cor 7:13), Rome, and Dalmatia (2 Tim 4:10), mainly it seems as another agent of Paul. What does seem clear from the text is not that they were bishops, but that both Timothy and Titus were evangelists. Supporting this view was Whitby whom Edwards did not often cite favorably. From his commentary on Titus, "he ingenuously confesses, that these two Instances absolutely taken, afford us no convincing Arguments for a settled Diocesan Episcopacy."[98]

The argument for the diocesan episcopacy was also based on the claim of historic succession of bishops in various cities. Edwards

---

95. Edwards, *Discourse of Episcopacy*, 224-25.
96. Edwards, *Discourse of Episcopacy*, 226.
97. Edwards, *Discourse of Episcopacy*, 227.
98. Edwards, *Discourse of Episcopacy*, 229; Whitby, *Paraphrase*, 2:22.

reported that some Fathers, including Eusebius, Jerome, Chrysostom, and Theodoret believed that Timothy and Titus began this process as the first Bishops of Ephesus and Crete. In addition to Timothy and Titus, "*Bishops* were constituted by the Apostles themselves to succeed them in great Cities [. . .] *James* at *Jerusalem, Linus* or *Clement at Rome, Mark* at *Alexandria, Ignatius* at *Antioch, Polycarp* at *Smyrna*." Edwards dismissed all of this for lack of evidence, but added that even if it were so, there is still no case for a bishop having authority over presbyters.[99]

Ancient sources in support of James as Bishop of Jerusalem include Cyril, Jerome, Augustine, Epiphanius (ca. 310/320–403), and Ambrose. Edwards responded that if James was bishop, the relief from Antioch would have been sent to him, rather than to "*the Elders*" (Acts 11:29–30). When the debate about circumcision was held in Jerusalem, there was no mention of a bishop to hear the matter, but only the "*Apostles* and *Elders*" and "the *whole Church*." (Acts 15:2, 6, 22). Edwards concluded that James was a member of the presbytery and any thought that James was Bishop or Archbishop of Jerusalem is "but a Dream."[100]

According to Edwards, neither is there evidence that Linus or Clement served as Bishops of Rome, as that term is presently used. From Irenaeus we can surmise that Linus and Clement did succeed Paul and Peter as pastors, where they had been serving the Gentile and Jewish congregations, respectively. But church fathers Irenaeus, Eusebius, Tertullian, and Epiphanius often cited as sources on apostolic succession do not agree with each other on either, whether or not Paul, Linus, Anacletus, and Clement served as bishop, or if they did, in what order.[101] Edwards said that the cases for Mark at Alexandria, Ignatius at Antioch, Erastus at Macedonia, Epaphroditus at Philippi, and Polycarp at Smyrna are similarly weak. Edwards quoted Eusebius who said of Mark's bishopric that "*it is said* it was so." Edwards did believe that the elevation of bishops over presbyters began to take place during the second and third centuries, but that it was not commonplace.[102]

Some have claimed that Ignatius was the first Bishop of Antioch. Edwards countered that the church at Antioch was co-founded by Apostles Peter and Paul who focused on the Jewish and Gentile converts

---

99. Edwards, *Discourse of Episcopacy*, 229–30.
100. Edwards, *Discourse of Episcopacy*, 230–32.
101. Edwards, *Discourse of Episcopacy*, 232–34.
102. Edwards, *Discourse of Episcopacy*, 233–34.

respectively, just like they did in Rome. Yet, no one has suggested that Peter or Paul served as Bishop of Antioch. Similarly, Polycarp is often called the first Bishop of Smyrna. But what does Polycarp write to the church in Philippi? "Be obedient to the Presbyters and Deacons," hardly evidence for the episcopacy. Edwards's final argument was that given by Eusebius, whom he called "this best of Church-Historians," writing four hundred years after the apostles: "there is no depending upon *Tradition* concerning the *Succession* of Bishops."[103]

It might seem that Ignatius of Antioch substantiated the episcopacy in his epistles. But Edwards was convinced by the testimony of numerous scholars that these epistles show clear evidence of interpolation.[104] Illustrating the interpolation, Edwards, quoted a questionable passage which shows an uncharacteristic and exaggerated description of the bishop's power: "Obey your Bishop as you would obey Christ [. . .] My Son, honour God and the "King," but I say, Honour God and the Bishop as High Priest, according to his priesting, and after him honour the King."[105] From the epistles of Ignatius commonly accepted as genuine, Edwards could only substantiate one bishop as an ordinary pastor of one church. At most he was merely the presbyter chosen to preside over the presbytery on certain occasions, not someone of a different order or higher rank. Not only that, Ignatius accorded presbyters and deacons equal "Respect and Honour."[106]

Clement, a contemporary of Ignatius, wrote to the church at Corinth regarding the dismissal of their pastor. In that letter, Edwards noted, the Corinthians are told *"to be subject to their Presbyters"* and when he referred to a bishop, it was equivalent with presbyter. Likewise, Hermas did not distinguish between bishops and presbyters. In his letter to Philippi, Polycarp did not mention a bishop distinct from presbyters. According to Edwards episcopacy proponents have ignored all these examples. Instead

---

103. Edwards, *Discourse of Episcopacy*, 234-36.

104. Edwards, Discourse of Episcopacy, 237-38. Anastasius Bibliothecarius (c. 810-c. 878), librarian of the Church of Rome, Jesuit Robert Bellarmine (1542-1621), David Blondel (1591-1655), Jean Daillé (1594-1670), Jean Morinus (1591-1659), Martialis Mastræus (fl. 1608), Nicephorus (c. 758-828), Patriarch of Constantinople, and Claudius Salmasius (1588-1653).

105. Edwards, *Discourse of Episcopacy*, 237.

106. Edwards, *Discourse of Episcopacy*, 238-40. Edwards also cited Ussher for his work in identifying spurious letters of Ignatius, but he did not mention that Ussher's interest was to identify authentic sources for the purpose of documenting Episcopalian government in the early church.

they have attempted to bolster their case by attacking the heretic Aerius who maintained that all church offices were equal, as if refuting a heretic is corroboration.[107] Edwards responded by quoting Stillingfleet:

> Upon the strictest Enquiry it will prove true that *Jerom, Austin, Ambrose, Sedulius, Primasius, Chrysostom, Theodoret, Theophylact,* were all of *Aërius's* Judgment as to the Identity of both Name and Order of Bishops and Presbyters in the Primitive Church; but here lay the Difference, *Aërius* from hence proceeded to Separation from Bishops and their Churches because they were Bishops.[108]

Edwards's final point of disagreement was over the claim that bishops were successors to the apostles. This Edwards found to be completely absurd as the apostles had a personal relationship with Jesus that could not be transferred. Edwards cited John Lightfoot (1602–75) and papal defender Isaac Barrow (1612/13–80) who declared that the office of apostle was distinct from all others, making such succession impossible.[109]

Edwards added to his list of supporters other ancient writers in addition to Clement and Ignatius. Justin Martyr mentioned only deacons and presbyters in his *Second Apology*. Cyprian, Bishop of Carthage, in his best known work, *On the Unity of the Catholic Church*, stated that the bishops are the basis for that unity. Yet, what did he mean by "bishop"? Edwards said that it is clear from his writings that bishop in Cyprian's context was understood to be the president or moderator of the presbyters and quoted Cyprian referring to the presbyters in Carthage as "*Collegues* and *Fellow-presbyters*." Edwards also quoted Bishop Cornelius (d. 253) of Rome as saying that he did nothing "*without his presbyters*."[110] Bishop Ambrose of Milan, Augustine, and Chrysostom held similar views. Augustine wrote that bishop is only a name of honor. Jerome recognized that some bishops thought themselves to be superior to presbyters. Edwards translated his rejection of that notion:

> They ought to know that they are not Lords, but Priests or Presbyters [. . .] Before the Time that there were Parties and

---

107. Edwards, *Discourse of Episcopacy*, 241–43. Edwards mistakenly identified the Hermas of Romans 16:14 as the author of *Shepherd of Hermas*.

108. Edwards, *Discourse of Episcopacy*, 245; Stillingfleet, *Irenicum*, 276. Apparently, Aerius did not think that the elder temporarily presiding could be named a bishop.

109. Edwards, *Discourse of Episcopacy*, 246.

110. Edwards, *Discourse of Episcopacy*, 247–48.

> Divisions in Religion, by the Instinct of the Devil, the Government of the Church was carried wholly by the common Advice of Presbyters: But afterward, when Parties and Contentions arose, it was universally agreed upon, that one would be chosen out of the Number of Presbyters, to preside above the rest [...] to prevent Schism.[111]

For anyone doubting whether these eminent fathers did not carry enough weight, Edwards cited certain canons approved unanimously by more than two hundred bishops who attended the Fourth Council of Carthage in 398:

Canon 22: "A Bishop must not ordain Any without the Counsel of his Clergy."

Canon 23: "He must hear no Man's Cause unless his Clergy be present; otherwise the Bishop's Sentence shall be void."

Canon 34: "Whilst a Bishop sits, he shall not suffer a Presbyter to stand."

Canon 35: "He must know that he is but a Colleague of the Presbyters."[112]

In Edward's understanding then, the structure of early church government is best described as Presbyterian from the days of the Apostles and over some indeterminate period of time, underwent a gradual shift to the Episcopalian diocesan system. But with the Reformation, many doctrines were questioned and challenged, including the Roman Catholic Episcopalian structure. Concluding his historical survey, he cited a number of recent men who believed that bishops and priests were of the same office, i.e., whatever authority a bishop might have over a presbyter was granted by the presbyters in his diocese and was most likely temporary. In addition to those mentioned above, he identified Laurence Humfrey (1527?-90) of Oxford, William Fulk (1538-89) of Cambridge, Bishop Thomas Bilson (1546/7-1616), William Whitaker (1548-95) of Cambridge, Richard Hooker (1554-1600), Francis Mason (1566?-1621), Elnathan Parr (1577-1622), Archbishop Ussher, Herbert Thorndyke, Nicholas Bernard (1600-1661), and Bishop Stillingfleet.[113]

Edwards's case would have been stronger had he excluded Ussher. Ussher's "view" was his proposed accommodation with the Scottish

---

111. Edwards, *Discourse of Episcopacy*, 249-50.
112. Edwards, *Discourse of Episcopacy*, 254.
113. Edwards, *Discourse of Episcopacy*, 256-60.

Presbyterians, whereby a "president" or bishop would be selected from among the elders of a given city or diocese and an "archbishop" would be selected to preside as moderator over the synod of bishops in a given province.[114] Although Ussher was willing to compromise, he believed that "The ground of episcopacy is derived partly from the pattern prescribed by God in the Old Testament, and partly from the imitation thereof brought in by the apostles, and confirmed by Christ himself in the time of the New."[115] He found support for the episcopacy beginning with the Old Testament ranking of the high priest above priests, who were in turn above the Levites.

Although Edwards faced stiff opposition among the conforming clergy, Bishop Stillingfleet was an interesting ally. His first major work *Irenicum* reflected his Latitudinarian outlook and was an attempt to make peace with the Presbyterians.[116] He did not address the question of the proper form of church government exegetically as had Edwards. Though he was well-connected, he did not defend the episcopacy either; he simply said that it did not matter that Scripture failed to clearly prescribe the correct form of church government. In his historical survey, he concurred with many of Edwards's points, including that Cranmer and many others held that "at first Bishops and Presbyters were the same." He acknowledged that the Presbyterian understanding has more to commend it. "The Episcopal men will hardly find any evidence in Scripture, or in the practice of the apostles [. . .] nor in the Primitive Church." His prescription was

> *That Form of government is the best according to the Principles of Christian Prudence, which comes nearest to Apostolical practice, and tends most to advancing the peace and unity of the Church of God.* What that Form is, I presume not to define and determine.[117]

The Episcopacy came about "only as a prudent constitution of the Civil Magistrate for the better governing of the Church." What mattered was unity and unity required one institutional form for a given national church.[118]

---

114. Ussher, *Reduction of Episcopacy*, 12:532–36.
115. Ussher, *Original of Bishops*, 7:43.
116. Irenicum comes from εἰρήνη, meaning "peace."
117. Stillingfleet, *Irenicum*, 414–15.
118. Stillingfleet, *Irenicum*, 393; 414–16.

In the last section of his book, Stillingfleet addressed the power of the keys in the context of the "peace, unity and purity" of the church. Standards of purity obviously establish the grounds for excommunication, but what did he mean by purity? Before answering the question he asked where the power of the church comes from. It is not the consent of the governed, but rather Christ himself. Stillingfleet reasoned that the Lord's Supper is the most obvious mechanism to exclude someone from the visible communion. But when it comes to the question of purity, Stillingfleet only seemed to see it in moral terms, citing passages from 1 Corinthians chapters 4 and 5:

> that where any persons in a Church do by their open and contumacious offences, declare to the World that they are far from being the persons they were supposed to be in their admission into the Church, there is a power resident in the Pastors of the Church to debar such persons from the privileges of it.[119]

Edwards observed that moderate leaders of the Church of England like Stillingfleet—supporters of the episcopacy—agree that there are "True Churches" [in Europe] which have no bishops, proving that the episcopacy is "not a divine institution, and to be necessarily maintained in the Church; for if it were, there could not be a True Church without it."[120]

Of course by Edwards's day, the Church of England was operating as a straightforward diocesan episcopacy . . . or was it? Referring to the official polity for ordaining priests in the church, Edwards pointed out that the Scripture used to ordain priests is taken from Acts 20, while the passage used for bishops is from 1 Timothy, which means either that the church is disregarding Scripture or that the bishops in Acts and Timothy are presbyters. A second problem Edwards raised was that some deans and arch-deacons were not subject to the bishop in whose diocese they resided and had assumed duties thought to be the bishop's alone, such as the power of excommunication. This, he said, is further proof that the Church of England follows man-made laws, rather than Scripture.[121]

One-by-one, Edwards dismissed the arguments of English divines who defended the episcopacy. Richard Hooker challenged anyone to find "but one church upon the Face of the whole Earth" without a

---

119. Stillingfleet, *Irenicum*, 431, 443–44.
120. Edwards, *Discourse of Episcopacy*, 262.
121. Edwards, *Discourse of Episcopacy*, 262–64.

bishop; Edwards replied there were no bishops initially."[122] Chillingworth claimed that "between the Apostles Times and those soon after there was not Time enough for, nor Possibility of changing the Government of Presbyters into that of Bishops: therefore there was no such Alteration, consequently Episcopacy was of Apostolical Institution." Edwards called this a "Sophistical way of Arguing [like] *Rome*."[123] Dr. Beveridge argued that the reason we do not see the establishment of diocesan rule universally in the patristic era was because of persecution and lack of Christian rulers. Edwards remarked that Beveridge was usually quite skilled at clear explanations, but in this case he was "much mistaken." He did not discuss in detail the case made by Dr. Henry Maurice (1648–91) in his *Defence of Diocesan Episcopacy*, describing it as "Trick and Evasion," full of contradictions.[124] Dodwell he condemned for doubting and twisting Scripture in order to defend the episcopacy.

But it was Bishop Joseph Hall, whom Edwards judged that his passion had completely overcome his common sense. Claiming that the Episcopalian structure was founded by Christ, he wrote, "I am, for my part, so confident of the divine institution of the majority of bishops above presbyters, that I dare boldly say there are weighty points of faith which have not so strong evidence in holy scriptures."[125] Hall went so far to say that episcopacy determines correct doctrine and where it is absent, there is heresy and confusion. Edwards pointed out a few counterexamples, including European Reformed churches and the Jacobite Churches.[126]

For Edwards, the ancient, biblical approach to church government was a healthy balance between congregational "Popular Disorder" and modern Episcopalian "exorbitant Ambition and Affection of Superiority." Despite his firm convictions against the present system, he concluded,

> Providence may in time restore the *Substance* to us. 'Till then let us be contented with the Ecclesiastical Government which we have. [. . .] Though there are many Deficiencies and Flaws in the Constitution itself, yet there are many more in the Officers. The Office itself is not so much to be found fault with as the Persons that are employed in it, who generally execute it either

---

122. Edwards, *Discourse of Episcopacy*, 269.
123. Edwards, *Discourse of Episcopacy*, 270.
124. Edwards, *Discourse of Episcopacy*, 274, 275.
125. Hall, *Episcopacy*, 9:190, 208.
126. Edwards, *Discourse of Episcopacy*, 276.

Carelessly, or Partially, or too Rigorously, and pervert the Ends of the Office and Constitution.[127]

Notwithstanding his commitment to Scripture and firm disagreement with the Episcopalian system of which he was a part, for Edwards, this was not a reason to leave the Church of England. The church would never be perfect on earth. In sermons and essays, he often identified with the Church of England, enjoining others to take their commitment seriously. "Let us not say we are of the *Church of England,* and yet deny some of the Chief Doctrines contain'd in her *Articles.*"[128]

> I hope the serious Consideration of this will make you improve the Time of *Fasting* and *Humiliation* which is set apart Monthly by our Church to the great and worthy Designs of it, namely the Abhorring of your former evil Ways, and the speedy Reforming of your Lives.[129]

For Edwards, the unity of the church was an overriding aspect of ecclesiology, largely ignored by most everyone else. Division over ecclesiastical matters was especially troubling since Jesus emphasized unity and elsewhere the New Testament clearly spoke of one church, using metaphors which were inherently indivisible without serious problems: a body, a bride, a family, a temple, and a building. As ecclesiological issues were a common excuse for division, Edwards stressed that most divisive issues were far less important than unity. Though he was in the minority on many of these issues, he submitted to the prevailing position and practices of the Church of England for the sake of unity.

---

127. Edwards, *Discourse of Episcopacy*, 277–78.
128. Edwards, "How Ministers of the Gospel," 117.
129. Edwards, "True Causes," 219–20.

7

ON CHURCH UNITY AND SCHISM

AUGUST 24, 1662 BECAME known as Black Bartholomew Day[1] for the Act of Uniformity which silenced approximately two thousand ministers who would not conform, claiming that to do so violated their consciences as they understood the commands of Scripture. However great this was, it was similar in size to the Presbyterian ejections of Episcopalians during the prior two decades. Most occurred during 1642–47, a conservative estimate being about sixteen hundred who were removed from their churches and unable to find other positions.[2]

It is important to recall the context of 1662. The struggle for control of the Church of England, at least since the break with Rome, had been continual. Initially, it was Cranmer's attempt to transition from Catholicism to a Reformed Protestant faith, which cost his life when Mary succeeded Edward VI. Following the death of Mary, Elizabeth repealed her edicts designed to restore Catholicism, but resisted attempts at further reform by Puritans. However, the major concern of the Queen was not religious reform but political loyalty, as neither Catholics nor Presbyterians recognized the crown as the head of the church and there were more than enough rabble-rousers to alarm the authorities.[3] In the seventeenth century, with the success of Laud and Charles I at promoting Arminianism along with certain aesthetic preferences which resonated more with Catholic traditions, Puritans were forced to retreat, some geographically

---

1. Ninety years after the St. Bartholomew's Day massacre in Paris.
2. Green, "Persecution," 523, 525.
3. Ha, "Spiritual Treason," 66–68.

to Holland or Massachusetts. Then, reflecting the changing consensus against Laud, Parliament changed course, leading to Laud's demise. Even before the archbishop's execution, Charles was quite aware of his weakening political standing, perhaps leading him to appoint John Williams as Archbishop of York.[4]

During the sixteenth and seventeenth centuries, government ordinances specifying lawful religious beliefs and practices changed repeatedly, dividing the nation religiously into two broad groups which became known as conformists and nonconformists.[5] As the tide began to turn against Archbishop Laud in the 1640s, the conformists included Laudians and anti-Laudians, along with some moderate Puritans who were concerned about extremist dissenters. Among the nonconformists were moderates like Baxter who worked for a more accommodating episcopacy and Independents who opposed any structure of church government except at the local level.[6] With the failure of the Commonwealth government, Charles II returned with his promises of religious toleration, raising the hopes of many for comprehension measures to heal the nation.

From the viewpoint of the Laudians returning to power in 1660, the Presbyterians were being held accountable for executing the king and the archbishop, along with (officially) abolishing the monarchy, episcopacy, liturgy, ceremonies, church courts, and the church calendar. In short, they saw English civil and religious tradition along with culture itself being discarded. But though this is somewhat true, what transpired in the 1640s did not happen so suddenly, absolutely, or so universally as the events of the Great Ejection. Of twenty-six active bishops (in 1643), only fourteen lost their posts and six of the remaining bishops were invited to join the Westminster Assembly.[7] In 1645 copies of the *BCP* were to be destroyed, but according to inventory records, that ordinance was ignored in more than one third of all parishes and there is no record of penalties (fines and imprisonment) on any violators. Records also indicate that less than one quarter of the parishes purchased its replacement, the *Directory of Public Worship*. A 1644 ordinance outlawed the church calendar,

---

4. Earlier, Williams was not in favor with Charles or Laud, having opposed Laud's Arminianism and his ceremonial reforms. See Tyacke, *Anti-Calvinists*, 209–10.

5. Members of the Westminster Assembly included nonconformists along with conformists like Bishop Edward Reynolds, a Presbyterian.

6. Fincham and Taylor, "Episcopalian Identity," 459.

7. Morrill, "Church of England," 93.

but it also seems to have been inconsequential.[8] In 1646, the episcopacy was officially terminated, but Episcopalian ordination continued with approximately 2500 ordained during 1646–60.[9] These illegal ordinations represent about 50–60 percent of what would have been expected based on statistics prior to 1646 and following 1660, indicating that the level of dissent was comparable to that of 1662.[10]

Consistent with the king's promise of accommodation, the Savoy Conference was called in 1661 to draft yet another revision of the *BCP*, which nonconformists hoped would provide more freedom in how the liturgy was to be used. Presbyterian Baxter was optimistic that his moderate proposals would be adopted. Unfortunately, the surviving High Churchmen were in no mood to grant concessions, despite promises made by the king to the Presbyterians, so that of the few changes adopted, most were requested by the Laudians.[11] But the real problem for the nonconformists came with passing the 1662 Act of Uniformity which, among other things, required each minister to "openly and publickly before the Congregation there assembled, declare his unfeigned Assent and Consent to the use of all things in the said Book contained and prescribed, in these words and no other."[12]

This had not been expected by Presbyterians and other nonconformists when welcoming Charles II back from exile. On May 1, 1660, he had sent a letter to Parliament which stated "that no man shall be disquieted, or called in question, for differences of opinion in matters of Religion, which do not disturb the peace of the kingdom."[13] On October 25 in "His Majesty's Declaration to all his loving Subjects," he began, "How much the peace of the State is concerned in the peace of the Church."[14] The conciliatory tone of his declaration of October 25, 1660, encouraged all but his most skeptical opponents.

---

8. Morrill, "Church of England," 93–94, 104–06.
9. Fincham and Taylor, "Episcopalian Identity," 474.
10. Fincham and Taylor, "Vital Statistics."
11. Spinks, "Liturgy and Worship," 165–66.
12. Baxter, *Reliquiæ*, Part 2, 393; *Act for the Uniformity of Publick Prayers*. Along with the Act of Uniformity, ministers were required to renounce the Solemn League and Covenant, which had been adopted in 1643 to establish and preserve a Puritan-inspired reformed religion in England and Scotland. This was similar to the distress of the Episcopalians in 1643. See Keeble, "Settling the Peace."
13. Cobbett, *Cobbett's Parliamentary History*, 4:17.
14. Cobbett, *Cobbett's Parliamentary History*, 4:131.

> When we were in Holland, we were attended by many grave and learned ministers from hence, who were looked upon as the most able and principal asserters of the Presbyterian opinions [. . .] and to our great satisfaction and comfort, found them persons of full affection to us, of zeal for the peace of the Church and State, and neither enemies (as they have been given out to be) to Episcopacy or Liturgy; but modestly to desire such alterations in either, as, without shaking foundations, might best allay the present distempers. [. . .] We have not the least doubt but that the present Bishops will think the present concession, now made by us to allay the present distempers, very just and reasonable, and will very chearfully conform themselves thereunto.[15]

And what was meant by "present concession"? The king promised six reforms with respect to Episcopalian government, including improving criteria for selecting bishops, reducing the size of large dioceses, establishing closer working relations between bishops, presbyters, and deans, and eliminating the "exercise [of] any arbitrary power" by bishops. Regarding the liturgy, he promised to appoint a commission of divines, equal in number of "both persuasions" to make appropriate revisions. Until then, he asked that ministers "not totally lay aside the use of the Book of Common Prayer." Concerning other contested practices, no one was to be denied the Lord's Supper for failing to kneel, no one was to be denied baptism for failing to sign the cross, no one was to be forced to bow at the name of Jesus, and no minister would be forced to wear the Surplice.[16] And to impress everyone that his message of toleration was genuine,

> We are content, and it is our will and pleasure, (so they take the Oaths of Allegiance and Supremacy) that they shall receive ordination, institution, and induction, and shall be permitted to exercise their function, and to enjoy the profits of their livings, without the said Subscription or Oath of Canonical Obedience.[17]

The freedom from taking an oath was also promised to the university staffs. The King repeated his promise of religious freedom made from Breda and spoke of the day when England's Protestant faith would be a beacon to the world and

15. Cobbett, *Cobbett's Parliamentary History*, 4:132–33, 136.
16. Cobbett, *Cobbett's Parliamentary History*, 4:138–39.
17. Cobbett, *Cobbett's Parliamentary History*, 4:140.

all our good subjects will, by God's blessing upon us, enjoy as great a measure of felicity, as this nation hath ever done, and which we shall constantly labour to procure for them, as the greatest blessing God can bestow upon us in this world.[18]

Charles II's politically astute declaration reflected much of what a delegation of Presbyterian leaders to the Hague had requested in person just after his May 1 letter.[19] That delegation was led by Edmund Calamy, Thomas Case (1598–1682), Thomas Manton (1620–77) and Edward Reynolds.[20] The following year, Calamy declined the bishopric of Coventry and Lichfield, Manton declined the Deanery of Rochester and Reynolds was appointed Bishop of Norwich.

There is no record of Edwards's thoughts at the time. He could not help being aware of the extent of the controversy. His theological views were perhaps not that mature, but given his education under Dr. Tuckney and the report that he was unable to continue his fellowship at St. John's due to his Calvinist views which clashed with Gunning and Turner,[21] it seems reasonable to conclude that he chose ordination in the Church of England despite (possible) serious misgivings about where it was headed. There is no reason to think that his outlook changed later in life, except that through study, he become more established in his convictions.

For three decades following the Great Ejection, various options were suggested to accommodate those excluded by the Act of Uniformity. Initially comprehension seemed to have the most support. A number of proposals to weaken requirements for conformity were discussed in Parliament. Nonconformists like Baxter and John Owen were kept engaged to varying degrees, hoping for a breakthrough. But Parliament was reluctant to act, persuaded in part by arguments that they might undermine the integrity of the church, indirectly promote schism, and give ground to papists. In the course of national debate, a second course of action

---

18. Cobbett, *Cobbett's Parliamentary History*, 4:141.

19. Given Charles' subsequent vacillation on measures to fulfill his promises, finally settling on a Declaration of Indulgence in 1672, which included Catholics, some have concluded that his Presbyterian initiative was merely a ruse, or perhaps that he was too weak to oppose the Royalist parliament upon his return to England. Whatever the case, Parliament in 1673 forced him to cancel his declaration, replacing it with the 1673 Test Act requiring that anyone in public service deny the doctrine of Transubstantiation and join the Church of England. See Rose, "Law Established," 25–26; Southcombe, "Dissent," 199; Fritze and Robinson, *Historical Dictionary*, 512–13.

20. Proctor, *History*, 104–09.

21. Robinson, "John Edwards."

was taken by Charles II and James II. Royal declarations of indulgence were granted in 1672, 1687 and 1688, essentially eliminated penalties for nonconforming behavior.

Religious freedom was given a further boost by the Glorious Revolution. With the ascendancy of William and Mary and passage of the Succession to the Crown Act of 1707, paranoia concerning the perceived papal political threat mostly evaporated, allowing more freedom to promote toleration. Within their first three years, sixteen bishops and both archbishops were appointed, largely the work of Mary, filling vacancies resulting either from death or those refusing to swear allegiance. These new appointments constituted a rather abrupt shift for the church, being typically Low Church, Whig men who were more inclined toward toleration.[22]

This final chapter will complete the picture of Edwards as someone more committed to the unity and the Reformed and orthodox identity of the Church of England than any of his public square contemporaries. In Chapter 4, we saw evidence of his commitment to the integrity of the church, in his opposition to those who would redefine the church by disregarding or contravening its fundamental tenets. In Chapter 5, we saw how accommodating he was to those who satisfied his broad definition of orthodoxy, but with whom he had serious theological disagreements. Both of these chapters primarily referenced his polemical writings. Chapter 6 summarized Edwards's position on those non-nebulous issues most often given by dissenters for their nonconformity. This chapter will focus on the debate over schism and conformity from both sides followed by Edwards's response, primarily from his more systematic writings, of which there were three multivolume works: *Theologia Reformata*, *Veritas Redux*, and *The Preacher*.

RATIONALE OF THE NONCONFORMISTS

Most seventeenth-century conformers viewed schism as unlawful and a great evil. Most nonconformists attempted to justify their separation or rationalize that they were not actually in a state of separation. For most who separated from the Church of England, the primary issues could be reduced to three: the Episcopalian government, liturgy prescribed by the *BCP*, and certain ceremonial practices. The debate over all of these

22. Pincus, 1688, 402, 404, 410–11, 425.

issues eventually reverted back to supposed practices of the apostolic and patristic eras. Unfortunately, both sides seemed to be able to satisfy themselves that available evidence from ancient sources supported their positions.

Richard Baxter was respected as a nonconformist leader who worked for church unity and was invited to the Savoy Conference, where his moderate proposals for compromise, consistent with the King's declaration, were rejected. He declined the offer of a bishopric and did not conform. Baxter was well acquainted with many of the dissenters and explained some of the reasons given by ministers who did not conform, including those who

1. simply opposed having such requirements imposed on their manner of worship;
2. did not want to be part of a church characterized as "Profane and Vitious and Debaucht and Scandalous;"
3. did not want to strengthen a church they saw as "*Usurpers*" of "God's Heritage;"
4. feared that they may succumb to the prelates whose goal is to "root out godly Ministers and Christians;"
5. believed that conforming would cause them to break their personal covenants to reform the church;
6. believed that the Church of England was under God's judgment and therefore did not want to "be partakers of their Plagues;"
7. saw conforming requirements as "Engines of Division" and did not want to be associated with such schism;
8. believed that these measures were completely unnecessary and would only inhibit their ability to preach the gospel;
9. opposed the episcopacy for a variety of reasons including, weak pastoral care, corruption, and failure in discipline, which they described as "unlawful," unbiblical, and one that "destroyeth the *Pastoral Office*," leading to the conclusion of the Brownists that "our Churches are no true Churches;"
10. saw the episcopacy as contrary to Christ's teaching against allowing the church to adopt the hierarchical administrative structures found in secular institutions;

11. saw a conflict between subscription and serving God, which they believed led to perjury;
12. opposed taking vows;
13. were confused and troubled by a number of issues concerning oaths, petitions, law, Parliament, the King, and the church, along with the respective authority of each;
14. opposed the Oath of Canonical Obedience because they thought it could be in conflict with their allegiance is to the Word of God. However, many of these same nonconformists stated their willingness to respect and obey bishops without an oath;
15. opposed re-ordination;
16. opposed the *"unfeigned assent and consent"* requirement as an offense to conscience, because it is open to wide interpretation;
17. opposed reading the Apocrypha in church as Scripture, which it is not;
18. opposed the new clause on baptizing infants, including baptizing non-covenantal children and the requirement to have godparents, along with the tendency to teach baptismal regeneration;
19. opposed treating unregenerate people as regenerate when administering the Lord's Supper or at a burial, by declaring such a person to have entered the presence of God;
20. opposed the requirement for ministers to use the cross and surplice.[23]

Twenty and more years after the ejection, wounds remained. Especially onerous was the requirement to *"declare my assent and consent"* to the *BCP*.[24]

Baxter replied to a minister who had spoken of his (Baxter's) contempt for his nonconformity:

> This, you say, *may be one of my chief scruples, that I could not prevaricate with Authority; had there been allowed a little Equivocation, and might I have been permitted to give an assent and consent which were not unfeigned, the task had not been so intollerable; but to require such an assent and consent, searches men*

---

23. Baxter, *Reliquiæ*, Part 2, §301–428.
24. *Statutes*, 744.

> to the bottom, and beats the Hypocrite out of all his Subterfugies; who can bear it? I answer, The declaring of my unfeigned assent and consent is a great scruple to me, though not hereby to be kept from a little Equivocation with man, but from a down-right lying before God, and against mine own Conscience.[25]

Baxter's accuser suggested that he should consent, given that there may have been errors in printing the *BCP*. He responded that the authors of the ordinance left him no option with the wording of the ordinance, "pretending to an Infallibility."[26] Even though Baxter desired comprehension and spoke in favor of a modified episcopacy, he was not an Erastian. Against Stillingfleet and others he argued that state control was one of the major problems with the church in Catholic countries.

But another less tangible, but for some even more crucial, issue was the heart of the gospel. How is grace to be understood? Puritans saw Arminian free will as an obstacle to understanding divine grace. And how was the Laudian concept of ecclesiastical authority different from Rome's? As a young student at Queen's College, Oxford, John Owen found himself in the middle of the Arminian-Calvinist controversy with the arrival of William Laud as chancellor in 1630. Owen completed his BA (1632) and MA (1635), but left in 1637, while working on his BD, to avoid being expelled for refusing to submit to new regulations regarding ceremonies directed by Laud.[27]

Unlike Baxter, Owen was not eager to be included in the Church of England as it was in his day. Apart from all the theological and ecclesiological disputes, he raised the issue of authority, essentially questioning the jurisdiction of the Church of England over nonconformists in the same manner that Protestants questioned the authority of Pope. In response to Stillingfleet's *The Unreasonableness of Separation*, Owen wrote,

> Who is it that shall make these orders and constitutions, that must be observed for the preservation of the unity and peace of the church? It can be none but those who have the power so to do by being uppermost in any place or time. Who shall judge them to be lawful? No doubt they that make them.[28]

---

25. Baxter, *Nonconformists Advocate*, 33.
26. Baxter, *Nonconformists Advocate*, 35.
27. Gribben, *John Owen*, 35–36.
28. Owen, *Inquiry*, 15:276.

Rome claimed authority for itself and proclaimed unity on its own terms, declaring *de facto* those who refused to submit as schismatics. Echoing common sentiment of the day, Owen called Rome that church "which pretends itself to be catholic or universal, comprehensive of all true believers."[29] Owen saw little difference between Canterbury and Rome. He affirmed that Christians are to practice "love, union, peace, and order" because it was commanded by Christ and if they would only do so, there would be no schism, regardless of affiliation with established ecclesiastical bodies. But he saw no basis in Scripture for men "to invent and appoint a new kind of union and order." So to dissent from the presumed authority of the Church of England is "no more schism than it is adultery."[30]

Owen had many of the same concerns as Baxter including freedom from certain elements of liturgy and ceremonies imposed on worship. But his primary concern was the Latitudinarian influence on contemporary theology. Though quite satisfactory when first drafted, he thought the XXXIX Articles were inadequate to defend against recent Arminian and Socinian encroachments.[31] It was Arminianism, with its emphasis on human self-sufficiency and consequent diminishing of divine grace, that Owen believed to be the major corrupter of the Reformed doctrine formulated under Cranmer. "Never did any men [. . .] more eagerly endeavour the erecting of this Babel, than the Arminians, the modern blinded patrons of human self-sufficiency." He accused them of effectively denying God's attributes of immutability and sovereign will and minimizing his absolute foreknowledge and providence. Among other things, they sought to establish human dignity not beset by the curse of original sin, ascribe to individuals free will independent of divine predestination, and "deny the efficacy of the merit of the death of Christ." For Owen, divine grace was all-sufficient and completely unmerited. Without it, every person was dead in sin, completely unable to seek God.[32]

Owen wrote extensively on the nature of a "true church," but never said that the Church of England was not a true church, in part because he viewed the question at the local level. In other words, some individual congregations of the Church of England could be true churches, while

---

29. Owen, *Inquiry*, 15:333.
30. Owen, *Inquiry*, 15:437.
31. Owen, *Inquiry*, 15:450.
32. Owen, *Display of Arminianism*, 10:28–31.

others were not. He certainly did not believe that one could be accused of schism simply for leaving a particular local church, regardless of its affiliation.

> It must be remembered that *communion with particular churches is to be regulated absolutely by edification.* No man is or can be obliged to abide in or confine himself unto the communion of any particular church any longer than it is for his edification. And this liberty is allowed unto all persons by the church of England. For, allow a man to be born in such a parish, to be baptized in it, and there educated; yet if at any time he judge that the ministry of the parish is not useful unto his edification, he may withdraw from the communion in that parish, by the removal of his habitation, it may be to the next door.[33]

And so, individuals like Owen neither felt much allegiance to the Church of England, nor any guilt over separating from it.

BAXTER AND STILLINGFLEET ON SCHISM

Given the national disorder during the seventeenth century and the complex interdependency between government, universities, and the church, the occurrence of serious schism in the church is not at all surprising. As events unfolded, there was widespread concern over the potential danger for the church caused by all the dissension, not the least because love was supposed to be the hallmark of the church. During Edwards's adult life, hundreds of authors published thousands of works in London, the primary purpose of which was to defend conformity or nonconformity. They varied in intensity from abusive and intolerant to understanding and compromising.

If one were to select a prominent leader each from the nonconformists and the Church of England who possibly could have forged a reunion, Richard Baxter and Edward Stillingfleet would be candidates.[34] Up until about 1680, Baxter, thirty years Stillingfleet's senior, had quite a positive view of Stillingfleet, *"whom I once thought more unlikely than most to be*

---

33. Owen, *True Nature*, 16:37.

34. This point is debatable. Writing of the Savoy Conference, Gilbert Burnet believed that Baxter was "most unfit to heal matters," but that opinion is probably based more on his unrefined diplomacy than his fervent aspirations, given Baxter's perseverance over many years. See Burnet, *Bishop Burnet's History*, 1:295–97.

*come our Accuser."*³⁵ Baxter recognized that he himself was not a skilled negotiator, being rather direct and blunt. It did not help that he came from a poor background without the benefit from the education, culture, and connections that came from attending Cambridge or Oxford, as had Stillingfleet. But despite his failure at the Savoy Conference, his efforts to work for church unity were as long lasting and long suffering as anyone and cannot easily be dismissed, simply because he was not skilled at negotiating with formidable opponents defending church and civil law. In contrast to Baxter were men like Edwards's professor Anthony Tuckney, who did not bother to attend the Savoy Conference, having decided that prospects for genuine compromise were nil.

Of course, negotiating a mutually agreeable settlement requires two committed parties and it has often been said that the bishops were not sincere participants and they did little to disguise that perception.³⁶ There were numerous attempts to resolve differences involving many others, including Tillotson and John Howe before Parliament, but from the Restoration until the Act of Toleration, 1689, little changed. Of course, individual perspectives often change with time. In the 1660s, Wilkins and Tillotson were promoters of comprehension, whereas Patrick and Stillingfleet were far more critical of nonconformity and did not firmly support comprehension until the reign of James II.³⁷

Of all those participating in the public debate on conformity and dissent in the late seventeenth century, Baxter was the most prolific, with over thirty published works. He wrote passionately against separation, but he did not conform. He probably worked as hard for unity as any in the seventeenth century, but failed to convince the Church of England to adopt what he viewed as reasonable latitude. He was not opposed to the episcopacy, but he and others were startled and dismayed by the determined and unaccommodating bishops after Charles had promised reasonable toleration and cooperation.

The issue of conformity first confronted Baxter as a young man in 1640 when the Convocation of the Church of England passed seventeen new canons which, among other things, were designed to preserve the ceremonial innovations of Laud and more firmly establish the principle of divine right. Charles requested a canon which would require all clergy

---

35. Baxter, *Third Defence*, Preface.
36. Cooper, *John Owen*, 192.
37. Rivers, *Reason, Grace, and Sentiment*, 1:33.

to take an oath to observe established standards for "doctrine and discipline." Initially the archbishop said the oath would protect clergy from being charged with popery with a phrase stating, "I will not endeavour by myself or any other, directly or indirectly, to bring in any popish doctrine contrary to that which is so established." But in the final version, the word "popish" was removed and the word "et cetera" was added, making the oath even more ambiguous and alarming.[38] Thereafter Canon 6 became known as the "Et Cetera Oath," which Baxter described as "a chief means to alienate me, and many others from it," being "imposed on us for the unalterable subjecting of us to Diocesans."[39]

Baxter had remarkable success as a pastor for nineteen years at Kidderminster, but faced many trials, including conflict between Presbyterians, Episcopalians, and Independents, along with the civil wars, arrests, and imprisonments. His first dispute relative to church unity was with John Saltmarsh (d.1647) who maintained that presbyters ordained by bishops were illegitimate because Scripture requires only congregational ordination.[40] In his reply Baxter accused him of being so narrow as to essentially be "against all Church Government, Church Censures, Church Officers, Church Ordinances, even Baptism it self."[41] Later at Kidderminster, Baxter overcame some of the ecclesiastical opposition to church unity by organizing an association of Presbyterian, Episcopalian, and Independent ministers in Worcestershire. They met monthly to cooperate on such matters as catechizing, evangelism, and discipline.[42] Before being forced to leave Kidderminster, Baxter wrote another work calling for church unity among "Abassines, Arminians, Greeks, Romanists, Lutherhanes, Calvinists, Arminians, Contra-remonstrants, Episcopalians, Presbyterians, Independents, and moderate anabaptists." He emphasized that all Christians should agree on the necessary things and allow freedom on other matters. His list of essentials, based on the Apostles' and Nicene Creeds, along with the Ten Commandments, was similar to that of Edwards.[43]

---

38. Davies, *Caroline Captivity*, 275–76.
39. Baxter, *Reliquiæ*, Part 1, §22.
40. Saltmarsh, *Divine Right*.
41. Baxter, *Plea for Congregationall Government*, 1.
42. Baxter, *Christian Concord*; Lim, *In Pursuit of Purity*, 117–55.
43. Baxter, *Universal Concord*, To the Reader, 55.

With the return of Charles II, Baxter was named one of the king's chaplains and invited to the Savoy Conference. Baxter drafted an alternative to the *BCP*, which allowed more freedom in use of the liturgy, but all was for naught. Nevertheless, even after the 1662 ejection, he continued to make the case for comprehension and compromise, while challenging error where he saw it. In *The Judgment of Mr. Baxter Concerning Ceremonies and Conformity* he refuted a work by John Humfrey which claimed that saving grace came through the Lord's Supper.[44] In one of his replies to separatist Edward Bagshaw (1628–71), Baxter hearkened back to the Worcestershire Agreement, calling it "sin" to exclude those "whom Christ receiveth and would have us receive."[45]

In 1679, he made another strong appeal to the conforming clergy to reconsider not only their decisions on toleration and comprehension, but also how they understood the problem. He reported reading more than twenty of their works and from "these accusations, my conscience urged me to acquaint the accusing Clergy with our Case," but his friends persuaded him to "leave it all to God."[46] Baxter recognized that the views of the conformists and nonconformists varied widely, portraying men like himself as truly seeking reconciliation with few demands. The following year a sequel addressed to Bishops George Morley (1598–1684) and Peter Gunning appeared, where he attempted to define unity, causes and effects of schism, and terms necessary for union. He repeated his point that the conditions sought by the dissenters prior to the ejection were most reasonable, framing the conflict starkly in spiritual terms:

> It grieveth my soul to see what advantage Satan hath got in England, against that Christian Love which is the life and character of Christ's disciples, and to cause wrath, envy hatred and strife, when God saith, *"He that hateth his brother is a murderer, and no murderer hath eternal life in him."*[47]

That same year, his opinion of Stillingfleet changed.

As a young cleric Stillingfleet established himself as a future leader with a keen interest in church unity by publishing *Irenicum* at the age of twenty-four. Seeing disputes over church government as a major cause of separation, Stillingfleet contended that the question over church

---

44. Humfrey, *Humble Vindication*.
45. Baxter, *Defence*, 17.
46. Baxter, *Nonconformists Plea*, Introductory Epistle.
47. Baxter, *True and Only Way*, Preface

government was incorrectly posed by those who asked which form of government most closely follows that of the Apostles. The proper question is whether "any one individual form be found so upon Divine Right, that all ages and Churches are bound unalterably to observe it."[48] From natural law, he argued that the basic purpose of the church is worship and toward that end the church must be governed in a manner conducive to proper worship, which requires unity—the unity clearly taught in the New Testament. Stillingfleet stressed his idea of unity with the phrase "peace and unity," a frequent theme. [49] But since Scripture fails to prescribe a divinely instituted structure, Stillingfleet concluded that we adopt that form which best advances the peace and unity of the church and as long as that form does not violate Scripture, it is reasonable to let the civil authorities decide.[50]

> The Unity then of the Church, is that of communion, and not that of approbation; and different opinions are no further liable to censures, than as men by the broaching of them, do endeavour to disturb the peace of the Church of God.[51]

For Stillingfleet unity required a tolerant community, not common beliefs. Beliefs may differ as long as they do not disrupt the peace, in which case we no longer have communion, but the beginning of schism. So in order to maintain the peace and unity of the church, members must not attempt to require agreement when issues are divisive, but to "acquiesce" to the established authorities.[52]

On the lookout for allies in his cause, the *Irenicum* caught Baxter's eye and he included it in his list of recommended books that "plead best the cause of Love and Peace."[53] But, from Baxter's perspective, love and peace were not advanced in May 1680, when Stillingfleet attacked nonconformists in a sermon before London Mayor Robert Clayton (1629–1707) at Guild Hall Chapel. By then Stillingfleet was quite prominent in London, having been appointed Dean of St. Paul's two years earlier. He made it clear that schism does not refer to separation of the Church of England from Rome, which is no different than England being independent of the

---

48. Stillingfleet, *Irenicum*, Preface.
49. Stillingfleet, *Irenicum*, 10, 105–07, 124, 157, 261, 275, 277, 314, 347, 415.
50. Stillingfleet, *Irenicum*, 414–16.
51. Stillingfleet, *Irenicum*, 108.
52. Stillingfleet, *Irenicum*, 124.
53. Baxter, *Cure*, 303.

Roman Empire. Just as people in each nation are united, so should Christian people in that same country be united "under the same Profession of Faith, the same Laws of Government, and rules of Divine Worship."[54] Very regrettably, it was the dissenters who were disrupting the unity of the church in England and Stillingfleet saw no good reason for their separation. "They do not deny that we have all the essentials of true Churches, *true Doctrine, true Sacraments,* and an *implicite Covenant between Pastors and People.*" But nonconformists have separated themselves from the Church of England, even though "they unanimously confess they find no fault with *the Doctrines of our Church.*"[55] Their rationale was difficult for Stillingfleet to comprehend.

Equally difficult for Stillingfleet were some dissenters who claimed that physical separation was not sin because, even though they met in a different place, it was not really separation. They justified their disunion by claiming that Christ instituted only individual congregations. Stillingfleet asked whether Christians are not required to have fellowship beyond their local body. Where do we read this in Scripture? "It is very strange, that those who contend so much for the Scriptures being a perfect Rule of all things pertaining to Worship and Discipline, should be able to produce nothing in so necessary a Point."[56]

Stillingfleet identified another faction of nonconformists who agreed that separation was sin, but also claimed they were not separated. This he found absurd, citing apostolic practice of not allowing "*Brethren who agree in all substantials of Faith and Worship, to separate from one another.*"[57] Dissenters claimed that what is sin is to go against one's conscience, but he dismissed their "tenderness of Conscience" claim as something that "can never justifie Separation."[58] There are "*Willful Errors of Conscience*" when people follow unfounded prejudice instead of asking God to illumine the truth of his Word and so believe that division and separation is necessary to satisfy their conscience. Such heedlessness, Stillingfleet labeled "*Willful and Damnable Sins.*"[59] In addition to disrupting the peace of the church, nonconformists, he concluded, were

---

54. Stillingfleet, *Mischief of Separation*, 19.
55. Stillingfleet, *Mischief of Separation*, 21.
56. Stillingfleet, *Mischief of Separation*, 26.
57. Stillingfleet, *Mischief of Separation*, 41.
58. Stillingfleet, *Mischief of Separation*, 39.
59. Stillingfleet, *Mischief of Separation*, 44–45.

making the "pretended *Unity*" of "*Papal Tyranny*" seem attractive and endangering the future of the church.⁶⁰ He called all Christians to work for peace and unity. He admonished the dissenters to recognize that the church will never be perfect in this world, to exercise love, humility, and discretion in seeking the common good rather than our own interests, to see separation as sin, and to realize that division weakens the church, which faces other, very formidable enemies.

Stillingfleet's printed sermon was one of a great number of publications to appear in the national debate over conformity, especially following the Great Ejection. Some Church of England clergymen such as Latitudinarian Bishop Patrick were more respectful of the nonconformists than Stillingfleet.⁶¹ But others like future Bishop of Oxford Samuel Parker caused greater offense. Parker accused nonconformists of having a superstitious view of God and gave no ground on their conscience defense, claiming that religion and conscience must submit to government authority for the sake of peace: "Most mens minds or Consciences are weak, silly and ignorant things, acted by fond and absurd principles, and imposed upon by their vices and their passions" justifying all sorts of evil, including "Murder, Treason, and Rebellion."⁶² It would appear that he viewed the conscience more as a curse than a blessing: "The last Refuge for *Godly Disobedience* is the Pretence of a Doubtful, Scrupulous, and Unsatisfied Conscience."⁶³ By the end of his 300-page harangue, there were few disreputable qualities with which he failed to condemn his caricatured dissenter. "He pretends Conscience only to vouch his humor, and his insolence, i.e. he is a villain and an hypocrite," arrogant in his biblical understanding, accountable to no one and a "*Notorious Heretick*."⁶⁴ He concluded where he began by stating that it is certainly acceptable to follow one's conscience, but only in private; in the public sphere, it is our obligation to submit to public authority.⁶⁵

For Baxter who had labored so hard at reunion, Stillingfleet's sermon was too much to take. He made it clear that not all nonconformists shared the same views. As for himself, he said that the Act of Uniformity was so

---

60. Stillingfleet, *Mischief of Separation*, 59.
61. Patrick, *Friendly Debate*.
62. Parker, *Discourse*, 6, 7.
63. Parker, *Discourse*, 267, 279.
64. Parker, *Discourse*, 273, 319.
65. Parker, *Discourse*, 312–14.

much more restrictive than any prior ecclesiastical canons and that were Hooker, Bishop Bilson, and Archbishop Ussher alive, they would have been nonconformists.[66] Baxter respectfully asked Stillingfleet to clarify some specific points, particularly to provide the reason why "that sinful *separation* which you mention as mine," because he was concerned that he might be "guilty of sinful Separation."[67] In his reply (printed in Baxter's book), Stillingfleet said that he did not have Baxter in mind when speaking of sinful separation, but was simply asking the question of

> whether the upholding Separate Meetings for Divine Worship, where the Doctrine established [i.e. by the Church of England], and the substantial parts of Worship are acknowledged to be agreable to the Word of God, be a sinful separation, or not? [. . .] By Separate Meetings, I mean such as pretend to a purer way of worship and are kept up in opposition to the legal establishment of Religion among us.[68]

Baxter replied that he did not understand what Stillingfleet meant by "separation." Returning to the offending sermon, he concluded that Stillingfleet's "separation" is predicated on his belief that "*God hath authorized the Magistrate*" to sanction pastors, their preaching, public prayers, and their practices.[69]

Baxter proceeded to give Stillingfleet what appears to be a brief lecture on the ancient history of conflict over civil investiture and of the corruption of human power, asking him to reflect on who was at fault with his separate meeting charge, when "you know that you have cast them out."[70] As power and authority comes only from God, "Those who rightfully give Orders, must give such Orders as God hath instituted."[71] Baxter challenged the idea of absolute conformity. He asked how Stillingfleet could be so firm on a national church when he admitted in his *Irenicum* that Scripture does not clearly mandate a particular form for church government.[72] He raised many provocative questions on separation, such as "Is it Separation for Men to refuse Pastors that are Usurpers?," given

66. Baxter, *Richard Baxter's Answer*, Preface.
67. Baxter, *Richard Baxter's Answer*, 8.
68. Baxter, *Richard Baxter's Answer*, 11.
69. Baxter, *Richard Baxter's Answer*, 14.
70. Baxter, *Richard Baxter's Answer*, 15–17.
71. Baxter, *Richard Baxter's Answer*, 20.
72. Baxter, *Richard Baxter's Answer*, 31.

that it is no crime in civil cases.[73] "Is it *Schism*, or Sinful *Separation*, to Disobey a Command about Religion, which no Man hath true Authority to Give?"[74] What follows are more deferential remarks, where Baxter acknowledged the validity of some of Stillingfleet's points. In conclusion, Baxter thanked Stillingfleet for his advice and counsel, but refused to accept the charge of separation.

Baxter was not the only one who took issue with Stillingfleet's sermon. In response to some of his critics, Stillingfleet wrote a third volume against schism, beginning with a history of dissent from the English Reformation. He reduced the reasons given by nonconformists to four: church government, certain stipulations that must be accepted, the issue of conscience, and comparisons with the Protestant separation from Rome, each of which he refuted.[75] Even though he did not believe that Scripture mandated a particular form of church government, he did argue that "our *Diocesan Episcopacy* is the same for *substance* which was in the *Primitive Church*" (a statement somewhat at odds with his *Irenicum*).[76] Not surprisingly he concluded, "I cannot find any Plea *sufficient* to justify in point of *conscience*, the *present Separation* from the *Church of England*."[77] Baxter responded with a very detailed critique, accusing Stillingfleet of historical errors, false accusations, and weak reasoning.[78] He continued writing, suggesting means to achieve unity and defending moderate nonconformists against accusations of schism until he died in 1691.

Baxter named the Catholic Church as most responsible for schism, despite their claim historically for universality and unity. "There is no Sect of Christians which maketh so great use of their pretence to Unity, and crying down Heresie, Schism and Separation, as the Papists do," presuming to know the truth, they claim absolute authority for the church and pope and excommunicate and persecute those who do not submit.[79] In addition to Catholics, he named those who believed that every true church must follow episcopal succession, along with anabaptists,

---

73. Baxter, *Richard Baxter's Answer*, 49.
74. Baxter, *Richard Baxter's Answer*, 53.
75. Stillingfleet, *Unreasonableness of Separation*, 219.
76. Stillingfleet, *Unreasonableness of Separation*, 244.
77. Stillingfleet, *Unreasonableness of Separation*, 394.
78. Baxter, *Second True Defence*.
79. Baxter, *Search*, 1–3.

Brownists, Seekers, Quakers, and Ranters as major contributors to discord and division.[80]

Apparently seeing no reason to continue engaging the nonconformists, Stillingfleet focused on other matters until the arrival of William and Mary set off the nonjuring controversy. For that, Stillingfleet offered practical arguments against those who opposed oaths in general and this one in particular. To those who claimed they could not break their oath to King James II, he argued that in reality that oath was no longer in force, being "repugnant to the publick Good."[81]

Stillingfleet was a respected Latitudinarian. Unlike the high-flying High Churchmen, he was tolerant on liturgy; he was not rigid on the form church government, believing there was no specific form was taught in Scripture; on doctrine, he was relatively liberal, unlike conservative Arminians or Calvinists. What he was not flexible on was the existence of a single national church as the only church and, as he believed, the only means by which to ensure his ultimate goal of peace and unity.

Among the nonconformists, Baxter was quite willing to compromise. He was not opposed in principle to the *BCP*, nor a national episcopacy. Biblical doctrine was much more important to him than Stillingfleet, but he was closer to Stillingfleet theologically than was John Edwards.[82] Given his more moderate Calvinism, it would seem to have been easier to find common ground with Stillingfleet. As noted above, his essentials for establishing church unity were similar to Edwards. What he and others desired was some latitude. He wanted a Church of England more tolerant of dissenting positions.

Both men spoke with great passion and urgency for church unity. Baxter thought of himself as willing to accept the most reasonable terms. "You could not (except a Catholick Christian) have truelier called me

---

80. Pastoor and Johnson, *Historical Dictionary*. The first principle of the Brownists was independence of the local church. Seekers emphasized contemplation, believing that all existing seventeenth-century churches were corrupt. Ranters did not trust the Bible as divine revelation or human reason, disregarded moral laws, and leaned toward pantheism.

81. Stillingfleet, *Discourse Concerning the Unreasonableness*, 12.

82. Baxter differed from most Calvinists in a number of significant respects: e.g., universal redemption, conditional election and denial of reprobation (see Richard Baxter, *Universal Redemption*), on the role of works for full justification, which was more of a process than a single event, although inferences from Baxter's strong anti-antinomian views have clouded his position. See Boersma, *Hot Pepper Corn*; Packer, *Redemption and Restoration*, 241–65.

than an *Episcopal-Presbyterian-Independent*," recognizing that "the three Parties have some *Truths* and some *Errors*."[83] After all, he admitted that his proposal for church government came from Archbishop Ussher.[84] Baxter worked very hard for a more tolerant church, but he was unwilling to accommodate himself to certain positions, such as the "unfeigned assent and consent" clause. Unfortunately for Baxter, Stillingfleet's side held the power.

EDWARDS ON SCHISM

It was into this continuing and unresolved national debate that Edwards addressed the issues of church unity, schism, and dissent on a number of occasions, having faced them since his ordination. Forty-five years later on May 1, 1707, his sermon celebrating the political union of England and Scotland was another call for church unity. With Ezekiel 37:22 as his text, he preached against two groups of dissenters, one of which he clearly saw as the more egregious contributor to dissension than the other. Those commonly called dissenters are so named because they dissent from some of the ceremonial requirements such as use of the surplice and kneeling when receiving the sacrament, but "our *Arminian* Clergy" are also, because they dissent from some important doctrines of the church, such as original sin and eternal election.[85] Edwards was actually more sympathetic to the first group in the church. Rather than finding them guilty of schism, Edwards harkened back to Luther at Worms: "I plainly see that they had a license given them even by our Spiritual Fathers and Representatives of the Church to exercise their Religion according to the Dictates of their Consciences, and that with Impunity."[86]

Although it was common to identify those usually called dissenters as schismatics because most of them had left the church, Edwards had a broader view of both dissent and schism. Most of his fellow churchmen spoke of schism as separation, which they called unlawful. He pointed out that schism according to First Corinthians is "an unlawful Breach

---

83. Baxter, *Third Defence*, 110.

84. Baxter, *True and only Way*, Preface. Baxter also reported speaking with Ussher who told him that "*Councils were but for Counsel and Concord, and not for the Government of each other or any of the members.*" See Baxter, *True and only Way*, 110.

85. Edwards, *One Nation*, 10–11.

86. Edwards, *Arminian Doctrines*, 214.

of the Orders and Institutions of the Christian Church."[87] Members of the Corinthian church were disruptive in various ways when the church assembled. So, as Edwards understood Scripture, one aspect of schism for an individual meant failing to do what a lawfully established church requires or doing things contrary to what is required, either of which could occur without physical separation.[88]

Of the one hundred and forty-one canons of the church, he claimed that "there are not a quarter of them observed by our churchmen" and proceeded to list some of the canons in this category. For example, Can.55 required a Bidding Prayer by the preacher prior to his sermon; Can.59 required the minister to catechize every Sunday and holy day before the evening prayer. In addition, to these sins of omission, "Illegal and Uncanonical Practices" were being observed by many clergymen.[89] Can.67 stipulated that ministers must not allow anyone to take the Lord's Supper if they are known to be living in unrepentant sin; Can.75 prohibited ministers from frequenting taverns, playing cards, and dice, etc.[90] These plus more examples led Edwards to a conclusion that did not endear him to the church. "If everyone be a *Schismatick* that conforms not to all things Prescribed by the Church of *England,* then most certainly great numbers of our Clergy lie under the just Imputation of Schism."[91]

Even more serious for Edwards, however, were those in the church who dissented from church doctrine as set out in the XXXIX Articles. Those who did not really believe the Creeds and Articles were the real dissenters, not the nonconformists who studiously held to most of them. "How can we blame the Dissenters for disgusting the Rites and Ceremonies of the Church, when we ourselves disrelish its Articles?" He thanked God for the so-called dissenters who recognized the importance of sound doctrine and maintained biblical orthodoxy despite the waywardness of some leaders of the Church of England.

> If there had been none of that Party, the Church of *England* had been long since ruin'd, for if the High Churchmen had had no check, they would have brought in Popery before this time, by

---

87. Edwards, *Theologia*, 1:750.
88. Edwards, *Preacher, Third Part*, 141–42.
89. Edwards, *Preacher, Second Part*, 182.
90. Edwards, *Preacher, Third Part*, 142–43.
91. Edwards, *Preacher, Third Part*, 148.

a Sidewind of *Arminianism* and by their over-valuing of *Ceremony* and *Pomp* in Divine Worship.[92]

Edwards lectured the church for emphasizing the principles of "*Unity* and *Uniformity* among us," while failing to take appropriate measures to achieve it. "Talk no longer of Union in the Church, till you unite in Doctrines."[93] He called the Church of England "self–condemned" for complaining about Catholics trying to "corrupt our religion" when we are doing it to ourselves.[94] He said it was shameful that many of those who have been labeled as schismatics were more orthodox in following the "Doctrines of our Church" than "we who have subscribed to them" yet "disregard them."[95] Ultimately unity and peace of the church depends upon the restoration of the "Ancient Truths of the Gospel" as the centerpiece of preaching so that all orthodox Christians will understand them, believe them, and live by them.[96]

Contemplating the orthodoxy of the church in the early eighteenth century, Edwards was startled to read the preface of Cotton Mather's *Old Paths Restored*. What surprised him was that the preface was written by William Whiston and it was Whiston who decided to have the book reprinted in London. In condemning Calvinist theology, Whiston actually confirmed Edwards's view that the church had departed from its original understanding of the XXXIX Articles. Whiston assured his readers that he did not "at all believe the main part of the Doctrine therein contained; that being next to impossible for any one to do that is so much in Love with a Rational Religion [. . . and] the Original Writings of Christianity." But he was impressed by six things he learned from Mather. First, that Edwards, an avowed Calvinist "without actually leaving the Church of England, shall be so admir'd, and caressed, and celebrated [. . .] as if he were the grand Pillar and Support of the Church and of pure Christianity." Last, which caught Edwards's attention, was Whiston's assessment of the state of the XXXIX Articles within the church.

> 'Tis certain those Articles favor the Doctrines of Calvin; and 'tis as certain that the Body of the Members of our Church do not now believe those Doctrines; nay do so vehemently

---

92. Edwards, *Preacher, Second Part*, 182–83.
93. Edwards, *Preacher, Second Part*, 179.
94. Edwards, *Preacher, Second Part*, 181.
95. Edwards, *Preacher*, x.
96. Edwards, *Preacher, Second Part*, 190–91.

oppose them. Yet do we [. . .] go on in what is too like to Open Prevarication [. . .] and no longer give a handle to our own Consciences.[97]

So according to Edwards, Whiston called the nonconformists the "True Churchmen," but the conforming Arminians, "false and *perfidious*" because they did not conform to the XXXIX Articles.[98] Having named Whiston the "*False Prophet of our Age*," he welcomed Whiston's observations and compared him to Balaam, "*He came to Curse this People, but behold, he hath altogether Blessed them.*"[99]

In addition to accusing many of his fellow divines of disregarding certain prescribed liturgy and official doctrines, Edwards saw their attitude toward the orthodox dissenters as especially unchristian and a major contributor to schism. Those who call these nonconformists "*Damn'd Schismatics*" are the hypocritical high-flyers who do not themselves attend services and are not embarrassed to publicly justify their behavior.[100] Even worse was to pronounce the dissenters as "*Damn'd,*" when the same men repeat the words "at the Burial of the most profligate Wretch, *In sure and certain hope of the Resurrection to eternal Life.*"[101]

Is "Brotherly *Love*" not an essential for church unity?, Edwards asked.[102] Yet, "we have knock'd People on the Head for God's sake and for Religions's sake. Whilst we have decried the Persecution which the *Papists* are guilty of, we have Imitated it."[103] Against those who opposed his toleration of dissenters as detrimental to the church and state, Edwards responded that basic Christian charity would reduce animosity, bigotry and division while promoting peace and good will. He went even further to state that both the established church and the moderate dissenters actually need each other. "If both Parties among us did not *Poise* one another, they would soon be Wanton and Skittish, and the High-Mettled Bigots on either side would shew themselves Disorderly, Mutinous and

---

97. Tuttle, "William Whiston and Cotton Mather," 200–4. Following his correspondence with Whiston, Mather decided to write a book against Whiston. Edwards wrote the preface as requested, but it was never published, possibly due to Edwards's unexpected death.

98. Edwards, *Some New Discoveries*, 115, 117, 119.

99. Edwards, *Some New Discoveries*, 118, 119.

100. Edwards, *Arminian Doctrines*, 214, 215.

101. Edwards, *Arminian Doctrines*, 216–17.

102. Edwards, *Preacher, Second Part*, xxxviii, 141.

103. Edwards, *Preacher, Second Part*, xxx.

Unruly."[104] Edwards summarized his own view of the "*Sober and Moderate Dissenters*":

> I consider that they are our Fellow-Christians [. . .] They believe and acknowledge the same Articles of the Christian Faith [. . .] they serve and worship the *same* Blessed Jesus [. . .] They profess to live according to the *same* Holy Rule [. . .] They have the *same* Principle of Conscience in their Breasts [. . .] and we can't be so uncharitable as not to think that when they leave this World they go to the *same* Place of Happiness that we look for. And shall we meet them there, and yet persecute them here? No, by no means.[105]

In a discourse on Galatians 5, he said that "*Unity* is the genuine consequent of [Love]."[106] More incisive than that was his commentary on the Second Commandment that those who love God "must" love fellow believers, and "if we love our Brethren, it is an infallible Sign we love God." He reminded his readers that the distinguishing mark of "the True Professors of Christianity" given by Jesus and reiterated in the epistles, especially by the Apostle John is "*that you love one another*." He summarized the power of Christian love to make people happy because it "ties all Bodies, Churches and Societies together" and "links all virtues and Graces together." Love is fundamental to who we are and essentially "consummates" all other virtues.[107] He admonished the Church of England to be more engaging and disarming in persuading nonconformists and to be sensitive to their "Tender Consciences": "Let us treat them as Brethren, with Meekness, Moderation and Forbearance."[108]

Edwards was not only criticizing the high-flyers for their lack of brotherly love toward dissenters, he implicated the leaders of Church of England for consenting to the separation in the first place. But Lightfoote (quoted by Edwards) claimed the issue was not whether the bishops had consented to any separation, but

> "*what Grounds and Reasons there are for separating*: As if our Bishops, the lawful Governors of our Church, who consented to the tolerating of the Separation which we are speaking of,

---

104. Edwards, *Preacher, Second Part*, xxxii–xxxiii.
105. Edwards, *Arminian Doctrines*, 217.
106. Edwards, *Fruits*, 3.
107. Edwards, *Theologia*, 2:470–71.
108. Edwards, *Arminian Doctrines*, 218.

did not know what Grounds and Reasons there are for it; or as if they had done what they did in this Affair without good *Grounds and Reasons*."

To Edwards it was a vacuous excuse of the bishops to claim that they did not know why the separation occurred, as the dissenters "have a thousand times told us." They follow their own consciences in deciding to separate. "Should not our Charity, as well as our Prudence, prompt us to be cautious in stigmatizing the Orthodox and Conscientious Dissenters with the infamous Brand of *Schism?*" And yet the relationship between the Church of England and its nonconformists Edwards concluded was little different in principle from the circumstances that led to the Protestant separation from Rome.[109]

He recalled that John Hales often said that "*Schism and Heresy are Theological Scare-Crows*," meaning that they are used to terrorize those who do not "subscribe to that particular Set of Doctrines which I maintain" or "submit to such Terms of Communion as I approve of." He found it "*deplorable*" that there were folks on both sides who were so intolerant that they could not imagine anyone in the opposing camp to be upright in their character and sound in their judgment. Again, he challenged everyone to heal their relationships on earth, given that they will likely meet in heaven.[110]

Conforming was not an easy decision for Edwards, especially considering the church's treatment of these dissenters. But for him, compliance with church polity was necessary to preserve unity. Even though he was quite sympathetic with the dissenters on many of their positions, he himself was not a dissenter.

> I adhere to the Doctrine, I joyn with the Worship, I embrace the Communion, and I acquiesce in the Government of our Church, and I have always shew'd my self conformable to these: but I could never prevail with my self to condemn all those who separate from us. For tho' I can with a good Conscience give an account to my self of my own practice, yet I have no Authority to censure and judge the Perswasions and Conscience of other Persons in this affair.[111]

---

109. Edwards, *Arminian Doctrines*, 216–17.
110. Edwards, *Preacher, Second Part*, xxxv, xxxviii.
111. Edwards, *Preacher, Second Part*, xxvii–xxviii.

But conforming did not mean that he was timid to defend important doctrines. He believed that some confused his bold defense of Calvinism for anger against Arminians. He reported receiving numerous rebuttals, some unsigned, often containing errors he felt necessary to correct. Some thought that all doctrines necessary for salvation were easy to understand, but those he emphasized were *"intricate and perplex'd."* Edwards responded that *"even the plainest doctrines, such as Faith and Repentance"* generate considerable controversy. Another one claimed that Edwards's favorite doctrines were not found in the Gospels, to which he said, "I'm heartily sorry for these Divines that they have lived so long and have not look'd into the *Gospels*."[112] Still another accused him of serving the interests of Scotland and Geneva and being disloyal to the Church of England. For this view, he quoted Dr. Sanderson: "the *Arminians* seek to draw Persons of those that dissent from them into dislike with the State, as if they were *Puritans* [. . . which] is the most unjust and uncharitable course."[113]

Despite his sharp disagreements with Arminians, Edwards concluded that we have two choices: either tolerate those with whom we disagree on non-essential matters or seek to destroy them. "This is an unquestionable Truth that our Power in Matters that are Indifferent, is not to be used to the Scandal of those that are Weak": otherwise First Corinthians 9 is not Scripture. And to reject Romans 14:14, is to say that "It is the Conscience that makes the Crime."[114] As for himself, he professed to respect others for their learning and piety, regardless of their theology. Though he believed Arminians were misled by error, he also believed there were "many good Men" among them. He adamantly opposed treating his opponents with "angry Censuring." "I hold it no small delinquency to malign and traduce those that differ from us, as Infidels and Outcasts."[115] Edwards did not see himself engaged in a contest to win a theological debate; he continued to pray that Whitby (before his apostasy) and others whom he called "my Brethren" would see the error of their ways.

> I reckon it as a Duty and Service owing to my *Religion*, to my *Profession*, to my *Conscience*, and to the *Church* of which I am a Member, to assert and vindicate these Divine Truths [. . .] and I

---

112. Edwards, *Veritas*, xxiv–xxv.
113. Edwards, *Veritas*, xxvii.
114. Edwards, *Preacher, Second Part*, xxix.
115. Edwards, *Veritas*, xxii.

hope I shall have Courage enough to defend this Post to the last, seeing I contend not for *Victory*, but *Truth*.[116]

According to Edwards, the unity of the church is based on the principle that the members constitute "but *one Body*"—a body which has Christ as its head. On this point he was very emphatic: "There is no one Point of Christianity, that is more plainly delivered than this, tho' it is less taken notice of, than any whatsoever; I mean the Union of Believers with Christ." He cited a number of passages in Scripture, including John 17:21, where Jesus prays that church would be one as is the Trinity.[117] For at least the last thirty years of his life, he worked to define and defend what that meant. Theologically, one issue was, what is the true church? He agreed with Bucer, Beza, and Vermigli that the three marks of a true church are "Pure and Sound Doctrine, the Sacraments Ministered according to Christ's Holy Institution, and the Right Use of Ecclesiastical Discipline."[118] His main concern was not the holiness of the members or even of its leaders, but with the ordinances, including prescribed prayers, administration of the sacraments and preaching. And he was not speaking of "*Disputable* Matters" or "Things *Indifferent*" or where the Scripture is not clear.

Edwards often wrote about sound doctrine, *Theologia Reformata* and *Vertias Redux* being his two major works. In his instructions to young preachers, he addressed five key doctrines under fire from Arminians: eternal election, original sin, imputation of Christ's righteousness, justification by faith alone, the necessity of special and supernatural grace.[119] Sound doctrine was not only the basis for defining beliefs and practices of the true church, it was also "the Foundation which must be laid for a Christian Life." A poor foundation will not lead to a good life. "The Practice of Godliness will vanish without Faith." He was particularly critical of Latitudinarians. "Those among us that talk most of *Charity* and *Piety* are the least concerned for *Soundness* of *Doctrine*: those that are most for *Living* well have the least regard for what they *Believe*."[120]

---

116. Edwards, *Arminian Doctrines*, 115.
117. Edwards, *Theologia*, III (1726), 128.
118. Edwards, *Brief Confutation*, 289-90; Parker, "Moral Agency," 45.
119. Edwards, *Preacher, Second Part*, 4-28.
120. Edwards, *Preacher, Third Part*, 139-40.

In response to those within the Church of England for whom the episcopacy was nonnegotiable, Edwards separated the essential from the nonessential:

> I never heard any sober Man assert that Episcopacy and the Discipline that goes along with it are *Essential* nor absolutely necessary to the Church, that is, that the Church ceases to be, if they be wanting. Our Church (according to the Concessions of some of the Learnedst Men among us) might be a True Church without these, but she can't without her Doctrine. It is this that makes the Substantial Distinction between a True and a False Church, but the other things do not.

Doctrines he called the "Shibboleth" of the church because by these we have our identity.[121] In his works there are frequent references to the creeds as orthodox expressions of essential, sound doctrine, all of which were part of the Church of England liturgy. It was to these creeds that he turned for succinct statements when challenged by heterodoxy. He wrote an extensive commentary on the Apostles' Creed. He proved Whiston's heresy by comparing his views to the Nicene Creed, calling it nothing more than "plain Scripture."[122] He defended the Athanasian Creed against attack by Samuel Clarke, but admitted that the beginning text was rather "*harsh and severe*," where it says that unless you believe in the "*Catholick Faith*," you will go to hell.[123] However elsewhere, reflecting on the truth of the Gospel, he asked, "what can be more harsh and severe than St. Paul's reproving the *Galatians* Apostacy from the Truth?"[124]

Although Edwards recognized the creeds as critical landmarks of the faith, he realized that the creeds themselves could be misused and fail to serve their intended purpose. He warned against saying, "I believe in God the Father" and simply meaning "*I believe God to be, and to be almighty, etc.*" Reviewing the teachings of a number of Greek and Latin fathers, he made clear the difference between "*I believe in*" as "*Trusting or Relying upon*," which pertains alone to God, and "I believe" as "naked Belief or Assent," which pertains to everything else, including creeds and the church.[125] No doubt this was behind his debate with Locke on the

---

121. Edwards, *Preacher, Second Part*, 178.
122. Edwards, *Some Brief Observations*, 61.
123. Edwards, *Supplement*, 67–80; Edwards *Theologia*, 1:639.
124. Edwards, *Preacher*, 186.
125. Edwards, *Doctrine of Faith*, 100–07.

Apostles' Creed: "If a man believe no more than is in *express* terms in the *Apostle's Creed*, his Faith will not be the *Faith* of a Christian" and "this Creed hath more in it than he [Locke] and his brethren will subscribe to."[126]

Protestants in England were divided on whether or not Rome was a true church and also on the definition of a true church. On one extreme were those who asserted that Rome was apostate prior to the Reformation, guilty of persecuting true believers. Some Puritans compared Rome to Old Testament Amalek.[127] On the other hand, despite obvious corruptions, Rome did profess allegiance to foundational truths as expressed in the three creeds. Article XIX left open the question of what it means for the Word to be preached "purely" or the sacraments administered "duly."[128] Prior to his appointment as bishop, George Carleton wrote that Rome could not be the true church because they accept as members those who "make onely an externall profession" but have no "inward grace," they have made the Pope, not Christ, head of their church, and because they do not exhibit unity of the Spirit or of faith.[129] Rome continued its historic claim as the true church, convinced that Protestants could not be included, having rejected Rome, not to mention their many divisions.[130]

The continuing controversy prompted Edwards to write a short book on the topic. He summarized both sides of the debate, drew from Scripture and the Fathers to conclude that even though Rome was said to "own the *three Creeds* as we do," she was not a true church because of serious corruptions: a lack of true faith in preaching (e.g., soteriology) and failure to properly administer the Sacraments (e.g., the Mass).[131] The problem was not that they denied any essentials, but that (quoting William Sherlock) their "'Imposing of New Doctrines and Practices upon Christians as necessary to Salvation, which were never taught by our Saviour and his Apostles.'" Following Paul's instructions to his assistants Timothy and Titus, first in Edwards's mind was sound doctrine, because

---

126. Edwards, *Socinianism Unmask'd*, 47, 48.
127. Milton, *Catholic and Reformed*, 36, 99.
128. Milton, *Catholic and Reformed*, 131–72.
129. Carleton, *Directions to Know*, 9–22.
130. Milton, *Catholic and Reformed*, 46.
131. Edwards, *Brief Confutation*, 292–96.

"we are ascertained that the Church is the Pillar and Ground of the Truth. 1 Tim. 3:15" and Rome failed because of their additions.[132]

Though firm that no one should separate from a true church, Edwards was not unconditionally bound to the established Church of England.[133] He recognized that there have always been "corruptions" in the church and there is no reason to expect a perfect church in this life. He implored his readers and especially the clergy, who are called to exercise discipline, to be vigilant in addressing problems that arise. But if the official ordinances are revised to go against Scripture on foundational doctrines like the deity of Christ, Christians are obligated to leave the church because "whatever is disown'd by God Himself, and is repugnant to His Word, is *substantially Evil*." Without clear evidence of such corruptions however, we must remain.[134] To put it simply, if our church is true, we are bound to remain; if it fails to be true, we must depart.

Except for Rome's imposition of essentials in addition to those found in the three creeds, Edwards did not discuss the problem of determining which corruptions were allowable (as in the Church of England) and which were not (as in Rome). He saw the XXXIX Articles as being well-founded on the three creeds. He admitted that he differed with Augustine on whether baptism by a heretic was acceptable even if it was trinitarian. Neither did he accept ordination from heretical churches.[135] Despite the "Pollutions of the Roman Church" which obscured the Gospel, he saw salvation as a divine work so that "in the Times of Popery many were saved" being "*in* the *Roman* Church, but not *of* it."[136] For Edwards it was logically inconsistent to remain a Protestant and consider Rome a true church. To do so would invalidate the Reformation.

> If the general Assertion of our Clergy be true that the Papists are Right as to *all Essentials*, and in a *salvable* State, it is absurd and unreasonable to contend with them so much as we do, and to defend our Separation from them.[137]

Regarding physical separation, Edwards called it schism if there was no "*just Cause*." But "when the Society requires us to comply with gross

---

132. Edwards, *Brief Confutation*, 293.
133. Edwards, *Brief Confutation*, 311–17.
134. Edwards, *Theologia*, 1:551–52.
135. Edwards, *Brief Confutation*, 319–20.
136. Edwards, *Brief Confutation*, 324.
137. Edwards, *Brief Confutation*, 326.

Errors and vicious Practices, it is not to be questioned but that a Departure from that Society is lawful and warrantable." Furthermore, when a church places such unbiblical stipulations on its members, it is the church that is guilty of schism, which Edwards noted was exactly what Chillingworth accused Rome of causing.[138] Edwards recognized that "just cause" was not so easy to define because it does touch on matters that are *"Indifferent"* and relates to the somewhat conflicting principles of Christian liberty and causing offense. As an example, he referred to some who refused to worship with the Church of England because they claimed it would offend *"their weak Brethren."*[139] He recalled the fact that Paul had Timothy circumcised, but not Titus. Edwards's guidance in such situations was that we submit to those in authority over us, carefully consider the situation of our brother is in, and practice brotherly love and humility as a witness to the essence of the Christian life.[140]

For Edwards, corruption of doctrine was serious, which is why separation from heretics is necessary. He cited Justinian's *Codex* where a heretic is defined as anyone who does not accept the first four church councils, namely Nicaea, Constantinople, Ephesus, and Chalcedon.[141] Edwards summarized the foundational doctrines of the Scriptures topically:

> The Being of a God; The Doctrine of the Trinity; The Divinity and Satisfaction of Christ; His Resurrection and Ascension, and His Coming again to Judgment; The Immortality of Humane Souls; The Rewards of Heaven, and The Torments of Hell. And he is truly an Heretick who denies any of these Articles.[142]

Edwards emphasized that being accused of heresy does not make one a heretic. Neither are they who follow false teaching out of ignorance, but those who maintain their deviant beliefs "with great *Willfulness* and *Obstinacy*."[143]

---

138. Edwards, *Theologia*, 1:752.

139. Edwards, *Theologia*, 1:754.

140. Edwards, *Theologia*, 1:762.

141. Edwards, *Theologia*, 1:717. Roman Emperor Justinian the Great (482–565) reorganized and corrected civil law of the empire. He legalized Christian orthodoxy against Arians and other heretics.

142. Edwards, *Theologia*, 1:717.

143. Edwards, *Theologia*, 1:718.

8

Conclusion

WHAT DID JOHN EDWARDS do to save the Church of England? First, he recognized that the true church is not a human institution. If the Church of England was to continue as part of the divinely instituted church of Christ, certain *essential,* defining characteristics upon which it was established could not change because God is immutable and his truth as revealed in Scripture does not change. Edwards often spoke and wrote about truth, especially in *Veritas Redux: Evangelical Truths Restored.* Among the truths necessary for maintaining the church as a true church were those doctrines spelled out in the three creeds: Apostles', Nicene, and Athanasian, all foundational for the Church of England and its XXX-IX Articles. He did not view these creeds as authoritative above Scripture, but as summarizing the essential truths of Scripture.

It was from this perspective that he was very concerned about men like John Locke, Samuel Clarke, William Whiston, and Daniel Whitby who promoted a more inclusive definition of orthodoxy by making optional such doctrines as the Trinity and the deity and atoning work of Christ. Edwards was uncompromising in his defense against those who refused to accept as essential the traditional orthodox understanding of these central doctrines, basing his arguments first on Scripture, second on the Fathers, and third on the Reformers and respected men in the Church of England. In short, the church, like any institution depends on a set of defining marks for its identity and reason to exist. Edwards saw peace, unity, and toleration as important, but not as important as defining and upholding essential truth. For unity to be real and lasting, that unity must be based on established doctrinal foundations.

A second emphasis for Edwards was to convince professing Christians that unity must take precedence over non-essentials. If the church is founded on divine truth, the church is one, because God's truth is a unified whole. Unity demands that all members subscribe to the same essentials as expressed in the creeds as traditionally understood. Although unity is secondary to these essential truths, it must take precedence over other, non-essential doctrines. Since the fourth century, all orthodox Christians have been held the doctrines expressed in the Nicene Creed as essential. In practice, however, most everyone adds to the Nicene Creed whatever else they held dear—often those beliefs that set them apart from other branches of the church. For example, Baptists require adult baptism and Roman Catholics, submission to the authority of the church and pope. In effect, although everyone sees the Nicene Creed as necessary and essential, very few really believe that it is in any respect sufficient.

Edwards often referred to the three creeds as essential, along with doctrines which they summarize. He used them to distinguish heresy from orthodoxy in practice. First, he followed the historic standard that those who deny the Nicene Creed are outside the church. Second he did not separate himself from those who upheld these central doctrines, but with whom he disagreed on other doctrines, aside from papists due to Rome's corrupted understanding. Third, on a linear scale of importance, he placed the unity of the church below the creedal essentials and above all other doctrines.

On non-essential doctrines (those not specified or implied by the creeds) there is freedom, but not freedom to add to the essentials. In Edwards's thinking, this meant that it is not absolutely necessary that all Christians agree, for example, on all aspects of soteriology (e.g., Arminian or Calvinistic), church government, or forms of worship. Edwards had his own views on non-essential and disputable matters. Many of them were important to him and he felt compelled to help other Christians come to what he believed to be a more biblical understanding. For example, he believed that Arminianism was in error, not supported by the XXXIX Articles as understood by Archbishop Cranmer and his colleagues. He believed that the Presbyterian understanding of church government was more faithful to Scripture than the Episcopal system. However the church is big enough for Arminians and Calvinists and an Episcopalian government is acceptable.

Nonconformists objected to Episcopalian government, preferring Presbyterian or congregational; Baptists did not accept paedobaptism; others objected to prescribed liturgy and certain ceremonial stipulations. For these and other reasons, they chose not to conform. For them, unity was not so important. On the other hand, the Church of England, especially in 1662 was no more interested in church unity than the dissenters as the Act of Uniformity required "unfeigned consent and assent" by all clergy in the use of the *BCP*—clearly a nonessential in Edwards's mind. Even Latitudinarians like Edward Stillingfleet exercised their latitude only selectively (on matters not deemed to be important to them).

Were there not other contemporary conforming Calvinist clergy in the Church of England? Yes, but as his published works attest, none were nearly as vigilant and determined to protect the identity of the church by their public opposition to heterodoxy as was Edwards. None were as bold in articulating a Reformed apologetic within the church. And none pursued the unity of the church with the fervor and personal commitment of Edwards. He understood that schism was not simply a matter of physical separation. Theological and spiritual separation were not only more serious, but also more ruinous, which was why he emphasized doctrinal unity. Though he did not condone the decision of the nonconformists, he was very sympathetic to their theological understanding because he believed that they generally conformed more closely to the essentials than did the Latitudinarian leaders of the Church of England.

Third for Edwards was that Christians treat other believers with genuine love and respect. He recognized that the tension over conformity was exasperated by a lack of love between conformers and dissenters. Sadly, the topic of Christian love, which is emphasized so widely in the New Testament, did not often enter the national discussion. He recognized the Reformation principle that each person must follow their own conscience as they seek to honor God and the commands of Scripture. As a consequence, he showed deference to Latitudinarians in the church, such as Bishops Stillingfleet and Patrick, though he sharply disagreed with some aspects of their theology. But he did not think it was acceptable to malign the character of a fellow believer with whom he disagreed. In this respect, he was different from many of his contemporary pamphleteers in the church. Near the end of his life he wrote, "I part friendly and charitably with those that concur not with me in my Apprehensions;

yea those of the *Arminian* Cut, that have reproach'd my late Undertakings without any shadow of Reason."[1]

To put it in the seventeenth-century Lockean context, Edwards practiced genuine toleration to all who conformed to the defining doctrinal documents of the Church of England and in particular, toward those who held beliefs in opposition to doctrines which were important to him. Historically, relatively few people, including Christians, have given more than lip service to toleration. Yet toleration is simply a weak version of Jesus' command to "love thy neighbor as thyself," Edwards's theme on many occasions.

Instead of Edwards, Locke has been regarded as the chief prophet of toleration, but how tolerant was he? As has been noted, he was not very tolerant of criticism. Yes, he was more amenable in identifying heterodox people like himself as Christians than was Edwards and most others of the time. But he was not so tolerant of those who interpreted Scripture differently from himself, like Edwards, nor of Catholics, nor atheists.[2] Locke wanted people to be tolerant about things that were important to them, but not to him. Most people have Locke's sense of tolerance, being tolerant regarding those issues that are not of great concern to them.

Edwards, on the other hand, was an unabashed Calvinist. Calvinist doctrine was very important to him, which is obvious in his preaching and writing. Yet he respected Latitudinarians in the church and practiced genuine toleration toward them. He respected their right to interpret Scripture as they did and he was determined to unite with them in the Church of England because unity is essential for the peace of the church and its witness to the world.

Put another way, toleration was, perhaps along with peace, most essential for Locke. Christian doctrines, even those such as the Trinity, were not, and viewed as obstacles to peace and toleration. For Edwards, toleration was important as an expression of Christian love, but he was not willing to dispense with central doctrines like the Trinity for the sake of peace and unity in the church for in his mind, without the doctrine of the Trinity, the church would not be Christian. Perhaps he was more tolerant of those who kept their heresy relatively private, which is why he did not launch a major attack on Newton, but he was not tolerant of heretical views being propagated in print because such activity would lead

---

1. Edwards, *Doctrine of Faith*, xix.
2. Marshall, *John Locke*, 47, 68, 73, 76.

people astray. As stated in his sermon on the plague, nothing is more important for any individual than eternal salvation and salvation depends on the eternal truth of God.

Fourth, Edwards saw the Church of England as one with the historic catholic church. Copious citations to numerous authorities throughout his works demonstrate Edwards's deep awareness of one church separated by time and geography, but united in its biblical understanding and commitment to Christ. Though Edwards was not afraid to identify himself as a Calvinist, Calvin was not his authority.

> I do not urge upon you that *Calvin* speaks thus, or the *Synod* of *Dort* teaches thus, but I chiefly inculcate that the *Sacred Writ* saith thus, that our *Saviour himself* saith thus, and that the *Inspired Apostles* say the same.[3]

He simply thought that what had generally been understood as Calvinism was the most faithful interpretation of biblical truth. He agreed with Bishop Wilkins of Chester who named in addition to Calvin as "*Eminent for their Orthodox sound Judgment*" reformers Peter Martyr, Wolfgang Musculus (1497–1563), Heinrich Bullinger (1504–75), Ludwig Lavater (1527–86), Lambert Danaeus (c.1535–c.1590), Anton Praetorius (1560–1613), Johannes Piscator (1546–1625), Girolamo Zanchi (1516–90), Franciscus Junius (1545–1602), and others.[4] Though Scripture was authoritative for Edwards, he recognized that its interpretation is a nontrivial enterprise, fraught with numerous pitfalls. He did not consider biblical hermeneutics to be a solo exercise. To avoid error, it must be undertaken with care and humility, consistent with orthodox believers historically. Such an approach he believed would reinforce and maintain church unity.

Fifth, Edwards worked to save the church by perpetuating orthodoxy within the Church of England along with churches in the American colonies through many of his works that were used in theological education of young ministers. His books included biblical commentaries, systematic theology, and disputations with heretics and non-Calvinists. With considerable dexterity in Hebrew, Greek, and Latin, he was adept at comparing the Septuagint with the Hebrew text and reading the Greek New Testament along with the Fathers who wrote in Greek or Latin. He

---

3. Edwards, *Preacher, Third Part*, 296.
4. Edwards, *Preacher*, xxi–xxii.

often pointed out flaws in the logic, hermeneutics, and ancient language facility of his opponents.

What he did not do, based on available evidence, was to engage men like Stillingfleet as did Baxter and appeal for a more accommodating comprehension. Neither does it seem that he contacted nonconformists to suggest that they reconsider some of their demands. Nor does it seem that he made any attempt to form alliances with other like-minded men, but he did welcome the efforts of others who joined him in warning about the Socinian threat. Perhaps he did not sense a calling or have the energy to organize a movement. More likely, he believed that his pen was his most effective means of mobilization and writing a more propitious use of his time.

Edwards provided a model of sorts for how a minister should preach, engage the church and the world, and counsel others. In his instruction to the clergy, he charged them to

> not despair of Success. Let us enlighten the dark World, and call men off from their vicious Courses, and warn them of the Judgments of God, and invite and allure them by the tenders of Grace and Mercy, and commend Religion to them by our own Examples, and every way approve our selves to God in the discharge of our Pastoral Duty.[5]

Given the spread of his books in various libraries, including those of influential men like Increase and Cotton Mather, George Whitefield, Timothy and Jonathan Edwards, and Joseph Bellamy, it is difficult to estimate his influence on the eighteenth-century church and beyond.

While not a particular thrust of Edwards's endeavors, a sixth aspect of his second career rescue effort was the unrelenting zeal, commitment, and urgency with which he pursued his mission until his last days. This is evident not only in the volume but also the content of his published works. His published output was impressive, even if we ignore the report that on his death, he left almost as many manuscripts unpublished as he had published. However it is the content of his works, which demonstrates that his retirement was not one of leisure and cerebral tranquility. Looking back on all he had written, he described his work as "uneasie" but "necessary," "very daring and hazardous," attempting "to recall those Doctrins which were almost extinguished in this Generation." Yet he wrote,

---

5. Edwards, *Preacher*, 356.

> I could not in Conscience omit it; for I thought my self oblig'd, seeing all others were silent, to take notice of the Degeneracy of the Times, as to some of the Truths and Doctrines of Christianity, and of the Dangerous and Scandalous Passages in the Writings of some of our Preachers."

But even in the last decade of his life, he was not about to put down his pen, not discouraged by "Mens Raileries and Reproaches," which he took to be against Scripture as much as himself. Instead, he prayed that with God's help he would continue with "Resolution and Patience," submitting his work to the "Censure of those who have Judgment to examine it."[6]

Finally, Edwards conformed. He conformed to the established Church of England, a church whose center of gravity he believed had departed from its historic roots and official defining documents. But rather than salving his conscience in the interest of ecclesiastical peace by accommodating himself to significant, adverse discrepancies between where the church was and where he believed it should be, his pen was never dry. Repeatedly he called the church to adhere to the XXXIX Articles following the reformed understanding of Thomas Cranmer, leading the church leadership to consider him a rabble-rousing dissenter. He called on the church to avoid its Romish liturgical leanings and rigid adherence to the prayer book, giving greater freedom to the clergy; but church leadership was inflexible. He rejected the episcopal form of government as lacking foundation both in Scripture and the ancient church, yet he served in that structure. He conformed because he believed that the unity of the church was both, most clearly taught in Scripture *and* most ignored in practice of any tenet of the Christian faith.

He pointed out that many of the ostensibly conforming clergy, including some bishops, did not conform either to the rubric, the XXXIX Articles as traditionally understood, or in some cases, even basic Protestant orthodoxy. But neither the deviation and defiance of the conformers, nor the rationale and grievances of the non-conformers persuaded Edwards break his commitment to the unity of the church. It is no exaggeration to say that had conformist and nonconformist parties alike followed his example of employing as the necessary and sufficient basis for ecclesiastical unity the doctrinal essentials of Christian orthodoxy as historically understood, while at the same time accommodating with love and respect all those who accept these standards, but disagree on non-essentials, Church of England schism could have largely been avoided.

6. Edwards, *Doctrine of Faith*, xvi, xix.

Appendix A

THE WORKS OF JOHN EDWARDS

Although Edwards is best known for his polemical works against non-trinitarians and Arminians, they amount to less than 20% (in volume) of his published works, which can be grouped into six categories. Aside from those identified as sermons, biblical exposition or theological explication, most can be considered apologetic: either he was defending doctrine which he believed to be under attack, or he was attacking works which he believed were leading people astray.

Sermons

Edwards's first publication was a sermon given at Holy Trinity when Cambridge was being ravaged by the Black Death (§1 below). Although he likely preached well over a thousand other sermons only about a dozen are known to have been published individually, with another dozen in a collection of sermons. Most of these are associated with special occasions such as preaching before Charles II (#1 in §2 below), before courts and magistrates (#2 and #3 in §2), before an assembly of clergy (#4 in §2), before the mayor and aldermen (#8 in §2), at Cambridge (#13 in §2), or commemorating a special event: the opening of a fair (Stourbridge?) (#5 in §2), declaration of war against France (#6 in §2), a Fast Day declared by the monarch (#7 in §2, §5, §9), Cambridge commencement (§3, §4), the union of England and Scotland (§6), deliverance from the gunpowder plot and the arrival of King William (§8), the accession of King George (§10), or unsettled public issues such as the use of apparel (#9 & #10 in §2) and Socinianism (#12 in §2). Others topics included exhortations for personal piety (§11, §13) and calls for national repentance (§7, §12). Edwards's sermons were structured like a persuasive argument and based on a single biblical text. He carefully enumerated his points in lists of explanation, observation, application, and conclusion, liberally drawing on supporting Scripture. His applications were direct, personal, and unavoidable.

1. *The Plague of the Heart* (1665), 1 Kgs 8:38.
2. *Sermons on Special Occasions and Subjects* (1698), John 18:38; Ps 82:6, 7; Exod 18:25; 1 Cor 14:12; Ezek 27:27; Gen 14:14; Josh 7:12; Mark 3:24; 1 Tim 2:8, 9; 1 Tim 3:16.
3. *The Eternal and Intrinsick Reasons of Good and Evil* (1699), Ps 119:142.
4. *Concio Determinatio pro Gradu Doctoratus in Sacra Theoligia* (1700).
5. *The Heinousness of England's Sins* (1707), Lam 1:8.
6. *One Nation and One King* (1707), Ezek 37:22.
7. *The Surest Way of Prospering in Our Military Affairs the Ensuing Campaigns,* (1708), Ps 60:12.
8. *Great Things Done by God for Our Ancestors, and Us of This Island* (1710), Ps 126:3.
9. *How England Hath Left Her First Love* (1711), Rev 2:4, 5.
10. *How to Judge Aright of the Former and the Present Times* (1714), Eccl 7:10.
11. *The Fruits of the Spirit* (1713), Gal 5:22, 23.
12. *Against Indifference in Religion* (1731), 1 Kgs 18:21.
13. *Christ, a Christian's Life; and Death in His Gain* (1731), Phil 1:21.

Biblical Exposition

In three works (§1, §2, §5) Edwards provided commentary on twenty-eight texts, the meaning of which he found to be shrouded in mystery or controversy, such as the identity of the spirits in prison (1 Pet 3:19), Jephtha's vow (Judg 11:30–31), and the meaning of Baal-zebub (2 Kgs 1:2). The third title below is a three-volume work which continues in the same vein discussing seventy-four additional difficult passages selected because of translation difficulties, challenges from non-Christians, historical disputes, and remarkable teachings. In addition to offering insights into the particular texts, these discourses are organized to illustrate three themes concerning Holy Scripture: truth and authority, style (focusing on grammatical and hermeneutical challenges), and excellency and perfection (by which he means the incomparable beauty of expression as wells at profound content). *Polpoikilos Sophia* is overview of biblical history presented as successive dispensations, highlighting the sovereign purposes of God and his triumph over false religions.

1. *An Enquiry into Four Remarkable Texts of the New Testament* (1692).
2. *A Farther Enquiry into Several Remarkable Texts of the Old and New Testament* (1692).
3. *A Discourse Conerning the Authority, Stile, and Perfection of the Books of the Old and New Testament,* 3 vols (1694–96).
4. *Polpoikilos Sophia: A Compleat History or Survey of all the Dispensations and Methods of Religion* (1699).
5. *Exercitations Critical, Philosophical, Historical, Theological: On Several Important Places in the Writings of the Old and New Testament* (1702).

Theological

Measured by word count, Edwards's theological works comprise the largest of these six categories. The first and eighth listed below are concerned with the epistemological issues of reason and revelation and the nature of truth and error in relation to various Fathers and philosophers. Though Edwards frequently cited the Fathers, he was very concerned about the practice of regarding them as authoritative by virtue of their antiquity, given that "the Antient fathers of the Church are made Patrons of some of the most Unjustifiable Doctrines and Practices that prevail among us."[1] He believed that they contributed greatly to our theological understanding, but cannot be read uncritically. Edwards wrote the second book at an elementary level so that parents could lead their children in family devotions to instruct them in the basic knowledge and practice of the

---

1. Edwards, *Patrologia*, 4.

Christian faith.² Probably the most referenced work of Edwards for theological education was *The Preacher*, which appeared in three volumes. In it he provided practical advice on the duties of a pastor, with an emphasis on preaching sound doctrine. In the third volume, he responded to critics of his first volume like Robert Lightfoote and critiqued Richard Allestree's *The Whole Duty of Man*. The fourth and fifth works comprise a two-volume set in defense of Reformed soteriology, the first being Edwards's *ordo salutis* and the second a lengthy exposition of faith and justification. *Theologia Reformata* includes an extended commentary on the Apostle's Creed, the Lord's Prayer, and the Ten Commandments in the first two volumes. The third volume, subtitled, "Graces and Duties" is instruction for the Christian life from regeneration and sanctification to admonition from the Beatitudes to moral guidance, which was largely his own statement on "the whole duty of man." Edwards dedicated the seventh to the Bavarian-born Princess of Wales, wife of future King George II, believing that she was interested to understand the scriptural basis for Calvinism because of her grandmother's interest in these doctrines. He also desired to explain the prevalence of Calvinism among Germans historically, beginning with Gottschalk of Orbais (808–867?) and continuing to recent times, explaining that though "his Disciples abandon'd their Master's Principle [. . .] Your Luther was a *Calvinist*."³ The eighth, and twelfth titles clearly state their contents. The tenth is a biblical and historical review of the justification for the episcopacy, which Edwards found to be wanting. *The Time of Reformation* is a call for a genuine, national, and spiritual renewal led by the example and preaching of the clergy leading to peace and unity in both civil and ecclesiastical realms.

1. *A Free Discourse Concerning Truth and Error* (1701).
2. *The Whole Concern of Man* (1701).
3. *The Preacher* (3 parts) (1705, 1706, 1709).
4. *Veritas Redux. Evangelical Truths Restored* (1707).
5. *The Doctrine of Faith and Justification Set in a True Light* (1708).
6. *Theologia Reformata*, 3 vols (1713, 1726).
7. *The Scripture-Doctrine of the Five Points* (1715).
8. *A Treatise of Repentance* (1718).

2. Edwards, *Whole Duty*. A second edition was published in Boston, 1725.
3. Edwards, *Scripture-Doctrine*, iii–vii.

9. *Patrologia: A Brief Discourse Concerning the Primitive Fathers and Antient Writers of the Christian Church*, in *Remains of John Edwards* (1730).

10. *A Discourse of Episcopacy*, in *Remains* (1730).

11. *The Time of Reformation*, in *Remains* (1730).

12. *A Resolution of This Query: Whether the Doctrine of Non-Resistance and Passive-Obedience Is to Be Understood without Any Limitation and Restriction* in *Remains* (1730).

Polemical against Those He Considered to Be within the Church

Edwards wrote against two Calvinists, Tobias Crisp for his extreme view of grace, and Lawrence Fogg for the confusion he generated by contradicting himself (§1, §3) on doctrinal fundamentals such as grace, divine sovereignty, and election. Bishop Burnet's interpretation of the XXXIX Articles was criticized for failing to recognize their clear affirmation of Reformed theology (§2). Archbishop William King was too willing in a sermon to compromise truth concerning God and salvation for the sake of peace with Unitarians (§4). Edwards's attack on aggressive Arminianism was prompted by a work of Whitby's before he became Arian (§5). Some in the Church of England held that Rome is the true church and that ministers are priests in the traditional sense of that word. Edwards wrote the last of these work for those in the Church of England who might be open to these two teachings of Rome.

1. *Crispianism Unmask'd* (1693).
2. *The General Exceptions against the Bishop of Sarum's Exposition of the XXXIX Articles* (1704).
3. *A Letter to the Reverend Lawrence Fogg, DD* (1705).
4. *The Divine Perfections Vindicated* (1710).
5. *The Arminian Doctrines Condemn'd by the Holy Scriptures* (1711).
6. *A Brief Confutation of These Two False and Dangerous Positions* (1730).

Polemical against Those He Considered to Be outside the Church

Edwards launched major attacks against three non-trinitarians: John Locke, primarily in the first four works listed in this section, although he criticized him for a number of other issues in several other works. In works §5, §7, and §8 below, he attacked the more explicitly defined Arian-like position of Samuel Clarke. The sixth work focused on William Whiston, whose trinitarian heterodoxy cost him the Lucian Professorship at Cambridge. Locke responded with two works to Edwards and one to Bishop Stillingfleet who joined the debate against Locke. Whiston responded briefly, but Clarke ignored Edwards, at least in print. In the final work listed in this section, Edwards offered a refutation both of Catholic doctrines traditionally opposed by Protestants and also objections to Protestantism often given by Catholics.

1. *Some Thoughts Concerning the Several Causes and Occasions of Atheism, Especially in the Present Age* (1695).
2. *Socinianism Unmask'd* (1696).
3. *The Socinian Creed* (1697).
4. *A Brief Vindication of the Fundamental Articles of the Christian Faith* (1697).
5. *Some Animadversions on Dr. Clark's Scripture-Doctrine of the Trinity* (1712).
6. *Some Brief Observations and Reflections on Mr. Whiston's Late Writings* (1712).
7. *A Supplement to the Animadversions on Dr. Clarke's Scripture-Doctrine of the Trinity* (1713).
8. *Some Brief Critical Remarks on Dr. Clarke's Last Papers* (1714).
9. *The Doctrines Controverted between Papists and Protestants* (1724).

Philosophy/Natural Philosophy

Edwards had a strong interest in natural philosophy, believing that it confirmed biblical truth. In *Cometomantia*, he argued that the heavenly bodies provide signs from God (frequently of judgment, but also for salvation), but have no power of causation.[4] The second work provided a teleological argument for the existence and providence of God by examining the science of astronomy, geology, climatology, biology, and human anatomy and physiology. For much of his life, Edwards followed the thinking of respected men like John Milton and William Harvey (1578–1657) who doubted or rejected the Copernican view. Even as late as 1714, he stated that "no Man alive can certainly tell which of these [Ptolemy, Copernicus, Tycho, Descartes] is True."[5] *Brief Remarks* was a critique of Whiston's theory of creation which Edwards found to be in serious conflict with the Genesis account. The fourth listed work was an overview of developments in the liberal arts and sciences coupled with seemingly unrelated commentary against his various adversaries. The last work listed is a critique of the traditional answers provided by philosophers and others to the question of how we find genuine happiness.

1. *Cometomantia, A Discourse of Comets* (1684).
2. *A Demonstration of the Existence and Providence of God* (1696).
3. *Brief Remarks Upon Mr. Whiston's New Theory of the Earth* (1697).
4. *Some New Discoveries of the Uncertainty, Deficiency and Corruptions of Human Knowledge and Learning* (1714).
5. *A Brief View of the Mistakes about Happiness* (1724).

Collected Works

After his death, at least one collection of works unpublished in his lifetime appeared. Another collection advertised as "All the Works" was also published.

1. *Remains, A Discourse of Comets* (1684).
2. *All the Works of John Edwards, D.D. in Ten Volumes* (1702?)[6]

---

4. Edwards, *Cometomantia*, 136.
5. Edwards, *Some New Discoveries*, 69.
6. Evans, *Holy Emulation Urged*, 275. This work is advertised under "Some BOOKS Printed for J. Robinson, at the Golden Lion in St. Paul's Church-Yard," a book seller who sold many of Edwards's works. It appears to be lost.

Publishers

Edwards's first publication in 1665 was printed by John Field (d. 1668) who, with his connections to Cromwell, had been appointed ten years earlier to the lucrative position of official printer at Cambridge University Press.[7] Field's successor, John Hayes printed Edwards's first biblical commentary and two other sermons, both given at the university.[8] Field and Hayes printed a good number of prominent works, including Bibles and prayer books.[9] They also printed sermons, especially those associated with the university. Given the prestige of the university press, university printers could be more selective in accepting work. Like his first sermon, Edwards's final work, a posthumous collection titled, *Remains of the Late Reverend and Learned John Edwards, D.D.*, was printed at Cambridge University Press, where Cornelius Crownfield had been appointed as "Printer" in 1705.[10] There is no evidence that Edwards used the university press for any other works but it must be noted that the printer is named in only about one quarter of his titles.

He attempted to use the university printer for his 1709 sermon given at St. Mary's, Cambridge, commemorating divine deliverance from the 1605 Gunpowder Plot along with the blessed arrival of King William in 1688. Despite the fact that three of his previous Cambridge sermons were printed at the university press and that this sermon was one of his least controversial, he was denied and had it printed elsewhere. John Byrom (1692–1763), not yet eighteen, wrote to a friend concerning the state of the church following two very public controversies. One was Parliament's vote to impeach Sacheverell for high crimes and misdemeanors, suspending his preaching for three years for his controversial November 5, 1709 sermon which failed to recognize resistance to the Glorious Revolution and link it to the Gun Powder plot. His letter cited a second dispute between Bishop Hoadly and Bishop of Exeter Ofspring Blackall regarding resistance in the 1688 revolution. Byrom wondered if the university's refusal to publish Edwards's recent sermon was related but said that he would "buy it to see why our University refused to license it."[11]

---

7. Blagden, "Early Cambridge Printers," 282.

8. Edwards, *Four Remarkable Texts*; Edwards, *Eternal and Intrinsic Reasons*; Edwards, *Concio*.

9. Plomer, *Dictionary*, 150.

10. McKenzie, *Cambridge University Press*, 56.

11. Byrom, *Private Journal*, 1:10.

Twelve years earlier, Edwards had another problem with the university press after requesting and receiving permission for a Cambridge imprimatur for *A Brief Vindication of the Fundamental Articles of the Christian Faith*, which was his fourth attack on Locke.[12] As soon as Locke saw the book, he wrote to John Covel, mockingly condemning it as "such a just model of manageing controversie in Religion, to be a pattern [. . .] in the rest of the Universitie to immitate" and questioning Covel's betrayal of their long friendship for approving Edwards's request. Still not admitting his authorship of *The Reasonableness of Christianity*, which set off the firestorm, Locke wrote on Sept. 29, 1697, "Tis not that I pretend to be interested in the Controversie wherein Mr. Edwards is a party: but hearing he had named me in the title of his booke, I thought my self concerned to read it."[13] In his reply of October 4, Covel claimed that although he gave Edwards permission to use his name, he had not seen the book at all, relying on the judgment of his colleagues.[14] On December 21, Archbishop Tenison wrote to Locke that he had been visited by Henry James and Bishop Patrick. James told him that he had instructed Edwards to edit out some objectionable passages, which Edwards assured him he did and it was subsequently approved by Beaumont.[15] Tenison's reply did not satisfy Locke, who remained distressed because the world would see Cambridge University as having approved of Edwards's book.[16]

Aside from these two incidents, Edwards's relationship with publishers does not appear remarkable. At least thirty-six named individuals were employed as printers or booksellers of his works. They varied from High Church to nonconformist Whigs. Except for the following three booksellers, no one handled more than three titles. With considerable overlap, John Lawrence (fourteen), Jonathan Robinson (twenty), and John Wyat (twenty-three) sold over half of his titles. Robinson and Wyat primarily sold nonconformist literature. Lawrence was a Presbyterian and is described as "upright" and "honest." John Humphreys printed

---

12. Given to him by Joseph Beaumont, Regius Professor of Divinity, Peterhouse College; John Balderston (d. 1719), Master of Emmanuel College; John Covel (1638–1722), Master of Christ's College; Henry James (d. 1717?), Master of Queen's College.

13. Locke, *Correspondence*, 6:210–11.

14. Locke, *Correspondence*, 6:217–18.

15. Locke, *Correspondence*, 6:275–76.

16. Locke, *Correspondence*, 6:299–301 (Locke to Tenison, January 15, 1698). The following were printed in London, but given an imprimatur from Cambridge: Edwards, *Farther Enquiry*; Edwards, *Discourse Concerning*.

for John Lawrence and possibly John Robinson and John Wyat.[17] Of the remaining printers and sellers, Brabazon Alymer, Thomas Cockerill, Joseph Downing, and Edmund Jeffrey specialized in theology, sermons and classical works.[18] Pro-Whigs Richard Baldwin and John Morphew were fairly prominent, no doubt for publishing political pamphlets, newspapers, popular literature, and satire, often controversial.[19] Benjamin Motte handled wide-ranging religious and scientific literature and along with Thomas Ilive (d.1724) was considered a high-flyer.[20] Samuel Keimer (1689–1742) was a religious vagabond who later emigrated to Pennsylvania as a Quaker and hired Benjamin Franklin as an apprentice.[21]

Correspondence

Undoubtedly, most of the correspondence between Edwards and other individuals has been lost. The largest extant collection is between Edwards and geologist John Woodward on the scientific understanding of Genesis.[22] Although Edwards's recipients are not always identified other than "my good friend," other letters can be found in several libraries between Edwards and Bishops Richard Kidder and Simon Patrick, pastors Lawrence Fogg and Cotton Mather, and bookseller John Wyat.[23] When serving as rector of St. Peter's in Colchester, Edwards wrote to Bishop Henry Compton of London on behalf of Alderman Thomas Green, a resident of his parish, who had been accused of being a nonconformist.[24]

Manuscripts

Older biographical dictionaries state that upon his death, Edwards left a considerable collection of manuscripts, "nearly as many" as his printed

   17. Plomer, *Dictionary*, 165, 184, 256, 322.
   18. Plomer, *Dictionary*, 11, 76, 106, 171; McKitterick, *Cambridge University Press*, 1:421.
   19. Plomer, *Dictionary*, 15–17, 210.
   20. Plomer, *Dictionary*, 167, 212–13. See Chapter 6 for a discussion of high-flyers.
   21. Bloore, "Samuel Keimer," 255–87.
   22. Cambridge University Library, Ms Add 7647/114–120.
   23. See bibliography. One letter to Lawrence Fogg was published, but other correspondence with him is referenced.
   24. Timothy Glines, "Politics and Government," 186, 205.

works. Of the fifty separate publications listed above, not more than eight were not printed until after Edwards died. The Cambridge Library appears to contain the largest repository of Edwards manuscripts, but that amounts only to an incomplete manuscript of sermons, along with another partial manuscript whose topic is ecclesiology. If Edwards left many more manuscripts, they remain to be discovered and catalogued. On the other hand, in addition to his manuscripts, Edwards did leave a good number of published works and together with the works of those with whom he interacted, we have a good selection of material to study.

Appendix B

SCHOLARSHIP FOCUSED ON EDWARDS

Until now, only five studies in modern history have focused on Edwards. Earlier in the twentieth century, Ronald Crane wrote a long essay naming Edwards "the pioneer of the movement" to restore the idea of progress in Christian thought with his *A Compleat History or Survey of All the Dispensations and Methods of Religion*. According to Crane, the idea of progress had been recognized throughout church history, seen in the works of such men as Tertullian, Hugh of St. Victor, and Thomas Aquinas. But with the rise of Deism and the Enlightenment, "the hold on men's minds of the ancient dogma of the world's perpetual decay had at last been decisively weakened if not altogether destroyed." As the new source of authority, natural philosophy supplanted revealed religion, which was dismissed as irrational and superstitious. In leading the revival of "Anglican Apologetics," Edwards refuted the idea that religion and natural philosophy are in opposition, observing that knowledge of both has advanced throughout history by the express design of God who reveals "divine truths to men."[1] Inspired by Edwards, others such as Edward Young (1683–1765) and Bishop Edmund Law (1703–87) gave greater prominence to this theme in the mid to late eighteenth century with expanded and more compelling expressions, in response to Matthew Tindal and other prophets of Deism.[2]

Hermon Ray's 1956 PhD thesis at Edinburgh provided a thematic survey of Edwards's theological works, seeing him as "a stalwart

---

1. Crane, "Anglican Apologetics," 273–306.
2. Crane, "Anglican Apologetics," 361, 368, 373, 382.

Trinitarian," "a Puritan preacher of salvation," and "a dogmatic controversialist." Ray corrected earlier thinking by showing that it was John Edwards, not American Jonathan Edwards, who influenced George Whitefield to adopt Calvinist theology.[3] In *Shapers of English Calvinism, 1660–1714*, Dewey Wallace included Edwards as one of six influential seventeenth-century theologians, recognizing that Edwards's abrasiveness was to some extent shaped by his context: consternation over the decline of Calvinian leadership and influence in the church and the coincident advance of open heterodoxy. Edwards is seen as a transition—harkening back to the established Reformed theology of the previous century with its roots in the Fathers and also as a forerunner of the evangelical revival to come.[4] In 2013, Jeongmo Yoo published an analysis of Edwards's view of free will based on his PhD at Calvin Theological Seminary under Richard Muller, showing how Edwards's understanding allows for absolute divine sovereignty while avoiding metaphysical determinism and providing for genuine human freedom.[5]

Most recently in 2019, Jake Griesel completed his PhD at Cambridge, addressing the question of Edwards's stature in the later Stuart Church of England. Griesel counters earlier scholarship on two counts. First, rather than being a relatively insignificant cleric because of his Calvinism as some had dismissed him, he maintains that Edwards was actually fairly prominent. Second, despite opposition from Arminians within the church, he was actually accorded a more positive reception because, contrary to some earlier studies, the Reformed perspective continued to be well represented within the church into the eighteenth century. In arriving at this conclusion, he builds on the work of Stephen Hampton.[6]

---

3. Ray, "Religious Thought," 320–21.
4. Wallace, *English Calvinism*, 221, 241–42.
5. Yoo, *John Edwards*.
6. Hampton, *Anti-Arminians*. Griesel's full work has not been made public, but summaries of his general thesis have appeared online.

Appendix C

Edwards and His Critics

Edwards most often appears in contemporary historiography as the lead antagonist of the pamphlet war that erupted with the publication of John Locke's *The Reasonableness of Christianity*. Typical of those who clearly have an unfavorable view of Edwards's attack on Locke's theology is John Higgins-Biddle in his critical edition of Locke's work. Although he does not accept the verdict of those who have concluded that Locke was a Deist, Socinian, Unitarian or Hobbist, he does recognize that "most subsequent interpreters of Locke's religious views have confirmed one or more of these accusations."[1] He also believes that Edwards clearly influenced how Locke's religious ideas have been understood from Locke's day until the present.[2] It seems that one of his objectives in writing this critical introduction is to restore Locke's tarnished reputation, not by objective analysis, but by discrediting his opponents, especially Edwards through distortion and innuendo. Several examples follow.

1. Higgins-Biddle begins by stating that "theological controversy of the most heated and zealous sort was something of a tradition in the Edwards family" and "but either from his dead father's books or from his theological education, Edwards had also acquired a pious zeal for heresy-hunting."[3] Certainly Thomas Edwards fit this description. But since we know nothing about the father of Thomas Edwards, this statement simply assumes as established fact that

---

1. Locke, *Reasonableness*, critical ed., viii, xv.
2. Locke, *Reasonableness*, critical ed., xliii.
3. Locke, *Reasonableness*, critical ed., xlii, xliii.

John followed in his father's disruptive and schismatic footsteps, not to mention that he perverts the meaning of tradition.

2. "The crux of Edwards's case was that Socinianism was a cause of atheism, if not atheistic itself."[4] Edwards did think that Socinianism led to atheism because it denies the orthodox understanding of God. But the crux of Edwards's case against Locke was not the linkage between Socinianism and atheism, but that Locke, like all antitrinitarians refused to affirm the doctrine of the Trinity, which has been accepted historically by Catholic, Protestant, and Orthodox churches as a necessary doctrine of orthodox Christianity.

3. Related to the above claim is the question of how "Socinian" is defined. Like many of Locke's defenders, Higgins-Biddle raises the question of whether or not Locke was truly a Socinian, even as he acknowledges the ambiguity of the term.[5] Did Locke hold to all the Socinian articles of faith? Certainly, having Unitarian friends, possessing Socinian books, or even taking notes from those books does not make one a Socinian. Edwards was actually more careful than most in his day who leveled charges of Socinianism, but as he wrote, the distinctions between Arian, Socinian and other antitrinitarian doctrines were not nearly as significant as what they shared in common. What he saw in Clarke, Locke, Whiston, and later Whitby were efforts "to destroy the true and proper Divinity of the Son of God, and of the Holy Ghost."[6] None of these men would affirm the doctrine of the Trinity, which for Edwards (and historic orthodox Christianity) was a fundamental and essential tenet. Framing the debate on the exact definition of Socinian, which Edwards also noted was not so well-defined, is simply a red herring.[7]

4. Typical of Higgins-Biddle's innuendo against Edwards is his description of the first attack on Locke which appeared in a book dedicated to Archbishop Thomas Tenison, which "won Edwards no advancement."[8] Was there ever a hint that Edwards sought any advancement in his entire career? To the contrary, Edwards repeatedly

---

4. Locke, *Reasonableness*, critical ed., xliv.
5. Locke, *Reasonableness*, critical ed., xlii.
6. Edwards, *Some Animadversions*, 4.
7. Edwards, *Some Thoughts*, 67–68.
8. Locke, *Reasonableness*, critical ed., xliii.

spoke of the prevailing anti-Calvinist sentiment and the "very hard Censures" and abuse that he expected, rhetorically asking,

> Do I seek to conciliate the Favour of Men, by propounding a Doctrin to them that I know will be very pleasing and grateful to them? [...] If I should make it my Work to gratify any Man's Humour, I should betray the Truth, and thereby shew that I am unworthy to be a Minister of Christ.[9]

5. Higgins-Biddle states, "there is no reason to doubt Locke's claim that in formulating the ideas expressed in *The Reasonableness* he turned to the Scriptures alone."[10] No reason? Yes, Locke studied the New Testament carefully, but how it is understood is a matter of interpretation. What about Locke's library, notebooks, and close friends? Despite his denials, it is much more likely that Locke was influenced by heterodox sources than not.[11]

6. Higgins-Biddle admits that many of those who may have influenced Locke were at one time accused of Socinianism."[12] That does not prove that Locke or any of them were Socinian, but it does suggest that Locke and his accused associates had something in common and not necessarily that "Edwards and his followers were [...] faulty [in] their judgement [as it appears] to modern evaluation."[13] And what evidence is there that any of Locke's accusers were "followers" of Edwards? Was Latitudinarian Bishop Edward Stillingfleet? Jonathan Edwards of Oxford? Polymath Gottfried Leibniz? Higgins-Biddle gives Edwards a lot of credit, while producing no evidence that any of Locke's critics were "followers" of Edwards.

7. Higgins-Biddle attempts to shore up Locke's orthodoxy by suggesting that his view was similar to Richard Baxter's: "In his *Second Vindication* he [Locke] called his readers' attention to an incident in which Baxter had proposed the ancient threefold formula of the Apostles' Creed, the Lord's Prayer, and the Decalogue as a body of fundamentals."[14] When Locke recalled that incident, he was address-

---

9. Edwards, *Doctrine of Faith*, xiii–xv.
10. Locke, *The Reasonableness*, critical ed., lxv.
11. See Chapter 4.
12. Locke, *Reasonableness*, critical ed., lviii-lxvi.
13. Locke, *Reasonableness*, critical ed., lxi, lxvii.
14. Locke, *Reasonableness*, critical ed., lxvii.

ing the problem "that almost every distinct Society of Christians Magisterially ascribes Orthodoxy to a select set of Fundamentals distinct from those proposed in the Preaching of our Saviour and his Apostles"—which is most definitely a problem.[15] However when Baxter made that statement, the context was distinguishing between the "*Sense*" and the "*Words*" used to express Essentials of the Christian faith. By "sense," Baxter was referring to how words are interpreted or understood and he warned though we can attempt to express our essentials clearly, "some Heretics will put their own Sence on them, and Subscribe them," rendering their subscription useless to the orthodox.[16] Whether or not Locke read Baxter carefully is difficult to know, but Higgins-Biddle should have. Baxter and his fellow ministers in Kidderminster were concerned about the personal salvation of their congregants because "the Liturgy [...] had little more explicatory value than the Words themselves of the Creed, Lord's Prayer, and Decalogue."[17] Therefore he offered to draft a catechism for them to use with adults. In that catechism Baxter clearly affirms the doctrine of the Trinity and full deity and humanity of Jesus Christ as "necessary to us to be believed."[18]

8. Referencing Robert Wallace, Higgins-Biddle wrote that "loyal sons of the Church of England found they could not agree among themselves on the proper exposition of the doctrine" of the Trinity. This is to be expected since among these "loyal sons" are those such as Arthur Bury and Stephen Nye who, though ordained in the Church of England, would not pass the traditional test of orthodoxy, having explicitly denied doctrines expressed in the Nicene Creed to which they formerly subscribed.[19]

A much more even-handed assessment of the Locke-Edwards debate was provided by Victor Nuovo in his contribution to the Clarendon edition of Lock's works. He judges Edwards as a moderate Calvinist whose works "include one of the most comprehensive accounts of

---

15. Locke, *A Second Vindication*, first ed., 216–17; Locke, *Vindications*, critical ed., 127.
16. Baxter, *Reliquiæ*, Part 2, §51–52.
17. Baxter, *Reliquiæ*, Part 2, §40.
18. Baxter, *Catechizing of Families*, 37–42, 92–96.
19. Locke, *Reasonableness*, critical ed., lxviii.

Calvinist theology composed in the English language." In conclusion to his commentary he wrote of Edwards that

> anyone who takes the trouble to survey his achievement as an author, both of controversial works and constructive theology, cannot fail to recognize how successful he was in accommodating to polite society and its discourse, and this, notwithstanding the total incompatibility between his views and those of deists and free-thinkers and moderate Christians who purportedly represented the intellectual fashions of the day. As a defender of what he took to be fundamental Christianity, it is arguable that he was no more and no less enlightened that [sic] his great adversary John Locke. Both were uncompromising defenders of the infallible truth of Christian revelation.[20]

The difference of course was how they interpreted this infallible truth.

There have been other scholarly critiques of Edwards where the primary focus was someone else (most often Locke) or a particular topic such as antitrinitarianism.[21] But too often, passing references to Edwards have been misleading, perpetuating the caricature that he was little different from his father, portraying him as "hostile" and "intemperate," a "bitter opponent," "vulgar," "extreme," "fanatical," "implacable," "narrow-minded, persecutory," "rigid," "distinctly eccentric," "remarkably vulgar and unrestrained," "a scurrilous opponent," and "that irascible Reformed polemicist."[22] One writer identified him as "an embittered, heresy-hunting Anglican Calvinist, [who] denounced *The Reasonableness of Christianity* as poisonous Socinianism, the enemy of true revelation and of ecclesiastical organization"; another "as bigoted an adversary as his father Thomas Edwards."[23] But was Edwards embittered, angry, intolerant and lacking in self-control? Although he was sometimes harsh and uncompromising with heretics, a closer look gives evidence of a different man and indicates that a number of writers have confused Edwards's strong convictions, direct talk, occasional sarcasm, and rejection of heresy in

20. Locke, *Vindications*, critical ed., xxxvii–xxxviii, lxxiii.
21. Sell, *John Locke*; Haycock, "Claiming Him," 301.
22. Spellman, "Locke," 220, 225; McLachlan, *Socinianism*, 290; Dunn, *Political Thought*, 82; Marshall, *John Locke*, 415; Plumtre, *Thomas Ken*, 2:135; Parker, *Biblical Politics*, 32; Stanton, "Hobbes and Locke," 67; Walker, *Reason and Religion*, 224; Oakes, *Conservative Revolutionaries*, 123; Wilson, *Merchant-Taylor's School*, 840; Hampton, *Anti-Arminians*, 35; Locke, *Questions*, 26; Bourne, *John Locke*, 2:495; Hampton, *Anti-Arminians*, 60.
23. Young, *Religion and Enlightenment*, 27; Champion, *Pillars*, 111.

the church with quite different and less admirable qualities of arrogance, anger, spite, and general intolerance, perhaps because they fail to distinguish him from his father or find his Calvinistic convictions objectionable. Edwards's summary of his critics:

> Those who are displeas'd with an Author's Matter, do always blame his Language and Expressions; and they will says he is Scurrilous, because he speaks Truth with some Keeness and Sharpness. But I have always taken care to observe the Rules of Civility, when Persons have been capable of it.[24]

Those who continue to describe Edwards in the manner of his seventeenth-century opponents need to more thoroughly examine the contexts, issues, and sources, but above all, what he actually wrote.

Not only are attributes of his father Thomas Edwards too often ascribed to John, but also those of some of his contemporaries who were careless and caustic in condemning their opponents. One scholar's broad brush casts Edwards with William Sherlock, Robert South(1634–1716), John Wallis, Francis Fullwood (d. 1693) and Edward Fowler. The only reference to Edwards cited as evidence actually belongs to his contemporary Jonathan Edwards of Oxford.[25] John Edwards reserved his strong language for heretics, but these five, all clergy in the Church of England were malicious toward some in the church as well as orthodox nonconformists. Fowler referred to nonconformist John Bunyan as "a most Black-mouthd Calumniator" and "true Successor of the Pharisees" and to his books as the "most Abominable Scurrilities."[26] South condemned not only Catholics and Socinians, but also Presbyterians, Puritans, and members of the Church of England, such as non-juring Sherlock (as a tritheist).[27] Some other references to Edwards are simply in error, on one hand calling him a "High Churchman" and on the other, "a very intemperate and pugnacious clergyman, who afterwards became a nonconformist."[28] This second source had little regard for any of Locke's critics, describing Edwards as "a very contemptible antagonist" and Stillingfleet as "a more

---

24. Edwards, *Doctrine of Faith*, xvii.

25. Bulman, *Anglican Enlightenment*, 264–65. Other examples of misattribution: Sweeney and Barshinger, *Jonathan Edwards*, 57; Muller, *Reformed Dogmatics*, 3:149.

26. Fowler, *Dirt Wip't Off*, 2, 3, 69.

27. South, *Tritheism*, 31, 170. See Appendix D.

28. Buchwald and Feingold, *Newton*, 121; Bourne, *John Locke*, 2:290. There is no evidence that Edwards ever gave a thought to conforming.

influential, though hardly a more honest or able opponent."²⁹ Some years earlier another writer had referred to *A Preservative Against Socinianism* by Jonathan Edwards as "almost as notorious for its violence and scurrility, as the attacks of his namesake, John Edwards."³⁰ Not only is there considerable confusion regarding Edwards's character traits and a general ignorance of his contributions, but historiographic assessment of the theological context in which he worked is also unsettled, particularly the orientation of the Stuart church vis-à-vis Calvinism.

Despite the dismissive and inaccurate references, some recent scholars such as Thomas Pfizenmaier have cited Edwards in a neutral or positive light. Some such as Richard Muller and Stephen Snobelen have commended Edwards for his insights and contributions.³¹

29. Bourne, *John Locke*, 2:407, 2:415.

30. Wallace, *Antitrinitarian Biography*, 1:344.

31. Pfizenmaier, *Trinitarian Theology*, 142–43, 180–81; Muller, *Reformed Dogmatics*, 3:149; Snobelen, "God of Gods," 192.

Appendix D

WAS EDWARDS A LONELY REFORMED VOICE IN THE CHURCH OF ENGLAND IN 1700?

Though Calvinism did not evaporate suddenly in the Church of England from the Great Ejection, what was the situation in 1700? Until recently, the general consensus was that relatively few Calvinists remained in the Church of England. The near-contemporary biographer of Archbishop Tillotson, no friend of Calvinism, identified Edwards as "the reviver of *Calvinism* in the church of England, after the gradual extinction of it there."[1] The late eighteenth century saw the publication of a laudatory biography of non-juror Charles Leslie, whose author, speaking of theological controversies and heresies, attempted a bit of humor in condemning Edwards for resurrecting Calvinism:

> No sooner had this subject [John Asgill's teaching that death is not necessary for Christians] been dismissed from consideration, than the doctrines of Predestination and Election reappeared for agitation under the auspices of one Edwards, a Calvinistic doctor at Cambridge. These questions have been worn so threadbare by discussion in all times, that it is quite unnecessary to touch upon them here, or refer to him and his sermon for "re-establishing Calvinistic doctrines long stifled, and to extirpate Arminianism," further than to say that "if he had no free-will he could not help it, that may be his excuse"[2]

---

1. Birch, *Life*, 336–37.
2. Leslie, *Life*, 369.

More recently, Roland Stromberg calls Edwards "about the only remaining example of a prominent Anglican Calvinist" by the beginning of the eighteenth century.³ However, Peter White, Julian Davies, and most recently Stephen Hampton have attempted to challenge this view.⁴ Hampton's position is that previous scholars have erroneously concluded that the Reformed element within the Church of England following the 1662 Restoration was impotent and "thoroughly marginal," but the evidence he cites to support his claim is far from conclusive.⁵

There are four significant problems with his argument. Essentially, he attempts to dismiss the more established view by misrepresenting it. His thesis amounts to a response to a straw-man version of late twentieth-century scholarship. First, the scholars Hampton cites refer to Calvinism's demise at the end of the seventeenth or beginning of the eighteenth centuries.⁶ Hampton shifts the focus to the 1662 Restoration. Stromberg and the others noted that Calvinism was in decline within the Church of England following 1662, but not that it was nearly extinct until forty years later.

Second, the scholars Hampton cites refer not to Reformed theology, but to Calvinism. But in making his case, Hampton substitutes Reformed for Calvinism, arguing that it is "broader and more ancient."⁷ To be sure, Reformed is broader and more historic and Calvinism is often a problematic term. It has been used by some interchangeably with Reformed and pejoratively by others, sometimes narrowly referring to Presbyterian ecclesiology, other times to the doctrine of election, and not so often to a theological orientation with which Calvin himself would identify. Citing Richard Muller, Hampton notes that the meanings of both Calvinism and Reformed were continually evolving and involved many strands so that "identifying any conforming Anglican as Reformed is never a straightforward matter."⁸ Unfortunately, Hampton himself offers no definition of either term. But by substituting what is generally understood as a much broader term for Calvinism, his case is easier to make. The fact is, that of the quotations included in his book from the above scholars,

3. Stromberg, *Religious Liberalism*, 111.
4. White, "Rise of Arminianism"; Davies, *Caroline Captivity*.
5. Hampton, *Anti-Arminians*, 36.
6. Hampton, *Anti-Arminians*, 3–5. In addition to Stromberg, D.W. Bebbington, G.R. Cragg, N. Tyacke, J. Spurr.
7. Hampton, *Anti-Arminians*, 6.
8. Hampton, *Anti-Arminians*, 8.

"Calvinism," not "Reformed" is the only identifying label to be found. Those scholars could have used the word Reformed instead of Calvinist; certainly all of them understand the distinction Hampton has in mind. But they chose not to, perhaps because they are using Calvinist in the same sense as Edwards, which, as will be seen, as somewhat equivalent to Reformed. Perhaps as a tactic to bolster his argument, Hampton seems to be using the term in its narrower, stigmatic sense, like many of Edwards's contemporary critics.

In contending that Reformed is to be preferred over Calvinist, Hampton calls our attention to Bishop George Morley, who neither he nor Morley himself identify with Calvinism.[9] Hampton refers to Morley's "Reformed theological sympathies."[10] Both Cragg and Spurr had claimed Morley as a Calvinist which suggests that they may be using it as somewhat equivalent to Reformed.[11] In attempting to shift the argument from Calvinism to Reformed, Hampton also tries to enlist John Edwards who did agree that Reformed is a broader and more useful term, but *did* claim to be a Calvinist, although he certainly did not see Calvin as infallible.[12] As Edwards is said to be "about the only remaining example of a prominent Anglican Calvinist," whether or not Edwards considered Reformed to be a broader term than Calvinist is quite irrelevant.

In addition to shifting from 1700 to 1662 and trading Calvinist for Reformed, Hampton alters Stromberg's statement in a third, more subtle way by broadening his meaning of prominent. By prominent Calvinist, Stromberg was referring no doubt to men who were prominent theologically in their preaching and writing, not simply prominent in a public or scientific sense, but not so Hampton as will be seen below.

Fourth, Hampton cites as evidence individuals who died before 1700 to counter Stromberg's claim concerning the beginning of the eighteenth century, while at the same time quoting Bebbington: "within the eighteenth-century Church of England, 'the doctrine of justification by

---

9. Hampton, *Anti-Arminians*, 5–6. Morley identified a Calvinist as someone who favors the Presbyterian form of church government and opposes the Episcopalian system.

10. Hampton, *Anti-Arminians*, 14.

11. Cragg, *Puritanism*, 19; Spurr, *Restoration Church*, 11, 31.

12. Despite the changing, ambiguous and confusing uses of the term, Edwards did not shy away from using it, holding to a moderate understanding as noted in the main text.

faith had well-nigh disappeared. Calvinism was at a discount after the Restoration.'"[13]

As evidence that Stromberg and the others are in error, Hampton names thirty-five individuals. But in addition to Morley, sixteen of those thirty-five died before 1700.[14] Obviously they were not among those "remaining" at the beginning of the eighteenth century. What do we know about the other eighteen? Were they prominent in their defense of Calvinism or Reformed theology as was Edwards? First, consider the seven who were healthy and active when Edwards died in 1716.

Three certainly held prominent positions. William Delaune (1659–1728), St. John's College, Oxford, BA, MA, BD, DD, served as president of St. John's, Oxford, canon of Winchester, vice-chancellor of Oxford and chaplain to Queen Anne. William Nicolson (1655–1727), BA, MA, fellow, Queen's College, Oxford held bishoprics in Carlisle and Derry and was elected a fellow of the Royal Society. William Stanley (1647–1731) BA, MA, BD, DD, St. John's College, Oxford was president of Corpus Christi College, vice-chancellor of Cambridge and Dean of St. Asaph Cathedral. And as prominent churchmen, what were they known for? Was it their defense of Calvinism or Reformed theology?

The thrust of Delaune's biography was his life-long financial crisis resulting from a gambling addiction. It also appears that he owed his ecclesiastical advancement to his wealth. But despite his considerable inheritance, he found it necessary to embezzle over £2000 from Oxford's Clarendon Press during his four-year tenure as vice-chancellor in order to cover gambling losses. By the age of fifty-two, he had lost his inheritance and all that he had borrowed from friends and the university. The purpose of his only publication in the year of his death, *Twelve Sermons upon Several Subjects and Occasions* was to pay off some of his debt.[15] It seems that his priority in life was maintaining social connections regardless of political affiliation to enhance his personal standing and remain solvent. Judging from his activities and Thomas Wagstaff's view that

13. Hampton, *Anti-Arminians*, 3.

14. Thomas Barlow, Isaac Barrow, Sir Robert Boyle (1627–91), John Conant, Samuel Crossman (1625–84), William Dillingham (1617–89), Francis Fullwood, John Hacket, Ezekiel Hopkins, Thomas Horton (d. 1673), Thomas Marshall (1621–85), John Pearson, Edward Reynolds, Thomas Tully, Seth Ward, John Wilkins.

15. The selected sermons do not provide clear evidence of Delaune's Reformed theology, in part because the biblical texts do not touch directly on those doctrines which divide Arminians and Calvinists.

Delaune "knew little of theology," it would be difficult to call Delaune a prominent theologian of any stripe.[16]

William Nicolson's primary interest was politics, both civil and ecclesiastical. For most of his twenty-five years as bishop of Carlisle and then Derry, he was involved in personal, political, and legal controversy. Aside from managing his ecclesiastical affairs, a major interest was collecting manuscripts, rather than doing theology. His most significant works were the *English Historical Library*, followed by the *Scottish Historical Library* and the *Irish Historical Library*. They were impressive and extensive bibliographies of manuscripts and printed material relating to national history. Although the diocese of Derry contained a significant number of dissenters, he opposed toleration for the Presbyterians. Hampton claims that Nicolson's Reformed credentials are demonstrated in a 1716 sermon on justification wherein he expounds the doctrine of imputation. But although it was denied by some Arminians such as John Goodwin, others affirmed it, such as Francis Duke (fl.1642–60), known as "broadly Arminian [. . .] rejecting absolute or personal predestination and affirming the salvific potency of universal grace."[17] The doctrine of imputation is generally seen as Protestant, but not attestation of reformed credentials. Nicolson was definitely prominent, but his theological persuasion is not clear, except for strong opposition to Rome.[18]

William Stanley supported Henry Compton's (1631/2–1713) education at Oxford. Compton rose to become Bishop of London and was able to appoint several Reformed men to their positions, but does that make Stanley a prominent Calvinist or Reformed divine? He did publish *The Faith and Practice of a Church of England Man*, which is clearly Protestant in its rejection of Rome's "Additions," but not clearly Reformed.[19] The XXXIX Articles are mentioned in passing, but he did not discuss them in any detail. The term "Arminian" does not appear at all in this work and neither Calvin nor Reformed theology is mentioned in relation to their respective theological distinctives. What Stanley is remembered for is helping to commission the construction of fifty new churches in London and publishing a catalog of manuscripts at Corpus Christi College.

16. Curthoys, "William DeLaune."

17. Ollerton, "The Crisis of Calvinism," 112; Arminius himself upheld imputation in a letter to Hippolytus a Collibus; see Fesko, "Arminius on Justification", 6–7.

18. Hayton, "William Nicolson."

19. Stanley, *The Faith and Practice*, 65–67, 159–88.

APPENDIX D

Henry Sacheverell (1676–1724), BA, MA, DD, Magdalen College, Oxford was certainly prominent, not for his ecclesiastical offices, but for his rousing and inflammatory sermons. One in particular preached on November 5, 1709, sold an unprecedented one hundred thousand copies, resulting in his impeachment by Parliament for high crimes and misdemeanors. Unlike traditional sermons on the anniversary of the Gunpowder Plot, he barely acknowledged the papal political threat. Whigs also associated that day with the 1688 arrival of William of Orange, who was believed to have saved England from the impending Catholic domination of James II. Instead of either historical event, Sacheverell compared the momentous Gunpowder Plot to the execution of Charles I. Using the reference to false brethren in 2 Corinthians 11:26 as his point of departure, he railed against all forms of dissent. Not only heretics and atheists, but Latitudinarians who advocated toleration, the Toleration Act itself, and occasionally conforming dissenters all threaten the identity and very existence of the Church of England. Sacheverell's trial resulted in a guilty verdict and a sentence prohibiting him from preaching for three years. Sacheverell capitalized on the publicity, became a folk hero, and the political fallout probably contributed to Tory victories in the next election.

Hampton's line of reasoning by which he understands Sacheverell to be Reformed likely follows from the House of Commons majority which had taken issue with Bishop Gilbert Burnet's reading of the XXXIX Articles as being too broad, allowing for both Arminian and Reformed interpretations. In response, Richard West (1670?–1716), Burnet's chaplain, wrote that Burnet based his understanding of the Articles on his understanding of Scripture, acknowledging no more than that an Arminian understanding is at times at odds with a Calvinistic understanding.

> I subscribe and give my unfeigned assent to the Articles of the Church in such a sense as only as the Scriptures will justifie me in; and if I think the Scriptures most favour the Arminian Tenets, as they are called, I am sure I can't honestly assent to them in a Calvinistical sense.[20]

Hampton derives his view of Sacheverell's theology from this statement by West in conjunction with an extract of Sacheverell's assessment of the Low Church view that the articles are too narrow as traditionally understood: "*He Thinks the* Articles of the Church *too* Stiff, Formal and

---

20. West, *True Character*, 21.

Strait-lac'd a Rule *to* Confine *His Faith in, and Complements 'em out of their Rigour and Severity.*"[21]

From this interchange Hampton concludes that Burnet allowed for a broader interpretation than the Reformed-leaning House thought reasonable and that West "assumed that the looseness to which he [Sacheverell] was objecting was one which permitted an Arminian reading of the Articles."[22] But Sacheverell makes no mention of Arminianism or Calvinism and it is instructive to see Sacheverell's statement in context. In his tirade against his prototypical Low Churchman, he includes every conceivable heretic and nonconformist whom he accuses of destroying the faith, but Arminians are not among them.

> *He believes very Little or no Revelation, and had rather lay His Faith upon the Substantial Evidences of His Own Reason, than the precious Authority of Divine Testimony. So that if He does* Suppose *the Being of a God, as for the Nature of* Jesus Christ, *He is not concern'd about His* Divinity, *whether His Union is* Hypostatical *or* Accidental, *being an utter Enemy to* Hard Terms in Religion. *And therefore the* Scholastick Jargon *of the* Trinity *will ill suit with One of so* Polite a Genius, *so that he had rather be a* Deist, Socinian or Nestorian, *than to Affront his Own Understanding with Believing what is* Incomprehensible, *or be so Rude as to Obtrude on Others what He cannot Himself Explain. He Thinks the* Articles of the Church *too Stiff, Formal and Strait-lac'd a Rule to Confine His Faith in, and Complements 'em out of their Rigour and Severity. He sets Loose All Opinions, can Embrace those of Every Sect, and is too Good Natur'd to Prosecute any One for* Heresy *or* Schism. *He looks upon the Censuring* Atheism, Infidelity *or* False Doctrine, *as a* Dogmatical Usurpation, *as an Intrusion and Breaking in upon That* Human Liberty, *which He sets up as the* Measure *and* Extent *of* His Belief.[23]

An honest reading of the XXXIX Articles would certainly lead any of those subscribing to the heresies he names to conclude that this theology was much too narrow. Perhaps Sacheverell was Reformed or even an anti-Arminian Calvinist. But the evidence presented by Hampton is far from convincing.[24]

21. Sacheverell, *Character*, 5.
22. Hampton, *Anti-Arminians*, 31.
23. Sacheverell, *The Character*, 5–6.
24. Speck, "Henry Sachervell."

The other three who were living when Edwards died were certainly less prominent. Benjamin Jenks (bap. 1648–1724) graduated from Queen's College, Oxford, BA, and served the church faithfully for fifty-six years following his installation as curate in Shopshire. His published works include a few sermons, several books on prayer and meditation, and a translation of Bellarmine's *Heaven Opened*. Whether teaching or writing, his most notable theme was moralizing on questionable practices of the day. Nothing in his laudable career, however, would lead someone to conclude that he was a prominent Calvinist.[25]

Peter Newcome (1656–1738) was the youngest son of ejected minister Henry Newcome (bap. 1627–95). Like his elder brother Henry, he decided to conform following his graduation from Brasenose College, Oxford, BA, MA. After ordination he served in several churches, but little is known about his life, particularly his theological inclination. He wrote a two-volume work called, *A Catechetical Course* to explain basic doctrine in fifty-two sermons, most of which are based on the Apostles' Creed, the Ten Commandments, the Lord's Prayer, and the sacraments. He did relate the covenant to salvation, but primarily in reference to baptism of a regenerational nature with little mention of grace and faith. For example, "As sure therefore as we have been *named in Baptism*, so surely are we Persons in *Covenant* with God."[26] When faith is mentioned it is in reference, not to trusting in Christ, but to believing the Creed: "And the *Object* hereof, which our *Catechism* teacheth us to believe, is, *All the Articles of the Christian Faith*."[27] Instead of warning about faith without works, he was concerned about baptism without works:

> For to be a *Christian* (we see) is not only to be *Baptised*, but to Answer our *Baptism* and make good the Promise that was the Condition thereof. A Wicked Life doing more to *Unchristian* us, than ever *Baptism* did to make us *Christians*.[28]

Losing salvation as the result of one's works is not a typical Reformed theme. But regardless of his questionable theology, if Newcome did not warrant an entry in the *ODNB*, he was probably not too prominent either.

Edward Welchman (1665–1739), BA, MA, Magdalen College, Oxford, dedicated his life to the church, rising to the position of prebendary

---

25. Johnston, "Benjamin Jenks."
26. Newcome, *Catechetical Course*, 1:32.
27. Newcome, *Catechetical Course*, 1:39.
28. Newcome, *Catechetical Course*, 1:54.

at the cathedrals in St. David's and Lichfield. The clearest writings revealing his theological alignment are found in *The Thirty-nine Articles of the Church of England Illustrated with Notes*. Here he explained that salvation is by grace alone through faith alone. Because of the Fall, we are completely unable to do any good works.

> Works done before the Grace of Christ may have some specious Appearance of Good, from whence they are called *good*, but improperly. [. . .] For neither can we *believe* unless God *open our Hearts*, (Acts xvi.14) neither can we *will* or *do, unless* He *of his good Pleasure work in us* for those Ends.[29]

He endorsed Article XVII on predestination and election, but warned against attention to the doctrine of reprobation. Though his Calvinism was not displayed in his writings nearly as prominently as that of Edwards, he was a prominent churchman and active well into the eighteenth century.[30]

What do we know about the remaining twelve who died between 1700 and 1716, when Edwards died? The career of Lancelot Addison (1632–1703), BA, MA, Queen's College, Oxford, later BD, DD, did not get off to a promising start when he was publicly humiliated after giving a particularly intemperate speech against Puritanism at Oxford. After ten years as a military chaplain in Tangiers, he returned home to serve as rector at Milston, followed by Dean at Lichfield. His earlier writings concerned Islam and Morocco, based on his experience there. Later he published a few theological works, including *A Christian's Manual*, from which Hampton says we can discern "Reformed leanings," although he offers no evidence.[31] Reformed leanings, perhaps; but the Arminian leanings seem to be more pronounced. To categorize him as prominently Reformed, much less Calvinistic, does not seem reasonable.

Though he talks about grace, Addison emphasizes faith much more. But the object of his faith is not Christ, but Scripture, or "the Doctrine of Christianity, summed up in the Apostles Creed. [. . .] I begin with Faith [. . . which] signifies my Assent unto [. . .] I take the Scriptures to be the

---

29. Welchman, *XXXIX Articles*, 30.

30. Cooper, "Edward Welchman."

31. Addison, *Christian's Manual* is largely a commentary on the Apostles' Creed, Ten Commandments and Lord's Prayer, supplemented by instruction for baptism and the Lord's Supper.

general Object of my Faith."[32] Trust, particularly trust in Christ for salvation is missing. Calvin did not teach that infant baptism washed away original sin, yet Addison writes, "Forgive me, O Lord, whatever I have transgressed against thee, from the time of my Baptism."[33] And does an individual's effort at repentance determine the extent of that forgiveness? "There is no Repentance so great, as that it entirely destroys all Sin."[34] Perhaps that is hyperbole, but, as a whole, there is more reason than not to doubt Addison's theology as Reformed.[35]

William Beveridge, BA, MA, St. John's College, Cambridge, was noted for his proficiency in oriental languages. His outstanding scholarship paved the way for advancement from his initial vicarage at Yealing to bishop at St. Asaph as he diligently carried out his duties at each post. Beveridge was clearly a prominent Anglican and also Reformed, but not everyone would call him a "prominent Anglican Calvinist." Perhaps reflecting his own bias, the author of the preface which introduced the Works of William Beveridge stated,

> There are, as has been frequently observed, in the works of Bishop Beveridge, occasional tinges of those opinions which were so rife in his early years, and of which Dr. Tuckney, the Master of his College and Professor of Divinity, was the well-known maintainer in his day; and there are, on the other hand, here and there in his Sermons, those occasional protests against the characteristics of the Church of Rome, common, more or less, to all our divines. But his mind was too essentially practical to entertain Calvinistic opinions and he was too entirely in earnest in teaching positive truth, and providing real food for his flock, to spend his time and waste his energies in the bare contradiction of error.[36]

His works, which contain one hundred and forty six sermons, commentaries on church catechisms and the XXXIX Articles and notes on the Old and New Testaments, do not exactly corroborate that assessment. Although references to Calvin, Luther or any Reformed theologians are sparse, he did say that the Articles of the Church of England

---

32. Addison, *Christian's Manual*, 6, 10.
33. Addison, *Christian's Manual*, 57.
34. Addison, *Christian's Manual*, 124.
35. Hamilton, "Lancelot Addison."
36. Cowie, "William Beveridge"; Beveridge, "Preface," 1:ix.

are consistent with the Apostles' Nicene and Athanasian Creeds.[37] When refuting Arminian notions of universal redemption, Augustine was cited, but not Calvin.[38] In his commentary on the XXXIX Articles, he cited Calvin twice and Luther three times, but not in articles IX, "Of Original or Birth Sin"; X, "Of Free Will"; XI, "Of the Justification of Man"; XII, "Of Good Works"; XVII, "Of the Works before Justification"; XVII, "Of Predestination and Election", where distinctly Reformed doctrines are most visible. Despite his lack of explicit references to Calvin, his Calvinism is evident in his commentary on the XXXIX Articles and throughout his sermons. Speaking of fallen human nature Beveridge wrote, "For his will being itself corrupted, it cannot but choose and delight in corruption."[39] Regarding predestination he stated that although we may explain some of the other articles by Scripture, the Fathers, and reason, this doctrine, being a "Mystery of Mysteries" is beyond "Carnal Reason."[40] Quoting Augustine or Fulgentius (460–533), he wrote that predestination follows from God's infinite goodness from before the world began and "that neither any of them, whom God predestinated to the Kingdom of Heaven can perish, nor any of those whom he did not predestinate unto Life can be saved."[41] Furthermore, as God's call to salvation is universal, the issue is not "whether God elected me from Eternity, but whether I obey him in time, if I obey him in time, I may certainly concluded that he elected me from Eternity."[42] On the relationship between man's will and God's will:

> Neither will it avail any thing here to say, God will will it efficaciously if man wills it (as our adversaries are forced to say); for then the efficaciousness of God's will would depend upon the determination of the will of man, and so the first cause be determined by the second, which is against all, even philosophical principles.[43]

So although Beveridge may have been reluctant to call himself a Calvinist and seldom cited Calvin, he did not evade or understate Reformed

---

37. Beveridge, "Sermon LX," 3:150.
38. Beveridge, "John iii.16," 10:586–90.
39. Beveridge, *XXXIX Articles*, 7:275.
40. Beveridge, *XXXIX Articles*, 7:343–44.
41. Beveridge, *XXXIX Articles*, 7:347. Apparently it was not clear whether the source of this quotation was Augustine or Fulgentius.
42. Beveridge, *XXXIX Articles*, 7:350.
43. Beveridge, "John iii.16," 10:590.

doctrines most often associated with Calvinism. He did oppose the 1706 Act of Union with Scotland, concerned that Scottish Presbyterians would adversely affect the Church of England.[44]

William Burkitt (1650–1703), BA, MA, Pembroke College, Cambridge was known for the very personal way in which he carried out his parish ministry in Milden and Dedham. His New Testament commentary, published as *Expository Notes with Practical Observations*, gives clear evidence by which he would be considered a Calvinist. He was also a friend of Puritan Anglican William Gurnall (1616–79). Whether he was prominent beyond his own parish is difficult to say. Certainly he was evangelistic and caring.[45]

As the son of the second earl of Northampton who was killed in an early battle of the English Civil War, Henry Compton was thrust into seventeenth-century political conflict at the young age of eleven. After dropping out of Oxford, he traveled abroad, received his MA at Cambridge, and served as an army officer before being recruited by the Dean John Fell (1625–86) of Christ Church, Oxford to join him as a canon commoner. Bishop George Morley installed him as master of St. Cross Hospital in Winchester the following year and two years later he was made canon. Compton was politically astute and along with his natural abilities and his noble heritage, it seems that he was accorded preferential treatment for appointments within the Church of England.

There is little doubt that Compton was anti-Catholic and orthodox in his theology, but it is not clear that he should be considered Reformed. In his *The Bishop of London's Tenth Conference with his Clergy*, he cited Jonathan Edwards of Oxford in condemning Socinians. Remonstrants such as Simon Episcopus (1583–1643), Étienne de Courcelles (1586–1659), and Philipp van Limborch (1633–1712) were censured, not for drafting the five articles which prompted the Synod at Dort, but for making "a Shew of asserting the Doctrin of the Trinity; but (alas!) it comes to nothing [. . .] They make Original Sin but a transient Punishment, and proportion the Efficacy of Christ's Satisfaction and the Sacraments accordingly."[46] He denounced as "Schismaticks" anabaptists, Independents, and Quakers, but called Hugo Grotius (1583–1645) "that Great and Learned Person" whom

---

44. Grosart, "William Beveridge."
45. Ginn, "William Burkitt."
46. Compton, *Tenth Conference*, 16–17.

we should "hearken to."⁴⁷ Hence, given Compton's career details, we must, along with his biographer Edward Carpenter, question his motivation. Carpenter's assessment is that Compton had "an almost complete lack of interest in theological discussion for its own sake."⁴⁸ Compton came from a prominent family and was prominent in his own right as Bishop of London, but if he had little real interest in theology and his motivation was essentially political, it certainly diminishes his stature as a prominent Anglican Calvinist.⁴⁹

John Hall, BA, MA, BD, DD, was both scholar and Master of Pembroke College, Oxford and later appointed Bishop of Bristol. His Puritan background engendered some opposition, but Hall was so effective at working within the system that Latitudinarians even supported him for Archbishop of Canterbury when Tillotson died. As an indication of his mastery of Reformed theology, Edmund Calamy the Younger (1660–1731) wrote, "He could bring all the Catechism of the Westminster Assembly, out of the Church of England. I never heard Mr. Gilbert [Presbyterian Thomas Gilbert] applaud any one more than this bishop."⁵⁰ When William III became king, Hall was in good stead because of his Calvinism, the new king observing that few clergymen were sympathetic to that view.⁵¹

Timothy Halton (bap.1633–1704) graduated from Queen's College, Oxford, BA, MA, BD, DD, and rose eventually to the position of vice-chancellor. He apparently published no books and there is little from which to infer his theological predilection. Hampton says that sermon manuscripts give evidence of "Reformed leanings." But the evidence Hampton cites is a book of hand-written sermons, based on texts such as Galatians 5:25, Isaiah 54:14–17, and Ephesians 4:30, which are clearly orthodox, but give little evidence of Arminian or Calvinist leanings.⁵² In any case, "Reformed leanings" do not seem to support the label of "prominent Calvinist."⁵³ Halton's lasting contributions included the construction of a new library and other buildings at Queen's College, to

47. Compton, *Tenth Conference*, 18, 39.
48. Hampton, *Anti-Arminians*, 14.
49. Coleby, "Henry Compton."
50. Calamy, *My Own Life*, 1:272.
51. Marshall, "John Hall."
52. Queen's College Library, Oxford, MS 497.
53. Hampton, *Anti-Arminians*, 11; Halton's sermons, Queen's College Library, Oxford, MS 497.

which he personally contributed a significant sum besides raising funds from other sources.[54]

William Jane (bap.1645–1707), Christ Church, Oxford, BA, MA, BD, DD, served as canon of Christ Church and St. Paul's, archdeacon of Middlesex, Dean of Gloucester and Regius Professor of Divinity at Oxford. He was appointed to the 1689 commission tasked to revise the *BCP*, where he opposed any changes, including an effort to remove readings from the Apocrypha. He challenged the legality of the commission and failing that, resigned from it. Colluding with the Earls of Rochester and Clarendon, he engineered his own election as prolocutor of the convocation to receive the commission's report and also defeated a proposed plan of comprehension. Calamy says Jane was a Calvinist "with respect to doctrine," but it is clear that his primary focus was ecclesiastical politics and opposing Catholicism, Socinianism, and Unitarianism.[55] As a staunch High Churchman, he was more concerned with maintaining the traditions of the Church of England and its standing in English society, along with his own. In other words, though prominent as a churchman, his Calvinism was neither consistent, nor prominent.

Nathaniel Parkhurst (1643–1707), BA, MA, Queen's College, Cambridge, served faithfully for forty-two years as vicar in Yoxford, described as a relatively obscure rural community. Judging from his published sermons, his primary ministry emphasis appears to be the salvation of his congregants, moral decline in society and division in the church. As to his Calvinist or Reformed leanings, little hint is given in his sermons, although historical consensus is that his overriding concern was to avoid doctrinal controversy, which would have been difficult for a prominent Calvinist in his day.[56]

Robert South, BA, MA, BD, DD, Christ Church, Oxford, achieved some prominence, but not as much as he sought. What he most desired was the bishopric of Oxford, but neither that nor any other promotion that he deemed acceptable was offered, despite his direct appeal to Archbishop Sancroft in 1686. He was appointed orator of Christ Church at the age of twenty-six, but apparently felt unfairly denied the canonship at the same time. He had to wait ten more years which was the typical age

---

54. Hegarty, "Timothy Halton."
55. Calamy, *Historical Account*, 1:275; Hegarty, "William Jane."
56. Blatchly, "Nathaniel Parkhurst."

for most appointed to that position.[57] In 1713 he was chosen to succeed Thomas Sprat (1635–1713), Bishop of Rochester and Dean of Westminster, but declined, being near eighty years old.

South built a reputation as an engaging but fairly intolerant preacher. His sermons were more political than those of his contemporaries and were often unrestrained in their acrimonious satire toward those he did not agree with, including Presbyterians, Puritans, Socinians, and Catholics.[58] This demeanor no doubt affected his reputation. Biographical sketches from different perspectives appear in some of his sermon collections. According to Gerard Reedy, two written by South's contemporaries tended to exaggerate: one, somewhat hostile, by Anthony Wood, the other favorable by an anonymous admirer.[59] Two later ones seem more balanced, but whether praising or criticizing, the points made are similar. From an anonymous nineteenth-century sketch we read,

> South's faults and his excellencies lie upon the surface. His sincerity and his earnestness, his uncompromising honesty, his shrewd, clear insight, his sound judgment, his robust, vigorous, common-sense appear on every page of his writings. But, at the same time, there are few of his discourses, in which he does not display intolerance, inveterate prejudices, and vehement partisanship, and in which the reader is not pained by the bitter scorn and fierce sarcasm which pours out upon his opponents. He hated the Puritans with a blind and undiscerning hatred. He made no allowance for them, expressed no sympathy with their evangelical creed and devoted labours, attempted no discrimination between the good and the bad men of the party, but assailed them all with unrelenting hostility.[60]

In appraising South's theological bent, we discover a man quite unlike Parkhurst, who was afraid that his Calvinistic or Reformed views might incite division. Surely someone with Reformed leanings would find something of merit among the Puritans over against Laud's disciples. Instead, "The ejections which followed the 1662 Act of Uniformity supplied more provisions of pluralism for Laudian avengers such as South" and "South's Laudian loyalties survived his accommodation with the

---

57. Reedy, *Robert South*, 14.
58. Reedy, *Robert South*, 53.
59. Reedy, *Robert South*, 11.
60. South, *Wisdom of Our Fathers*, xx.

revolution."[61] Jonathan Peele Dabney's (1793–1868) biographical portrayal, provided as a preface to a collection of South's sermons, includes this summary taken from the Christian Observer for 1823:

> Between Dr. South's extravagant and most ungovernable wit, and his hatred for Puritans and Socinians, added to the still lingering scholastic orthodoxy, the armour he always buckles on for conflict, he must be allowed to exhibit a most grotesque appearance; semi-Calvinist and semi-Arminian, semi-boxer and semi-buffoon, but always eloquent, profound, moral and bold for God and for truth.[62]

The anonymous source quoted above also appraised his theology:

> Whilst South was thus essentially orthodox and evangelical, it must be admitted that his views of truth were in many respects defective. The atonement of Christ, the work of the Spirit, the salvation of the sinner by grace alone through faith, were all maintained by him, but not with the fulness and frequency we must desire. They formed parts of his theological system, but they are co-ordinate where they should be supreme. They held their place amongst other doctrines, but they did not pervade, irradiate, and vitalize the whole. The reader of the following pages, amidst all his admiration of the genius of the writer, will often miss the fervour, the unction, and the fulness of evangelical teaching, with which the same subject would have been treated by many of South's contemporaries.[63]

Hampton seems to see South's Reformed convictions most clearly in his debate with William Sherlock on the doctrine of the Trinity. Sherlock was accused of following the thinking of Remonstrant theologians Etienne de Courcelles and Jean Leclerc (1657–1736). He also refers to South's debate with Sherlock on divine nature where he argued that all of God's attributes are of equal importance. But does refuting a tritheistic view of the Trinity or asserting that God's attributes are all of equal importance make one Reformed? South condemned the idea of middle knowledge as a way to understand God's omniscience, certainly an issue separating Reformed and Arminians.[64] However, South made a number of other statements, leading critics such as the *Christian Observer* above

61. Griggs, "Robert South."
62. South, *Discourses*, xxii.
63. South, *Wisdom*, xxii–xxiii.
64. Hampton, *Anti-Arminians*, 258.

to call him "semi-Calvinist and semi-Arminian," as noted above. His sermon on Genesis 1:27 does not sound so Reformed:

> That to assert, that God looked upon Adam's fall as a sin, and punished it as such, when, without any antecedent sin of his, he withdrew that actual grace from him, upon the withdrawing of which, it was impossible for him not to fall, seems a thing that highly reproaches the essential equity and goodness of the divine nature [. . .] We were not born crooked.[65]

So, to consider someone as unpredictable and inconsistent as South to be a Calvinist, or even Reformed is not tenable.

Mathematician and cryptographer John Wallis was certainly prominent as founding member of the Royal Society and Savilian Professor of Geometry at Oxford for over fifty years. Having studied natural philosophy, ethics, metaphysics, theology, anatomy and medicine at Cambridge, he had wide-ranging interests. In his primary profession of mathematics, despite being largely self-taught, he was well respected and made significant contributions. His prominence in theology was clearly secondary, but enhanced remarkably in 1644 when he was selected to assist chief scribe Adoniram Byfield (1602–60) at the Westminster Assembly. This gave young Wallis an amazing education as the foremost English theologians deliberated over the major theological issues of the day. Later in life after being awarded a DD, this theological foundation no doubt prompted him to enter the public debate on the Trinity, which had received considerable attention from the writings of Milton, Newton, and Locke as well as a number of prominent divines, such as Tillotson and Sherlock. Wallis attempted a rather novel defense of the Trinity in eight letters, comparing the Trinity to a geometric cube.[66] Although he managed to stay orthodox, he left some people then and now thinking that he strayed too close to modalism.[67] Wallis became a moderate Presbyterian during the interregnum, opposed the execution of Charles I, and retained his chair at Oxford with the return of Charles II. It can be reasonably inferred that his theology was reformed, but his renown was due to his mathematics. His most significant works in theology were written to refute anti-trinitarianism, hardly qualifying him as a prominent Calvinist.

---

65. South, "Sermon Preached," 1.41.
66. Wallis, *Doctrine*, 11–15.
67. Muller, *Reformed Dogmatics*, 4:120–21, 128–29; Rampelt, "Three Persons," 62.

Sir Joseph Williamson (1633–1701) intended to follow an academic career following his Queen's College education, BA, MA. However the promise of personal advancement and financial security attracted him to government service. His success in the field of intelligence helped him advance and he eventually served as Secretary of State and president of the Royal Society. Hampton's reason for naming him was that he secured preferment for certain individuals including Henry Compton and Timothy Halton and "seems to have been sufficiently interested in Reformed theology to have been sent a copy of Tully's *Iustificatio Paulina.*" Even if they were prominent Calvinists, which seems doubtful as noted above, his association with them does not make him one.[68]

Josiah Woodward (1657–1712) was educated at St. Edmund Hall, Oxford, BA, MA, BD, DD, and served as minister at Poplar, Middlesex, a crowded, disadvantaged part of sprawling London until shortly before he died. He was an influential writer and speaker in social reform and moral guidance, being active in moral reformation societies and a founding member of the Society for the Promotion of Christian Knowledge, which published many of his penny tracts.[69] Hampton includes him because of "Reformed sympathies" found in his *Short Catechism*. Again, "Reformed sympathies" hardly qualify one as a prominent Calvinist. Woodward's prominence is not due to his Reformed or Calvinist theology, but rather his activity as a life-long moral reformer, exhibited for example, in exhortations directed especially to soldiers, sailors, and young people that they engage in activity which is pleasing to God, such as prayer, reading Scripture, and observing the sacraments, while abstaining from that which is not, such as slander, drunkenness, lust, and profanity.[70]

So, of the thirty-five men given as examples by Hampton, we are left with Beveridge, Burkitt, Hall, and Welchman, for whom there is unambiguous evidence of their Reformed credentials at the beginning of the eighteenth century. Prominence is obviously a matter of judgment and degree. Certainly Beveridge and Hall rose to positions of greater prominence than Edwards, but it is clear that in the early eighteenth century, none of them were nearly as prominent in their Calvinism publicly as

---

68. Hampton, *Anti-Arminians*, 15; Meli, "John Wallis."

69. Spurr, "Josiah Woodward"; Craig, "Movement", 232; Woodward, *An Account of the Rise and Progress of the Religious Societies in the City of London* (London, 1712).

70. Hampton, *Anti-Arminians*, 13. To his credit, Woodward's works were published in many editions long after he died, e.g., *An Account, The Baseness, The Seaman's Monitor, A Short Catechism, The Soldier's Monitor, The Young Man's Monitor.*

was Edwards. Consequently there is little reason to doubt the claim of Stromberg and others that by 1700 Edwards was "about the only remaining example of a prominent Anglican Calvinist." Edwards proudly called himself a Calvinist and wrote extensively on the errors of Arminianism. At the same time, his effort to refute his opponents was not motivated by personal ambition, vengeance, or maliciousness. He considered Arminians brothers in Christ. His concern was to promote truth as he understood it from Scripture.

Bibliography

MANUSCRIPTS

American Antiquarian Society, Wooster, MA.

Cotton Mather to John Edwards, undated, MS II-58.

British Library

John Edwards to John Wyat, 1708, Add MS 4275/205.

Richard Kidder, Bishop of Bath and Wells to John Edwards, 1702, Add MS 4274/49.

Cotton Mather to John Edwards October 10, 1712, Add MS 4276/49.

Simon Patrick, Bishop of Chichester and [1691] of Ely to John Edwards, dated November 8, 1692, Add MS 4274/167.

Cambridge University Library

Multiple letters between John Edwards and John Woodward, from February 4, 1696/7 to August 23, 1699, MS Add 7647/114–122.

John Edwards to "My Good Friend," February 22, 1716, MS Add 7647/122.

John Edwards, untitled partial manuscript, April 19, 1714, MS Add 58.

Simon Patrick to John Edwards, August 11, 1692, MS Add 4274/167.

Notes of John Woodward in response to Edwards' understanding of life on earth before and after the Fall as explained in His book *A Compleat History* and His recent letters, June 26, 1699, MS Add 8286/11.

Oxford: Queens's College Library

Timothy Halton, Bound sermon manuscripts, MS 497.

PRIMARY WORKS

An Act for the Uniformity of Publick Prayers; and Administration of Sacraments and Other Rites and Ceremonies; And for the Establishing the Form of Making, Ordaining, and Consecrating Bishops, Priests, and Deacons in the Church of England. London, 1662.

Addison, Lancelot. *The Christian's Manual*. London, 1710.

Anon, *Censura Temporum: The Good or Ill Tendencies of Books, Sermons, Pamphlets, &c, Impartially Consider'd*. London, 1709.

Anon. *The General Exceptions against the Bishop of Sarum's Expositions of the XXXIX Articles Considered*. London, 1704.

B., F. *A Free but Modest Censure: On the Late Controversial Writings and Debates of the Lord Bishop of Worcester and Mr. Locke; Mr. Edwards and Mr. Locke; the Honorable Charles Boyle, Esq; and Dr. Bently*. London, 1698.

Bailey, Samuel. *Essays on the Pursuit of Truth and on the Progress of Knowledge*. 2nd ed. London: Longman, Brown, Green, and Longmans, 1844.

Barrett, B.F. *Beauty for Ashes: The Old and the New Doctrine Concerning the State of Infants after Death Contrasted*. New York, NY: Appleton, 1855.

Baxter, Richard. *The Catechizing of Families: A Teacher of Householders How to Teach Their Households*. London, 1683.

———. *Christian Concord, or, The Agreement of the Associated Pastors and Churches of Worcestershire*. London, 1653.

———. *The Cure for Church-Divisions, or, Directions for Weak Christians to Keep Them from Being Dividers or Troublers of the Church*. London, 1670.

———. *A Defence of the Principles of Love Which Are Necessary to the Unity and Concord of Christians and Are Delivered in a Book Called The Cure of Church-Division*. London, 1671.

———. *The Judgment of Mr. Baxter Concerning Ceremonies and Conformity*. London, 1667.

———. *A Dissuasive from Enquiring, or, A Further Account of Their Judgment in Certain Things in Which They are Misunderstood*. London, 1680.

———. *The Nonconformists Advocate, or, A Farther Account of Their Judgment in Certain Things in Which they Are Misunderstood*. London, 1680.

———. *The Nonconformists Plea for Peace, or, An Account of Their Judgment in Certain Things in Which They Are Misunderstood Written to Reconcile and Pacifie Such As by Mistaking Them Hinder Love and Concord*. London, 1679.

———. *A Plea for Congregationall Government, or, A Defence of the Assemblies Petition against Mr. John Saltmarsh.* London, 1646.

———. *Reliquiæ Baxterianæ.* London, 1696.

———. *Richard Baxter's Answer to Dr. Edward Stillingfleet's Charge of Separation.* London, 1680.

———. *A Search for the English Schismatick by the Case and Characters: I. Of the Diocesan Canoneers; II. Of the Present Meer Nonconformists, not As an Accusation of the Former, but a Necessary Defence of the Later, So Far as They Are Wrongfully Accused and Persecuted by Them.* London, 1681.

———. *A Second True Defence of the Meer Nonconformists against the Untrue Accusations, Reasonings and History of Dr. Edward Stillingfleet, Dean of St. Pauls.* London, 1681.

———. *A Third Defence in the Cause of Peace Proving 1. The Need of Our Concord; 2. The Impossibility of It on the Terms of the Present Impositions.* London, 1681.

———. *The True and Only Way of Concord of All Christian Churches: The Desirableness of It and the Detection of False Dividing Terms.* London, 1680.

———. *Universal Concord.* London, 1660.

———. *Universal Redemption of Mankind by the Lord Jesus Christ Sated and Cleared by the Late Learned Mr. Richard Baxter.* London, 1694.

Bennet, Thomas. *A Discourse of the Everblessed Trinity in Unity with an Examination of Dr. Clarke's Scripture Doctrine of the Trinity.* London, 1718.

Beveridge, William. *An Exposition of the XXXIX Articles of the Church of England.* London, 1710.

———. "John iii. 16." In *WWB*, 10:574-94.

———. "Preface." In *WWB*, 1:iii-x.

———. "Sermon LX, The Sufficiency of Scripture." In *WWB*, 3:144-58.

———. *The Theological Works of William Beveridge.* 12 vols. Oxford: Parker, 1842–1848.

———. *Thesaurus Theologicus, or, A Complete System of Divinity Summ'd up in Brief Notes upon Select Places of the Old and New Testament Wherein the Sacred Text Is Reduc'd under Proper Heads, Explain'd and Illustrated with the Opinions and Authorities of the Ancient Fathers, Councils, &c.* 4 vols. London, 1710-11. Reprinted in *WWB*, vols 9-10.

Biddle, John. *A Confession of Faith Touching the Holy Trinity according to the Scripture.* London, 1648.

———. *Twelve Arguments Drawn out of the Scripture Wherein the Commonly Received Opinion Touching the Deity of the Holy Spirit is Clearly and Fully Refuted.* London, 1647.

Biddulph, Thomas T. *Essays on Some Select Parts of the Liturgy of the Church of England, Being the Substance of a Course of Lectures Delivered in the Parish Churches of St. Werburgh, Bristol.* 3rd ed. Bristol, 1799.

Birch, Thomas. *The Life of the Most Reverend Dr. John Tillotson, Lord Archbishop of Canterbury, Compiled Chiefly from His Original Papers and Letters.* London, 1753.

Blackall, Ofspring. *Fourteen Sermons Preach'd upon Several Occasions.* 2nd ed. London, 1706.

Blackmore, Richard. *The Accomplished Preacher, or, An Essay upon Divine Eloquence.* London, 1731.

Bold, Samuel. *A Short Discourse of the True Knowledge of Christ Jesus.* London, 1697.

———. *Some Passages in the Reasonableness of Christianity, &c. and Its Vindication with Some Animadversions on Mr. Edwards' Reflections on the Reasonableness of Christianity and on His Book Entituled, Socinianism Unmask'd*. London, 1697.

Bowman, Thomas. *A Review of the Doctrines of the Reformation, with an Account of the Several Deviations to the Present General Departure from Them in a Series of Letters to a Young Gentleman Designed for the Ministry*. Norwich, 1768.

Bradshaw, Henry. *Collected Papers of Henry Bradshaw, Late University Librarian*, edited by Francis Jenkinson. Cambridge: Cambridge University Press, 1889.

Burder, George. *Evangelical Truth Defended, or, A Reply to a Letter Containing Strictures on a Sermon Preached at Lancaster by the Rev. Mr. Housman*. Lancaster, 1788.

Bunyan, John. *The Works of That Eminent Servant of Christ Mr. John Bunyan, Minister of the Gospel and Formerly Pastor of a Congregation at Bedford*. 3rd ed. 2 vols. London, 1767.

Burnet, Gilbert. *Bishop Burnet's History of His Own Time*. 6 vols. London, 1725.

———. *An Exposition of the Thirty-Nine Articles*. London, 1700.

———. *The Mystery of Iniquity Unveiled in a Discourse Wherein is Held Forth the Opposition of the Doctrine, Worship, and Practices of the Roman Church to the Nature, Designs, and Characters of the Christian Faith*. London, 1673.

Burnet, Thomas. *Archaeologiae Philosophicae, or, the Ancient Doctrine Concerning the Originals of Things*. London, 1692.

———. *The Sacred Theory of the Earth Containing an Account of the Original of the Earth and of All the General Changes Which It Hath Already Undergone or Is to Undergo till the Consummation of All Things*. London, 1684.

Bury, Arthur. *The Naked Gospel Discovering I. What Was the Gospel Which Our Lord and His Apostles Preached; II. What Additions and Alterations Latter Ages Have Made in It; III. What Advantages and Damages Have Therefore upon Ensued*. London, 1690.

Byrom, John. *The Private Journal and Literary Remains of John Byrom*. 2 vols. Edited by Richard Parkinson. London: Chetham Society, 1854.

Calamy, Edmund. *An Historical Account of My Own Life*. 2 vols. London: Henry Colburn and Richard Bentley, 1830.

Carleton, George. *Directions to Know the True Church*. London, 1615.

Chillingworth, William. *The Religion of the Protestants: A Safe Way to Salvation*. London: Bell & Daldy, 1870.

Clarke, Samuel. *Dr. Clark's Sentiments Concerning the Eternal Generation of the Son and Process of the Holy Spirit; Together with His Reasons for Writing and Preaching on the Trinity as Delivered to a Committee of the Upper House of Convocation*. London, 1714.

———. *A Letter to Mr. Dodwell Wherein All the Arguments in His Epistolary Discourse Against the Immortality of the Soul are Particularly Answered and the Judgment of the Fathers Concerning That Matter Truly Represented*. 6th ed. London, 1731.

———. *A Letter to the Reverend Dr. Wells*. London, 1714.

———. *Observations on Dr. Waterland's Second Defense in Defense of His Queries*. London, 1724.

———. *A Reply to the Objections of Robert Nelson, esq: and of an Anonymous Author [i.e. James Knight] against Dr. Clarke's Scripture-Doctrine of the Trinity*. London, 1714.

———. *The Scripture-Doctrine of the Trinity*. London, 1712.

Clarke, Samuel and Anthony Collins. *The Correspondence of Samuel Clarke and Anthony Collins, 1707-08*, edited by William L. Uzgalis. Peterborough, ON: Broadview, 2011.

Clissold, Augustus. *The Spiritual Exposition of the Apocalypse as Derived from the Writings of the Hon. Emanuel Swedenborg*. London: Longman, Brown, Green and Longmans, 1851.

Collins, Anthony. *An Essay Concerning the Use of Reason in Propositions, the Evidence Whereof Depends upon Human Testimony*. London, 1707.

Compton, Henry. *The Bishop of London's Tenth Conference with His Clergy upon the Fifth and Tenth Injunctions Given by the King*. London, 1701.

Copleston, Edward. *An Enquiry into the Doctrines of Necessity and Predestination in Four Discourses Preached before the University of Oxford with Notes and an Appendix on the Seventeenth Article of the Church of England*. 2nd ed. London, 1821.

Crisp, Tobias. *Christ Alone Exalted: Being the Compleat Works of Tobias Crisp, D.D. Containing XLII Sermons on Several Selected Texts of Scriptures Which Were Formerly Printed in Three Small Volumes by That Late Eminent and Faithful Dispenser of God's Word Who Was Sometime Minister at Brinkworth in Wiltshire and Afterward Many of the Sermons Were Preached in and About London to Which is Now Added Ten Sermons, Whereof Eight Were Never before Printed*. London, 1690.

———. "Sermon II: Christ the Only Way [part II]." In *CAE*, 15.

———. "Sermon VI: To Lay Our Sins on Christ Is the Lord's Prerogative Only [part I]." In *CAE*, 322.

———. "Sermon VII: The New Covenant of Free Grace [part II]." In *CAE*, 100.

Culverwell, Nathanael. *An Elegant and Learned Discourse on the Light of Nature*. London, 1669.

de Thoyras, Rapin. *The History of England*. 3rd ed. 7 vols. Translated by N. Tindal. London, 1743.

Defoe, Daniel. *Tour through the Eastern Counties of England, 1722*. London, 1888.

Delaune, William. *Twelve Sermons upon Several Subjects and Occasions*. London, 1728.

Dodwell, Henry. *An Epistolary Discourse Proving from the Scriptures and the First Fathers That the Soul Is a Principle Naturally Mortal*. London, 1706.

———. *Separation of Churches from Episcopal Government As Practised by the Present Non-conformists Proved Schismatical from Such Principles As Are Least Controverted and Do Withal Most Popularly Explain the Sinfulness and Mischief of Schism*. London, 1679.

Edwards, John. *Against Indifference in Religion Which Is So Notorious in This Present Age*. London, 1730. Reprinted in *REM*, 490-516.

———. *All the Works of John Edwards, D.D. in Ten Volumes, 8vo. viz. On the Authority, Stile, and Perfection of the Holy Scriptures, and Explaining Several Difficult Texts and Several Defences of the Holy Trinity Against the Socinians, &c.* London, 1702?

———. *An Answer to Dr. Whitby's Second Pretended Defence*. London, 1711. Reprinted in Edwards, *The Arminian Doctrines*, 118-212.

———. *The Arminian Doctrines Condemn'd by the Holy Scriptures by Many of the Ancient Fathers by the Church of England and Even by the Suffrage of Right Reason: in Answer to the Revd. Daniel Whitby*. London, 1711.

———. *A Brief Confutation of These Two False and Dangerous Positions, Namely 1. That the Church of Rome Is a True Church and Consequently That Salvation May Be*

Attained in It; 2. *That Ministers of the Gospel Are True and Proper Priests and Have Their True and Proper Sacrifice and Altar Now on Earth.* London, 1730. Reprinted in *REM*, 280–376.

———. *A Brief Discourse or Sermon Shewing How England Hath Left Her First Love and How She May Recover It.* London, 1711.

———. *Brief Remarks on "The Difficulties which attend the Study of the Scriptures."* London, 1714.

———. *Brief Remarks Upon Mr. Whiston's New Theory of the Earth and upon an Other Gentleman's Objections against Some Passages in a Discourse of the Existence and Providence of God Relating to the Copernican Hypothesis.* London, 1697.

———. *A Brief View of the Mistakes about Happiness, or, the Chief Good of Man with Proper Directions for Redresses.* London, 1724.

———. *A Brief Vindication of the Fundamental Articles of the Christian Faith as Also of the Clergy, Universities, and Publick Schools from Mr. Lock's Reflections upon Them in His Book of Education.* London, 1697.

———. *Christ, a Christian's Life and Death in His Gain.* London, 1730. Reprinted in *REM*, 518–36.

———. *Cometomantia, A Discourse of Comets Shewing Their Original, Substance, Place, Time, Magnitude, Motion, Number, Colour, Figure, Kinds, Names, and More Especially, Their Prognosticks, Significations, and Presages ... Where Also Is Inserted an Essay of Judiciary Astrology, Giving Satisfaction to This Grand Question: Whether Any Certain Judgments and Predictions Concerning Future Events Can Be Made from the Observation of the Heavenly Bodies Both Occasioned by the Appearance of the Late Comets in England and Other Places.* London, 1684.

———. *Crispianism Unmask'd, or, A Discovery of the Several Erroneous Assertions and Pernicious Doctrins Maintain'd in Dr. Crisp's Sermons.* London, 1693.

———. *Concio Determinatio pro Gradu Doctoratus in Sacra Theoligia.* Cambridge, 1700.

———. *A Demonstration of the Existence and Providence of God: From the Contemplation of the Visible Structure of the Greater and the Lesser World.* London, 1696.

———. *Der Socinianische Glaube.* Berlin, 1719.

———. *A Discourse Concerning the Authority, Stile, and Perfection of the Books of the Old and New Testament.* 3 vols. London, 1694–96.

———. *A Discourse of Episcopacy, Wherein This Question Is Resolved, Whether in the Primitive Times There Was a Distinct Order of Bishops Different from That Of Presbyters, or Whether All Ministers Were Equal.* London, 1730. Reprinted in *REM*, 148–278.

———. *The Divine Perfections Vindicated; or, Some Brief Remarks on His Grace William Lord Arch-Bishop of Dublin's Sermon.* London, 1710.

———. *The Doctrine of Faith and Justification Set in a True Light.* London, 1708.

———. *The Doctrines Controverted between Papists and Protestants Particularly and Distinctly Consider'd and Those Which Are Held by the Former Confuted.* London, 1724.

———. *An Enquiry into Four Remarkable Texts of the New Testament Which Contain Some Difficulty in Them with a Probable Resolution of Them.* London, 1692.

———. *The Eternal and Intrinsick Reasons of Good and Evil: a Sermon Preach'd at the Commencement at Cambridge on Sunday the Second Day of July, 1699.* London, 1699.

———. *Exercitations Critical, Philosophical, Historical, Theological on Several Important Places in the Writings of the Old and New Testament*. London, 1702.

———. *A Farther Enquiry into Several Remarkable Texts of the Old and New Testament: Which Contain Some Difficulty in Them: with a Probable Resolution of Them*. 2nd ed. London, 1692.

———. *A Free Discourse Concerning Truth and Error Especially in Matters of Religion*. London, 1701.

———. *The Fruits of the Spirit*. London, 1713.

———. *The General Exceptions against the Bishop of Sarum's Exposition of the XXXIX Articles Considered*. London, 1704.

———. *Great Things Done by God for Our Ancestors and Us of This Island: A Sermon Preach'd before the University of Cambridge at St. Mary's, November 5, 1709*. London, 1710.

———. "The Hearer: A Discourse Shewing What Are the Qualifications That Are Required in Those Who Would Receive Benefit and Advantage by Hearing the Word Preached." In Edwards, *Preacher, the Second Part*, 1–85 (second pagination). London, 1706.

———. *The Heinousness of England's Sins Represented in That of Jerusalem's, or, In What Respects a Nation May Be Said to Sin Grievously*. London, 1707.

———. "How Ministers of the Gospel Are to Excel." In Edwards, *Sermons*, 92–133.

———. *How to Judge Aright of the Former and the Present Times: A Discourse on Eccles. 7.10, Occasion'd by the Late Happy Accession of King George to the British Throne*. London, 1714.

———. *A Letter to the Reverend Lawrence Fogg, D.D. and Dean of Chester Wherein His Pretended Vindication of Some Passages in His New and Inconsistent Scheme of Divinity Is Examin'd and Confuted*. London, 1705.

———. *One Nation and One King: A Discourse on Ezek. XXXVII.22, Occasion'd by the Happy Union of England and Scotland*. London, 1707.

———. *Patrologia, or, A Discourse Concerning the Primitive Fathers and Antient Writers of the Christian Church*. In *REM*, 19–146.

———. *The Plague of the Heart: Its Nature and Quality, Original and Causes, Signs and Symptoms, Prevention and Cure; with Directions for Our Behaviour under the Present Judgement and Plague of the Almighty*. London, 1665.

———. *Polpoikilos Sophia: A Compleat History or Survey of All the Dispensations and Methods of Religion from the Beginning of the World to the Consummation of All Things As Represented in the Old and New Testament; Shewing the Several Reasons and Designs of Those Different Administrations and the Wisdom and Goodness of God in the Government of His Church through All the Ages of It*. London, 1699.

———. *The Preacher. A Discourse Shewing What Are the Particular Offices and Employments of the Character in the Church*. London, 1705.

———. *The Preacher. The Second Part Shewing I. What Particular Doctrines Ought To Be Preached by the Dispensers of the Gospel; II. That These Doctrines are Generally Neglected or (Which is Most Usual) Preached against; III. What are the Causes of This Neglect and Opposition; IV. What are the Dreadful Consequences Hereof*. London, 1706.

———. *The Preacher. The Third Part Containing Farther Rules and Advices for the Right Discharging of the Sacred-Office of Preaching*. London, 1709.

———. *Remains of the Late Reverend and Learned John Edwards, D.D. Sometime Fellow of St. John's College in Cambridge*. London, 1731.

———. *A Resolution of This Query: Whether the Doctrine of Non-Resistance and Passive-Obedience Is to Be Understood without Any Limitation and Restriction*. In *REM*, 442–88.

———. *The Scripture-Doctrine of the Five Points (as They Are Commonly Called) Wherein the Texts in the Old and New Testament Relating to Those Points Are, According to the Calvinian Scheme, Faithfully Collected and Some of them Explain'd and Illustrated for the Better Understanding the True Meaning of Them*. London, 1715.

———. *Sermons on Special Occasions and Subjects*. London, 1698.

———. *The Socinian Creed, or, A Brief Account of the Professed Tenents and Doctrines of the Foreign and English Socinians: Wherein Is Shew'd the Tendency of Them to Irreligion and Atheism with Proper Antidotes against Them*. London, 1697.

———. *Socinianism Unmask'd: A Discourse Shewing the Unreasonableness of a Late Writer's Opinion Concerning the Necessity of Only One Article of Christian Faith*. London, 1696.

———. *Some Animadversions on Dr. Clark's Scripture-Doctrine (As He Stiles It) of the Trinity*. London, 1712.

———. *Some Brief Critical Remarks on Dr. Clarke's Last Papers Which Are His Reply to Mr. Nelson and an Anonymous Writer and the Author of Some Considerations &c.* London, 1714.

———. *Some Brief Observations and Reflections on Mr. Whiston's Late Writings Falsly Entitul'd, Primitive Christianity Reviv'd Shewing, the Unreasonableness, Partiality, and Inconsistency, of His Whole Performance and That It No Ways Answers His Audacious Design of Disproving the True and Proper Divinity of Our Blessed Lord and Saviour Jesus Christ*. London, 1712.

———. *Some New Discoveries of the Uncertainty, Deficiency, and Corruptions of Human Knowledge and Learning*. London, 1714.

———. *Some Thoughts Concerning the Several Causes and Occasions of Atheism, Especially in the Present Age with Some Brief Reflections on Socinianism and on a Late Book Entituled, The Reasonableness of Christianity as Deliver'd in the Scriptures*. London, 1695.

———. *A Supplement to the Animadversions on Dr. Clarke's Scripture-Doctrine (As He Stiles It) of the Trinity*. London, 1713.

———. *The Surest Way of Prospering in Our Military Affairs the Ensuing Campaigns and Thereby of Putting a Speedy Conclusion to the Expensive and Bloody War Which at Present We Are Involv'd in*. London, 1708.

———. *Theologia Reformata*. 3 vols. London, 1713–1726.

———. *The Time of Reformation: A Seasonable Discourse of the Effectual Means and Methods of Reforming the Lives and Manners of the Whole Body of This Nation*. London, 1730. Reprinted in *REM*, 378–440.

———. *A Treatise of Repentance, both Legal and Evangelical, More Especially and Chiefly of the Latter*. London, 1718.

———. "The True Causes of the Ill Success of War." In *Sermons*, 192–224.

———. *Veritas Redux. Evangelical Truths Restored: Namely Those Concerning God's Eternal Decrees, the Liberty of Man's Will, Grace and Conversion, The Extent and Efficacy of Christ's Redemption, and Perseverance in Grace*. London, 1707.

BIBLIOGRAPHY 257

———. *The Whole Concern of Man, or, What He Ought to Know and Do, in Order to Eternal Salvation Laid Down in a Plain and Familiar Way for the Use of All, but Especially the Meanest Reader*. London, 1701.

———. *The Whole Concern of Man, or, What He Ought to Know and Do, in Order to Eternal Salvation Laid Down in a Plain and Familiar Way for the Use of All, but Especially the Meanest Reader*. 2nd ed. Boston, 1725.

———. *A Woman with a Book Open to the Words "The Whole Concern of Man" Looks toward Heaven and the Eye of Providence*. London, [17—?].

Edwards, Jonathan (1629-1712). *The Doctrine of Original Sin As It Was Always Held in the Catholic Church and Particularly in the Church of England, Asserted and Vindicated from the Exceptions and Cavils of the Reverend Dr. Daniel Whitby*. Oxford, 1711.

———. *A Preservative against Socinianism: Shewing the Direct and Plain Opposition between It and the Christian Religion Particularly in Those Two Great Fundamental Articles of Our Faith Concerning Original Sin and the Redemption of the World by the Death and Sufferings of Our Blessed Saviour. The Second Part*. 2nd ed. Oxford, 1693.

———. *A Preservative against Socinianism Shewing the Necessity of Faith and That Socinus and His Followers on the Contrary, by Making the Perswasion of the Mind Concerning Divine Truths a Useless or at Best an Indifferent Matter Plainly Undermine All Revealed and More Especially the Christian Religion. The Third Part*. Oxford, 1697.

———. *A Preservative against Socinianism: Shewing the Falsehood and Impiety of That Pernicious Opinion Advanced by Socinus and His Followers, viz. That Reason Is to Be the Great Rule of Our Faith and the Supreme Judge of Revealed Religion. The Fourth and Last Part*. Oxford, 1703.

Edwards, Jonathan (1703-58). *The Works of Jonathan Edwards. Vol. 10: Sermons and Discourses 1720-1723*, edited by Wilson H. Kimnach. New Haven, CN: Yale University Press, 1991.

———. *The Works of Jonathan Edwards, Vol. 26: Catalogues of Books*, edited by Peter J. Thuesen. New Haven, CN: Yale University Press, 2008.

Edwards, Thomas. *The First and Second Part of Gangræna, or, A Catalogue and Discovery of Many of the Errors, Heresies, Blasphemies, and Pernicious Practices of the Sectaries of This Time, Vented and Acted in England in These Four Last Years; Also a Particular Narration of Divers Stories, Remarkable Passages, Letters; an Extract of Many Letters, All Concerning the Present Sects Together with Some Observations upon and Corollaries from All the Fore-named Premisses*. London, 1646.

———. *The Third Part of Gangræna, or, A New and Higher Discovery of the Errors, Heresies, Blasphemies, and Insolent Proceedings of the Sectaries of These Times with Some Animadversions by Way of Confutation upon Many of the Errors and Heresies Named*. London, 1646.

Evans, R., V.D.M. *Holy Emulation Urged, or, Arguments and Motives for Christians to Excel in Holiness, Enforced from Matth. 5:57*. London, 1702.

Fell, John. *The Life of the Most Learned, Reverend and Pious Dr. H. Hammond*. London, 1662.

Fogg, Lawrence. *God's Infinite Grace in Election and Impartial Equity in Preterition Vindicated, or, An Antidote Against Offences, Occasioned by Sundry Celebrated*

Parties Unwarily Contending about God's Eternal Prescience and the Internal Operations of His Grace in Its Leading Men Through Faith to Salvation. London, 1713.

———. *Theologiæ Speculativæ Schema*. London, 1712.

———. *Two Treatises: I. A General View of Christian Religion in Eight Positions; II An Entrance into the Doctrine of Christianity by Catechetical Institution*. London, 1712.

Fowler, Edward. *Certain Propositions by Which the Doctrin of the H. Trinity Is So Explain'd According to the Ancient Fathers As to Speak It Not Contradictory to Natural Reason Together with a Defence of Them in Answer to the Objections of a Socinian Writer in His Newly Printed Considerations on the Explications of the Doctrin of the Trinity*. London, 1694.

———. *Dirt Wip't Off, or, A Manifest Discovery of the Gross Ignorance, Erroneousness, and Most Unchristian and Wicked Spirit of One John Bunyan, Lay-Preacher in Bedford, Which He Hath Showed in a Vile Pamphlet Publish't by Him against the Design of Christianity*. London, 1672.

Gailhard, Jean. *The Epistle and Preface to the Book against the Blasphemous Socinian Heresie Vindicated*. London, 1698.

Gardiner, James. *The Duty of Peace amongst Members of the Same State, Civil, or Ecclesiastical, Impartially Laid Down and Recommended*. London, 1713.

Gastrell, Francis. *A Defence of Some Considerations Concerning the Trinity, &c. in Answer to the Reflections Made Upon Them in a Late Pamphlet Entitled, An Essay Concerning the Use of Reason, &c.* London, 1707.

———. *Remarks Upon Dr. Clark's Scripture-Doctrine of the Trinity*. London, 1714.

Hacket, John. *Bishop Hacket's Memoirs of the Life of Archbishop Williams, Lord Keeper of the Great Seal of England, Abridg'd, with the Most Remarkable Occurrences and Transformations in Church and State*. London, 1715.

Hales, John. *Golden Remains of the Ever Memorable Mr. John Hales of Eton College*. London, 1659.

———. *The Works of John Hales*. 3 vols. Glasgow, 1765.

Hall, Joseph. *The Episcopacy by Divine Right Asserted*. In Hall, *The Works*, 9:142-281.

———. *The Works of the Right Reverend Joseph Hall, D.D., Bishop of Exeter and Afterwards of Norwich, a New Edition, Revised and Corrected with Some Additions*. 10 vols. Edited by Philip Wynter, Oxford: Oxford University Press, 1863.

Hammond, Henry. *The Miscellaneous Theological Works of Henry Hammond*. 3rd ed. 3 vols. Oxford: Parker, 1849.

———. *A Paraphrase and Annotations Upon the Book of the Psalms*. 2 vols. Oxford: Oxford University Press, 1850.

———. *A Practical Catechism*, 16th ed. Oxford: Parker, 1847.

———. *Thirty-One Sermons Preached on Several Occasions*. 3 vols. Oxford: Parker, 1849.

Heylyn, P. *Cyprianus Anglicus, or, the History of the Life and Death of the Most Reverend and Renowned Prelate William, by Divine Providence, Lord Archbishop of Canterbury*. Dublin: 1719.

Hickes, George. *An Apologetical Vindication of the Church of England in Answer to Her Adversaries Who Reproach Her with the English Heresies and Schisms*. London, 1706.

———. *Some Discourses Upon Dr. Burnet and Dr. Tillotson: Occasioned by the Late Funeral Sermon of the Former upon the Later*. London, 1705.

———. *Two Treatises on the Christian Priesthood and on the Dignity of the Episcopal Order: with a Prefatory Discourse in Answer to a Book Entitled, The Rights of the Christian Church.* 4th ed. 3 vols. London, 1847.

Hill, Richard. *An Apology for Brotherly Love and for the Doctrines o the Church or England in a Series of Letters to The Revd. Charles Daubeny with a Vindication of Such Parts of Mr. Wilberforce's Practical View, as Have Been Objected to by Mr. Daubeny in His Late Publication, entitled A Guide to the Church.* London, 1798.

Hoadly, Benjamin. *A Letter to a Clergy-Man in the Country Concerning the Votes of the Bishops in the Last Session of Parliament Upon the Bill against Occasional Conformity.* London, 1704.

Humfrey, John. An Answer to t*he Unreasonableness of Separation So Far as it Concerns the Peaceable Designe* with Some Animadversions upon the Debate between Him and Mr. Baxter Concerning the National Church and the Head of It. London, 1682.

———. *An Humble Vindication of a Free Admission unto the Lord's Supper.* London, 1653.

Jackson, John. *An Examination of Mr. Nye's Explication of the Articles of the Divine Unity, the Trinity, and Incarnation wherein Is Briefly Shewn the Insufficiency of That Explication Both from Scripture and Reason with a Vindication of Dr. Clarke's Scriptiure-Doctrine and Replies from the Charge of Tritheism.* London, 1715.

———. *Three Letters to Dr. Clarke from a Clergyman of the Church of England Concerning His Scripture-Doctrine of the Trinity.* London, 1714.

Johnson, Samuel. *A Dictionary of the English Language.* 2 vols. London, 1755.

King, William. *Divine Predestination and Fore-knowledge Consistent with the Freedom of Man's Will.* Dublin, 1709.

Knight, James. *The Scripture Doctrine of the Most Holy and Undivided Trinity Vindicated from the Misinterpretations of Dr. Clarke.* London, 1714.

Laud, William. *The History of the Troubles and Tryals of the Most Reverend Father in God and Blessed Martyr William Laud, Lord Arch-Bishop of Canterbury.* 2 vols. London, 1693/4. Reprinted in Laud, *The Works,* 3.273-463, 4.1-461.

———. *A Speech Delivered in the Star-Chamber on Wednesday, the 14th of June 1637.* London, 1637. Reprinted in Laud, *The Works,* 6:Part 1, 35–70.

———. *The Works of the Most Reverend Father in God William Laud, DD.* 7 vols. Edited by William Scott. Oxford: Parker, 1857.

Laurence, John. *An Apology for Dr. Clarke.* London, 1714.

Leslie, Charles. *The Charge of Socinianism against Dr. Tillotson Considered.* London, 1694. Reprinted in *WCL,* 2:541–605.

———. *Reflections Upon the Present Controversie Concerning the Holy Trinity.* London, 1714.

———. *Some Reflections upon the Second of Dr. Burnet's Four Discourses Concerning the Divinity and Death of Christ.* London, 1694. Reprinted in *WCL,* 2:608–33.

———. "A Supplement upon Occasion of a History of Religion Lately Published." In *WCL,* 2:635–69.

———. *The Theological Works of the Reverend Charles Leslie.* 7 vols. Oxford: Oxford University Press, 1832.

———. *A View of the Times, Their Principles and Practices.* 2nd ed. 6 vols London, 1750.

Lightfoote, Robert. *Dr. Edwards's Vindication Consider'd in a Letter to a Friend.* London, 1710.

———. *Remarks Upon Some Passages in Edwards's Preacher, Discovering His False Reasonings and Unjust Reflections upon His Brethren the Clergy.* London, 1709.

Locke, John. *The Correspondence of John Locke.* 8 vols. Edited by E. S. De Beer. Oxford: Clarendon, 1976–2010.

———. *An Essay Concerning Human Understanding.* 5th ed. London, 1706.

———. *An Essay Concerning Human Understanding,* edited by Peter Nidditch. Oxford: Clarendon, 1975.

———. *A Letter Concerning Toleration, Humbly Submitted, etc.* London, 1689.

———. *The Reasonableness of Christianity As Delivered in the Scriptures.* London, 1695.

———. *The Reasonableness of Christianity As Delivered in the Scriptures,* edited by John Higgins-Biddle. Oxford: Oxford University Press, 1999.

———. *A Second Vindication of the Reasonableness of Christianity.* London, 1697.

———. *Mr. Locke's Reply to the Right Reverend the Lord Bishop of Worcester's Answer to His Second Letter.* London, 1699.

———. *Some Thoughts Concerning Education.* London, 1695.

———. *Questions Concerning the Law of Nature,* edited and translated by Robert Horwitz, et. al. Ithaca, NY: Cornell University Press, 1990.

———. *A Vindication of the Reasonableness of Christianity, &c. from Mr. Edwards's Reflections.* London, 1695.

———. *Vindications of the Reasonableness of Christianity,* edited by Victor Nuovo. Oxford: Clarendon, 2012.

Mather, Cotton. *Bonifacius: An Essay upon the Good That Is to Be Devised and Designed by Those Who Desire to Answer the Great End of Life and To Do Good While They Live.* Boston, MA, 1710.

———. *Diary of Cotton Mather 1709–1724.* 2 vols. Boston: Massachusetts Historical Society, 1892.

———. *Dr. Cotton Mather's Student and Preacher Intituled, Manuductio Ad Ministerium, or, Directions for a Candidate of the Ministry Wherein, I. A Right Foundation Is Laid for His Future Improvement, II. Rules Are Offered for Such a Management of His Academical and Preparatory Studies and Upon That for Such, III. A Conduct after His Appearance in the World As May Render Him a Skillful and Useful Minister of the Gospel.* London, 1781.

———. *The Minister: A Sermon Offer'd unto the Anniversary Convention of Minsters from Several Parts of New-England.* Boston, MA, 1722.

———. *The Palm-Bearers: A Brief Relation of Patient and Joyful Sufferings and of Death Gloriously Triumphed over.* Boston, MA 1725.

———. *Utilia: Real and Vital Religion Served in the Various & Glorious Intentions of It.* Boston, MA, 1716.

Mayo, Richard. *A Plain Scripture-Argument against Dr. Clark's Doctrine Concerning the Ever-Blessed Trinity.* London, 1715.

More, Henry. *The Theological Works of Henry More.* London, 1708.

Nelson, Robert. *The Life of Dr. George Bull.* London, 1713.

Newcome, Peter. *A Catechetical Course of Sermons for the Whole Year.* 2 vols. London, 1712.

Newton, Isaac. *Philosophiæ Naturalis Principia Mathematica.* 2nd ed. London, 1713.

Nicholls, William. *A Comment on the Book of Common-Prayer and Administration of the Sacraments, etc. Together with the Psalter or Psalms of David.* London, 1710.

Nicholson, Edward. *Short Notes on Dr. Edwards's Long Book to Which He Gives the False Title of Veritas Redux: Truth Return'd: Instead of Scabies Ecclesiæ Redux, the Scab of the Church Return'd.* London, 1712.

North, Roger. *The Autobiography of Roger North*, edited by Augustus Jessopp. London: Nutt, 1887.

———. *Notes of Me: The Autobiography of Roger North*, edited by Peter Millard. Toronto: University of Toronto Press, 2000.

Nye, Stephen. *An Account of Mr. Firmin's Religion and of the Present State of the Unitarian Controversy.* London, 1698.

———. *The Agreement of the Unitarians with the Catholick Church.* London, 1697.

———. *Considerations on the Explications of the Doctrine of the Trinity.* London, 1693.

———. *The Exceptions of Mr. Edwards in His Causes of Atheism against the Reasonableness of Christianity as Deliver'd in the Scriptures, Examin'd and Found Unreasonable.* London, 1695.

———. *A Letter of Resolution Concerning the Doctrines of the Trinity and the Incarnation.* London, [1691?].

Oldisworth, William. *An Essay on the Nature, Extent, and Authority of Private Judgment in Matters of Religion.* London, 1711.

Owen, Charles. *Plain Reasons I. For Dissenting from the Church of England; II Why Dissenters Are Not and Cannot Be Guilty of Schism in Peaceably Separating from the Places of Public Worship in the Church of England; and III Several Common Objections Brought by Churchmen against Dissenters Answer'd.* 4th ed. London, 1718.

Owen, John. *A Display of Arminianism Being a Discovery of the Old Pelagian Idol Free-Will with the New Goddess Contingency.* London, 1681. Reprinted in *WJO*, 10.12–169.

———. *An Inquiry into the Original, Nature, Institution, Power, Order, and Communion of Evangelical Churches.* London, 1681. Reprinted in *WJO*, 15.224–469.

———. *The True Nature of A Gospel Church and its Government* (second part). London, 1681. Reprinted in *WJO*, 106:4–275.

———. *The Works of John Owen.* 17 vols. Edited by William Goold. Carlisle, PA: Banner of Truth, 1997.

Parker, Samuel. *A Discourse of Ecclesiastical Politie Wherein the Authority of the Civil Magistrate over the Consciences of Subjects in Matters of Religion Is Asserted, the Mischiefs and Inconveniences of Toleration Are Represented, and All Pretenses Pleaded in Behalf of Liberty of Conscience Are Fully Answered.* London, 1670.

Parriett, Thomas. *The Doctrine of the Martyrs of the Church of England Vindicated from the Misrepresentations of Dr. Edwards in His Book Entituled, Evangelical Truths Restored, Shewing Wherein He Has Misrepresented the Doctrine of the Martyrs of the Church of England.* London, 1707.

P[atrick], S[imon]. *A Brief Account of the New Sect of Latitude-Men.* London, 1662.

Patrick, Simon. *The Christian Sacrifice.* London, 1701.

———. *A Friendly Debate Betwixt Two Neighbors, the One a Conformist, the Other a Non-Conformist about Several Weighty Matters.* London, 1669.

———. *The Witnesses to Christianity, or, The Certainty of Our Faith and Hope.* 2 vols. London, 1675–77.

Potter, Edward. *A Vindication of Our Blessed Saviour's Divinity Chiefly against Dr. Clarke*. London, 1714.
Pufendorf, Samuel. *The Divine Feudal Law*. London, 1703.
Pye-Smith, John. *First Lines of Christian Theology*, edited by William Farrer. London: Jackson and Walford, 1854.
Sacheverell, Henry. *The Character of a Low-Church-Man: Drawn in Answer to The True Character of a Church-Man*. London, 1702.
Saltmarsh, John. *The Divine Right of Presbyterie Asserted by the Present Assembly, and Petitioned for Accordingly to the Honourable House of Commons in Parliament*. London, 1646.
Sanderson, Robert. *Pax Ecclesiæ*. London, 1678. Reprinted in Sanderson, *The Works*, 5:253-77.
———. *The Works of Robert Sanderson, D.D., Sometime Bishop of Lincoln*. 6 vols. Oxford: Oxford University Press, 1854.
Scandret, J. *Sacrifice: The Divine Service from the Covenant of Grace to the Consummation of the Mystery of Man's Redemption*. London, 1707.
Scrivener, Matthew. *Apologia pro Sanctae Ecclesiæ Patribus adversus Joannem Dallaeum de Usu Patrum, &c*. London, 1672.
Sergeant, John. *Five Catholick Letters Concerning the Means of Knowing with Absolute Certainty What Faith Now Held Was Taught by Jesus Christ*. London, 1688.
———. *Sure-Footing in Christianity on the Rule of Faith*. London, 1665.
Sherlock, William. *A Practical Discourse of Religious Assemblies*. London, 1681.
South, Robert. *Discourses on Various Subjects and Occasions*. Boston, MA: Bowles and Dearborn, 1827.
———. "A Sermon Preached at the Cathedral Church of St. Paul's, November the 9th, 1662 (Gen. i.27)." In South, *Sermons Preached*, 1:28–52.
———. *Sermons Preached Upon Several Occasions*. 7 vols. Oxford: Clarendon, 1823.
———. *The Wisdom of Our Fathers: Selections from the Writings of Robert South, D.D.* London, The Religious Tract Society, 1867.
———. *Tritheism Charged upon Dr. Sherlock's New Notion of the Trinity*. London, 1695.
Spottiswoode, John. *History of the Church of Scotland Beginning the Year of Our Lord 205, and Continued to the End of the Reign of King James 6*. 3 vols. Edinburgh: Oliver & Boyd, 1851.
Stackhouse, Thomas. *A Compleat Body of Speculative and Practical Divinity*. London, 1743.
Stanhope, George. "Sermon VIII. The Conditions and Privileges of the Second Birth." In *Sermons Preach'd upon Several Occasions*, 224-251. 2nd ed. London, 1705.
Stanley, William. *The Faith and Practice of a Church of England Man*. London: Pickering, 1848.
Stennett, Joseph. *An Answer to Mr. David Ruffen's Book, Entitul'd Fundamentals without a Foundation, or, A True Picture of the Anabaptists, &c*. London, 1704.
Stillingfleet, Edward. *The Bishop of Worcester's Answer to Mr. Locke's Letter Concerning Some Passages Relating to His Essay of Humane Understanding Mention'd in the Late Discourse in Vindication of the Trinity with a Postscript in Answer to Some Reflections Made on That Treatise in a Late Socinian Pamphlet*. London, 1697.
———. *The Bishop of Worcester's Answer to Mr. Locke's Second Letter, Wherein His Notion of Ideas Is Prov'd to Be Inconsistent with It Self and with the Articles of the Christian Faith*. London, 1698.

———. *A Discourse Concerning the Doctrine of Christ's Satisfaction, or, The True Reasons for His Sufferings with an Answer to the Socinian Objections*. London, 1696.

———. *A Discourse Concerning the Unreasonableness of a New Separation on Account of the Oaths With an Answer to the History of Passive Obedience So Far as Relates to Them*. London, 1689.

———. *A Discourse in Vindication of the Doctrine of the Trinity With An Answer To the Late Socinian Objections Against It from Scripture, Antiquity, and Reason*. London, 1697.

———. *Irenicum, a Weapon-Salve for the Churches Wounds, or, The Divine Right of Particular Forms of Church-Government Discussed and Examined According to the Principles of the Law of Nature, the Positive Laws of God, and the Practice of the Apostles and the Primitive Church, and the Judgment of the Reformed Divines; Whereby a Foundation Is Laid for The Churches Peace and the Accommodation of Our Present Differences, Humbly Tendered to Consideration. The Second Edition with an Appendix Concerning the Power of Excommunication in a Christian Church*. London, 1662.

———. *The Mischief of Separation. A Sermon Preach'd at Guild-Hall Chappel, May 11. MDCLXXX. Being the First Sunday in Easter-Term, before the Lord-Mayor, &c*. London, 1680.

———. *Origines Britannicæ, or, the Antiquities of the British Churches to Which is Added an Historical Account of Church Government as First Received in Great Britain and Ireland*. London, 1710.

———. *A Rational Account of the Grounds of Protestant Religion Being a Vindication of the Lord Archbishop of Canterbury's Relation of a Conference, &c. from the Pretended Answer by T.C.* 2 vols. Oxford: Oxford University Press, 1844.

———. *Six Sermons with a Discourse Annexed Concerning the True Reason of the Sufferings of Christ Wherein Crellius His Answer to Grotius is Considered*. London, 1669.

———. *Two Discourses Concerning the Doctrine of Christ's Satisfaction, or, the True Reasons of His Sufferings with an Answer to the Socinian Objections*. London, 1700.

———. *The Unreasonableness of Separation, or, An Impartial Account of the History, Nature, and Pleas of the Present Separation form the Communion of the Church of England to Which Several Late Letters Are Annexed of Eminent Protestant Divines Abroad Concerning the Nature of Our differences and the Way to Compose Them*. London, 1681.

———. *The Works of That Eminent and Most Learned Prelate, Dr. Edw. Stillingfleet, Late Lord Bishop of Worcester Together with His Life and Character*. 6 vols. London, 1709–10.

Taylor, Jeremy. *A Discourse on the Liberty of Prophesying Shewing the Unreasonableness of Prescribing to Other Men's Faith and the Iniquity of Persecuting Differing Opinions*. London, 1702.

Thoresby, Ralph. *The Diary of Ralph Thoresby, Author of the Topography of Leeds*. 2 vols. Edited by Joseph Hunter. London: Colbern and Bentley, 1830.

Thorndike, Herbert. *An Epilogue to the Tragedy of the Church of England, Being a Necessary Consideration and Brief Resolution of the Chief Controversies in Religion that Divide the Western Church*. London, 1659.

Tillotson, John. "Concerning the Divinity of Our Blessed Saviour" (Sermons XLIII & XLIV). In *WJT*, 3:281–338.
———. "Concerning the Incarnation of Christ" (Sermons XLV & XLVI). In *WJT*, 3:339–81.
———. "Concerning the Sacrifice and Satisfaction of Christ" (Sermon XLVII). In *WJT*, 3:382–408.
———. "Concerning the Unity of the Divine Nature and the Blessed Trinity" (Sermon XLVIII). In *WJT*, 3:409–38.
———. "Of the Education of Children" (Sermons LI–LIII). In *WJT*, 3:483–551.
———. "The Fruits of the Spirit the Same with Moral Virtues" (Sermon CCI). In *WJT*, 3:465–84.
———. "Of Justifying Faith" (Sermon CCXXVI). In *WJT*, 9:312–27.
———. "Of the Testimony of the Spirit to the Truth of the Gospel" (Sermon CCXXII). In *WJT*, 9:246–57.
———. "On the Nature of Faith in General" (Sermon CCXVIII). In *WJT*, 9:173–189.
———. "The Rule of Faith, or, an Answer to the Treatise of Mr. J.S. Entitled, 'Surefooting, &c.'" In *WJT*, X.225–446.
———. *The Works of the Dr. John Tillotson, Late Archbishop of Canterbury*. 10 vols. London, 1820.
Tindal, Matthew. *Christianity as Old as the Creation, or, The Gospel, a Republication of the Religion of Nature*. London, 1730.
———. *A Defence of the Rights of the Christian Church Asserted against a Late Visitation Sermon Intitled, The Rights of the Clergy in the Christian Church Asserted*. London, 1709.
———. *The Rights of the Christian Church Asserted against the Romish and All Other Priests Who Claim an Independent Power over It*. London, 1706.
Toland, John. *Christianity Not Mysterious, or, A Treatise Shewing That There is Nothing in the Gospel Contrary to Reason Nor above It and That No Christian Doctrine Can Be Properly Called a Mystery*. London, 1695.
Toplady, Augustus. *Historic Proof of the Doctrinal Calvinism of the Church of England*. 2 vols. London, 1774.
———. *The Church of England Vindicated from the Charge of Arminianism*. London, 1769.
———. *More Work for Mr. John Wesley, or, A Vindication of the Decrees and Providence of God from the Defamations of a Late Printed Paper Entitled, "The Consequence Proved."* London, 1772.
Turner, John. *A Vindication of the Rights and Privileges of the Christian Church*. London, 1707.
Ussher, James. *The Original of Bishops and Metropolitans Briefly Laid Down*. Reprinted in Ussher, *The Whole Works*, 7:41–71.
———. *The Reduction of Episcopacy unto the Form of Synodical Government Received in the Ancient Church, Proposed in the Year 1611*. Reprinted in Ussher, *The Whole Works*, 12:527-36.
———. *The Whole Works of James Ussher*. 17 vols. Edited by Charles Elrington. Dublin: Hodges & Smith, 1864.
Wadworth, Daniel. *Diary of Rev. Daniel Wadsworth, Seventh Pastor of the First Church of Christ in Hartford*, with notes by George Leon Walker. Hartford, CT: Case, Lockwood & Brainard, 1894.

Wallis, John. *The Doctrine of the Blessed Trinity.* London, 1690.

Walter, Thomas. *A Choice Dialogue between John Faustus a Conjuror and Jack Tory, His Friend.* London, 1720.

Warne, Jonathan. *Arminianism, the Back-Door to Popery; Humbly Offered to The Consideration of the Arch-Bishops, Bishops, with the Rest of the English Clergy; and the Students in Both Universities.* London, 1738.

———. *An Attempt to Promote True Love and Unity between the Church of England and the Dissenters Who are Calvinists of the Baptist, Independent, and Presbyterian Perswasions by Setting Down the Thirty-nine Articles of the Aforesaid Church in One Column, and the Articles of Faith of Those Dissenters in Another That Every Impartial Person May, at One View, Discover, That They All Agree in Every Essential Point, That Concerns Our Eternal Salvation Which Will Be a Good Means to Create true Love, and Cordial Affection to Each Other.* London, 1741.

———. *The Church of England Turned Dissenter at Last: Clearly Proving That the Generality of Those That Profess Themselves Her Clergy, Have Forsaken Most of the Important Doctrines of Her Articles, Homilies, and Collects, Contained in the Common-Prayer.* London, [1740?].

———. *The Downfal of Arminianism: or, Arminius (who Falsly Calls Himself a Son of the Church of England.) Tried and cast (and in Him all his Adherents, Who Call themselves Sons of the Church of Eugland.) Before the Right Honourable The Lord Chief Justice Truth, For Holding and Propagating False Opinions, Concerning the Five Following Points, viz. 1. Absolute Election. 2. Particular Redemption. 3. The Efficacy of God's Grace in Conversion. 4. The Impotency of Man's Will in Conversion. 5. The final Perseverance of the Regenerate. Proved True from 1. The Articles of the Church of England. 2. Her Common-Prayer Book. 3. Her Homilies. 4. The Holy Scriptures. A List of the Names of the Right Rev. Jury. 1. Arch-Bp. Usher. 2. Bp. Ridley. 3. Bp. Latimer. 4. Bp. Jewel. 5. Bp. Davenant. 6. Bp. Hall. 7. Bp. Reynolds. 8. Bp. Cooper. 9. Bp. Babbington. 10. Bp. Downham. 11. Bp. Hopkins. 12. Bp. Beveridge. Humbly Offered to the Consideration of His Grace the Archbishop of Canterbury, the Bp. of London, the Bp. of Winchester, the Bp. of St. Davids, and the Bp. of St. Asaph.* London, 1742.

———. *The Dreadful Degeneracy of a Great Part of the Clergy, the Means to Promote Irreligion, Atheism, and Popery. To Which Is Prefix'd, a Letter to the Reverend Mr. George Whitefield.* London, 1739

Warne, Jonathan and Lancelot Andrewes. *The Bishop of London's Doctrine of Justification, in His Late Pastoral Letter, Proved by Bishop Andrews's Sermon on That Point, So Contrary to the Church of England, that it Rather Agrees with the Church of Rome. With a Postscript in Vindication of the Revd. Mr. Whitefield's Assertions, Relating to the Errors Contained in the Book Call'd the Whole Duty of Man, and Archbishop Tillotson's Works.* London, 1739.

Waterland, Daniel. *A Critical History of the Athanasian Creed.* Cambridge, 1728.

Watts, Isaac. *The Works of the Rev. Isaac Watts.* 9 vols. Leeds, 1813.

Welchman, Edward. *Dr. Clarke's Scripture Doctrine of the Trinity Examined.* London, 1714.

———. *The Thirty-nine Articles of the Church of England Illustrated with Notes.* London, 1743.

Wells, Edward. *An Essay Towards an Impartial Account of the Holy Trinity and the Deity of Our Saviour As Contained in the Old Testament.* London, 1712.

———. *Remarks on Dr. Clark's Introduction to His Scripture-Doctrine of the Trinity.* London, 1713.
West, Richard. *The True Character of a Church-Man: Shewing the False Pretences to That Name Together with the Character of a Low Church-Man Drawn in Answer to It.* London, 1702.
Wheatly, Charles. *A Rational Illustration of the Book of Common Prayer of the Church of England.* 8th ed. London, 1759.
Whichcote, Benjamin. *Moral and Religious Aphorisms of Doctor Whichcote,* edited by Samuel Salter. London, 1753.
Whiston, William. *A Collection of Authentick Records Belonging to the Old and New Testaments.* London, 1727.
———. "A Dissertation upon the Epistles of Ignatius." In *PCR,* 1:1–101 (second p. sig. B).
———. "An Essay on the Apostolical Constitutions." In *PCR,* 3:1–718.
———. "An Historical Preface." In *PCR,* 1:i–clxxv, 1–78.
———. *A New Theory of the Earth from its Original to the Consummation of All Things Wherein the Creation of the World in Six Days, the Universal Deluge, and the General Conflagration, As Laid Down in the Holy Scriptures, Are Shewn to Be Perfectly Agreeable to Reason and Philosophy.* 4th ed. London, 1725.
———. *Primitive Christianity Reviv'd.* 5 vols. London, 1711–12.
———. *A Proposal for Erecting Societies for Promoting Primitive Christianity.* London, 1712.
———. *Reflexions on an Anonymous Pamphlet.* London, 1713.
Whitby, Daniel. *A Discourse Concerning the True Import of the Words Election and Reprobation.* London, 1710.
———. *A Discourse of the Necessity and Usefulness of the Christian Revelation by Reason of the Corruption of the Principles of Natural Religion among Jews and Heathens.* London, 1705.
———. *A Discourse Shewing That the Expositions Which the Ante-Nicene Fathers Have Given of the Texts Alleged against the Reverend Dr. Clarke by a Learned Layman Are More Agreeable to the Interpretations of Dr. Clarke Than to the Interpretations of That Learned Layman.* London, 1714.
———. *A Dissuasive from Enquiring into the Doctrine of the Trinity.* London, 1714.
———. *Four Discourses Shewing I. That the Apostle's Words, Romans the Ninth, Have No Relation to Any Personal Election or Reprobation; II. That the Election Mentioned in St. Paul's Epistles to the Gentiles Is Only That of the Gentiles to Be God's Church and People; III. That These Two Assertions of Dr. John Edwards, viz. (1) That God's Fore-Knowledge of All Futurities Depends on His Decree and That He Fore-knows Them Because He hath Decreed Them; (2) That God Did from All Eternity Decree the Commission of All the Sins in the World, Are False, Blasphemous, and Render God the Author of Sin; IV. Being a Vindication of My Annotations from the Doctor's Cavils.* London, 1710.
———. *A Full Answer to the Arguments of the Reverend Dr. Jonathan Edwards.* London, 1712.
———. *A Paraphrase and Commentary on the New Testament.* 2 vols. London, 1703.
———. *A Reply to Dr. Waterland's Objections Against Dr Whitby's Disquisitiones Modestæ.* London, 1720.
———. *The Second Part of a Reply to Dr. Waterland's Objections.* London, 1721.

Whitefield, George. "College Rules." Reprinted in *WGW*, 3.497–99.

———. *A Continuation of the Reverend Mr. Whitefield's Journal, During the Time He Was Detained in England by the Embargo*. London, 1739.

———. *A Continuation of the Reverend Mr. Whitefield's Journal, from His Embarking after the Embargo to His Arrival in Savannah, Georgia*. London, 1740.

———. "Letter CCXXI. To the Rev. Mr. J. W., Boston, Sept. 25, 1740." Reprinted in Whitefield, *A Select Collection*, 210-12.

———. "A Letter to Some Church-Members of the Presbyterian Persuasion." Reprinted in *WGW*, 4.43–49.

———. "A Letter to the Reverend Mr. John Wesley in Answer to His Sermon Entituled, Free-Grace." Reprinted in *WGW*, 4.52–73.

———. "The Recommendatory Preface." In Bunyan, *The Works*, iii–iv.

———. *A Select Collection of Letters of the Late Reverend George Whitefield, M.A. Of Pembroke-College, Oxford, and Chaplain to the Rt. Hon. The Countess of Huntington; Written to His Most Intimate Friends, and Persons of Distinction, in England, Scotland, Ireland, and America, from the Year 1734 to 1770. Including the Whole Period of His Ministry with an Account of the Orphan-House in Georgia to the Time of His Death*. 3 vols. London, 1772.

———. *The Works of the Reverend George Whitefield, M.A., Late of Pembroke-College, Oxford and Chaplain to the Rt. Hon. the Countess of Huntington*. 6 vols. London, 1771–72.

Wilkins, John. *Of the Principles and Duties of Natural Religion*. London, 1710.

Williams, Daniel. *The Answer to the Report, &c. Which the United Ministers Appointed Their Committee to Draw up As in the Preface; Also Letters of the Right Reverend the Bishop of Worcester and the Reverend Dr. Edwards to Mr. Williams against Whom Their Testimony Was Produced by Mr. Lob*. London, 1698.

Winchester, S. G. *The Importance of Doctrinal and Instructive Preaching*. Philadelphia, PA: Presbyterian Board, 1839.

Wise, Thomas. *The Christian Eucharist Rightly Stated, or, An Occasional Proof That the Lord's Supper Is Not a True and Proper Sacrifice*. London, 1711.

Witing, John. *Truth the Strongest of All, or, An Apostate Further Convicted and Truth Defended in Reply to George Keith's Fifth Narrative*. London, 1706.

Woodward, Josiah. *An Account of the Rise and Progress of the Religious Societies in the City of London, &c. and of Their Endeavours for Reformation of Manners*. 4th ed. London, 1712.

———. *The Baseness and Perniciousness of the Sin of Slandering and Back-Biting*. 3rd ed. London, 1729.

———. *The Seaman's Monitor: Advice to Sea-faring Men with Reference to Their Behaviour before, in, and after Their Voyage with Prayers for Their Use*. 17th ed. London, 1806.

———. *A Short Catechism Explaining the Substance of the Christian Religion Suited to the Understanding of Children and the Meanest Capacities*. 2nd ed. London, 1720.

———. *The Soldier's Monitor Being Serious Advice to Soldiers to Behave Themselves with a Just Regard to Religion and True Manhood*, 7th ed. London, 1776.

———. *The Young Man's Monitor Shewing the Great Happiness of Early Piety and the Dreadful Consequences of Indulging Youthful Lusts*. 9th ed. London, 1770.

SECONDARY WORKS

Abbey, Charles J. *The English Church and Its Bishops 1700-1800*. 2 vols. London: Longmans and Green, 1887.
Abbey, Charles J. and John H. Overton. *The English Church in the Eighteenth Century*. 2 vols. London: Longmans and Green, 1878.
Adair, E.R. "Laud and the Church of England." *Church History* 5 (1936) 121-40.
Aikin, John, et. al. *General Biography, or, Lives, Critical and Historical of the Most Eminent Persons of All Ages, Countries, Conditions, and Professions*. 10 vols. London, 1804-18.
Allison, C. Fitzsimons. *The Rise of Moralism: The Proclamation of the Gospel from Hooker to Baxter*. Vancouver, BC: Regent College Publishing, 2003.
Anstey, Peter R., ed. *The Oxford Handbook of British Philosophy in the Seventeenth Century*. Oxford: Oxford University Press, 2013.
Ariew, Roger, et. al. *Historical Dictionary of Descartes and Cartesian Philosophy*. Lanham, MD: Rowman and Littlefield, 2015.
Atherton, Ian. "Cathedrals, Laudianism, and the British Churches." *The Historical Journal* 53 (2010) 895-918.
Atkins, Jonathan M. "Calvinist Bishops, Church Unity, and the Rise of Arminianism." *A Quarterly Journal Concerned with British Studies* 18 (1986) 411-27.
Baker, P.R.S. "Thomas Edwards." In *ODNB*.
Ball, Bryan. W. "Samuel Bold." In *ODNB*.
Bayne, Peter. *Documents Relating to the Settlement of the Church of England by the Act of Uniformity of 1662: with an Historical Introduction*, edited by George Gould. London: W. Kent, 1862.
Beiser, Frederick C. *The Sovereignty of Reason: The Defense of Rationality in the Early English Enlightenment*. Princeton, NJ: Princeton University Press, 1996.
Blagden, Cyprian. "Early Cambridge Printers and the Stationers' Company." *Transactions of the Cambridge Bibliographical Society* 2 (1957) 275-89.
Blatchly, J.M. "Nathaniel Parkhurst." In *ODNB*.
Bloore, Stephen. "Samuel Keimer." *The Pennsylvania Magazine of History and Biography* 54 (1930) 255-87.
Boersma, Hans. *A Hot Pepper Corn: Richard Baxter's Doctrine of Justification in Its Seventeenth-Century Context of Controversy*. Vancouver, BC: Regent College Publishing 1993.
Bonet-Maury, Gaston. *Early Sources of English Unitarian Christianity*. London: British and Foreign Unitarian Association, 1884.
Bourne, H.R. Fox. *The Life of John Locke*. 2 vols. New York: Harper, 1876.
Buchwald, Jed Z. and Mordechai Feingold. *Newton and the Origin of Civilization*. Princeton, NJ: Princeton University Press, 2013.
Bulman, William. *Anglican Enlightenment: Orientalism, Religion and Politics in England and its Empire, 1648-1715*. Cambridge: Cambridge University Press, 2016.
Campagnac, E. T. *The Cambridge Platonists: Being Selections From the Writings of Benjamin Whichcote, John Smith, and Nathanael Culverwell*. Oxford: Clarendon, 1901.
Carlton, Charles. *Archbishop William Laud*. London: Routledge and Kegan Paul, 1987.
Carroll, Robert and Stephen Pickett, eds. *The Bible: Authorized King James Version*. Oxford: Oxford University Press, 2008.

Carter, Benjamin Huw. "Politics, Theology, and Cambridge Platonism: The Trinity and Ethical Community in the Thought of Ralph Cudworth." PhD dissertation, Middlesex University, 2004.
Carter, C. Sydney. *The English Church in the Seventeenth Century*. London: Longmans and Green, 1909.
Chalmers, Alexander. *The General Biographical Dictionary: Containing an Historical and Critical Account of the Lives and Writings of the Most Eminent Persons in Every Nation, Particularly the British and Irish, from the Earliest Accounts to the Present Time*. 32 vols. London, 1812–17.
Champion, Justin. "'Directions for the Profitable Reading of the Holy Scriptures': Biblical Criticism, Clerical Learning and Lay Readers." In *Scripture and Scholarship in Early Modern England*, edited by Ariel Hessayon et al., 208–30. Aldershot, Hampshire: Ashgate, 2006.
―――. *The Pillars of Priestcraft Shaken*. Cambridge: Cambridge University Press, 1992.
Chappell, Vere, ed. *The Cambridge Companion to Locke*. Cambridge: Cambridge University Press, 1999.
Cleveland, Charles Dexter. *The Poetical Works of John Milton with a Life of the Author*. London: Sampson Low, Son, and Marston, 1865.
Cobbett, William. *Cobbett's Parliamentary History of England*. 36 vols. London: Bagshaw, 1806–08.
Coffey, John. *Persecution and Toleration in Protestant England, 1558–1689*. Essex: Pearson, 2000.
Coleby, Andrew M. "Henry Compton." In *ODNB*.
Collinson, Patrick. "Anthony Tuckney." In *ODNB*.
Collette, Daniel. "Pascal, Spinoza and Defining Cartesianism." *Society and Politics* 8 (2014) 81–99.
Collier, Jay. *Debating Perseverance: The Augustinian Heritage in Post-Reformation England*. Oxford: Oxford University Press, 2018.
Como, David R. "Predestination and Political Conflict in Laud's London." *The Historical Journal* 46 (2003) 263–94.
Cooper, Thompson. "Edward Welchman." Revised by Emma Major. In *ODNB*.
Cooper, Tim. *John Owen, Richard Baxter and the Formation of Nonconformity*. Surrey: Ashgate, 2011.
Cornwall, Robert D. "Charles Leslie." In *ODNB*.
Cosby, Matthew. "The Cambridge Platonists and the Pre-History of the English Enlightenment." PhD dissertation, University of Wisconsin, Madison, 2016.
Coudert, Allison P. "John Locke and Francis Mercury van Helmont." In *Everything Connects: In Conference with Richard H. Popkin*, edited by James E. Force et al., 87-114. Leiden: Brill, 1998.
Cowie, Leonard. "William Beveridge." In *ODNB*.
Cragg, Gerald. *From Puritanism to the Age of Reason*. Cambridge: Cambridge University Press, 1966.
―――, ed. *The Cambridge Platonists*. Oxford: Oxford University Press, 1968.
Craig, Andrew Gordon. "The Movement for the Reformation of Manners, 1688–1715." PhD dissertation, University of Edinburgh, 1980.
Crane, Ronald. "Anglican Apologetics and the Idea of Progress." *Modern Philology* 31.3 (1934) 273–306.

———. "Anglican Apologetics and the Idea of Progress, 1699-1745, Concluded." *Modern Philology* 31.4 (1934) 349-82.

Creighton, Mandell. "William Chillingworth," In *ODNB*.

Crisp, Oliver D. and Douglas A. Sweeney, eds. *After Jonathan Edwards: The Courses of the New England Theology*. Oxford: Oxford University Press, 2012.

Crocker, Robert. *Henry More, 1614-1687: A Biography of the Cambridge Platonist*. Dordrecht, Netherlands: Kluwer Academic, 2003.

Cross, F.L. and E.A. Livingston, eds. *The Oxford Dictionary of the Christian Church* Oxford: Oxford University Press, 1997.

Cumming, John, ed. *Supplement to Gibson's Preservative from Popery: Being Important Treatises on the Romish Controversy*. 18 vols + 7 suppl. vols. London: British Society for Promoting Religious Principles of the Reformation, 1850.

Curthoys, J. H. "William DeLaune." In *ODNB*.

Dacome, Lucia. "Resurrecting Numbers in Eighteenth-Century England." *Past & Present* 193 (2006) 73-110.

Davie, Martin. "Calvin's Influence on the Theology of the Reformation." *Ecclesiology* 6 (2010) 315-41.

Davies, Julian. *The Caroline Captivity of the Church: Charles I and the Remoulding of Anglicanism*. Oxford: Oxford University Press, 1992.

Dixon, Philip. *Nice and Hot Disputes: The Doctrine of the Trinity in the Seventeenth Century*. London: T&T Clark, 2003.

Doran, Susan. "Elizabeth I's Religion: The Evidence of Her Letters." *Journal of Ecclesiastical History* 51 (2000) 699-720.

Duncan, Stewart. "Toland and Locke in the Leibniz-Burnett Correspondence." *Locke Studies* 17 (2018), 117-41.

Dunn, John. *The Political Thought of John Locke*. Cambridge: Cambridge University Press, 1982.

Ellis, Mark. *Simon Episcopius' Doctrine of Original Sin*. Bern: Lang, 2006.

Fesko, John. "Arminius on Justification: Reformed or Protestant?" *Church History and Religious Culture* 94 (2014) 1-21.

Fincham, Kenneth. "William Laud and the Exercise of Caroline Ecclesiastical Patronage." *Journal of Ecclesiastical History* 51 (2000) 69-93.

Fincham, Kenneth and Peter Lake. "The Ecclesiastical Policies of James I and Charles I." In *The Early Stuart Church, 1603-1642*, edited by Kenneth Fincham, 23-49. London: Macmillan, 1993.

Fincham, Kenneth and Stephen Taylor. "Episcopalian Identity, 1640-1662." In *The Oxford History of Anglicanism, Volume 1: Reformation and Identity c.1520-1662*, edited by Anthony Milton, 457-82. Oxford: Oxford University Press, 2017-18.

———. "Vital Statistics: Episcopal Ordination and Ordinands in England, 1646-1660." *The English Historical Review* 126 (2011) 319-44.

Fincham, Kenneth and Nicholas Tyacke. *Altars Restored: The Changing Face of English Religious Worship, 1547-1700*. Oxford: Oxford University Press, 2007.

Force, James E. *William Whiston: Honest Newtonian*. Cambridge: Cambridge University Press, 1985.

Force, James E. and David S Katz, eds. *Everything Connects: In Conference with Richard H. Popkin*. Leiden: Brill, 1998.

Fritze, Ronald H. and William B. Robinson, eds. *Historical Dictionary of Stuart England 1603-89*. Westport, CT: Greenwood, 1996.

Gascoigne, John. *Cambridge in the Age of the Enlightenment*. Cambridge: Cambridge University Press, 1988.
Gatiss, Lee. *The Tragedy of 1662: The Ejection and Persecution of the Puritans*. London: The Latimer Trust, 2007.
Gaukroger, Stephen. "Descartes' Methodology." In *The Renaissance and Seventeenth-Century Rationalism*, edited by G. H. R. Parkinson, 156–86. London: Routledge, 1993.
Gibson, Edmund and John Cumming, eds. *A Preservative against Popery in Several Discourses upon the Principal Heads of Controversy between Protestants and Papists*. 18 vols. London: Society for Promoting the Religious Principles of the Reformation, 1848–50.
Ginn, Richard J. "William Burkitt." In *ODNB*.
Glines, Timothy. "Politics and Government in the Borough of Colchester, 1660–1693." PhD dissertation, University of Wisconsin, 1974.
Goldie, Mark. "Cambridge Platonists (Act. 1630s–1680s)." In *ODNB*.
———. *Roger Morrice and the Puritan Whigs: The Entring Book, 1677–1691*. Woodbridge: Boydell, 2016.
Gordon, Alexander. "Anthony Tuckney." In *DNB*.
Gorton, John. *A General Biographical Dictionary*. 3 vols. London: Whittaker, 1833–1838 and Bohn, 1851.
Green, I.M. "The Persecution of 'Scandalous' and 'Malignant' Parish Clergy During the English Civil War." *The English Historical Review* 94 (1979) 507–31.
Greig, Martin. "'Bishop Gilbert Burnet and Latitudinarian Episcopal Opposition to the Occasional Conformity Bills, 1702–1704." *Canadian Journal of History* XLI (2006) 247–62.
———. "Heresy Hunt: Gilbert Burnet and the Convocation Controversy of 1701." *The Historical Journal* 37 (1994) 569–92.
Gribben, Crawford. *John Owen and English Puritanism: Experiences of Defeat*. Oxford: Oxford University Press, 2016.
Gribben, Crawford and R. Scott Spurlock. *Puritans and Catholics in the Trans-Atlantic World 1600–1800*. Basingstoke, Hampshire: Palgrave Macmillan, 2015.
Griffin, Martin I.J. *Latitudinarianism in the Seventeenth-Century Church of England*. Leiden: Brill, 1992.
Griggs, Burke. "Robert South." In *ODNB*.
Grosart, A. B. "William Beveridge." In *DNB*.
Ha, Polly. "Spiritual Treason and the Politics of Intercession: Presbyterians, Laudians and the Church of England." In *Puritans and Catholics in the Trans-Atlantic World 1600–1800*, edited by Crawford Gribbben, et al., 66–88. Basingstoke, Hampshire: Palgrave Macmillan, 2015.
Hamilton, Alastair. "Lancelot Addison." In *ODNB*.
Hampton, Stephen. *Anti-Arminians: The Anglican Reformed Tradition from Charles II to George I*. Oxford: Oxford University Press, 2008.
Hargrave, O.T. "The Freewillers in the English Reformation." *Church History* 37 (1968) 271–80.
Harmsen, Theodor. "George Hickes." In *ODNB*.
———. "Henry Dodwell." In *ODNB*.
Haycock, David Boyd. "'Claiming Him as Her Son': William Stukeley, Isaac Newton, and the Archaeology of the Trinity." In *Heterodoxy in Early Modern Science and*

Religion, edited by John Brooke, et al., 297–318. Oxford: Oxford University Press, 2005.
Hayton, D.W. "William Nicolson." In *ODNB*.
Hazard, Paul. *The Crisis of the European Mind, 1680–1715*. New York, NY: New York Review, 2013.
Hegarty, R. A. P. J. "William Jane." In *ODNB*.
Hessayon, Ariel and Nichols Keene, eds. *Scripture and Scholarship in Early Modern England*. Aldershot, Hampshire: Ashgate, 2006.
Hill, Christopher. *The Century of Revolution 1603–1714*. New York, NY: Norton, 1980.
Hochberg, Herbert. "The Empirical Philosophy of Roger and Francis Bacon." *Philosophy of Science* 20 (1953) 313–26.
Howe, Daniel Walker. "The Decline of Calvinism: An Approach to Its Study." *Comparative Studies in Society and History* 14 (1972) 306–327.
Hoyle, David. "A Commons Investigation of Arminianism and Popery in Cambridge on the Eve of the Civil War." *The Historical Journal* 29 (1986) 419–25.
Hudson, Wayne. *The English Deists*. London: Pickering and Chatto, 2009.
Hughes, Ann. *Gangræna and the Struggle for the English Revolution*. Oxford: Oxford University Press, 2004.
Hunt, John. *Religious Thought in England in the Nineteenth Century*. 3 vols. London: Strahan, 1870–73.
Hutton, Sarah. "Debating the Faith: Damaris Masham (1658–1708) and Religious Controversy." In *Debating the Faith: Religion and Letter Writing in Great Britain, 1550–1800*, edited by Anne Dunan-Page, et al., 159–75. New York: Springer, 2013.
Israel, Jonathan. *Radical Enlightenment: Philosophy and the Making of Modernity, 1650–1750*. Oxford: Oxford University Press, 2001.
Jesseph, Douglas. "Mechanism, skepticism, and witchcraft: More and Glanville on the failures of the Cartesian philosophy." In *Receptions of Descartes*, edited by Tad M. Schmaltz, 183–99. London: Routledge, 2005.
Johnston, Warren. "Benjamin Jenks." In *ODNB*.
Jolley, Nicholas. "Leibniz on Locke and Socinianism." *Journal of the History of Ideas* 39 (1978) 233–50.
Johnson, G.W. *A New and General Biographical Dictionary*. 15 vols. London, 1798.
Jones, Mark. "John Calvin's Reception at the Westminster Assembly (1643–1649)." *Church History and Religious Culture* 91 (2011) 215–27.
Jones, Tod E., ed. *The Cambridge Platonists, a Brief Introduction with Eight Letters of Dr. Antony Tuckney and Dr. Benjamin Whichcote*. Langham, MD: University Press of America, 2005.
Kassler, Jamie C. *Seeking Truth: Roger North's Notes on Newton and Correspondence with Samuel Clarke c.1704–1713*. Oxon: Routledge, 2016.
Katz, David S. *God's Last Words: Reading the English Bible from the Reformation to Fundamentalism*. New Haven, CN: Yale University Press, 2004.
Keeble, N. H. *"Settling the Peace of the Church": 1662 Revisited*. Oxford: Oxford University Press, 2014.
Kim, Julius J. "The Religion of Reason and the Reason for Religion: John Tillotson and the Latitudinarian Defense of Christianity, 1630–1694." PhD dissertation, Trinity Evangelical Divinity School, 2003.
Kippis, Andrew. *Biographia Britannica, or, The Lives of the Most Eminent Persons Who Have Flourished in Great-Britain and Ireland from the Earliest Ages to the Present*

Times, Collected from the Best Authorities, Printed and Manuscript, and Digested in the Manner of Mr. Bayle's Historical and Critical Dictionary. 5 vols. London, 1793.
Kishlansky, Mark. *A Monarchy Transformed: Britain 1603-1714.* New York: Penguin, 1997.
Lake, Peter. "Calvinism and the English Church 1570-1635." *Past and Present* 114 (1987) 32-76.
———. "Serving God and the Times: The Calvinist Conformity of Robert Sanderson." *Journal of British Studies* 27 (1988) 81-116.
Lane, Calvin. "Before Hooker: The Material Context of Elizabethan Prayer Book Worship." *Anglican and Episcopal History* 74 (2005) 320-56.
———. *The Laudians and the Elizabethan Church: History, Conformity and Religious Identity in Post-Reformation England.* London: Routledge, 2016.
Leslie, R. J. *Life and Writings of Charles Leslie, M.A., Nonjuring Divine.* London: Rivingtons, 1885.
Letham, Robert. *The Westminster Assembly: Reading Its Theology in Historical Context.* Phillipsburg, NJ: P&R, 2009.
Lettinga, Neil. "Covenant Theology Turned Upside Down: Henry Hammond and Caroline Anglican Moralism: 1643-1660." *Sixteenth Century Journal* XXIV (1993) 653-69.
Lewis, Eric. "Cartesianism Revisited." *Perspectives on Science* 15 (2007) 493-522.
Lim, Paul Chang-Ha. *In Pursuit of Purity, Unity, and Liberty: Richard Baxter's Puritan Ecclesiology in its Seventeenth-century Context.* Leiden: Brill, 2004.
———. *Mystery Unveiled: The Crisis of the Trinity in Early Modern England.* Oxford: Oxford University Press, 2012.
Lord, Evelyn. *The Great Plague: A People's History.* New Haven, CN: Yale University Press, 2014.
Macaulay, Thomas Babington. *The History of England from the Accession of James II.* 5 vols. Chicago: Belford and Clarke, 1884-98.
MacCulloch, Diarmaid. *Thomas Cranmer: A Life.* New Haven: Yale University Press, 1996.
Mandelbrote, Scott. "Thomas Burnet." In *ODNB*.
Mander, W. J. *The Philosophy of John Norris.* Oxford: Oxford University Press, 2008.
Marshall, John. *John Locke: Resistance, Religion and Responsibility.* Cambridge: Cambridge University Press, 1996.
———. "Locke, Socinianism, 'Socinianism,' and Unitarianism." In *English Philosophy in the Age of Locke,* edited by M. A. Stewart, 111-82. Oxford: Oxford University Press, 2000.
Marshall, William. "John Hall." In *ODNB*.
Matthew, H. C. G. and Brian Harrison, eds. *Oxford Dictionary of National Biography.* Oxford: Oxford University Press, 2004.
McGiffert, Michael. "Henry Hammond and Covenant Theology." *Church History* 74 (2005) 255-85.
McKenzie, D.F. *The Cambridge University Press 1696-1712: A Bibliographic Study.* Cambridge: Cambridge University Press, 1966.
McKim, Donald. *Dictionary of Major Biblical Interpreters.* Downers Grove, IL: IVP Academic, 2007.
McKitterick, David. *A History of Cambridge University Press 1534-1698.* 3 vols. Cambridge: Cambridge University Press, 1992-2004.

McLachlan, H. John. *Socinianism in Seventeenth-Century England*. Oxford: Oxford University Press, 1951.
———. *The Story of a Nonconformist Library*. Manchester: Manchester University Press, 1923.
Meli, Domenico Bertoloni. "John Wallis." In *ODNB*.
Milton, Anthony. "Arminians, Laudians, Anglicans, and Revisionists: Back to Which Drawing Board?" *Huntington Library Quarterly* 78 (2015) 723-42.
———. *Catholic and Reformed: The Roman and Protestant Churches in English Protestant Thought 1600-1640*. Cambridge: Cambridge University Press, 1995.
———. *Laudian and Royalist Polemic in Seventeenth-Century England*. Manchester: Manchester University Press, 2007.
———, ed. *The Oxford History of Anglicanism, Volume I: Reformation and Identity, c.1520-1662*. Oxford: Oxford University Press, 2017.
Milton, John. *John Milton: Complete Poems and Major Prose*, edited by Merritt Y. Hughes. Indianapolis, IN: Hackett, 2003.
Morrill, John. "The Church of England, 1642-9." In *Reactions to the English Civil War 1642-1649*, edited by John Morrill, 89-114. London: Macmillan, 1982.
Mortimer, Sarah. *Reason and Religion in the English Revolution: The Challenge of Socinianism*. Cambridge: Cambridge University Press, 2010.
Muller, Richard A. *Calvin and the Reformed Tradition: On the Work of Christ and the Order of Salvation*. Grand Rapids: Baker Academic, 2012.
———. *Post-Reformation Reformed Dogmatics: The Rise and Development of Reformed Orthodoxy, Ca. 1520 to Ca. 1725*. 4 vols. Grand Rapids: Baker Academic, 2003.
Mullinger, J. Bass. *Cambridge Characteristics in The Seventeenth Century*. London: Macmillan, 1867.
———. *A History of the University of Cambridge*. London: Longmans and Green, 1888.
———. *The University of Cambridge*. Cambridge: Cambridge University Press, 1911.
Nicolson, Marjorie. "Early Stages of Cartesianism in England." *Studies in Philology* 25 (1929) 356-74.
Nuovo, Victor. *Christianity, Antiquity and Enlightenment: Interpretations of Locke*. London: Springer, 2011.
Oakes, John S. *Conservative Revolutionaries: Transformation and Tradition in the Religious and Political Thought of Charles Chauncy and Jonathan Mayhew*. Eugene, OR: Pickwick, 2016.
Ollard, S.L. *A Dictionary of English Church History*. London: Mowbray, 1919.
Ollerton, Andrew. "The Crisis of Calvinism and the Rise of Arminianism in Cromwellian England." PhD dissertation, University of Leicester, 2016.
Packer, J. I. *The Redemption and Restoration of Man in the Thought of Richard Baxter*. Carlisle, PA: Paternoster, 2003.
Palin, David A. "Should Herbert of Cherbury Be Regarded as a 'Deist'?" *The Journal of Theological Studies, New Series* 51 (2000) 113-49.
Parker, Charles. "The Moral Agency and Moral Autonomy of Church Folk in the Dutch Reformed Church of Delft, 1580-1620." *Journal of Ecclesiastical History* 48 (1997) 44-70.
Parker, Kim Ian. *The Biblical Politics of John Locke*. Waterloo, ON: Wilfrid Laurier University Press, 2004.
Parkinson, G. H. R. "Introduction." In *The Renaissance and Seventeenth-Century Rationalism*, edited by G. H. R. Parkinson, 1-14. London: Routledge, 1993.

Pastoor, Charles and Galen K. Johnson. *Historical Dictionary of the Puritans*. Lanham, MD: The Scarecrow, 2007.
Patterson, W.B. *King James VI and I and the Reunion of Christendom*. Cambridge: Cambridge University Press, 1997.
Pearce, Kenneth. "Berkeley's Lockean Religious Epistemology." *Journal of the History of Ideas* 74 (2014) 417–38.
Pederson, Randall. *Unity in Diversity: English Puritans and the Puritan Revolution, 1603-1689*. Leiden: Brill, 2014.
Pennington, Edgar Legare. "The Beginnings of the Library in Charles Town, South Carolina." *Proceedings of the American Antiquarian Society* 44 (1934) 159–87.
Perez-Ramos, Antonio. "Francis Bacon and Man's Two-Faced Kingdom." In *The Renaissance and Seventeenth-Century Rationalism*, edited by G. H. R. Parkinson, 130–55. London: Routledge, 1993.
Pfizenmaier, Thomas C. *The Trinitarian Theology of Dr. Samuel Clarke (1675-1729): Context, Sources, and Controversy*. Leiden: Brill, 1997.
———. "Was Isaac Newton an Arian?" *Journal of the History of Ideas* 58 (1997) 57–80.
Pincus, Steve. *1688: The First Modern Revolution*. New Haven: Yale University Press, 2011.
Plomer, Henry R. *A Dictionary of the Printers and Booksellers Who Were at Work in England, Scotland and Ireland from 1668 to 1725*. Oxford: Oxford University Press, 1922.
Plumtre, E.H. *The Life of Thomas Ken*. 2 vols. London: Isbister, 1890.
Powell, Thomas. *An Essay on Apostolical Succession: Being a Defence of a Genuine Protestant Ministry against the Exclusive and Intolerant Schemes of Papists and High Churchmen*. London, 1840.
Prest, Wilfrid. "The Religion of a Lawyer?: William Blackstone's Anglicanism." *Parergon* 21 (2004) 153–68.
Proctor, Francis. *A History of the Book of Common Prayer with a Rationale of its Offices*. Cambridge: Macmillan, 1855.
Purrington, Robert D. *The First Professional Scientist: Robert Hooke and the Royal Society of London*. Basel: Birkhäuser, 2009.
Pyle, Andrew, ed. *The Dictionary of Seventeenth-Century British Philosophers*. New York: Thoemmes Continuum, 2000.
Quantin, Jean-Louis. *The Church of England and Christian Antiquity: The Construction of a Confessional Identity in the 17th Century*. Oxford: Oxford University Press, 2009.
Rampelt, Jason M. "Three Persons in One Man: John Wallis on the Trinity." MTh thesis, Westminster Theological Seminary, 2002.
Ray, Hermon. "The Religious Thought of Dr. John Edwards of Cambridge (1637–1716)." PhD dissertation, University of Edinburgh, 1956.
Reedy, Gerard. *Robert South (1634-1716): An Introduction to His Life and Sermons*. Cambridge: Cambridge University Press, 1992.
Rivers, Isabel. *Reason, Grace, and Sentiment: Volume 1, Whichcote to Wesley: A Study of the Language of Religion and Ethics in England 1660-1780*. Cambridge: Cambridge University Press, 1991.
Roberts, Sydney Castle. *A History of the Cambridge University Press 1521-1921*. Cambridge: Cambridge University Press, 1921.
Robinson, C.J. "John Edwards." In *DNB*.

Robinson, C.J., revised by Stephen Wright. "John Edwards." In *ODNB*.
Rogers, G. A. J. "John Locke: Conservative Radical." In *The Margins of Orthodoxy*, edited by Roger Lund, 97–116. Cambridge: Cambridge University Press, 1995.
Rose, Hugh James. *A New General Biographical Dictionary*. 12 vols. London, 1839–57.
Rose, Jacqueline. "By Law Established: The Church of England and the Royal Supremacy." In *The Later Stuart Church 1660–1714*, edited by Grant Tapsell, 21–45. Manchester: Manchester University Press, 2012.
Rupp, Gordon. *Religion in England, 1688–1791*. Oxford: Oxford University Press, 1987.
Russell, Arthur. *Memoirs of the Life and Works of Lancelot Andrewes*. London: Saunders and Otley, 1863.
Russell, Conrad. "Introduction." In *The Origins of the English Civil War*, edited by Conrad Russell, 1–31. London: Macmillan, 1973.
Ryrie, Charles. *Dispensationalism*. Chicago, IL. Moody, 1995.
Sailor, Danton B. "Cudworth and Descartes." *Journal of the History of Ideas* 23 (1962) 133–40.
Savonius-Wroth, S.J., et al., eds. *The Continuum Companion to Locke*. London: Continuum International, 2010.
Schuman, Andrew. "Training Ministers of 'Light and Heat': Jonathan Edwards's Home-Based Educational Approach and its Legacy." In *The Global Edwards: Papers from the Jonathan Edwards Congress held in Melbourne, August 2015*, edited by Rhys Bezzant, 261–76. Eugene, OR: Wipf and Stock, 2017.
Seed, John. *Dissenting Histories: Religious Division and the Politics of Memory in Eighteenth-Century England*. Edinburgh: Edinburgh University Press, 2008.
Schmaltz, Tad M. *Early Modern Cartesianisms: Dutch and French Constructions*. Oxford: Oxford University Press, 2017.
Schwartz, Hillel. "Arminianism and the English Parliament, 1624–1629." *Journal of British Studies* 12 (1973) 41–68.
Scriba, Christoph J. "The Autobiography of John Wallis, F. R. S." *Notes and Records of the Royal Society of London*, 25 (1970) 17-46.
Secretan. C.F. *Memoirs of the Life and Times of the Pious Robert Nelson*. London: Murray, 1860.
Sell, Alan P. F. *John Locke and the Eighteenth-Century Divines*. Eugene, OR: Wipf and Stock, 2006.
Simpson, J. A. and E. S. C. Weiner, eds. *The Oxford English Dictionary*. Oxford: Oxford University Press, 1989.
Sinnema, Donald W. "Calvin and the Canons of Dordt (1619)." *Church History and Religious Culture* 91 (2011) 87–103.
Snobelen, Stephen D. "'God of Gods, and Lord of Lords': The Theology of Isaac Newton's General Scholium to the Principia." *Osiris* 16 (2001) 169–208.
———. "'To us there is but one God the Father': Antitrinitarian Textual Criticism in Seventeenth- and Early Eighteenth-Century England." In *Scripture and Scholarship in Early Modern England*, edited by Ariel Hessayon et al., 116–36. Aldershot, Hampshire: Ashgate, 2006.
Sommerville, C. John. *Popular Religion in Restoration England*. Gainesville, FL: University Press of Florida, 1977.
Southcombe, George. "Dissent and the Restoration Church of England." In *The Later Stuart Church 1660–1714*, edited by Grant Tapsell, 195-216. Manchester: Manchester University Press, 2012.

Southgate, Beverley. "John Sergeant." In *ODNB*.
Speck, W.A.. "Henry Sachervell." In *ODNB*.
Spellman, W.M. "Locke and the Latitudinarian Perspective on Original Sin." *Revue International de Philosophie* 42 (1988) 215–28.
Spinks, Bryan D. "Liturgy and Worship." In *The Oxford History of Anglicanism, Volume 1: Reformation and Identity c.1520–1662*, edited by Anthony Milton, 148-67. Oxford: Oxford University Press, 2017–18.
———. "Renaissance Liturgical Reforms: Reflections on Intentions and Methods." *Reformation & Renaissance Review* 7 (2005) 268–82.
Spurgeon, C.H. *TheTreasury of David*. 6 vols. London: Marshall Brothers, n.d.
Spurr, John. "'Latitudinarianism' and the Restoration Church." *The Historical Journal* 31 (1988) 61–82.
———. "Josiah Woodward." In *ODNB*.
———. *The Restoration Church of England, 1646–1689*. New Haven: Yale University Press, 1991.
Stanton, Timothy. "Hobbes and Locke on Natural Law and Jesus Christ." *History of Political Thought* 29 (2008) 65–88.
The Statutes: Revised Edition. 16 vols. London, 1870–88.
Steiner, Bernard C. "Rev. Thomas Bray and His American Libraries." *The American Historical Review* 2 (1896) 59–75.
Stephen, Leslie and Sidney Lee, eds. *Dictionary of National Biography*. New York: Macmillan, 1885-1900.
Stewart, Kenneth. *Ten Myths about Calvinism*. Downers Grove, IL: IVP Academic, 2011.
Stewart, Larry. "Newtonianism, and the Factions of Post-Revolutionary England." *Journal of the History of Ideas* 42 (1981) 53–72.
Stewart, M. A., ed. *English Philosophy in the Age of Locke*. Oxford: Oxford University Press, 2000.
Stoughton, John. *History of Religion in England from the Opening of the Long Parliament to 1850*. 8 vols. London: Hodder and Stoughton, 1901.
Stromberg, Roland N. *Religious Liberalism in Eighteenth-Century England*. London: Oxford University Press, 1954.
Sweeney, Douglas A., and David P. Barshinger. *Jonathan Edwards and Scripture: Biblical Exegesis in British North America*. Oxford: Oxford University Press, 2018.
Tapsell, Grant. *The Later Stuart Church, 1660–1714*. Manchester: Manchester University Press, 2012.
Tetlow, Joanne E. "The Theological Context of John Locke's Political Thought." PhD dissertation, The Catholic University of America, 2006.
Thiselton, Anthony. *The First Epistle to the Corinthians (NIGTC)*. Grand Rapids: Eerdmans, 2000.
Todd, Margo. "'All One with Tom Thumb': Arminianism, Popery, and the Story of the Reformation in Early Stuart Cambridge." *Church History* 64 (1995) 563–79.
Toon, Peter. *Hyper-Calvinism in English Nonconformity 1689-1765*. Weston Rhyn: Qunita, 2003.
Trevelyn, George Macaulay. *England under the Stuarts*. London: The Folio Society, 1996.
Trevor-Roper, Hugh. *Archbishop Laud 1573–1645*. Hampshire: Macmillan, 1988.
Trueman, Carl R. and R. Scott Clark, eds. *Protestant Scholasticism: Essays in Reassessment*. Carlisle: Paternoster, 1999.

Tulloch, John. *Rational Theology and Christian Philosophy in England in the Seventeenth Century*. London: Blackwood, 1874.

Tuttle, Julius Herbert. *The Libraries of the Mathers*. Worcester, MA: Davis, 1910.

———. "William Whiston and Cotton Mather." *Transactions of the Colonial Society of Massachusetts* XIII (1910–11) 197–204.

Tyacke, Nicholas. *Anti-Calvinists: The Rise of English Arminianism c.1590–1640*. Oxford: Clarendon, 1987.

———. "Archbishop Laud." In *The Early Stuart Church*, edited by Kenneth Fincham, 51–70. London: Macmillan, 1993.

———. *Aspects of English Protestantism c.1530–1700*. Manchester: Manchester University Press, 2001.

———. "From Laudians to Latitudinarians: a shifting balance of theological forces." In *The Later Stuart Church, 1660–1714*, edited by Grant Tapsell, 46–67. Manchester: Manchester University Press, 2012.

———. "The Rise of Arminianism Reconsidered." *Past and Present* 115 (1987) 201–16.

Tyerman, L. *The Life of the Rev. George Whitefield*. 2 vols. London: Hodder and Stoughton, 1876.

Vian, Alsager. "Thomas Edwards." In *DNB*.

Walker, Christopher J. *Reason and Religion in Late Seventeenth-Century England*. London: Tauris, 2013.

Wallace, Dewey D. "The Doctrine of Predestination in the Early English Reformation." *Church History* 43 (1974) 201–15.

———. *Shapers of English Calvinism, 1660–1714*. Oxford: Oxford University Press, 2011.

———. "Socinianism, Justification by Faith, and the Sources of John Locke's *The Reasonableness of Christianity*." *Journal of the History of Ideas* 45 (1984) 49–66.

Wallace, Robert. *Antitrinitarian Biography*. London: Whitfield, 1850.

Walsham, Alexandra. *Charitable Hatred: Tolerance and Intolerance in England, 1500–1700*. Manchester: Manchester University Press, 2006.

———. *Providence in Early Modern England*. Oxford: Oxford University Press, 1999.

Watson, William C. "Rethinking the Late Stuart Church: The Extent of Liberal Anglicanism, 1688–1715." *Anglican and Episcopal History* 70 (2001) 143–68.

Webster, C. "Henry More and Descartes: Some New Sources." *The British Journal for the History of Science* 4 (1969) 359–77.

Westfall, Richard S. *Never at Rest: A Biography of Isaac Newton*. Cambridge: Cambridge University Press, 1980.

White, Peter. "The Rise of Arminianism Reconsidered." *Past and Present* (1983) 34–54.

Wigglesworth, Jeffrey R. "Samuel Clarke's Newtonian Soul." *Journal of the History of Ideas* 70 (2009) 45–68.

Wilson, H.B. *The History of the Merchant-Taylor's School*. London, 1814.

Winchester, S.G. *The Importance of Doctrinal and Instructive Preaching*. Philadelphia: Presbyterian Board, 1839.

Wolterstorff, Nicholas. "Locke's Philosophy of Religion." In *The Cambridge Companion to Locke*, edited by Vere Chappell, 172–98. Cambridge: Cambridge University Press, 1994.

Woolhouse, Roger. *Locke: A Biography*. Cambridge: Cambridge University Press, 2007.

Wootton, David. "John Locke: Socinian or natural law theorist?" In *Religion, Secularization and Political Thought: Thomas Hobbes to J. S. Mill*, edited by James E. Crimmins, 39–67. New York: Routledge, 2013.

Yolton, John W. John Locke and the Way of Ideas. Oxford: Oxford University Press, 1968.

Yoo, Jeongmo. *John Edwards (1637–1716) on Human Free Choice and Divine Necessity: The Debate on the Relation between Divine Necessity and Human Freedom in Late Seventeenth-Century and Early Eighteenth-Century England*. Gottingen: Vandenhoeck and Ruprecht, 2013.

Young, B.W. *Religion and Enlightenment in Eighteenth-Century England: Theological Debate from Locke to Burke*. Oxford: Oxford University Press, 1998.

General Index

Abbot, George, 14
Abbot, Robert, 19
Act
   Succession to the Crown (1707), 119
   of Toleration, 178
   of Uniformity, 87, 167, 169, 171, 183, 201, 243
   Union with Scotland, 239
Aërius, 161
Allestree, Richard, 131–32, 210
Ambrose, 107, 123, 159, 161
anabaptist, 138, 141, 147, 179, 185, 240
ancient Christianity, 5, 91, 111, 139, 141, 153, 155–56, 159, 161, 165, 173, 184, 189, 205, 223
antinomian, 115–16, 130
   anti-, 186
Apocrypha, 174, 242
Apostle's Creed, 8, 21, 94, 114, 120, 179, 195–96, 223, 236–38
Apostolic Constitutions, 88–90, 92
apostolic succession, 42, 159–61
Arian, Arianism, 3, 8, 41, 45, 59, 64, 66, 70–71, 73–79, 81–82, 84, 87–89, 91, 93, 97, 107, 198, 211–12, 222
Aristotle, 84, 151
Arminian, Arminianism, vii, viii, 1, 5, 7–9, 12–14, 18–20, 22, 28, 33–34, 37–41, 45, 85, 87, 94, 97–98, 101–03, 107–12, 115, 118, 121–22, 127, 129–30, 132–35, 167–68, 175–76, 179, 186–87, 189–94, 200, 202–03, 207, 211, 220, 225, 229–30, 232–35, 237–38, 240–41, 243–44, 246
   anti-, 13, 19, 28, 220, 225, 230–31, 235, 240–41, 244, 246
Arminius, 5, 13, 129–30, 233
Athanasian Creed, Athanasius, 8, 21, 57, 75–76, 81, 93–94, 156, 199, 238
atheism, 9, 45, 47–52, 56–58, 71–72, 212, 222, 235
atonement, 51, 58–59, 65, 69, 130, 145, 244
Augustine of Hippo, 8, 14, 19, 34, 43, 80, 88, 101, 106–08, 123, 141, 159, 161, 197, 238–39

baptism, 129, 138–43, 148, 155–56, 177, 179, 179, 197, 200–01, 236–37
   baptismal regeneration, 141–43, 174, 236
Baptist, 19, 90, 200–01, 240
Baxter, Richard, viii, 32, 106, 115, 168–69, 171, 173–81, 183–87, 204, 223–24
Bellamy, Joseph, 40, 204
Beveridge, William, 40, 165, 238–39
Bible, 2, 4, 44, 48–49, 57–58, 67–68, 88, 90, 92, 125, 165, 186, 209, 214
Biddle, John, 53, 72
bishop, office of, 18, 152–65, 168, 170, 172, 174, 178, 191, 205
Blackall, Ofspring, 126, 142, 214

281

Bold, Samuel, 33, 62, 64–67, 70
Book of Common Prayer, 3–4, 11–12,
    16–17, 19, 30, 87, 134, 144,
    147–50, 168–69, 172, 174–75,
    180, 186, 188, 201, 205, 214, 241
Boyle, Robert, 73, 84, 232
Bray, Thomas, 35
Bull, George, 77–80, 82–83, 92
Burnet, Gilbert, 21–22. 45, 47–48, 74,
    96, 101–03, 121, 126, 177, 211,
    234
Burnet, Thomas, ix, 34, 68, 88
Bunyan, John, 38, 226
Bury, Arthur, 33, 50, 224
Bury, St. Edmunds, 30

Calamy, Edward, 28, 171, 241–42
Calvin, John, 6, 13, 15, 19, 22, 34,
    102, 144, 189, 203, 231, 233, 237,
    238–39
Calvinism, Calvinist, vii, viii, 1, 5–10,
    12–15, 17–24, 31, 34, 39, 41–42,
    86, 94–95, 97–98, 101, 103,
    105, 107, 109–12, 114–19, 128,
    132, 134–35, 171, 175, 179, 186,
    189, 189, 200–03, 210–11, 220,
    224–27, 229–46
    anti-, 12–14, 18, 33, 132, 168, 222
Cambridge
    St. John's College, x–xi, 14, 29–31,
        69, 171, 238
    Platonism, 8, 18, 75
    town, 25–26, 35, 207
    university, viii, 8–9, 12, 18, 23, 26,
        28, 30–31, 33, 35, 39–40, 61,
        67, 69–70, 84, 87–89, 162, 178,
        207, 212, 214–17, 220, 229, 232,
        239–40, 242, 245
Canterbury, xi, 13–14, 22, 47, 89, 121,
    142, 156, 176, 241
Cartesian, 8, 29, 84, 88
    anti-, 84
Catholic, Roman, Rome, vii, 4–5, 10,
    12, 14–16, 18–19, 21–22, 56–59,
    63, 92, 95, 97, 100–03, 113,
    122–23, 126, 129–30, 136, 138,
    146, 148–49, 155–56, 158–62,
    165, 167, 175–76, 179, 181,
    185–86, 189, 192, 196–98, 200,
    202, 211–12, 222, 226, 233–34,
    238, 243
    anti-, 56, 98, 108, 114, 143, 198,
        233, 240, 242
    papists, 14, 42, 102, 118, 125, 146,
        171, 185, 197, 200, 212
    popery, 28, 34, 39, 42, 121, 146,
        179, 188, 197
    universal, 8, 110, 138, 195, 203
Charles I, 11, 13–16, 128, 168, 234,
    245
Charles II, 12, 19, 30, 136, 169,
    171–74, 178, 180, 207, 245
Charles Town, Carolina, 35–36
Chillingworth, William, 69, 83, 91,
    101, 113, 128, 165, 198
Chrysostom, 109, 123, 153–55, 159,
    161
Church of England, vii–viii, 1–24,
    27–28, 30, 32–33, 35–36, 39–42,
    44–45, 47–48, 50, 52, 56, 60, 69,
    71, 74, 76–79, 82, 85–86, 89–90,
    92, 94, 96, 98–99, 102–03, 105,
    109, 111–14, 118–29, 133–34,
    136, 138, 141, 144, 147–50,
    155–57, 164, 166–95, 197–203,
    205, 211–12, 215, 220, 224–27,
    229–31, 233–36, 238–42
    canons (law) of, 15, 78, 162,
        178–79, 184, 188
    High, 7, 15, 20, 22, 45, 74, 103,
        119–21, 126, 169, 186, 188, 215,
        226, 242
    Low, 20, 172, 234–35
Civil War, 11, 13, 16, 18, 147, 179, 240
Clarke, Samuel, viii, 3, 9, 22, 33, 47,
    73–88, 90, 93, 96, 120, 140, 195,
    199, 212, 222
Colchester, 24, 31, 216
communion
    as in fellowship, 177, 181, 192
    Holy Communion. *See* Lord's
        Supper
Compton, Henry, 216, 233, 240–41,
    245
conformity, vii–viii, 2–4, 10, 15–16,
    19, 24, 94, 127, 149–50, 154, 163,

168, 170–73, 177–78, 180, 183, 190, 192–93, 201–02, 205, 230, 234, 236
Congregational (church), 1, 36, 40–41, 179
conscience, 10, 21, 29, 102, 112, 127, 132, 142, 146, 167, 174–75, 180, 182–83, 185, 187, 190–93, 201, 205
covenant, 139–40, 173–74, 182, 236
  of Grace, 128–31
  Halfway, 2
  New, 139, 140, 142, 145
  Old, 144–45
  of Works, 130
Cranmer, Thomas, 14, 21, 136, 143, 148, 150–51, 155, 163, 167, 176, 200, 205
Crellius, Johannes, 56, 81–82
Crisp, Samuel, 33
Crisp, Tobias, 115–17, 211
Cyprian, 107, 123, 138, 153–54, 157, 161

deacon, 152–53, 155–57, 160–61
Deism, Deist, 8, 21–22, 45, 50, 55–57, 61, 66, 70–71, 73, 79, 84, 88, 101, 104, 121, 124, 126, 219, 221, 225, 235
Descartes, 45, 49, 84, 88
diocese, 83, 154–55, 157–58, 162–65, 170, 179, 185, 233
dissent, vii–viii, 1, 10, 12, 19, 39, 103, 112, 122, 127, 136, 147, 149, 150, 168–69, 172–73, 176, 178, 180, 182–83, 185–93, 201, 205, 233–34
Dodwell, Henry, 120–23, 137, 156, 165
Dort, Synod of, 142, 203, 240

ecclesiology, 4–5, 10, 20, 24, 129, 137, 151, 153, 166, 175, 217, 230
Edwards, Jonathan (1629–1712), 110–11, 117, 223, 226–27, 240
Edwards, Jonathan (1703–58), vii, ix, 1–2, 23, 24, 40–41, 101, 204, 219
Edwards, Mary, 28

Edwards, Thomas, 28–29, 121, 128, 221, 225–26
Edwards, Timothy, 1, 41, 204
election, doctrine of, 86, 102, 108–09, 119, 129, 186–87, 194, 211, 229–30, 237, 239
Elizabeth, Queen, 12, 15, 148–49, 167
Episcopal, Episcopalian, 7, 8, 10, 20, 28, 129, 151–52, 154, 157–58, 160, 162–63, 165–70, 172, 179, 185, 187, 200–01, 205, 231
ethics, morality, 21–22, 92. 99, 101, 105–06, 128–31, 164, 186, 194, 210, 236, 242, 244–46
eucharist. *See* Lord's Supper
Eusebius of Caesarea, 73, 153, 159–60

faith, 98, 137, 139
  assent, 46, 92, 98–99, 103, 106, 195–96, 236–37
  and baptism, 141–43
  faith as a belief system, 4, 8–10, 20–22, 29, 45–46, 50–51, 56–57, 59–61, 70, 84–86, 89, 96–97, 100–01, 104, 133, 140, 143, 149, 165, 167, 170, 182, 191, 193, 195–96, 205, 209, 212, 215, 222–24, 233–36
  evidence of, 7, 66, 106, 140
  fideism, 56, 124
  imputed, 130–31, 141
  justification by. See justification
  and the Lord's Supper, 143–44, 146–47
  nominal, 147
  profession of, 76, 123, 182, 191, 196, 200
  trust, 106–07, 128–29, 132, 195, 236–37
  and works, 22, 115, 130, 194, 236
Fathers of the Church, 5, 6, 19, 73–76, 78–79, 81–82, 86, 91–93, 108–09, 120, 122–23, 125, 132, 153–54, 159, 162, 187, 195–96, 199, 203, 209, 211, 220, 239, 243
Firmin, Thomas, 53, 64, 233
Fogg, Lawrence, 23, 33, 117–19, 211, 216

GENERAL INDEX

foreknowledge, 56, 108–09, 176
Fowler, Edward, 20, 47, 55, 74, 96, 226

Glorious Revolution, 126, 172, 214
God,
   attributes of, 6, 48–49, 68, 73–74, 77, 81, 84, 99–101, 113, 115, 137, 176, 244
   Father, 52, 54–55, 59, 73–77, 80–82, 116, 195
   Godhead, 76
   works of God, 45, 63, 77, 87–88, 114, 137–38, 110, 129, 211
government,
   civil, 2, 87, 119, 168, 177, 183, 216, 245
   church, 5, 28, 38, 59, 147, 150–51, 158, 162–63, 165, 168, 177, 179–82, 184–87, 192, 200
   divine, 81
   congregational, 150, 165, 201
   Episcopalian, 7–8, 10, 129, 136–37, 150, 160, 165, 170, 172, 187, 192, 200–01, 205, 231,
   Presbyterian, 6, 28, 94, 147, 150, 162, 200–01, 231
grace, 36, 39, 59, 104–08, 116, 141, 146, 175–76, 194, 196, 211, 236–37
   effectual, 119, 139
   free, 14, 38, 108, 130
   irresistible, 119
   salvation by, 65–66, 100, 106, 109, 128, 180, 236, 244
   universal, 134–35, 233
   unmerited, 66, 107, 176
Great Awakening, 1, 3, 8
Great Ejection, 9, 19, 23, 30, 32, 136, 168, 171, 174, 180, 183, 229, 243
   unfeigned assent, 169, 174–75, 187, 201, 234
Grotius, Hugo, 130, 240
Gunpowder Plot, 207, 214, 234

Hammond, Henry, 112, 114, 128–35, 139, 152

Hampton, Stephen, 20, 220, 225, 230–31, 233–35, 237, 240–41, 244–46
Hereford, 28, 103
Hickes, George, 84, 103, 121–24, 156
Higgins-Biddle, John, 78, 221–24
High-flyers, 9, 119–21, 125, 136, 156, 190–91, 216
Hoadly, Benjamin, 22, 103–04, 126, 214
Hobbes, Thomas, 45, 48, 97, 124, 225
Hobbist, Hobbism, 69, 97, 121, 126, 221
Holy Spirit, Holy Ghost, 39, 41, 51, 54, 59, 61, 63, 74–77, 79, 81, 99, 105–06, 116–17, 119, 121, 137, 139–41, 143–46, 196, 208, 222, 244
Holy Trinity Church, Cambridge, 25–27, 30, 207
human nature, 59, 120
   free will, 14, 39, 99, 107–08, 175–76, 220, 229, 238
   of a regenerate person, 118, 129, 132
   of an unregenerate person, 27, 99, 141, 239
   hypocrisy, 48, 103, 121, 137, 146, 175, 183, 190

Ignatius, 15, 89–90, 92, 154, 159–61
Independents, 28, 168, 179, 240

James, New Testament church leader, 106, 154, 159
James I, 13–14
James II, 137, 172, 178, 186, 234
Jerome, 80, 108, 138, 143, 153, 155–57 159, 161
Jesus Christ,
   atonement of, 51, 58–59, 65, 69, 130, 145, 244
   deity of, 4, 10, 54–55, 59, 74–76, 81, 95, 137, 197, 199, 224, 249
   humanity of, 6, 63, 76, 82, 224
   Incarnation, 22, 49–51, 54–55, 57–58, 69, 82, 89–90, 96, 102, 125, 128

messiah, 4, 46–47, 52–53, 59–60, 62, 64–65, 137
  miracles of, 46–47, 52–53, 62
  relative deity of, 81–82, 84
  resurrection of, 22, 51–52, 62, 65, 68, 69, 91, 198
  Son of God, 51–54, 64, 69, 74, 80, 222
  subordinationism, 55, 73, 75–77, 82–83
justification, 39, 210, 231, 233, 238
  by baptism, 142
  by faith alone, 39, 103, 106, 116, 128, 194, 231, 236
  and sanctification, 130–31
  and works, 186

Kidder, Richard, 23, 33–34, 216
Kidderminster, 179, 224
King, William, 99–101, 211
Kippis, Andrew, 23, 29, 31, 33–35

Lambeth Articles, 12–13
Latitude, Latitudinarian, Latitudinarianism, 5, 8–10, 12, 18, 20–22, 44, 47–48, 51, 56, 69, 91, 96–114, 122, 126, 137, 163, 176, 183, 186, 194, 201–02, 223, 234, 241
Laud, William, 7, 11–18, 20, 28, 45, 101, 113, 127, 134, 143–44, 147–49, 167–68, 175, 178, 243
Laudian, Laudianism, 5, 8, 10, 12, 15–18, 20, 120, 144, 146–47, 168–69, 175, 243
  anti-, 168
Leibniz, Godfreid, 47, 68, 70, 223
Leslie, Charles, 45–46, 125–27, 229
Lightfoote, Robert, 33, 104–07, 191, 210
Limborch, Philipp van, 71–73, 240
liturgy, 5–6, 11, 18–19, 75–77, 85, 123, 136–37, 147–50, 168–70, 172, 176, 180, 186, 190, 195, 201, 205, 225
Locke, John, 46–74, 79, 84, 87–88, 124, 137, 195–96, 199, 202, 212, 215, 221–26, 245

Lord's Prayer, 143, 148, 210, 223–24, 236–37, 246
Lord's Supper, 10, 16, 34, 78, 121–22, 138–39, 143–48, 155–56, 164, 170, 174, 180, 188, 237
love, 7–8, 40, 115, 146, 176–77, 180–81, 183, 190–92, 194, 198, 201–02, 205
Luther, Martin, 6, 15, 187, 210
Lutheran, 5, 101, 141, 142, 147, 179

Mather, Cotton, vii, 2, 23, 36–37, 93, 189–90, 204, 216
Mather, Increase, vii, 2, 36–37
Middlesex, 70, 85, 241, 246
Milton, John, 29, 124, 213, 245
Morley, John, 25, 27
Muller, Richard, 5, 42, 220, 226, 230, 245

Nelson, Robert, 33, 77–80, 82–84, 86
Newcombe, Catharine, 31–32
Newton, Isaac, 2–3, 26, 33, 47, 53, 81–82, 84, 87–88, 202, 226, 245
Nicaea, 93, 95, 198
Nicene Council, Fathers, 86, 92
Nicene Creed, 4, 8, 10, 55, 94–96, 136, 179, 195, 199–200, 224, 238
Nicholson, Edward, 33, 111–14
nonconformity, 2, 4, 23–24, 28, 30, 34, 36, 42, 69, 115, 127, 136, 167–69, 171–78, 180–88, 190–92, 201, 204–05, 215–16, 226, 235
Nuovo, Victor, 50–51, 53, 61, 67, 224
Nye, Stephen, 33, 47, 49, 50, 53–56, 63–64, 66–67, 70, 89, 224

Origen, 73, 75, 108, 110, 153
Orthodox Church, 4, 95, 101, 142, 222
Owen, John, 34, 69, 171, 175–78
Oxford university, 12, 14–15, 20, 35, 50, 61, 74, 101, 117, 120, 124, 162, 175, 178, 223, 226, 232–33, 235–37, 240–42, 245

papists. See Catholic

Parliament, 11, 16–17, 29, 84–85, 129, 136, 148, 168–71, 174, 178, 214, 233
Passover, 138–39, 145
Patrick, Simon, 23, 44, 48, 51, 97–98, 114, 121, 178, 183, 201, 215–16
patristic church, 138, 144, 156
patristic era, 91, 148, 165, 173
Paul, 29, 34–35, 69, 103, 110, 132, 142, 147, 152, 154–55, 157–60, 195–96, 198
peace, ecclesiastical, 4, 14, 18, 21, 33, 95, 101, 113, 136–37, 163–64, 169–70, 175–76, 181–83, 186, 189–90, 199, 202, 205, 210
Pearson, John, 20, 26, 77, 79, 82, 153–54, 232
Pelagian, Pelagianism, 36, 110
  semi-, 12, 14
Polycarp, 15, 153, 159–60
popery. See Catholic
prayer, 27, 39, 111, 114, 129, 144, 146, 148–50, 155, 169, 184, 188, 194, 235, 246
predestination, 99, 100, 102, 107–09, 127, 229, 233, 237, 239
presbyter, 122, 151–57, 159–65, 179
Presbyterian, Presbyterians, 9, 16, 22, 30, 38–39, 41, 69, 115, 119, 121, 125, 148, 163, 167–71, 179, 187, 215, 226, 233, 239, 241, 242, 245
presbytery, 157–59, 160
priest, priesthood, 16, 30, 122–23, 125, 151–53, 155–56, 161–64, 211
  high, 127, 151–53, 160, 163
primitive Christianity, 88–93, 122, 161, 163, 185, 211
Puritan, 13–14, 16, 18, 20–22, 34, 38, 128, 130, 134, 137, 157–69, 175, 193, 196, 219, 226, 231, 237, 240–43
purity, ecclesiastical, 7–8, 164

Quaker, 126, 139, 147, 186, 216, 240

rationalism, 20, 45, 49–50, 70, 113, 129, 189, 219

redemption, 61, 76–77, 145, 186
  universal, 39, 186, 238
Reformation, 2, 6, 14–15, 40, 46, 104, 125, 136, 150, 162, 185, 196–97, 201, 210–11, 246
Reformed, 4–7, 12, 15, 33, 95, 97, 103, 128, 130, 133–34, 148, 165, 167, 169, 172, 176, 196, 201, 205, 210–11, 220, 225, 230–46
Remonstrants, 118, 135, 179, 240
Restoration, 20, 42, 178, 186, 189, 230–32
Reynolds, Edward, 20, 40, 168, 171, 232
righteousness,
  imputed, 39, 116–17, 128–30, 194, 233
  infused, 130
Rome. See Catholic
Royal Society, 115, 232, 245
Royalists, 16–18, 30, 87, 136, 171–72
rubric, 3, 11, 144, 205

sacrament, 5, 19, 27, 59, 123, 136–47, 155, 182, 187, 194, 196, 236, 240, 246
salvation, 72, 77, 113, 132, 193, 197, 203, 211–13, 219, 224, 239, 242
  by baptism, 129, 139, 141–42, 236
  by faith, 61–62, 71, 103–05, 115, 132, 139, 237, 244
  by grace, 65–66, 100, 106, 109, 128, 130, 180, 236, 244
  universal, 18, 39, 52, 186, 238
  by works, 104, 106, 128, 130, 239
sanctification, 106, 116, 122, 131, 128, 131–32, 210
Sanderson, Robert, 18, 30, 106, 124–35, 193
Savoy Conference, 30, 169, 173, 177–78, 180
schism, 180–81, 185, 187–98, 201, 205, 221, 235, 240
Scotland, vii, 17, 40, 169, 187, 193, 207, 239
separation, 121, 127, 137, 161, 172, 175, 178, 180–85, 188, 191–92, 197–98, 201

Septuagint, 44, 151, 203
Sherlock, William, 33, 46, 142, 196, 226, 244–45
sin, 27, 47, 59, 65, 69, 76, 103, 106, 109–10, 116, 118, 121, 123, 128–33, 137, 139, 141–43, 145–47, 157, 176, 180, 182–85, 188, 208, 238, 244
 original, 47, 51, 59, 63, 86, 108, 110, 129, 133, 141, 176, 187, 194, 237–38, 240
Socinian, Socinianism, 53–67, 69–74, 79, 82, 96, 98, 101–02, 118, 120–21, 125–26, 128–30, 139, 146, 176, 196, 204, 207, 212, 221–23, 225–27, 235, 240, 242–43
Socinus, Faustus, 3, 56, 58, 66, 129
soteriology, 4, 10, 19–20, 129, 131, 137, 196, 200, 210
 Arminian, 20, 238
 Calvinist, 18, 239
 saved by good works, 104
 universalist, 18, 39
South, Robert, 226, 242, 244–45
St. Andrew the Great Church, Cambridge, 32
St. John's College. *See* Cambridge
St. Paul's Cathedral, London, 47, 96, 181, 213, 241
St. Peter's Church, Colchester, 31, 216
St. Sepulchers Church, Cambridge, 31
Stillingfleet, Edward, 47–48, 54–58, 67, 69–70, 72, 74, 96, 114–15, 122, 137, 147, 152, 156, 161–64, 175, 177–78, 180–87, 201, 204, 212, 223, 226
Stoddard, Samuel, 1–2
Stromberg, Roland, 229–31, 246

Ten Commandments, 179, 210, 216, 236–37
Tenison, Thomas, 22, 47, 84, 97–98, 215, 222
Tertullian, 150, 153, 157, 159, 219
theology, 2–10, 23, 33, 35, 38, 42, 49, 57, 61, 73, 95–96, 98, 110, 117, 119, 148, 193, 176, 201, 203, 216, 225, 227, 232, 235–36, 238, 240, 244–45
 Arian, 91
 Arminian, 1, 9, 20, 33, 129, 233, 244
 Bull's, 83
 Calvinist, 1, 6–7, 9–10, 189, 220, 224, 232–33, 246
 Chillingworth's, 113
 Clarke's, 82, 84, 86
 covenant, 130–31
 Edwards's, 35, 96
 Hammond's, 129, 133
 Laud's, 18, 127
 Locke's, 3, 61, 70, 221
 Newton's, 82, 84
 rational, 113, 124
 Reformed, 6–7, 33, 95, 130, 211, 232–33, 238, 241, 244–46
 Sacheverell's, 234
 Socinian, 59
 Tillotson's, 113
 Whitefield's, 38
Tillotson, John, 20–22, 45–48, 69, 83, 88, 96–99, 104–07, 113, 121, 125–26, 178, 229, 241, 245
Tindal, Matthew, 53, 121, 124, 219
Toland, John, 21, 46, 53, 57–58, 68, 124
toleration, vii, 3–4, 7, 9, 17–18, 20–22, 29–31, 33, 47–48, 64, 95, 122, 137, 168, 170, 172, 178, 180–81, 186–87, 190–91, 193, 199, 202, 234. *See* Act of Toleration
 intolerance, 3, 5, 11, 20, 22, 70, 95, 119, 177, 190, 192–93, 202, 225, 233, 242–43
Trinity, Holy, 3–4, 47–48, 55, 57–59, 64, 69, 71, 73–74, 78, 82–83, 85, 128, 194, 235, 245
 anti-trinitarian, viii, 3, 44–93, 207, 212, 222, 225, 227, 245
 doctrine of, 9–10, 21–22, 44, 47, 49–51, 54, 57–58, 69, 74, 79, 84, 87, 89–90, 93, 96, 98, 102, 112, 198–99, 202, 212, 222, 224, 240, 244
 modalism, 53, 76, 245

(Trinity, Holy continued)
  order of, 76–77, 82
  Trinitarian, Trinitarianism, viii, 3–4, 48, 55, 57, 74, 85, 197, 219,
  tritheism, 53, 63, 79, 226, 244
Tuckney, Anthony, 30, 171, 178, 238
Tyacke, Nicholas, 12–14, 16, 20, 168, 230

uniformity, ecclesiastical, 15–16, 148. *See* Act of Uniformity
Unitarian, Unitarianism, 49, 53, 55, 63–64, 70, 72, 74, 98, 102, 112, 126, 211, 221–22, 242
unity, ecclesiastical, 3–4, 7–8, 10, 14–15, 18, 24, 33, 94, 98, 102, 113–16, 127, 133, 136–37, 161, 163–64, 172–73, 175–76, 178–83, 185–87, 189–92, 194, 196, 199–203, 205, 210
Ussher, James, 15, 40, 90, 160, 162–63, 184, 187

Wallis, John, 47, 74, 96, 226, 245
Warne, Jonathan, 1, 23, 35, 39, 40

Waterland, Daniel, 85, 87
Wells, Edward, 74, 78, 83–84
Westminster,
  Abbey, 242
  Assembly, 11, 30, 128, 168, 241, 245
  Confession of Faith, 133
Whig, 22, 172, 215–16, 234
Whiston, William, viii, 9, 22, 33, 47, 66, 70, 81–82, 86–93, 95, 120, 189–90, 195, 199, 212–13, 222
Whitby, Daniel, 33, 66, 85–87, 107–11, 133, 158, 193, 199, 211, 222
Whitefield, George, vii, viii, 1, 23, 38–40, 204, 219
Wilkins, John, 48, 114, 178, 203, 232
William of Orange, 121, 172, 186, 234, 241
Williams, Daniel, 115, 117
Worcestershire Agreement, 179–80

XXXIX Articles, 3–4, 6–7, 9, 12–13, 19, 21, 36, 70, 78, 87, 101–03, 113, 123, 137, 149, 166, 176, 188–91, 197, 199–200, 205, 211, 233–39

Scripture Index
Authorized (King James) Bible

OLD TESTAMENT

Genesis
1:27	244
14:14	208

Exodus
18:25	208

Numbers
31:14	151

Joshua
7:12	208
24:15	132

Judges
11:30–31	208

1 Samuel
15:22	123

1 Kings
8:38	27
18:21	208

2 Kings
1:2	208

2 Chronicles
34:12	151

Ezra
	91

Nehemiah
11:22	151

Psalm
51:16–17	123
53:1	48
60:12	208
66:13–14	132
82:6	208
96:9	15
119:115	132
119:142	208
126:3	208

Ecclesiastes
4	142
7:10	208

Song of Solomon
7:2	138

Isaiah

54:14–17	241

Lamentations

1:8	208

Ezekiel

18:24	131
18:34-45	131
21:27	34
27:27	208
37:22	187, 208

NEW TESTAMENT

Matthew

7:23	142
15:2	151
16:24	132
18:34–45	131
20:25-26	154

Mark

1:4	139
3:24	208
16:16	139
17:21	194

Luke

1:15	141
1:38	53
3:38	52
4:3	52
10:25	103
21:34	132

John

1:14	126
3:16	238n38, 239n43
4:1	129
14:28	82
17:21	194
18:38	208
20:31	52, 106

Acts

2:17	151
2:36	62
2:41	140n14
4:27-28	133
8:37	53
11:29–30	159
15:2, 6, 22	159
17:14	158
18:3–5	140n14
18:5	158
18:25	140n14
19:22	158
20	164
20:5, 6	158
20:17	154, 158
20:17–28	152

Romans

1:20	80
8:29-30	100
9	118
10:9	62
12:1	122
14:14	193
16:14	161

1 Corinthians

4	132, 164
4:17	158
5	164
7:14	140
10	138
10:4	145
11:28	147
14:12	208
16:10	158

2 Corinthians

2:12–13	158
5:17	132

7:6	158	4:14	155, 157
7:13	158	5:10	157
8:12	117	5:19	157
11:26	234	5:22	157

Galatians

4:8	85
5:22, 23	208
5:25	241

2 Timothy

1:6	157
4:10	158

Ephesians

1:18	80
2:8	103
3	132
4:30	241
5:15–16	132

Titus

1:5	152, 158
1:7	152
1:11	158
2:15	158
3:5	138
3:10	158
3:12	158

Philippians

1:1	154
1:21	208
2:6	125
3:8	65

Hebrews

1:2	77

1 Peter

3:19	208
3:21	141
5:1–2	152

Colossians

1:1	158
1:15	77
2:9	80

2 Peter

1:20	124

1 Thessalonians

3:2	158

1 John

5:20	80

1 Timothy

1:2–13	157
1:3	157
1:17	75
2:8, 9	208
3:15	197
3:16	208

Revelation

2:4, 5	208
3:11	132
20:4	87

www.ingramcontent.com/pod-product-compliance
Lightning Source LLC
Chambersburg PA
CBHW070234230426
43664CB00014B/2302